# PROPERTY, INSTITUTIONS, AND SOCIAL STRATIFICATION IN AFRICA

In this book, Franklin Obeng-Odoom seeks to carefully explain, engage, and systematically question the existing explanations of inequalities within Africa and between Africa and the rest of the world using insights from the emerging field of stratification economics. Drawing on multiple sources – including archival and historical material and a wide range of survey data – he develops a distinctive approach that combines key concepts in original institutional economics, such as reasonable value, property, and the distribution of wealth, with other insights into Africa's development and underdevelopment. While looking at the Africa-wide situation, Obeng-Odoom also analyzes the experiences of inequalities within specific countries. Comprehensive and engaging, *Property, Institutions, and Social Stratification in Africa* is a useful resource for teaching and research on Africa and the Global South.

FRANKLIN OBENG-ODOOM is Associate Professor in the Discipline of Development Studies and the Helsinki Institute of Sustainability Science at the University of Helsinki, Finland, where he chairs the Finnish Society for Development Research.

# Property, Institutions, and Social Stratification in Africa

### FRANKLIN OBENG-ODOOM
University of Helsinki

## CAMBRIDGE
### UNIVERSITY PRESS

University Printing House, Cambridge CB2 8BS, United Kingdom

One Liberty Plaza, 20th Floor, New York, NY 10006, USA

477 Williamstown Road, Port Melbourne, VIC 3207, Australia

314–321, 3rd Floor, Plot 3, Splendor Forum, Jasola District Centre, New Delhi – 110025, India

79 Anson Road, #06–04/06, Singapore 079906

Cambridge University Press is part of the University of Cambridge.

It furthers the University's mission by disseminating knowledge in the pursuit of education, learning, and research at the highest international levels of excellence.

www.cambridge.org
Information on this title: www.cambridge.org/9781108491990
DOI: 10.1017/9781108590372

First published 2020

Printed in the United Kingdom by TJ International Ltd, Padstow Cornwall

A catalogue record for this publication is available from the British Library.

Library of Congress Cataloging-in-Publication Data
Names: Obeng-Odoom, Franklin, author.
Title: Property, institutions, and social stratification in Africa / Franklin Obeng-Odoom, University of Helsinki.
Description: Cambridge, United Kingdom ; New York, NY : Cambridge University Press, 2020. | Series: Cambridge studies in stratification economics | Includes bibliographical references and index.
Identifiers: LCCN 2019040441 (print) | LCCN 2019040442 (ebook) | ISBN 9781108491990 (hardback) | ISBN 9781108590372 (epub)
Subjects: LCSH: Social stratification – Africa. | Equality – Economic aspects – Africa. | Economic development – Africa. | Economics – Sociological aspects.
Classification: LCC HN780.Z9 S6175 2020 (print) | LCC HN780.Z9 (ebook) | DDC 305.5/12096–dc23
LC record available at https://lccn.loc.gov/2019040441
LC ebook record available at https://lccn.loc.gov/2019040442

ISBN 978-1-108-49199-0 Hardback

# Contents

# Figures

# Tables

# Preface

It is intrinsically important to explain and, ultimately, resolve social stratification in Africa, but these aspirations have not yet been satisfactorily executed. Human capital explanations, offered by neoclassical economists, can be enticing, especially when they appear to explain the meteoric rise of the "Asian Tigers," including South Korea whose high levels of education, and commitment to a so-called culture of hard work tend to be the focus of much praise. However, many lay and learned Koreans dispute these claims. Over the years, I have visited the country a few times, become friends with South Korean scholars, presented papers in that country at the invitation of organizations such as the Korean Institute for Health and Social Affairs, and even taken a position as a Visiting Scholar at Yongsei University, South Korea's leading institution of higher studies. The achievements of Korea in education and health are outstanding, but I doubt the weight that is placed on human-capital explanations. The more systematic analyses of experienced scholars, including Anne Haila (2016), Ha-Joon Chang (2002, 2003), and Nigel Harris (1987), clearly show that more candor is needed in telling the story of the "Asian Tigers."

Explaining Africa's unequal position requires even deeper analysis. Conceptualizing the problem in terms of the absence of physical capital and the presence or dominance of natural resources is quite common, as is positing the need to reduce the transaction costs of transnational corporations, presumably working to resolve the challenges of development in Africa.

However, as this book shows, neither African culture, human capital, physical capital, nor the natural resource curse explains Africa's underdevelopment. None of these can sufficiently unravel the startling economic inequalities in Africa between various social groups, nor those disparities between Africa and the rest of the world. In this regard, the idea that new cultures of land would enhance "Africa's catch up" process is mistaken also. Although the reverse case – the idea that African land cultures are pristine – might be used to counter this central thesis, I find that similarly unconvincing. This tendency to express the African condition according to a trichotomy of either cultural pessimism, cultural triumphalism, or the scarcity of capital is not only limiting, it is also obfuscating and diversionary.

My argument is that neither orthodox nor heterodox development economics explanations of stratification in Africa can be deemed satisfactory. Both are overly focused on labour and capital struggles, while neither systematically addresses the problems of widespread "spatial apartheid" in Africa (Baker, 2019a, 2019b). Although helpful to some extent, this singular focus on capital neglects how stratification is created, aggravated, and maintained by landed property relations and a system of rent both spatially and temporally. Marxists pay some attention to land, of course, but they suggest, with their disproportionate focus on capital, that its relevance as explanation declines over time. Yet, the persistence of the land question casts doubts on this formulation. The recent land-grab debate might suggest a rapprochement, but this body of work is neglectful of the possessory or ownership structure of land and even more neglectful of land rent theory. In this debate, I contest the "state of affairs" in explaining stratification in Africa, signalling how I develop a relatively new explanation of stratification in Africa, drawing, among others, on stratification economics, a new field of economics pioneered by black economists and other economists of colour.

In the lead-up to writing this book, I have spent time in West and East Africa as well as North and South Africa, where I co-organized a conference on growth and inequality in Africa at the University of Witwatersrand in Johannesburg. Thanks to Lochner Marias, I also visited several mining sites as part of a University of the Free State study group on mining, economy, society, and environment in Free State, sometimes called the heartland of the apartheid regime. During this period, I spent time talking with both blacks and whites, whether lay or learned.

Dubbed "The World's Most Unequal Country" in a cover story by *Time* magazine of May 13, 2019 (see the full story by Baker, 2019a), the South African experience requires additional comments. As I stepped into the country, the different realities of black, colored, and white Africans hit me like a tsunami, in a way I had never before experienced as an African myself. These are all Africans – like me. But they face very different realities. After a long silence in the taxi in which I was travelling, I posed a question to the black taxi driver about inequalities in South Africa. He pointed to the spatiality of wealth and how it is underwritten by the intersectional forces of race, class, and gender.

Why, I asked him, has this persisted? He began an explanation that, as a black African land economist, I understand quite well: "We do not have any land," he said. "We have nothing." He continued, "Mandela did well to include everybody, but we were sold out because the land is in the hands of the whites." With the fear of becoming like Zimbabwe looming, the leaders of South Africa demurred from a radical land reform. They also stopped short of destroying settler colonialism. "What if we became like Zimbabwe?" the driver asked rhetorically, but also pointed out that even if Zimbabwe is poor, it is far safer than South Africa where crime, grime, and strife are commonly discussed, and the limits of the grit and hard work of black Africans are widely known. At the same time, however, he also said something about the spectre of absentee landowners after land reform.

Land is both the roots and the branches of this "spatial apartheid" (Baker, 2019a, p. 39), a point that the *Time* article makes quite well: "The source of the inequality that plagues South Africa is multifaceted ... But the largest dividing line is land" (Baker, 2019a, p. 37). In turn, not only have the conditions in slums worsened sociologically, they have also expanded spatially such that, between 1994 when apartheid was officially ended and 2019, the number of slums in South Africa has increased from 300 to 2,700 (Baker, 2019a). Cyril Ramaphosa, South Africa's current president, is right, then, to call the land question "the original sin that was committed against the people of South Africa" (cited in Baker, 2019b, p. 41), but the land question is much deeper. As this book shows, it is also the original and continuing sin that is committed by "conservatives," "radicals," and "revolutionaries" against Africa more widely.

Yet, development economists have been busily analyzing everything apart from land, a limited diagnosis that has made a bad situation worse. Indeed, in contrast to the taxi driver's emphasis on concrete claims to land, the mother of all wealth, the economists at the Witwatersrand conference made no systematic mention of land. Their emphasis was typically on income. A few times, casual references were made to wealth but only in terms of bonds and stocks. The conference, an assembly of seasoned and young African economists, showed the continuing dominance of mainstream (development) economics in the repertoire of African economists. All but one paper gave the nod to a heterodox challenge, albeit a soft one: new institutional economics. Neither institutional economics nor stratification economics, let alone Marxist economics, was given even a polite mention. Yet, almost everyone present, certainly the keynote speakers, stressed the importance of developing the field. It is, indeed, significant that the editors of the journal that co-sponsored the conference cast their votes unanimously for the maiden A. K. Fosu Prize to be given to the most heterodox of the papers presented, the work on new institutional economics, while recognizing the need to develop the work along even more critical lines.

Those paths must lead to, but also strengthen and ultimately sharpen, both stratification and institutional economics, as well as property economics in the postcolonial tradition; that is the analytical contribution that this book seeks to make. In doing so, many colleagues have helped me to develop this alternative stratification economics. Reviewers for Cambridge University Press have provided much guidance, as have readers for several journals that have published aspects of my analyses. In particular, I must acknowledge the referees and editors of *American Journal of Economics and Sociology, Forum for Social Economics, International Critical Thought, Habitat International, Research in Political Economy*, and the *Journal of Australian Political Economy*.

In developing this treatise, I also have benefited considerably from the advice, encouragement, and resource of many people. Clifford Cobb, editor of the *American Journal of Economics and Sociology*, deserves special thanks for his relentless encouragement for me to develop my analysis of land economics in Africa, publishing some of my papers and going above and beyond to support my effort to nuance others. I thank Wolfram Elsner for encouraging me to take on a more active role in the Association for Social Economics and, crucially, for inviting me to become one of the associate editors of the *Forum for Social Economics*. The opportunity given to me by Paul Alagidede to edit the *African Review of Economics and Finance* has been very helpful because the journal has exposed me to cutting-edge scholarship that I would otherwise have missed. Many thanks to Frank Stilwell for bringing me to political economy, where I started learning ways of replacing development economics with political economy of development; to Liz Hill and Elisabeth Riedle for giving me the chance to teach the latter; and to Spike Boydell for encouraging and supporting me to develop my work in property and political economy.

I am mightily grateful to Annie Herro whose persistent encouragement supplied me much-needed strength and enduring inspiration to complete this book. Together with her insights, generosity of spirit, and abundant wisdom, this book is much better than it could ever have been. To Leo Zeilig of the *Review of African Political Economy*, thanks for excellent feedback on developing my analysis of the political economy of people's power. David Primrose's helpful feedback on the book is also gratefully acknowledged. I have learnt a great deal from working alongside my colleagues in Development Studies and the Helsinki Institute of Sustainability Science at the University of Helsinki in Finland and I must, as a result, thank them for this social learning and for the opportunity to teach "Theories of Development" in our "Critical Development Studies Program." I thank Jeremy Gould, Ilona Steiler, Gutu Wayessa, and the other members of the "African studies network" at the University of Helsinki for inspiration and feedback on this book. Barry Gills, my official University of Helsinki mentor, deserves special thanks for a wide range of advice on the practical philosophy and the sociology of being an academic including, but transcending, the writing process.

It would be remiss not to thank William Darity Jr., my editor, and the leading thinker on stratification economics to which this book tries to make a contribution. He has been patient with me, critical where he has to be, but always encouraging throughout the journey. Thanks, Sandy, for the faith you have reposed in me and for your unwavering support for this book. To Karen Maloney Sara Doskow, Adam Hooper, Rachel Blaifeder, and to the Cambridge University Press team in New York and elsewhere, as well as the many other people involved in producing this book, I thank you for your excellent editorial support. In particular, I must thank Ursula Acton for carefully editing the book and Raghavi Govindane for patiently effecting my many changes at the proofs stage.

In the final sprint for the book, when I raced with time to meet the publisher's deadline, Kofi Boye woke up at dawn one morning asking, "What's the sound?" As he saw me struggling to put my final touches to the book on a computer that was clearly overworked, he noted: "Appa, don't do computer. Rest. Do computer tomorrow." I appreciate his care.

# PART I

# THE PROBLEM

# Introduction: The Global South in a "Compartmentalized World"

The Global South is relatively neglected in research about our "compartmentalized world." The volume of publications on inequality has increased five-fold since 1992, but many of these focus on the top 1 per cent of households located in the Global North (International Social Science Council, 2016), much like Thomas Piketty's work (e.g., Piketty, 2014), and others published in leading journals and magazines such as *Social Forces* (see, for example, Kwon, 2016), *Regional Studies* (see, for example, Kane and Hipp, 2019), and *The Economist* (see, for example, *The Economist*, 2019). Yet, both spatial and social inequalities are widespread and increasing within and between groups in Africa and between Africa and the rest of the world (Obeng-Odoom, 2013b, 2014a; Smet, 2019).

So, in this book, my focus is on stratification in the Global South or what Frantz Fanon (1961) called "the wretched of the earth"; their experiences of appalling economic inequalities; the dire implications for society, economy, and environment; why this compartmentalization continues to deepen; and what can be done about it. Analytically, the focus on stratification provides a more comprehensive approach to studying the Global South because the concern about stratification leads to additional questions about inequality in relation to whom, what, where, why, and how, and hence throws the searchlight on the bigger question of "economic backwardness" in the Global South.

According to Alude Mahali and her colleagues (2018, p. 3), we should understand the Global South to be "the countries of Africa, Central and Latin America, the Pacific and Carribean islands, and most of Asia." I accept this geographical interpretation of the phrase, but I apply it in a broader sense to include those social relations in the Global North that resemble or shape conditions that pertain to geographical Global South (think of, for example, black Americans and the Indigenous peoples of Australia). Politically, the focus on the Global South emphasizes its revolutionary potential, as Samir

3

Amin repeatedly stressed (see, for example, Aly Dieng, 2007). Analytically, focusing on the Global South more widely addresses the widespread problem of methodological nationalism (Gore, 1996; Connell, 2007; Marois & Pradella, 2015) in explaining development, underdevelopment, and alternative development. Although there is the danger of overgeneralizing, the countries in the Global South share many experiences, including chattel slavery.

Yet, almost all the political-economic analyses of the current extreme global economic inequalities focus mainly on capitalism quite a recent economic system, as the root of the problem and neoliberalism as the conveyor belt. Indeed, Alfred López's (2007, p. 1) introduction to the journal, *The Global South*, delimits the periodical's mission to only "three areas: globalization, its aftermath, and how those on the bottom survive it." Although useful, this diagnosis must be situated in a broader view of the nature of Western civilization and its aggressive expansion into the Global South. Historically built on a philosophy of exclusion, monopoly, and a superiority complex, Western civilization fueled chattel slavery, imperialism, colonialism, neo-colonialism, environmental pillage, and shocking forms of patriarchy (Ince, 2018). Its "discourse upon the origin and foundation on the inequality among mankind," to quote Jean Jacques Rousseau (1776), is patronizing. Its apostles tend to claim that the root of inequality can be either nature or nurture and that even conventions impelling inequality are patterned after natural forces (Rousseau 1776). These claims are insidious and toxic, but they continue to be accolated when disguised as academic research, seeking to 'prove' that all these forces are 'history' (see, for example, Maseland, 2018).

The Euro-American historical experience recalls the penetrating analysis by Frantz Fanon (1961) of the compartmentalization of the world in which nobody cares about "the Wretched of the Earth," Fanon's version of the Global South. Slaves were disproportionately colored and the colonizer subjected colored peoples to the most degrading forms of work only to force them out into townships and shanty towns as they were considered "subhuman" (Beckles, 2013), or, as tools, human capital (Hodgson, 2014). The justifying veil of "cultural difference" used as the logic for compartmentalization was eventually torn apart and burnt by fiery revolutions which, for a while, appeared to disrupt the shocking levels of compartmentalization and appeared to be bringing the "wretched of the earth" to the fore. Yet, with the rails and the chains of the veil and the system unbroken, racialized compartmentalization continues to reassert its ugly soul moulded in the furnace of neo-colonialism, capitalism, and imperialism.

Further, the drama of compartmentalization continues, and is arguably magnified, in today's gilded age. With some prevarication, the International

Social Science Council appears to jubilate that the number of publications on the issue has increased in recent times, However, inequality was always an issue: as has been evident in the plunder of resources in Latin America and Africa and the underdevelopment of the Pacific, the Middle East, and many parts of Asia. Many in Indigenous communities have been living in traumatic conditions while many of their white neighbors have so much more to eat than they need and more than is healthy to consume. Such stark contrasts have been the focus of Latin American scholars and many others researching the "development of underdevelopment" (e.g., Frank, 1966). So, why has the intense interest in inequality reemerged? The simple answer is – as Thomas Piketty's *Capital in the Twenty First Century* (2014) demonstrates – inequality is increasingly becoming a major issue in the West. The West has always had a fever of compartmentalization, but this increase in temperature has reached threatening levels, which many fear that it could undermine continuing class- and race-based privileges. For once, it appears that there is some sort of shared interest with "the Wretched of the Earth" for a genuinely global approach to fight a common enemy. But even then, the focus continues to be placed on "the top 1 per cent" in the global core.

In principle, the field of "development economics" has adopted a mandate to broaden this narrow focus. Indeed, the idea of "development" was, for a long time, understood as a general social change in societies everywhere (for a brief history, see Obeng-Odoom, 2013a). However, in practice, development economics is quite limited even in terms of its sources of inspiration. Often drawing mainly on narrow neoclassical and new institutional economics (Akbulut et al., 2015), it has often tended to focus on how rich countries can help poor ones, usually through producing a cadre of Western-educated development specialists who travel from their homelands to help or criticize other nations and peoples. These self-appointed prophets, in turn, tend to train national and global cadres to develop local plans for local progress or pontificate on global ideals without any detailed understanding of local processes (Currie-Alder, 2016). Indeed, in many cases, development economics has created a situation where "public discourse has become public disco" with comedians and musicians performing on stage using preposterous stories to solicit aid to help the poor (Moyo, 2009: chapter 2). In the slums of Indonesia, development has created a theater where the poor recite poems about their poverty as entertainment for the rich who pass some crumbs to them for being able to artistically describe their material deprivation (Peters, 2013).

It seems that the "New Directions in the Political Economy of Development" (Rapley, 1994) in the 1990s have been rolled back. There is an emergent emphasis on "postdevelopment." Characterized by the celebration of localist interventions and ways of life, postdevelopment seeks to write the obituary of development itself because the life of development is the death of many (Rapley 2004; Ziai, 2015). Universalist claims popularized by celebrities often create cacophonous noise in the ears of diligent students of development genuinely pondering alternatives, but does a retreat to self-help, tradition, and pre-industrial society ideals address unresolved issues? A minute of silence is needed to ponder the words of the late Aime Césaire:

> It is not a dead society that we want to revive. We leave that to those who go in for exoticism. Nor is it the present colonial society that we wish to prolong . . . It is a new society that we must create with the help of all . . ., a society rich with all the productive power of modern times, warm with all the fraternity of olden days. (Césaire, 1972: 52)

In my own contribution to the *Journal of Developing Societies* (Obeng-Odoom 2011), I tried to highlight some of the dangers of self-help and localism, including affinities between localism and some mainstream economic thought, the tendency of localist analyses to misdiagnose the development malady as a gigantism issue, and the penchant for localist advocates to overlook the power of reconstructing social relations and institutions across the globe. How do we close the gap, if we focus only on basic needs 'in the Global South' and do nothing about the startling high ceilings in the Global North and across the world (Stilwell, 2019)?

With all its weaknesses, development economics has been the source for insights on global economic inequalities. A focus on inequality started in the 1960s, as demonstrated in H. W. Arndt's work, *Economic Development: The History of an Idea* (1987, pp. 97–100). However, this emphasis on inequality quickly petered out. Economists put the case for growth instead because 'something must be grown before it is redistributed'. Since then, "inequality" has crawled on but more often slipped off the development agenda. Currently, development economics pays more andmore attention to inequality, but only as "risk," as a brake on economic growth, or as a hindrance to poverty reduction; not because it is the root of what W. Arthur Lewis, in analyzing economic development, called "racial conflict" (Lewis, 1985) or other conflicts in the Global South (Obi, 2009; Obeng-Odoom, 2019); not because inequality kills more than disease or limits the potency of healthcare programs (Obeng-Odoom & Marke, 2018; Wilkinson & Pickett, 2010; 2018); not because inequality helps explain the current socioecological crises and, indeed, undermines the struggle for a green and clean planet (Stilwell, 2017, 2019); and certainly not because inequality is unjust.

The relentless pursuit of economic growth is, in essence, the Holy Grail in development economics. As exemplified in the contribution of economists to the special issue of *Foreign Affairs* (vol. 95, no. 1, 2016) on "Inequality: what causes it, why it matters, what can be done," if growth can be sustained then inequality will take care of itself (see Bourguignon, 2016). Indeed, even without exploring different types of growth and how they arise (Gore, 2007), or whether commonly utilized notions of well-being in the West are similarly useful in the Global South (Mahali et al., 2018), mainstream economists like David Dollar and Aart Kraay (2002) hastily declared that "growth is good for the poor", an argument which, more recently, has been emphasized as "growth still is good for the poor" (Dollar et al., 2016).

In practice, whether it is growth, poverty, inequality, or any of the many changing goals and ends of development, development has become a patronizing notion that creates an idealized image of the West in the South or a unique/exotic image of the South as an "other." Development has become an orgy of *Orientalism* (1978), to recall Edward Said's masterpiece. Helping the poor is a common language, as is "sympathy," whether it is in terms of evaluating interventions (program/project aid), or goals – be they Millennium Development Goals (MDGs), Sustainable Development Goals (SDGs), or both. The award of the 2019 Nobel Prize in Economics for what the awardees call "the experimental approach to development economics" (see Banerjee and Duflo, 2009) further legitimizes the zeal to come across as "helping the poor". Much less attention is paid to nuanced conceptualization of these goals (on SDGs, see Gore, 2016; on MDGs see Obeng-Odoom, 2012; and Obeng-Odoom & Stilwell, 2013). Questions about the growing power of unaccountable NGOs and foundations are seldom asked and even more rarely answered. As Clifford Cobb (2015) has recently publicized, without the accountability and scrutiny to which national bodies are subjected, foundations set the agenda and frequently divert attention away from structural causes of inequality to effects such as corruption of national governments, backward cultures, and differential levels of human capital.

## POLITICAL ECONOMY, INEQUALITY, DEVELOPMENT, AND UNDERDEVELOPMENT

The political economy of development is sometimes seen as a salvation for these deficiencies in mainstream development discourses and practices. On the one hand, this optimism is appropriate. Political economists have offered analytical studies that show that what purports to foster development, in fact, could lead to its very opposite, underdevelopment. The "development of underdevelopment" happens on a world scale but also within and across countries. From this perspective, undeveloped (a state of being untouched) is distinct from underdeveloped, which is a state of suppression and oppression (Frank, 1966). Many dependency theorists take the view that development is, in fact, underdevelopment. Geovanni Arrighi, for example, argues that development is an illusion (Arrighi, 1991; Reifer, 2011). He demonstrates that the pursuit of development leads to inequalities through assumptions and practices that reinforce a global system of dependency.

This development-inequality nexus, then, is structural. As a modernizing project, characterized by a compartmentalized world in which the "West" is "modern" and the rest is "traditional" and the latter has to look to the former (Njoh, 2009a, 2009b), the vision of development makes princes of the West and servants of the South. Similarly, within the West, development glorifies opulent white privilege, while downgrading other ways of life. The emphasis on GDP, as the ultimate measure of economic progress, for example, elevates commodified and wasteful ways of life detailed in J. K. Galbraith's book, *The Affluent Society* (Galbraith 1958/1998), by measuring them positively. In contrast, as I note elsewhere (Obeng-Odoom, 2013a), the many informal economies that characterize economic organization in the Global South such as the nurturing and useful roles of caring for the home, the elderly, and the weak are overlooked in GDP estimates.

Thus, although its claims to superiority have often been scrutinized by scientific studies such as J. M. Hobson's *The Eastern Origins of Western Civilization* (2004), this philosophy continues to destroy and extend its very logic of inequality. It creates dependency and mimicry that reinforces the privilege. According to Arrighi (1991), as the dominant groups set the agenda, they hide the fact that not all wealth can be democratically appropriated. Most wealth is oligarchic and, hence, is monopolized by a few. Even in terms of wealth supposedly obtained using some time-honored market principles, the few who control it actively seek to block the widespread access to its acquisition. This is what University of Cambridge political economist Ha-Joon Chang has called *Kicking Away the Ladder* (2002).

On the other hand, a new political economy is flourishing. Preaching social justice, a much bigger goal than to be found in mainstream development economics, the inclination of this new political economy is to seek respectability, technical correctness, and conventional policies for redistribution. Examples can be seen in Thomas Piketty's important work and, curiously, in many of its critical reviews, including those published in the *Review of Radical Political Economics* (Reitz, 2016), *Metroeconomica* (Skillman, 2016), *Cambridge Journal of Economics* (Rowthorn, 2014), and *After Piketty: The Agenda for Economics and Inequality* (Bousehey et al., 2017). The focus on big data and technical formulae is commendable but their neglect of class, race, gender, and space not only as individual constructs but also their intersectionality, indeed linkage with the wider problem of uneven development obfuscates (Crenshaw, 1991). As an historical example, Engels' book, *Origin of the Family, Private Property, and the State* (1884), gave us only a partial insight into patriarchy as it is centered on class formation and dynamics in capitalism without due consideration of precapitalist forms of patriarchy and how they shape patriarchy in diverse forms of capitalism. Simone de Beauvoir's *The Second Sex* (1949/2009) brilliantly broadens the terms of the debate by examining patriarchy in other modes of production preceding capitalism, but forgets or downplays race. It is correct, then, for the black feminist, bell hooks, to ask in her 1981 classic, *Ain't I a Woman?* (1981). Since that historic question, first posed by the black feminist Sojourner Truth, in 1851, the situation has worsened, or in optimistic analyses, remained the same or changed little as black feminists are recurrently marginalized, their work devalued, and their voices stifled in the major publications on feminism (Crenshaw, 1989; Medie & Kang, 2018). Such neglect weakens any *avant-garde*, as it did when Aime Césaire – a prominent black scholar and, notably, Frantz Fanon's teacher – resigned from the French Communist Party, citing, as his reason, an insensitivity in left circles to everything other than class.

Yet, these forces intermingle, whether in *favelas* (Brazil), *aashwa'I* (Egypt), *bidonvilles* (France), or ghettoes (USA). These spaces of color are created, (allowed to) exist, and expand to contain the colored peoples who served the colonial empire and to absorb the "reserve army of labor" after bouts of economic depression (resources extracted from colored peoples and their land) to its own race (UN-HABITAT, 2003; Njoh 2009a, 2009b; Milliar & Obeng-Odoom, 2012; Peters, 2013; Obeng-Odoom, 2015b; Fondevila and Quintana-Navarrete, 2019). It is, thus, futile to seek to explore – as mechanistic economics does – whether it is race or class that is more important in this drama of life. Truly dialectical and intersectional analysis can only show that it is both (for a detailed discussion, see Chibber, 2013; Warren, 2017) in addition to other forces. The slums of the "wretched of the earth" play an important role in absorbing redundant labor that simultaneously reduces the cost of the privileges enjoyed by white capitalist society. When this analysis cascades up, the entire Global South, the wretched of the earth, can be seen as the slums of the world. It is pertinent to ask why "the wretched of the earth" persist not in spite of but because of their subjection to the modernizing and patronizing logic of Western civilization, as this is at the heart of the compartmentalization of the world in which we live.

From these considerations, five key questions beg for answers; namely (1) what are the patterns and dimensions of inequality across the world? (2) What are the causes of inequality? (3) Why does inequality persist? (4) Why is inequality an important focus for political economic analysis? (5) What can and is being done about inequality and by whom? I seek to answer these questions with reference to Africa as a point of departure for preparing the ground for a new political economy of the global south.

## THE PROBLEM, CONVENTIONAL DIAGNOSIS, AND MAINSTREAM PRESCRIPTIONS

Why Africa? Africa is the poorest continent in the world. Of the twenty-six poorest countries globally, twenty-four are in Africa (Harrison, 2011). More than 40 per cent of the population in sub-Saharan African (SSA) lives in extreme poverty. Although this represents a decline from the 1990 level of 57 per cent, the rate of poverty reduction in SSA is the slowest in the world. Poverty in Africa's growing urban centers is on the rise (UN, 2015). Across the continent, inequality is also on the rise within and between countries, groups, and classes. In spite of great expectations that Africa will "catch up" and, until recently, the recent resurgence of economic growth, the effect of growth has not consistently reduced poverty levels nor increased the share of Africa's GDP in the world economy. While Africa's largest economies, Nigeria and South Africa, grew substantially, their poverty levels remained either unchanged or increased (Lawanson & Oduwaye, 2014, see also Chapter 6). This "progress and poverty," as Henry George ([1879] 2006) once described the co-existence of affluence and want, can also be seen in the global sphere where, in spite of rising economic growth in Africa, Africa's contribution to world GDP has remained stagnant at 2 per cent since 2005 (United Nations Office of the Special Advisor on Africa (OSAA) and the NEPAD-OECD Africa Investment Initiative, ca. 2016).

Persistent inequality and poverty in Africa is typically explained as a function of the scarcity of human capital, the lack of physical capital, and natural capital problems. It is common to lump these problems together as a cultural problem (Gīthīnji, 2015). Theoretically, this "culture of poverty" idea – first developed by the anthropologist, Oscar Lewis (Wilson, 1992) – can be explained in two ways. The more conservative view, perhaps best presented systematically by the political scientist Edward C. Banfield (1976a) in *The Unheavenly City*, is that Africans have a culture that keeps them impoverished and, hence, no amount of public intervention such as decent schooling facilities for Africans can address their problems. The only solution is to assimilate the black populations into white groups or to get blacks to copy the whites. A more liberal interpretation is that the "culture of poverty" arises from poverty itself. The poor devise this culture as a survival mechanism and, hence, public policy that is able to remove poverty can also remove the culture of poverty (Banfield, 1976b; Marmor, 1976). The work of African economist, Eiman Zein-Elabdin (2016), provides a detailed account of how economists treat culture in their analyses of Africa (see also Ramnarain, 2016), a point to which we shall return in Chapter 1.

At this stage in the analysis, it is sufficient to peel off the cultural label and unpack its contents. Figure I.1 attempts to do so.

This figure shows the interaction of three forms of capital that, the argument goes, individually, and in their relationships, spell doom for Africa. Africa lacks physical capital or the humanly produced factor of production. Human capital, considered to be analogous to health, education, and experience, is held by many leading economists to be the principal driver of productivity, wage levels, and whether there is a convergence of incomes and wealth across, within, and between social groups, but this human capital is also lacking in Africa (Schultz, 1951, 1961; Gylfason, 2001, 2011). Natural capital, or "natural stocks that yield flows of natural resources and services without which there can be no production" (Daly, 1990, pp. 249–250), are abundant in Africa yet Africa has not been able to utilize them for any special advantage.

The reasons for this state of affairs can be found in how the forms of capital relate to one another. These forms of capital are considered substitutable (Salih, 2001). That is, one could be used to obtain the other in the process of production. In this sense, total capital can be maintained by expanding physical capital, which is typically considered as the limiting factor. While ecological economists hold natural capital to be "special," as

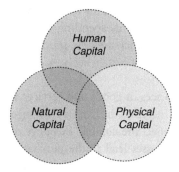

Figure I.1 Conventional diagnosis of poverty and inequality in Africa

it is the foundation of our existence, and the link between environment and development (Daly et al., 1994), mainstream economists tend to consider natural capital as an ordinary factor of production that must be utilized to increase the share of the other forms of capital to bring about economic growth.

Africa's natural capital, however, drives out all the other forms of capital. So, the natural capital problem has become a widely discussed issue in the study of Africa. Drawing on a wide range of theoretical positions, from "resource curse," "neopatrimonialism," to the "tragedy of the commons," the rich, diverse, and vast natural resources of Africa are seen as fundamental to the explanation of the continent's poverty and inequality problems (Hardin, 1968; Collier, 2006, 2009a, 2009b; Handelman, 2010; de Soto, 2011). Most of the existing work on minerals in Africa is framed around the resource curse thesis, which connotes the direct relationship between resource boom, and economic, social, as well as ecological pillage (for reviews, see Obeng-Odoom, 2014a, 2015a).

The original explanation for this paradox of abundance was framed around the so-called "Gregory Thesis" (Murray, 1981) after Robert George Gregory who showed how a boom in natural resources led to deindustrialization in Australia. The idea was recalibrated as "Dutch Disease" by *The Economist* magazine when it was describing how the Dutch economy experienced deindustrialization, following the dependence on the oil and gas sector in the North Sea (*The Economist*, 1977). Subsequently, Max Corden and Peter Neary (1982) provided a more systematic explanation of this paradox. According to them, in resource-rich economies, resources, including capital and labor, tend to move away from the manufacturing sector to the booming sector which can, in turn, cripple all other sectors – a process they called "resource movement effect." A "spending effect" sets in when, with the demise or contradiction of sectors other than the booming one, prices of goods and services in the non-booming sector rise as demand outstrips a declining supply. This spending effect can also set in when the sudden inflow of resources increases the purchasing power of some locals who, in turn, demand more of certain services – a process that tends to push up the prices of such services.

Either way, relative prices of goods and services increase in the booming economy. This, in turn, increases the *relative exchange rate*. While this process does not automatically affect the *nominal exchange rate*, it usually does in the sense that spending processes lead to the purchase of more local currency either because foreigners are buying more local currency in order to buy the country's natural resources or that foreigners are paying the country international currency which is used to buy local currency. As more local currency is bought, the price or exchange rate of that currency appreciates. A strong currency is usually viewed positively, but not so for manufactures that are exported because they become too expensive. Similarly, as the country obtains strong currency, it is cheaper for people to import more but that, too, can adversely affect manufacturing as fewer local manufactures are bought. Paul Collier, the University of Oxford-based development economist, has been a leading voice in the application, and further development of this idea. In his work, environmental problems, and socioeconomic and political tensions are all driven by resource booms, as exemplified in his vast scholarship on the subject (Collier, 2006, 2009a, 2009b).

Regarded as a "breakthrough," because it went against the prevailing "big push" approach to development at the time (Fosu & Gafa, 2018), the natural capital problem is not only restricted to minerals: it is much wider, usually extending to features of African land culture that inhibit investments and economic growth. Specifically, African communities have open-range land rights systems which are alleged to be inefficient and insecure, to impede access to credit, and to be inappropriate for the purpose of public administration, planning, and the provision of schooling. Indeed, the ready availability of land resources ostensibly drives out self-investment in human capital because working in such resource-based sectors requires little education and training (Gylfason, 2001). This strange case of natural capital driving out human capital serves as the basis for the argument that Africa has natural resource advantages (abundance of landed resources), but its customary land tenure system creates economic disadvantages (lack of human capital, lack of physical capital) (Collier & Venables, 2012).

Sharply critical of this view is a range of social scientists, especially social anthropologists and political scientists, who argue that it is precisely the erasure of African land culture that is the problem. What we have, then, is a debate in which one side condemns, while the other side romanticizes culture and traditions. Table I.1 contains a summary of the principal polarized positions in the debate.

The approaches summarized in Table I.1 are culture-centric, but they differ substantially in detail. Economists, especially those at the World Bank, frequently utilize cultural approaches to understand Africa in their engagement with the continent. In its seminal report on land, *Land Reform* (World Bank, 1975), the World Bank put forward the case for the use of formal title registers, individual tenure, and promoting market exchange in land.

Its lead economist with responsibility for land and development economics, Klaus Deininger, later coauthored a paper reporting that the

Table I.1 *Diverse cultural approaches to development*

|  | Economists | Political Scientists | Anthropologists and others |
|---|---|---|---|
| Unit of analysis | Customary institutions | Individuals and their clientelist relationships | Social identities, cultural groups, communities and community practices |
| Theories | Transactions costs | Public choice, neopatrimonialism | Social capital |
| Vision | Formalization and growth | Formalization and managing cultural expectations/results | Preservation of culture but also accepting that cultures change |
| Key proponents | Hernando De Soto, Klaus Deninger, Erica Field, Douglas North, Ronald Coase | A. K Onoma, Michael Ross | Carola Lentz, Liz Alden Wily |

World Bank had changed its views (Deininger and Binswanger, 1999). The revised World Bank position is stated in its 2003 report, *Land Policy for Growth and Poverty Reduction* (Deininger, 2003). Like the 1999 paper, the World Bank stresses its change in orientation, but a critical reading reveals that the basic argument remains the same or similar. Marketization of land is viewed as the key for economic development and poverty reduction. The report claims that customary land requires recording and state backing to be secure. Secure tenure is given by government through enforcing formal land rights. Women's rights are better guaranteed by formal rights. More formal tenure is the only reason credit can be given; customary tenure ought to evolve to individual tenure in the process of economic development; and land must be regarded as an "asset" and its exchange encouraged (Deininger, 2003, pp. xvii–xlvi).

Various agencies of the United Nations (e.g., FAO and UN-HABITAT), USAID, and an assortment of German development institutions (e.g., KFW Development Bank and GTZ) consistently have promoted this type of land reform. They offer the additional reason that it protects people from capricious and arbitrary evictions (Obeng-Odoom & Stilwell, 2013; Ehwi and Asante, 2016; Bertrand, 2019). In fairness, some economists, even in the World Bank, are more cautious about the pursuit of formalization, as is evident in the work of Hanan Jacoby (Jacoby & Minten, 2007).

Academic economists can be more nuanced too, but the tendency to emphasize titling is prevalent, often creating tensions between local context, inherited ideals, and imposed practices (Akiwumi, 2017). Duke University economist Erica Field, in several papers on the theme, seeks to demonstrate that the formalization of property rights leads to economic growth and redistribution of wealth and income, not only across the general population, but also between gender and ethnic groups. Registration is the route to access credit, to generate entrepreneurship, to improve urban housing, and to reduce urban poverty (Field, 2005). Some Asian economists also have given forceful support to this argument: the colonial adoption of registration that South Korea copied from Japan has been used to explain the rapid development of South Korea (Yoo & Harris, 2016) and the greater degree of liberation of its women (Yoo & Steckel, 2016).

Others, like MIT economist Daron Acemoglu and Harvard University economist James Robinson, take the approach to the global stage in explaining the social conditions of the poorer nations in their tome, *Why Nations Fail* (Acemoglu & Robinson, 2012). In doing so, their explanation draws heavily on the idea that the lack of clearly registered and formalized property rights holds African nations back and hence an aggressive marketization of landed property is the sure path to economic prosperity. This optimism is buoyed by research that appears to show that titling and hence security of tenure free idle labor by making it possible to draw people into the labor market who previously had wasted time taking care of unregistered land (Field, 2004). Indeed, these gains in efficiency arise from switching the role of guaranteeing security of tenure from local communities to the state. Also, titling leads to "substitution of adult for child labour" (Field, 2007, p. 1561).

Although widespread in academic circles and influential among policy makers, as Dan Bromley's (2008) review shows, this tendency to formalize has caused more harm than good (see Manji, 2006; Chapter 3). Not only are its assumptions unrealistic, its predictions are not borne out by real-world experiences in Africa. More fundamentally, the "social costs" (see Kapp, 1950/1971) of tearing apart property systems that have been communal for ages have manifested in widespread displacement and, hence, expulsion. Perhaps, the worst part of this process has been the transfer of landed wealth from the poor to the affluent, many of whom are also key advocates of this particular type of land reform.

There are, of course, major exceptions in the research on the economics of land reform. The work of economists such as Jean-Philippe Platteau, William Darity Jr., and Dan Bromley are clearly respectable exceptions. However, the *tendency* in the field is to pursue formalization, often in insidious ways of looking for – indeed creating – the precise conditions under which different types of formalization may produce beneficial effects. This "continuum" approach is also advocated by United Nations agencies such as UN-HABITAT. That is, there is a tendency – indeed a conceptual bias – to pursue formalization and to underestimate the power of other systems (Elahi & Stilwell, 2013).

In political science, this cultural approach is exemplified in A. K. Onoma's book, *The Politics of Property Rights Institutions in Africa* (2009). Onoma endeavors to show how patronage and clientelist relationships define the distributional effects of land reform. More fundamentally, he seeks to explain the nature of land reform primarily in terms of demographic and other internal factors such as ethnically informed ideologies. It is this approach to political science that is the source of inspiration for economists who pass some political comments about Africa, as exemplified in W. Arthur Lewis' (1965) book, *Politics in West Africa*. More recently, Ernest Aryeetey, a leading development economist, deployed this approach in his lecture at the United Nations University World Institute of Development Economics Research when he sought to answer the question, whether "democracy has failed African economies."[1] Although very closely linked to the public choice school of economics, the approach is, however, steeped in political science cultures that carry over to various "African Studies" departments.

Extreme forms of such analyses can be found in the idea of neopatrimonialism widely espoused by American political scientists. Highly influential, because it guides the approach of many key actors in the international community in dealing with African states, neopatrimonialism provides the basis for predicting the economic performance of Africa, and, reigning as the dominant political science approach to studying Africa (Mkandiwere, 2015), neopatrimonialism rests on the methodological claim that African politics is shaped by the "personality, management skills, and governing institutions of the incumbent ruler" (Bratton & van de Walle, 1994, p. 465). More fundamentally, this politics is inherently African:

---

[1] Aryeetey, E., 2018, "The political economy of structural transformation – has democracy failed African economies?", WIDER Annual Lecture 22, September 14, Helsinki, www.wider.unu.edu/event/wider-annual-lecture-22-political-economy-structural-transformation-has-democracy-failed (accessed 28 January 2019).

Our thesis is as follows: embedded in the ancien regime. Authoritarian leaders in power for long periods of time establish rules about who may participate in public decisions and the amount of political competition allowed. Taken together, these rules constitute a political regime. Regime type in turn influences both the likelihood that an opposition challenge will arise and the flexibility with which incumbents can respond. It also determines whether elites and masses can arrive at new rules of political interaction through negotiation, accommodation, and election, that is, whether any transition will be democratic. (Bratton & van de Walle, 1994, p. 454)

Even if the specific theories used in these analyses differ, the essence of the analysis – the emphasis on culture, difference, and internal factors to the fundamental neglect of international neocolonial and neoimperial factors, global markets, contexts, and the economic structure of the world system – makes this approach similar to the public choice theories used by diverse economists such as Duncan Black (Mueller, 1976). Indeed, the pre-analytic commitment to show that patronage and clientelist behavior is "rational" and the result of "self-interest" is often cast in terms of the new institutional economics credo of "transaction costs," as a reviewer of Onoma's book correctly points out (Lund, 2012).

The fundamental ontological, methodological, and empirical errors in neopatrimonialism have been systematically demonstrated. According to Thandika Mkandawire (2015, p. 602), "The attribution of all African ills to neopatrimonialism simply undermines internally driven change by occluding the real problems." Such problems, including Africa's unequal position in the world system, are conveniently glossed over by appealing to cultural defects in African leaders and hence building a framework that inevitably leads to Afro-pessimism founded on claims of causality that are suspect, metaphors that are better defined by their exceptions, false paradoxes, and non-sequiturs. A teleologically functionalist approach, neopatrimonialism has created what Mkandawire (2015, p. 602) calls "ontological despair" which, in popular parlance, has also fuelled much Afro-pessimism.

Many anthropologists of Africa have developed the opposite ontological and epistemological positions, which lead to quite different arguments. Drawing on ideas of "social capital," they contend that it is authentic African culture that will liberate the continent from the shackles of poverty, want, and inequality (for a critical review, see Fine, 2010). What is puzzling about this seeming challenge to the "cultural approach" is that, although it is not cast in "a general equilibrium framework . . . for the analysis of a host of issues related to property rights enforcement, corruption, and investment" (Acemoglu & Verdier, 1998, p. 1382), the standard trope for mainstream economists, it is also a variant of cultural determinism.

By focusing on cultural practices without systematically linking them to their evolution over time mediated by the economic system – especially the creation and distribution of rents locally and globally – this type of anthropological work produces another cultural "fetishism" (Alden Wily, 2011). Francis Nyamnjoh, the Chair of Anthropology at the University of Cape Town, famously pointed out that anthropology is guilty of failing the standard of social science scholarship; that is, engaging all possible evidence on an issue. Instead, the standard practice is to ignore major global structures and look, rather, at local stories – gleaned from interviews, whether done over two or a million years – without a wider political-economy engagement (Nyamnjoh, 2012a, 2012b, 2013).

One of the articles in which he made these points (Nyamnjoh, 2012b) drew prompt responses (or more precisely "defenses" of anthropology) from his fellow anthropologists (see, for example, Gordon, 2013, Niehaus, 2013, Teppo, 2013). However, as Nyamnjoh (2013) pointed out, they did not engage the cultural tokenism, mystification, and romanticization that, to this day, characterizes most anthropology of Africa.

Furthermore, the neoclassical conception of human capital problem – widely shared and promoted by the World Bank – manifests in the analysis of how Africa's mineral resources are governed. Here, the typical claim is that not only do Africans lack education but they also lack experience to govern their resources. It is in this sense that many African states are being directed to adopt "local content" in their minerals policy (see Chapter 4).

Within this framework, transnational resource corporations are the preferred governance institution for African resources. However, these corporations are required to support learning programs in the extractive industries and offer employment to this new cadre of specialists. In this way, such transnational corporations provide not only education but also experience to Africans in order to enhance the quantity and quality of human capital on the continent (Ovadia, 2016a).

According to the standard narrative, Africa's "capital problems" are mutually reinforcing. While different in their proximate theories, there are some crossovers. For example, the premises of conventional public choice theory are shared by economists and political scientists. More fundamentally, these approaches are influenced, more or less, by the intertwining theories of John Locke, Garrett Hardin, and Robert Lucas.

Locke's labor theory of property states that when land is not put to its highest and best use through private property investment and large-scale

commercial agriculture (of the kind not historically typical in African societies), we should expect poverty and economic stagnation (Andrew, 2012). For
Hardin, the consequences of common land are degradation, pollution, and
social chaos. Robert Lucas, the Nobel Prize winner in economics, famously
argued that capital is not moving to poorer regions through trade and hence
the regions are stagnating and falling behind other regions because of low
levels of human capital and a culture of property relations that is too communal (Lucas, 1990). Indeed, such regions could lose the limited human capital to
richer regions and hence become even more disadvantaged because of inadequate human capital. Centrally focused on national, not global, factors, the
Lucas model gives no room to explain international inequalities based on
initial historical conditions. Rather, the incomes of economies with similar
levels of human capital are expected to converge (Darity & Davis, 2005). These
prescriptions require additional comments to flesh them out.

## Mainstream Prescriptions

Centered on a three-way emphasis on "local content" minerals policy, an
expanded role for transnational corporations (and free trade), and the
formalization of land, advocates of mainstream prescriptions claim that
these economic reforms – diagrammed in Figure I.2 – will deliver Africa
from its crippling poverty and inequality problems.

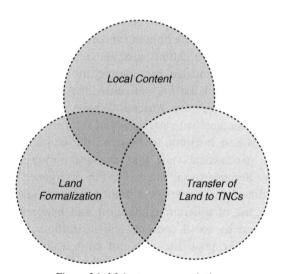

Figure I.2 Mainstream prescriptions

Designed as a rapprochement between Euro-American mission of "helping" Africa and "preserving" Afro African culture, the spirit behind this range of prescriptions is quite similar to the indirect rule system developed by imperial Britain. However, whether this mode of governance promotes "integration" or "assimilation," it resembles the French colonial policies around such genre (Njoh, 2007; see also Chapter 5).

For example, Europeanized African land reforms export the practices of the "successful" Western countries to the poor Africans, keeping Africans in charge through institutions such as customary land secretariats. This system of land tenure relations, the argument goes, explains the success of those economies. If Westernized, the argument continues, African countries will escape from poverty and close the gap between their material conditions and those of the West (de Soto, 2000). The characteristics of these Euro-American tenurial arrangements include formal title registration, regarding land as an asset that must be traded to be efficiently managed, and subdividing customary land. Variations of these ideas, incorporating state planning, and intended to enhance the operation of land markets, have also been advocated (Lai & Lorne, 2006). I shall revisit these characteristics in Chapter 3.

## Challenging the Mainstream?

Conceptual and empirical research in a variety of contexts (e.g., Darity & Williams, 1985; Folbre, 2012; Basu, 2017) provide a strong challenge to the mainstream lines of analyses in (development) economics. Their insights suggest that Africans may lack human capital, but mere credentialization does not eliminate discrimination based on color. Reasons for such discrimination vary. They include stereotyping, informed by past and continuing discourses about the backwardness of Africans, and deliberate biases intended to privilege non-Africans. Whatever the reasons, discrimination shapes agreements with Africans and informs assumptions about African practices and institutions. In turn, the conditions of Africans contradict the neoclassical view that markets only reward merit or human capital. Because social hierarchy, the divergence in wealth, the different and differential experiences among Africans (e.g., women and men; and Africans of different ethnicities) and between Africans and others, are shaped by social contexts and institutions, not only is the neoclassical human capital discourse not empirically verifiable, it also diverts attention from social provisioning and impedes efforts to interrupt the social contexts which reproduce disadvantage.

A rich body of literature challenges the idea of a "resource curse" on several grounds. Aspects of this body of work show that the nature of the neoliberal economic reforms imposed on African countries in the 1980s systematically led to a weakening of African states, the destruction of their social policies, and the creation of a generous tax climate for transnational corporations that led to a transfer of rent from producers to rentiers (Nwoke, 1984a, 1984b; Adésínà, 2012). In this sense, neoliberalism and neoliberalization could be seen as drivers of the resource curse rather than the panacea that its advocates contend they are.

Yet, it is a particular neocolonial type of neoliberalism that is in question here. Patterned after neocolonialism and imperialism, the reforms of the property rights system have privileged Western institutions and firms, giving them rights to exclude Africans from their own natural resources. With greater economic power and a global system that can shield powerful actors (compared with weakened African states) from being accountable, it is transnational forces and the institutions that support them rather than natural resources per se that create and sustain the present conditions in Africa (Rodney, 1972/2011; Harrison, 2008; Duchrow & Hinkelammert, 2010). The far more propitious experiences of resource-rich economies in the Global North give additional weight to the argument that a different set of institutions and property systems generate quite different outcomes.

Relying on the idea of "good governance," Paul Collier (2009a, 2009b), for example, argues that because strong institutions in the countries in the Global North were built *before* such countries discovered oil, they have tended to be blessed rather than cursed by oil. From this perspective, weak institutions are further weakened when economies become resource rich, a process which, in turn, creates a "natural resource trap". What is puzzling is that the Global North has benefitted substantially from these cursed minerals, allegedly because they have better institutions. Indeed, in contrast to the "natural resource traps" in Africa, countries with already strong institutions are said to be better able to govern fortuitous resources. Thus, some analysts have sought to argue that it is precisely the *staples* of mineral-rich economies such as Australia, Norway, and particularly Canada that best explain their higher standards of living (Watkins, 1963). These claims and Africanist responses are further explained in Chapters 5 and 8.

Yet, there is a danger in jumping from resource curse to resource blessing. Whether in Canada or Australia, resource optimism does not address the problems of resource pessimism. Historic and continuing dispossession of Indigenous or First Nations peoples, disastrous economic busts, wealth inequalities, and ecocide in these economies and the role of the extractive sector in this "accumulation by dispossession" (Harvey, 2003) cannot all be swept under the carpet of resource blessing (Rahnema & Howlett, 2002; Dow & Dow, 2004; Cahill & Stilwell, 2008; Mills & Sweeney, 2013). The nature of the institutions governing natural resources and how these institutions have been created, or are evolving within path dependencies established by historical processes, could be a more fruitful area of investigation.

However, the account of history in the conventional wisdom is far from satisfactory. Take the historical aspect of culture, as an example. Common to most of these analyses is a notion of history as "past" or as a "moment." In this view, the continuing and cumulative influences of historical processes, either in terms of shaping current and future institutions or in terms of their effect on the psychology of present-day society and its peoples, take the form of an equivalent ailment to "post traumatic slavery syndrome/disorder" (Darity, 2009). Indeed, with respect to Africa at least, New York University professor of history Frederick Cooper has shown that the "history" in cultural approaches is highly superficial and too short term. Cooper shows that the history is read in such a way that mimicking Western institutions becomes the only salvation (Cooper, 2014). Such historical approaches tend to have both weak predictive and weak explanatory power in the sense that they are not able to explain the heterogeneity in the trajectory of groups that have experienced similar past trauma. Just as critically, such approaches tend to neglect contemporary and ongoing discrimination and the crucial question of which past events are more damaging. Even more fundamentally, such historical approaches struggle to illuminate how historical forces intermingle with present-day, ongoing political economic processes of marginalization (Green & Darity, 2010). This history is not only "compressed," it is also based on highly problematic data-sets (Jerven, 2013, 2014, 2015).

While the challenge to mainstream development economics has been extensive so far, it has not as yet answered several important questions. Of these, three are particularly important because they raise fundamental issues about the structure of African economies. These questions are (1) how are rents generated and distributed, (2) what institutions maintain the current system, and (3) how best to recapture appropriated rents through expropriation of land, exploitation, and exclusion of black labor, particularly women and other minorities (e.g., migrants)? In short, as Rachel Kranton (2016) asks, "where do social distinctions and norms come from?"

The attempts to address these questions are unsatisfactory. Take the case of the economics of identity. As Ben Fine (2009) has shown, the nature of mainstream economics has clouded its vision and undermined its answers. The problem is that the economics of identity reduces fundamental questions to a narrow theory of social identity in which individuals select among identities without considering the social and economic structures and contexts within which such "free choice" must be made. Whether one of the sticks in the bundle of options is what is to be chosen or whether the choice is to be exercised over several bundles of choices, this approach to addressing the identity question is fundamentally flawed. A liberal alternative is to accept the status quo and the continuing production of inequality, social disadvantage, and poverty, and tax the advantaged classes for the purpose of redistributing their incomes to the marginalized. According to proponents, this approach is advantageous because it will ensure high levels of productivity, as only the best will be employed (Basu, 2017).

While an improvement over the economics of identity approach, this liberal alternative has the grave demerit of reinforcing the perception of inferiority of Africans, overlooking the grave psychological cost of unemployment, especially for women (Diette et al., 2015), and leaving unaddressed widespread inequalities in wealth *between* Africans and the rest and *among* Africans themselves. More fundamentally, these critical alternatives do not address the question of weak and strong sustainable development. Weak sustainable development is what is advocated by the mainstream. Informed by the idea of substitutability, the depletion of African resources is not a problem, as long as new technologies can be found and the externalities of ecocide can be internalized through putting a price on nature (Daly et al., 1994).

Yet, as Table I.1 and Figure I.2 suggest, this approach is highly inappropriate for studying Africa, not only because of the centrality of land to the identity of Africans and their economic systems, but also because of its inability to help in revealing the dramatic loss of biodiversity on the continent and its deleterious consequences for economy and society. Additional, more detailed and more nuanced analyses supporting these conclusions can be found in Chapters 3, 5, and 6, which go beyond the standard explanations of "Why development economics fails Africa" to which I now turn.

## Why Development Economics Fails Africa?

It is commonly claimed that development economics has failed because of problems intrinsic to economics (see, for example, Keen, 2003) or because of the problematic practices of economists (see, for example, Mäki, 2018). A more comprehensive position, contending that the reasons why development economics fails Africa is a bit of both, is developed by Polly Hill and Morten Jerven.

Polly Hill's principal challenge to development economics is both conceptual and pragmatic. For Hill, development economics tends to make conceptual mistakes, tends to over-rely on official statistics, and tends to neglect inequalities. In her words, she sought "to expose what I see as the old-fashioned, stereotyped, Western-biased, overgeneralized crudity and conceptual falsity of so many conventional economic premises, as well as economists' complacent attitude to bad official statistics" (Hill, 1986, p. xi).

Conceptual mistakes are fundamental to Hill's critique. Consider the idea of "peasant". If it is conceived as someone struggling, then, according to Hill, the idea does not apply to most of the people called peasants because they have much income from non-agrarian sources, which they combine with incomes from agrarian activities. Likewise, peasants are so diverse that their presumed shared objection to a common enemy is not often apparent.

The notion of "debt" is another conceptual faux pas. It is common to think of traditional money lenders as seeking to "rip off" other community members. However, Hill argues that, in many African communities, people tend to be simultaneously creditors and debtors. When a harvest is good, it is expected that one gives out credit in the form of seeds, for example. Also, even if there may be usurious conditions, much debt is not on usurious terms, as the debt relation is usually between friends, family members, and even lovers. It would help to have an estimate of the proportion of debt that is usurious to better understand the magnitude of the conceptual problem in the mainstream thinking. However, beyond expressions such as "invariably very high," Hill provides no clearer estimates. She notes that such exactness is itself problematic:

As for the number of debtors, this is invariably very high . . . as I have just said, people often borrow with one hand (for one purpose) and lend with another . . . the tendency to differentiate negates any urge to aggregate in order to arrive at net indebtedness, which means that the bald terms *debtor* and *creditor* are often meaningless. This is one of many reasons (three others being the secretiveness of creditors, the short-term nature of much credit, and the likelihood of default) why, as I have earlier insisted, the incidence of . . . "indebtedness" cannot be measured. (Hill, 1986, pp. 87–88, italics in original)

This conceptual critique of development economics leads to Hill's second concern: development economists' blind faith in statistics and the techniques for analyzing it. For Hill, the concepts used by statisticians are usually meaningless and they often misrepresent the landless and the powerless in

Africa either by overlooking, or by undercounting, such groups (see, for example, Hill, 1986, pp. 43 and 48). In essence, the available official statistical information is not reliable. If this is so, regardless of the rigor in the technique for analyzing the data, the results are likely to be questionable. Indeed, Hill argues that the more sophisticated the techniques, the less meaningful the results. In her words:

It is not fanciful to insist that as the sophistication of "data processing" increases, so the quality of the finished statistical product declines. Increasingly, so far as the rural third world is concerned, the power lies with those who have become so astoundingly proficient in manipulating the figures they receive "from below" – with the eager people who derive so much enjoyment from the advanced electronics. Infatuated by their technology, it is beneath their dignity to contemplate the *inherent unreliability* of their "basic data" – and their resultant impotence is never contemplated. Consequently, all the commands come from above, and the less ambitious, and far less clever, "data collectors" cower underneath. How can the international world be persuaded that the problems of collecting statistics, and allied material, at the ground level in the third world, are just as intellectually challenging, and far more important, than mere mathematical processing? (Hill, 1986, pp. 48–49, italics and quotation marks in original).

Hill is neither against econometrics per se nor is she against the use of data. Both are necessary for policy making and research. While modern political economists such as Ben Fine (2019) argue that, in practice, the elevation of big data and the use of econometrics as "better" research strategies lead to the crowding out of other strategies, what concerned Hill was rather different. She was against the reliance on problematic concepts, inadequately measured, and analyzed. As this problematic research design forms the basis of bold claims by those who know little or nothing about the African social context, this is a serious concern.

In developing this critique, Hill offers additional grounds for her analysis. She points out that the idea of "household" used in development economics is flawed fundamentally. Her reasoning is that there is substantial heterogeneity within the household. For example, Hill notes that in West African and South East Asian countries, even the standard definition that a household entails a group of people related by eating from the same bowl is mythical. Neither is the idea that everyone knows everything about other people in the household plausible because wives do maintain separate accounts, have separate economic activities, and sometimes live separately. In turn, the concept of perfect information, that belies much neoclassical development economics, is problematic. Indeed, in real-world households in Africa, information asymmetries can be regarded as the norm.

Long before Päivi Mattila-Wiro's (1999) review of the "economic theories of the household," Hill had shown that development economics tends to neglect (a) heterogenous complexities within the household, (b) the study of inheritance and the transmission of wealth, and (c) the peculiarities and complexities of women's experiences, including with land, men, and other women. Today, much research in home economics questions the unitary model of the household often associated with the economics of Gary Becker, but the resulting "new" models, such as the bargaining models, consensual models, and independent individual models (see Grossbard, 2010 for a detailed discussion), do not address the totality of Hill's critique, including the issue of wealth transmission. In this sense, development economics is centrally focused on growth, typically elides intergroup inequality, and obfuscates the nature of colonialism, neocolonialism, and imperialism, especially how their impacts are transmitted through generations.

Another serious defect of development economics is "The Golden Age Fallacy." This latter problem – elaborated in Chapter 6 of *Development Economics on Trial* – is what Hill calls "Aboriginal equilibrium" or the idea that there was "equality at the base" or that there was a pristine moment in the history of the poorer nations in which everyone was equal in rural society. Sometimes known alternatively as "the myth of Merrie Africa" (Hopkins, 1973, p. 10), this problematic explanation of African history (Emeagwali, 1980) leads neoclassical economists to suggest that it is not useful to study inequalities in rural areas because they do not exist, while Marxist economists only claim that, under precapitalist conditions, inequalities in rural areas are imposed by external factors.

The consequences of these conceptual and pragmatic problems are serious enough to unsettle society and economy. Hill identifies problems such as research that takes us nowhere, economics that misinforms or hides reality by neglecting it, and policies that make bad situations worse (see, for example, Hill, 1986, chapters 2–4). Development economics also peddles much misinformation, including the misleading claim that rural economies are entirely agrarian when, in fact, there are non-agrarian economic activities in such economies.

The policy mistakes identified by Hill are also important, particularly because they have had a more direct impact on Africans. For example, the bias of mainstream economists for mechanical farming – based on assumptions that small-scale farming is inefficient (Hill, 1986, chapter 2) – has led policy makers to neglect and to reject small-scale farming. Yet, as Hill (1963, 1966, 1986) shows, such farms can be – and often are – socially efficient. Indeed, cocoa farming of West Africa is done on a small-scale basis but it is able to supply the world's cocoa needs as well as meet the needs of the cocoa farmers.

Hill's criticisms (1) that mainstream development economics does not provide an effective approach to studying inequality, (2) that it is both Eurocentric and America-centric in both its concepts and vision of the good society, and (3) that these problems have contributed to worsening social conditions in Africa deserve the attention I have given them. They show the historical and continuing conceptual and epistemological limitations of development economics, a field that has supplied significant directions for policy-making in Africa.

However, Hill's diagnosis of the problems is limited. The problem is not just that the mainstream relies on problematic concepts and unreliable official statistics. Hill neglects questions about rent, space, and energy, overlooking how they are problematically treated in existing knowledge on stratification and, hence, treats lightly crucial conveyer belts of stratification in Africa (Mabogunje, 1980; Obeng-Odoom, 2013b, 2014a). Indeed, although modeled on the physics of energy (Mirowski, 1988a, 1988b), neoclassical economics has been unsuccessful in systematically theorizing energy, even in terms of narrow concerns about growth (Ayres et al., 2013) with much less to contribute about energy–space–rent and stratification interlinkages (Obeng-Odoom, 2014a). To neglect all these, as Hill does, is akin to discussing Catholicism without analyzing the papacy.

So, I caution against Hill's preference for an "indigenous economics" that is merely a marriage between anthropology and economics. While much stronger on analyzing entire economic systems (Marxist and old institutional economics versions), adapting methodological individualism to transaction costs (new institutional economics versions), and indeed addressing some of the problems identified by Hill (example, drawing on anthropological studies), *it does not succeed in probing inter-group inequalities shaped by multiple identities such as race, class, and gender and how these mould ecologically sustainable and inclusive development in poorer regions and among peoples of color.*

Similar problems characterize the book that answers the second question: Morten Jerven's (2015) *Africa: Why Economists Get It Wrong*. According to Jerven (2015), economists are entirely mistaken in their analyses of what is happening in Africa. Not only is their statistical information contrived, but also their description is wrong, their explanation is worse, and their policy advice is grotesquely awry. While this argument is not new, Jerven's book is the most recent, most extensive, and, perhaps, the most visible of the body of work that addresses these two interrelated questions, namely: the wrongs with development economics, especially in the African context, and why development economists get Africa so wrong.

Unfortunately, Jerven's contribution has been misunderstood. Some scholars, sensing his challenge to mainstream economics, confusingly regard his impressive oeuvre as Marxist or a rejection of market-based economic development. Others claim that even if his work is not Marxist, the book is a fundamental challenge to mainstream economics in its application to Africa (see Burbidge, 2016). Two contrasting interpretations of Jerven's book are common. On the one hand, some claim that Jerven's book "dismisses Karl Marx" (Wynne & Olamosu, 2015), but others such as Alfred Zack-Williams (2016) suggest that Jerven's work is Marxist, indeed equating it to the work of Andre Gunder Frank. Granted that Frank was influenced by Marx, it is debatable whether dependency theory, as constructed by Frank, was, in fact, Marxist.

Zack-Williams (2016) also suggests that Jerven's book is a radical green critique by pointing to some similarities with the work of René Dumont (see, for example, Dumont, 1966). Indeed, for the same book, some have interpreted it as showing that "if we can get the numbers right, we can help more people" (Gates, 2013), while others contend that Jerven's argument is "nice models ... do not tell the whole story" (Woodson, 2016, p. 579). Many others, who have correctly interpreted the book, have missed the political-economic context of his work, including Jerven himself (Jerven 2013b).

Therefore, it is important to set the record straight and provide a political-economic assessment of the book. According to Jerven, economists have been seeking to explain two things: first, a chronic failure of growth (first generation of economic growth literature, pre-2000s) and, second, slow growth trends (second generation of growth literature, post-2000s). By implication, they have been trying to explain uneven growth trends and the consequent "uneven development." However, neither of these trends is applicable to the African case in practice. In fact, Jerven argues, economists are chasing something that *never* happened. African economies grew recurrently after the continent gained independence (especially in the 1950s and 1960s) from various colonial regimes and, largely, have continued to grow since the 1990s. What economists frequently have done is use data collected in the late 1970s and 1980s (the period for which data are available and neoclassical economics became ascendant) and form impressions about Africa based on data sets that cover two decades when Africa experienced a major recession. Indeed, Jerven (2015, p. 4) argues that the first generation of economics literature confused the effects of the 1980s recession with an alleged general problem of slow African growth.

For Jerven, economists get Africa wrong because, although they pick ideas from history, they cherry-pick history and hence do not really understand the totality of African experiences. They seek, instead, to use shortcuts to become African experts but, depending on downloaded data sets often without knowing either the contexts within which the data were generated or the processes that are captured in the data, they become, instead, empty barrels.

Relying on unreliable data concerning countries they know little about and, hence, are unable to determine how much confidence to put in the data, their models are also ahistorical. They do not conduct detailed, careful long-term studies; they ask the wrong questions; and they err in interpreting social and economic phenomena. Even worse, these problems cannot be remedied easily because they are structural to the field. Unless economists are prepared to abandon years of perfecting a flawed approach, Jerven argues, the problems can only get worse.

Indeed, for Jerven (2015, p. 8), addressing the problem is only possible if the grand question asked about Africa changes. The question needs to move from why Africa has not grown/has grown slowly to how Africa grows and why African economies first grew, declined, and have regained growth. This reframing gets the history right, which, in turn, leads to focusing on the right contemporary policy issues. The focus for this rebirth of development economics should be on approaching Africa as a continent experiencing recurring growth, not newly occurring growth. And, of course, growth is not necessarily development.

Jerven (2015, p. 10) seeks to challenge African development economics by questioning its assumptions, evidence, interpretations, and the plausibility of the resulting "technical" economic advice. While non-economists will find Jerven's book helpful in empowering them to judge the work of the development economists, economists also will gain from reading this book, especially if they will take the author's advice: economists need to show "a bit more humility; in particular, a better understanding of the limits of their own datasets and statistical testing" (Jerven, 2015, p. 10). Indeed, economists and non-economists alike will learn that "A useful piece of general advice for cross-disciplinary work is that assumptions, data points and observations should roughly match the state of knowledge in other disciplines. It could be argued that this is not only useful advice but a fundamental principle" (Jerven, 2015, p. 70).

Political economists may well say, "we told you so," however, they would recoil at the near total absence of "the political economy of growth," to use Paul Baran's (1957) expression, from the analysis in Jerven's book. The book gives little attention to whether social progress is, in fact, accurately measured by GDP, in what ways GDP actually leads to a devaluation of labor given large informal economies in many African societies, the widespread existence of social enterprises whose activities are undervalued by an emphasis on growth or devalued by growth, and the direct link between GDP addiction and the brazen destruction of the environment in Africa (Fioramonti, 2013, 2014, 2017). Even worse, the book overlooks the invention of GDP as a springboard to enhance the power of Western countries, to force Africa to open its doors to plunder by transnational corporations, and massive displacements in Africa owing to the promotion of "growthmania," an idea developed at length in E. J. Mishan's (1967) book, *The Costs of Economic Growth*, let alone engage the debates generated by such ecological concerns, including Africanist concerns about "just transition" (Agyeman, 2013).

There is little discussion of the growing inequality within Africa and much less discussion of inequality between Africa and the global economy. Indeed, even in Jerven's own narrow framework of technical, data-based analysis of GDP, neither the limited contribution of Africa to global GDP nor its implications for society, economy, and environment are analyzed. In fact, as Matthias Schmelzer (2016) shows in his book, *The Hegemony of Growth*, the history of GDP says something completely different. There is nothing African about the political manipulation of GDP statistics nor the political manipulation of the conditions generating actual levels of GDP. This political number has always been manipulated to win wars, to maintain imperial power, to include some in, and to exclude others from, powerful clubs. The manipulation of the conditions that generate actual levels of GDP distract attention from pressing issues that confront power structures, as Lorenzo Fioramonti discusses in his book, *Gross Domestic Problem* (2015). Instead, Jerven's book adopts an idealist and technocratic epistemology that neglects materialist and historical concerns. In turn, it seeks paradigmatic change on the assumption that better quality technical power and quality numbers alone can save Africa.

The evidence, however, shows that growth – indeed the entire economics establishment – owes its success not to its superiority of ideas or methodology at all. Economics has attained its imperial status not just because of strong and rigorous methodology or even its better use of data, but also because it serves an ideological role of obfuscating interests such as class, race, and gender. As Michel de Vroey (1975, p. 416) famously noted: "in a class society, the ruling class cannot be indifferent to the type of social science developing in the society in which it holds power." This point has also been established systematically by Krisha Bharadwaj

(1986) in his book, *Classical Political Economy and the Rise to Dominace of Supply and Demand Theories*. More recently, John Weeks (2014) has put the case against economics differently, as expressed in the title of his book, *The Economics of the 1%*, emphasizing how the application of economic doctrines reinforces the wealth divide in favor of the owners of capital. It is, of course, important to study technical quality and Jerven does so brilliantly, but technical acuteness cannot be fully understood without an analysis of the political economy of measurement or of ideas more generally.

The far sightedness of Jerven is eclipsed by two cataracts. First, he does not link the turn to institutions and good governance in the 2000s to the rise of new institutional economics. In turn, he makes no analytical distinction between what Boettke, Fink, and Smith (2012) have called mainstream (neoclassical) and mainline (new institutional) economics, in turn, between the economics of individual choice and the economics of institutional exchange respectively. So, he conflates orthodoxy and heterodoxy in the form of new institutional economics. In this sense, the book does not succeed in showing that what has been happening in the economics of Africa is echoed in what is happening in the economics discipline more generally, as the account of Harold Demsetz (2002), a leading new institutional economist, suggests. The cataract is an unwillingness to extend his analysis from the doxy (orthodoxy of neoclassical economics and the so-called heterodoxy of new institutional economics) to the doxa (real world political economy), to use Pierre Bourdieu's nomenclature recently utilized for the analysis of global trade by Bill Dunn (2015).

Chapter 3 of Jerven's book, which is supposed "to focus less on aggregate growth and more on the political economy of growth, asking who benefits" (Jerven, 2015, p. 4), is centrally focused on growth with no analysis of inequality at all. Chapter 4 (p. 102) promises to go deeper than statistical issues, but the analysis remains data- and technique-driven – without attention to conceptual matters. Pertinent issues such as whether to take the ecological critique of growth seriously and deduct environmental bads (and other bads) from the gross measure to arrive at a net national product (NNP) are overlooked entirely. More fundamentally, the meaning of progress, its measurement, and how congruent it is with well-being are not even contemplated. Yet, as argued elsewhere (Obeng-Odoom, 2013a), these issues constitute crucial pieces in the jigsaw of analyzing African economies.

These concerns, in the wider context of the Global South, led scholars, such as Amartya Sen, Gustav Ranis, and Paul Streeten, working under UNDP Project Director, Mahbub ul Haq, to construct a human development index (HDI) (United National Development Programme [UNDP], 1990). Sen was later to develop the conceptual foundations of the HDI in the book, *Development as Freedom* (Sen, 1999). Nevertheless, this effort generated further questions about the measurement of economic performance. Indeed, writers such as Charles Gore (1997) suggest that many of the weaknesses that were raised against the GDP oozed into the estimation of HDI. Indeed, a critical ingredient in the estimation of the HDI is the GDP.

It is certainly important to deal with the statistical limits of GDP, but equally important are three additional aspects of GDP: first, its conceptual underpinnings; second, its philosophical basis; and, third, its historical journey to becoming what Fioramonti (2015) calls "the world's most powerful number." Trying to resolve these issues leads to questions about the relationship between GDP and inequality, GDP and poverty, GDP and environment, indeed GDP and happiness; and GDP and the structure of African urban economies, especially the dominance of informal economies (Obeng-Odoom, 2013a).

By ignoring the conceptual aspects of GDP, Jerven's work misrepresents the structure of African economies, especially the prevalence of informal economies. He misses how the most comprehensive improvement in techniques, benchmarks, and data quality in formal economies will overlook such economies and hence contribute to further misrepresenting African economies. Indeed, these neglected issues necessarily mean that we will need to focus on GDP and the idea of economic development itself, how it has evolved, and in what ways it has been measured over time.

Why did development change from being regarded as a colonial project to exploit resources in Africa to becoming a methodologically nationalist project for countrywide change? What led to this shift from being too economic to being socioeconomic?

Some of these issues are raised in H. W. Arndt's (1987) book, *Economic Development: a History of an Idea*, and, in more recent work (Rist, 2008; Obeng-Odoom 2013a), so Jerven had much work on which to build. Yet, he made a conscious choice that leads to the view that the growth problem is technical in nature. Questions of power, imperialism, patriarchy, and racism, even Eurocentrism, are missing in the book.

Not surprisingly, Jerven's reading list is seriously wanting in political economy research in Africa. There is little engagement with research in political economy journals – the exceptions being few indeed: two *New Left Review* articles by Arrighi (2002) and Lawrence (2010), and one *Cambridge*

*Journal of Economics* article by Mkandawire (2001). Research published in such journals as *Review of African Political Economy* and the *Review of Black Political Economy* do not get even a polite nod. There are a few references to the work of political economists such as Fantu Cheru, Cyril Obi, Frederick Cooper, Walter Rodney, and Mahmood Mamdani, but no preponderance toward political economy or even postcolonial analysis.

So, the question arises about where Jerven is going with his critique? He makes no appeal to justice or oppression. In turn, his critique is open to many interpretations. For instance, African statisticians worry that Jerven's work is aimed at dismissing the effort of African professionals in the many statistical bodies in Africa. Indeed, some African institutions have had to issue public statements against Jerven's work and, at least in one case, Jerven has been prevented from travelling to Africa by power brokers on the continent (Jerven, 2015, pp. 121–123). Part of the reason is, of course, that Jerven's book is centrally focused on state capacity – without acknowledging any significant improvement and certainly without looking at the structure of African economies (importantly, informal economies).

However, any claim that Jerven's intentions are to undermine African statistical bodies will also need to take into account some crucial observations he makes: for instance, on page 111, where he explicitly makes the case against those Bretton Woods institutions responsible for reducing the capacity of African institutions and, at the same time, asks them to work more effectively, while implicitly suggesting that the statistical authorities require more support.

Similarly, Jerven (2015, p. 125) also notes, "Africa's growth failure happened because of a combination of external economic shocks and a less-than-perfect policy response, from both international donors and national economic policy makers. But laying the blame solely on institutions and policies was a costly mistake."

However, many mainstream economists make similar claims. Daron Acemoglu, for example, makes the Eurocentric new institutional economics claim that settler colonies have developed precisely because of colonialism, while neo-colonial societies in which extractivism was the key focus of the colonialists, have lagged behind. Even if Acemoglu seeks to place the explanatory emphasis on how settler colonialism triggers incentives for investment rather than on the identity of the colonizers themselves, by prioritizing institutions of private property, allegedly the driver of greater economic development in the West, while downplaying the effects of slavery on draining Africa of its resources which helped build the West, Acemoglu's analysis is Eurocentric (for a detailed discussion, see Darity & Triplett, 2008, pp. 266–270).

Some of this Eurocentricism can be found in Jerven's own analysis. For example, he argues that Africa struggles because of colonial problems. However, it appears that, in his earlier book, *Poor Numbers* (Jerven 2013a), Jerven singled out, or focused almost entirely, on what, in his extensive review of that book, Michael Lipton summarizes as "Africa's national-accounts mess." Jerven critiques national institutions on the grounds that they are not sufficiently independent, the statisticians are poorly trained, and the other members of staff are not up-to-date on the use of the latest software, among others (see Lipton 2013 for a detailed review). So, in the book under discussion, Jerven might really be seeking to shut the stable doors when the horses have already bolted! That is why a clearer political commitment is needed from him. Yet, it is interesting to read how Jerven himself thinks the struggle can be won, including "getting African economies right":

> The solution is to refocus the study of economics on the study of economies. The increasing distance between the observers and the observed has created a growing knowledge problem. With the move to cross-country studies based on macro-analysis, country-level nuances have been lost. In other words, cross-country growth regressions can take us only so far. [pp. 130–131] ... It is the job of scholars to give tempered assessments that navigate between what is make believe and what passes as plausible evidence. That's how you avoid a statistical tragedy. (Jerven, 2015, p. 123)

Similarly, he states, "I hope I have shown that simply by asking questions – How good are the numbers? What are the assumptions? How convincing is the story? – one can engage critically with mainstream economics" (p. 132).

So, for Jerven, there is no place for power and ideology. Here, we see a non-materialist, positivist basis for social ideas: the view that ideas rise and fall only because they are "true." Yet, there are ideological elements in, for example, the fall of Ricardian economics (as Michael Reich showed in his work published in the *Review of Radical Political Economics* in 1980) and ideological elements in the rise of neoclassical economics (see, for example, the work of Mason Gaffney and his editor Fred Harrison in *The Corruption of Economics*, 1994).

Another example is the idea of the resource curse. As noted earlier, Jerven is critical of this concept. He says:

> When I wrote my own master's thesis at the London School of Economics in 2003–04, I was struck by the focus thus far on explaining only lack of growth, but I thought it was just a legacy of the 1990s. I was surprised to find that in 2007, three years later, major publications such as *The Bottom Billion* still stuck with the old line – there is no growth to explain here. (Collier 2007, cited on p. 25)

Jerven continues, commenting "The bottom line is that there is no "bottom billion." The evidence shows that the so-called traps are escapable and the so-called curses are not destiny" (Jerven, 2015, p. 132).

But the real problem with the idea of a resource curse is not so much that the calculations are wrong – important as that is. Rather, the idea – drawing on the metaphor of metaphysical forces of a curse and hence the impossibility of nations being able to do much about it – diverts attention from property and class relations as well as rent capture by transnational forces and corporations, the challenges of globalization, and the nature of uneven and unequal exchange, even imperialism (Emmanuel, 1972; Elhadary and Obeng-Odoom, 2012; Njoh, 2013; Obeng-Odoom, 2014d, 2015b). The resource curse analysis, in effect, is a grand scheme to undermine national authority and mercantilism, and it calls for more and more deepening of neoliberal globalization.

Of course, it is crucial to know why economists get Africa wrong. However, stopping at this stage without a radical political-economic analysis of the foundations of Africa's past, present, or future prosperity is insufficient. Jerven focuses on technical arguments, but GDP is more a political tool than a technical measure. The GDP has always been manipulated and contested for that reason. The Soviet Union was a victim of GDP manipulation, as Lorenzo Fioramonti shows in *Gross Domestic Problem* (Fioramonti, 2015, pp. 33–40). China, the USA, and others have all manipulated or refrained from correcting their GDP calculation for political reasons rather than technical ones.

The issue with the GDP is, therefore, not only technical, but also political. Africa's development has not always been tied to GDP: it has evolved from one matrix to another – for political-economic reasons intricately interwoven with matters of expediency. The GDP anoints the globalization turn, it promulgates a particular vision of progress, and it institutionalizes a particular type of power. This foundational focus is necessary to understand and transcend the roots of the complex social conditions in Africa. There are certainly more structural issues, including the appropriation of the African commons, the dynamics of the vast informal economies in Africa and their insertion into the global economy, and the growing inequalities within Africa and between Africa and the rest of the world. Neglecting these foundational matters and fine-tuning GDP only endorses – indeed worsens – the ongoing world order which tries to spit Africa out to the margins and tie it there. The technical, databased analysis of GDP can – indeed should – be part of a holistic political-economic critique of mainstream economics, especially in its deployment to understand Africa.

In short, although economic ideas are largely political, spread and sustained by various interests ((Schmelzer, 2016), leading J. K. Galbraith

(1979) to once claim that development economics emerged as a field to legitimize certain interests in Western nations, both Polly Hill and Morten Jerven provide idealist critiques, assuming that ideas are free-floating, unattached to any organizations, institutions, or interests. Analytically, this idealism is problematic because, as Michel de Vroey (1975, p. 416) famously noted, "in a class society, the ruling class cannot be indifferent to the type of social science developing in the society in which it holds power." Alternatives, beyond currently existing ones, are needed.

Mainstream development economics, conceptualized in this book as neoclassical development economics and its variants such as new institutional economics, is clearly limited. However, existing Marxist alternatives provide no panacea either. Both treat inter group and intra group stratification problematically. Both hide serious institutional processes with the mask of culture, as Eiman Zein-Elabdin's (2016) book, *Economics, Culture, and Development*, shows; and both neglect, or treat superficially, the questions of space, rent, gender and energy (see, for example, Obeng-Odoom, 2009, 2014a, 2014e, 2014f; Gore, 2017). The solution to these problems, however, cannot be further stretching the favored, but already over-stretched, explanatory framework, what J. K. Gibson Graham (1996/ 2006) called "capitalocentricism." Ironically, it is this capitalocentric framework that guides the latest books on African political economy, including Lee Wengraf's (2018) excellent book, *Extracting Profit: Imperialism, Neoliberalism and The New Scramble for Africa*.

### "The Beautyful Ones Are Not Yet Born"

The state of the literature, then, demonstrates the Ayi Kwei Armah paradox. During the decolonization period, there was much hope for a new Global South. Revolutionary leaders arose, promising a new world, and offering powerful ideas. Yet, colonial compartmentalization remained and, in many cases, birthed neoliberal compartmentalization. The reason was that the social relations bequeathed by the colonizer's philosopher (slavery, feudalism, capitalism, and imperialism) had not been repudiated. Instead, the logic was that the more that legacy or outgrowth of its roots in the form of capitalist and other modes of production could be embraced through forces of modernization/denied through "villagization" projects, the more developed/post-developed the ex-colonies would be. It is this limitation that the novelist Ayi Kwei Armah captured in his now classic novel, *The Beautyful Ones Are Not Yet Born* (1968).

The real problem of the existing knowledge on stratification in Africa is not that it fails in its exposition, but that it succeeds in obfuscating reality. It conveniently overlooks what R. T. Ely called "the ground under our feet." It strenuously claims that we now live in an era when fundamental questions about land and rent no longer matter; such an emphasis, we are told, is "too narrow." In short, it obfuscates the crime of stratification.

Like other crimes, deflecting attention is a defensive strategy of the crime of stratification. The appeal to culture is to mask shocking forms of rentierism, the view of Africa rising serves to legitimize the status quo, while the stubborn insistence on only capital serves as a strategy by both the left and the right, progressive and mainstream writers, to hide their complicity as beneficiaries of the historical and ongoing system of land, property, and rent appropriation.

It is insufficient to call for a change. What is needed is not just change; but a just change. I propose stratification economics as one route toward that change. Pioneered by black economists and other economists of color, the field aspires to be a formidable alternative to both the orthodoxy and existing heterodoxies (Darity et al., 2015). The nature of this sub-field together with its features is discussed in the next chapter.

1

# The Foundations for a New Beginning

As we have seen, "The Beautyful Ones Are Not Yet Born." From neoclassical economics to Marxist economics and institutionalism between them, "culture" has been an important focus for explaining inequality within Africa and between Africa and the rest of the world. In addition to suggestions made in the previous chapter, Eiman Zein-Elabdin's latest book, *Economics, Culture and Development* (2016), clearly establishes the various ways in which cultural explanations have been central to the key schools of economic thought, as has "modernization".

K. B. Anderson's book, *Marx at the Margins: On Nationalism, Ethnicity, and Non-Western Societies* (2010), shows that, at least early in his writings, Marx was quite pro-colonial. Although Marx's position on the colonial question became far more critical, according to Anderson, the relevance of many concepts in Marxist analyses to non-Western societies continue to be debated today. The principal polarized position, represented by the Chibber-Spivak debates that have been extensively covered in the book *The Debate on Postcolonial Theory and the Specter of Capital* (Warren, 2017), is whether to adopt or to jettison Marxist analyses. A possible middle ground is adapting, rather than adopting, these concepts wholesale, a line of analysis that even committed Marxists (see, for example, Barnes, 2012) accept and, hence, suggest that the foundations for a new beginning must be built.

Neoclassicals have been even more dismissive of African ways of life, viewing them as noneconomic barriers to progress. Alfred Marshall (1890), in *Principles of Economics*, focused on defects in Africa when he claimed that the continent is backward because of its savage cultures, harsh climate, and poor working habits of its peoples. Lord Peter Bauer (1971), in similarly focusing on the defects in Africa, claimed that Africa and Africans had "those attitudes and customs which most inhibit material advance" (p. 38). Indeed, Bauer contended that Africans lacked capital as well as "administrative skills, thrift, the ability to perceive and take advantage of economic opportunity, and various other aptitudes and attitudes, derived, in part from the background of societies long accustomed to the ways of a money economy" (p. 347). Modern neoclassical economists, under the aegis of the World Bank and the IMF, also tend to focus on defects in Africa. Their argument that Africa was has been backward because of the size of state interventions, as exemplified in the work of the prominent Oxford University economist Sir Paul Collier (e.g., Collier, 2006, 2009a, 2009b), is a case in point.

Institutionalists – whether of the old or new stock – tend to either celebrate or condemn culture, although they also insist that cultures are dynamic and their effects on economic development in Africa are contingent, for example, on the weather (Poirine and Dropsy, 2019). Part of a bigger problem of dualism or, better still, Manicheanism, the tendency is to teleologically conceive of African countries as moving from tradition, from collectivist cultures, from under/less development, and from particularity to modern, individualist, developed, or universal societies, as canonically explained by W. W. Rostow (1959) in his version of modernization theory. This thinking has always been part of economics, but it has been particularly intense or less intense at different periods, a pattern Zein-Elabdin (2016, pp. 9–13) has called "hospitality, retreat, and return."

Beyond questions of culture, other explanations for the persistence of inequality in Africa have been similarly simplistic, whether they relate to the lack of (human) capital or the presence – indeed abundance of and dependence on – of natural capital and the resource curse (as this introduction tries to make clear). More systematic and comprehensive explanations need to be developed. Doing so must involve building new foundations, but the question is where to begin: How do we build the conceptual foundations for a new beginning? In what ways can these be defended or reinforced against counter currents? When built, what sorts of arguments can they support? It is these questions that this chapter answers in three sections, respectively examining the nature of the foundations that can be built for a new beginning; clarifying the aims, paradigm, and arguments; and providing the overall structure of the book.

## What Foundations Can Be Built for a New Beginning?

The most developed social science tradition that can handle these relatively neglected aspects of political economy is the Georgist tradition. Its method of analysis – first developed in full in *The Science of Political Economy* (George, 1898) – is simply the systematic reconstruction of political economy (currently largely centered on capital and profit) to re-centering it on land and rent in their relationship with capital and labor. Modern Georgist theorists, however, tend to be quite ahistorical, quite sectoral, quite nationalist, quite idealist, and neglectful of stratification in Africa (see, for example, Gaffney, 1994; Foldvary, 2008; Giles, 2016, 2017).

To address these problems, my approach is to draw on the original work of Henry George and the ideas of stratification economists and black philosophers such as William Darity Jr. of Duke University and Sir Hillary Beckles of the University of West Indies. A formidable alternative, stratification economics is pioneered by black economists and other economists of colour (Darity et al., 2015). This field is characterized by at least three features. First, the acknowledgement of the existence – indeed persistence – of income, but especially wealth, inequalities between and within groups whether subnationally, nationally, regionally, or across the world system as the central problem. Second, the rejection of cultural and scarcity-of-capital (physical and human) explanations of stratification or structural inequalities. Third, investigating alternative explanations that take seriously the structural and institutional relationships between the privileged and the underprivileged, and probing the dialectical relationship between the conditions of the affluent and the afflicted. Emphasizing the interconnections between institutions and identities such as race, gender, and class is a major focus of analysis, as is how these identities shape and maintain diverse political economic experiences.

The field borrows from previous schools of economics, especially institutionalism, and, hence, the use of the term in the title of this book. For example, the idea of social provisioning or context as developed in original institutional economics is useful in stratification economics (Stewart, 2010). Here, the "context" or institutional foundations of social stratification becomes a focus of analysis. However, stratification economics is a distinct field in itself. So, neither development nor underdevelopment is taken as given. So-called habits or cultures of poverty, often seen as embedded within complex and dynamic social structures (Wilson, 1987), must also be related to wider global processes. Clearly, in stratification economics, so-called "culture" is irrelevant as explanation (Haila, 2016). Not only is the emphasis on culture inadequate, it also deflects attention from social realities that are unpalatable for privileged groups (Williams, 2017).

This orientation makes stratification economics critical of approaches that are based on the idea of the "free" individual devoid of any social bonds and critical of the so-called "rational *man*" of neoclassical economics whose identity is freely chosen. Like original institutional economics, the individual is an 'institutionalized mind' (Commons, 1934b/2009, pp. 73–74), showing sociality; not 'possessive individualism' as claimed by neoclassical economists (for a new critique of "possessive individualism", see Bromley, 2019). Yet, much original institutional economics itself was complicit in eugenics or the "scientific" justification of racism (Zouache, 2017), which stratification economics rejects. So, the book adapts, rather than adopts, institutional economics. This need to modify institutional economics has been recognized by many institutional economists, including Yoshinori Shiozawa (2004) in his manifesto of institutional and evolutionary economics in the twenty-first century. In *Reconstructing Urban Economics* (Obeng-Odoom, 2016d), I showed why we need to revise the work of Gunnar Myrdal, for example, therefore, I will not repeat myself here. I have also put the case for adapting, rather than adopting, the work of institutionalists such as J. R. Commons in my recent contribution to *Evolutionary and Institutional Economics Review* (Obeng-Odoom, 2018), and, hence, a repeat analysis here is not warranted. I revisit the work of others such as Karl Polanyi, Thorstein Veblen, and Joseph Schumpeter later in the book (see, for examples, Chapters 2, 3, and 7): for now, I will focus on the work of J. K. Galbraith only to illustrate the need for serious engagement that leads to adaption rather than adoption.

The choice of Galbraith is not arbitrary. He played a pioneering role in providing the contours of radical institutional development economics. Not only was he the first to try to develop courses on development economics, he was also one of the first economists to be consulted by the US government on development economics. The detailed account of the close interrelations between the politics and economics of development economics (see Galbraith, 1979, pp. 23–43) makes him a pioneering figure in the political economy of development. Indeed, although the recent flurry of interest in his work generally, as shown by Mike Berry in *The Affluent Society Revisited* (2013), is mainly because of his progressive analysis of inequality in the West, Galbraith also moved beyond other institutional economists by providing a bulwark against conventional thinking on development economics in Africa and elsewhere in the Global South. Indeed, for these reasons, Adam Sneyd (2014) has recently put the case for African political economy to embrace what he calls "Conceptual adventures via John Kenneth Galbraith." He is not clear, however, on which specific concepts, frameworks, and adventures that ought to be prioritized.

Scholars such as Zein-Elabdin (2016) point to ideas in Galbraith's book, *Economic Development* (1964), as *the* defining features of the Galbraithian approach to the political economy of development. However, this work is superceded by Galbraith's more specific and later classic, *The Nature of Mass Poverty* (1979). Galbraith himself considers this latter work to be the complement of his well-known book, *The Affluent Society* (1958/1998), which deals with that poverty "which afflicts the few or, in any case, the minority in some societies" ("case poverty"). *The Nature of Mass Poverty*, on the other hand, deals with "the poverty that afflicts all but the few in other societies" ("mass poverty") (Galbraith, 1979, p. 1). As the contrast between case poverty and mass poverty is also the focus of this book's conception of social stratification, *The Nature of Mass Poverty* (1979) requires additional discussion.

That book provides a critique of development economics, an appraisal of its alternatives, and a synthesis that transcends the typical claims about the causes of and solutions to mass poverty. The central critique of mainstream development economics (see especially chapters 1 and 2 of *The Nature of Mass Poverty*) is that it invents the causes of development to fit what mainstream society would like to hear, or would like to give (think of development aid). From this perspective, poverty has to be analyzed in mainstream accounts as a function of the lack of physical and human capital. In turn, resources can be given in the form of aid to engender such missing qualities. These explanations focus on almost everything that absolves the rich of responsibility. So, questions of culture, of nature, and of environment as causes of poverty are often raised, but they are usually intermixed with other "causes" (e.g., inefficient bureaucracy and inability to effectively manage resource endowments) that the West can help to redress. Development economics, then, serves to obfuscate interests of mainstream society rather than illuminate the structural drivers of poverty and inequality.

Galbraith is also critical of alternative lines of analysis. In particular, he considers as simplistic the exclusive focus on the capitalist economic system, on capitalists and on landlords, and how this system acts as a disincentive to high levels of productivity. He identifies several countries with the same so-called faulty economic system that are doing much better than others which suffer mass poverty. So, he argues that such explanations, while not invented, are not entirely plausible especially when we do not know for how long they should remain relevant.

On the other hand, *The Nature of Mass Poverty* not only rejects, it also accepts some prevailing explanations. Galbraith is particularly interested in developing the work of Raùl Prebisch whose mode of explanation highlighted the relative trade and employment (dis)advantages from specializing in labor-absorbing industry and the labor-expelling nature of agriculture.

For Prebisch, as African countries tend to specialize in agriculture, they are likely to have two problems. First, the terms of trade would tend to decline on the world market. Second, the surplus of labor would keep wages low. The uneven balance of power or terms of trade between small firms (that dominate the market structure of Africa) and oligopolistic giants (predominantly centralized in Western countries) would tilt the advantages of such specialization away from the poor.

Galbraith extends this explanation by adding a third line of analysis, which he calls: "the equilibrium of poverty." According to Galbraith, this new equilibrium cancels out attempted progress by the poor in two ways. First, economic deprivation tends to stifle motivation for economic success not because the poor are innately unmotivated but because their economic circumstances lead to what Galbraith calls "accommodation" (see Chapter 4 "accommodation"). In his words: "The tendency of the rich country *is* to increasing income; the tendency of the poor country *is* to an equilibrium of poverty. And, in each there is accommodation, in the one case to the fact of improvement, in the other to the hopelessness of the prospect" (Galbraith, 1979, p. 46). This tendency is not a conservative line of analysis that emphasizes an innate culture of poverty. Rather it is "accommodation to the culture of poverty" (p. 60), maintained by certain forces of "circular causation":

Since life is near the bare level of subsistence, there is no saving. Without saving and the resulting capital investment, there can be, from within the agricultural economy itself, no investment in improved agricultural technology – in irrigation, hybrid seeds, pesticides, fertilizer, improved machine cultivation. Without such investment, there can be no improvement in income that allows of saving and further investment. (Galbraith, 1979, pp. 52–53)

This dynamic is compounded by institutions such as the church, indeed all religions that preach "hope" for the poor (Galbraith, 1979, p. 63) to acquiesce. Galbraith differs from Marx: he contends that religion is not meant to create a "false consciousness." Rather, according to Galbraith, "It is, more specifically, a formula for making the best of a usually hopeless situation" (p. 63). Indeed, for Galbraith, merely accommodating does not mean acceptance of the inevitability of poverty (p. 69). Instead, Galbraith draws a different conclusion from accommodation by putting the case for major interventions to energize the poor and reconfigure their environment to sustain a different attitude. According to him:

There are two broad lines of attack on poverty that are consistent with the circumstances as here identified. The first is to combat accommodation – to seek to enlarge the number of people who, resisting or refusing accommodation, are motivated to escape the equilibrium of poverty. The second is to facilitate that escape. (Galbraith, 1979, pp. 92–93)

Seeking to question both accommodation and the equilibrium of poverty, as well as significantly increasing the number of people who reject accommodation, Galbraith puts the case for redesigning industrial policy to lift people out of poverty through employment and promoting migration as an escape from poverty to environments where nonaccommodation can be developed (in order to increase the pulse of struggle rather than the comforts of accommodation). The type of migration he favours is the one in which migrants' rights to work are guaranteed and the migrants are supported and, indeed, considered citizens. For him, migrants make a contribution to the economy that is so dynamic that the admission of migrants need not be regarded as an attempt to dispossess natives of their jobs for the benefit of migrants. Migrants can share in a dynamic economy.

Galbraith's approach to poverty and inequality in *The Nature of Mass Poverty* (1979) appears to be comprehensive, but it has important flaws. Three require special emphasis because they are very serious. First, its strong appeal to the culture of accommodation is questionable. As Dorrit Posel and Michael Rogan (2018) have recently shown, the poor and the marginalized have not accommodated. Indeed, the protests and uprisings in Africa, why they have arisen, and how they have spread across the continent and the world provide further empirical evidence to refute claims of accommodation (see Amin, 2011, 2014; Murrey, 2018). The neglect of global forces is the second weakness in Galbraith's work. Of course "equilibrium of poverty" might occur, but why is the local the only constraining force? What about international or global forces and the relationship between the local and the global?

Galbraith's posited solutions are similarly contestable. Consider land reform. Galbraith's appreciation of this age-old idea is limited to reform only in terms of physical redistribution of land explained only as rural physical land. Even more narrowly, the power of landlords is limited only to their control of the police or the military (see Galbraith, 1979, pp. 69–75). This conceptualization leads Galbraith to problematically wonder whether there is enough land for everybody to work without thinking about rents at all. In turn, the question of the redistribution of rents as land reform does not arise in Galbraith's analysis. Finally, Galbraith's substantial focus on the *behaviour of the poor* (accommodation) leads him to conclude that colonialism was a positive force against accommodation (attitudes by Africans and the poor generally) because it provided "strong tutelary aspects which acted in many and varied ways against accommodation" (pp. 90–91). This conclusion is factually wrong in the light of the history of mass poverty (Rodney, 1972) and the history of the violence of colonial education (Nyamnjoh, 2012a, 2012b) or what C. G. Woodson (1933/1990) famously called *The Mis-Education of the Negro*.

Stratification economics can significantly enhance (Galbraithian) institutional economics and, indeed, all the other key schools of economic thought, ranging from neoclassical to Marxist economics. An effective response to what Polly Hill (1966) once called "A Plea for Indigenous Economics," stratification economics is a field developed by and for peoples of color for whose emancipation existing theses and anti-theses of social science methodologies have not fully served, that is, if they were ever created to serve them. Stratification economics, in short, is the attempt by political economists of colour to contribute to the decolonization of economics methodologies (Smith, 1999), an aspiration that cannot be found even in the most refined form of "the institutionalist theory of economic development," as clarified by James Street (1987), but which is crucially important to better explain stratification in Africa.

Under the inspiration of leading black economists, especially William Darity Jr., stratification economics is slowly becoming an established approach for investigation (Arestis et al., 2014; Price, 2018; Stewart, 2018). For example, this framework has successfully served as a guide to research on immigration, labor conditions, and the racialization of the distribution of wealth in ways that existing methodologies have not been able to grasp (Darity, 2009; Arestis et al., 2014). Stratification economics has also inspired some historical research such as Jessica Gordon Nembhard's recent important work, *Collective Courage* (2014), and Gladys Mitchell-Walthour's book, *The Politics of Blackness* (2018). In these applications, this approach has generated much deeper and more comprehensive insights than the economics of identity, or neoclassical, behavioral, or new institutional economics. Stratification economics has also shown greater promise for more comprehensive insights than anthropological studies that romanticize "African culture" and some Marxian economic analyses that "fetishize" "class" and overlook other crucially important institutions such as race and how they interact with class. So, the approach is fruitful and can usefully inform a better understanding of inequality in Africa to complement the existing political economic analyses of inequality.

Such advances look more broadly at economic inequalities by considering space, class, gender, and race (Stilwell, 1993; Stilwell & Jordan, 2007; Stilwell, 2019). So, they substantially demonstrate that inequality is not a monolith and, hence, has to be addressed multidimensionally. Consequently, the multidimensional approach has been widely embraced, including by the

International Social Science Council in its latest *World Social Science Report: Challenging Inequalities: Pathways to a Just World* (2016).

Yet, using this multidimensional approach, some political economists tend to estimate inequalities separately for different dimensions such as gender (Brewer et al., 2002), leading to mechanistic claims such as women get less than men, Indigenous people have worse health conditions, developed countries do this or that, while developing countries do such and such. Methodologically, this multidimensional approach can create binaries and, hence, can be criticized for being only partially dialectical, as Samir Amin (1977, pp. 191–193) reminds us in his magisterial work, *Imperialism and Unequal Development*.

Stratification economics develops a rather different approach. By embracing the idea of "intersectionality," developed by the black feminist scholar, Kimberlé Crenshaw (1989, 1991), for example, it looks not only at *dimensions* but also the *intersections* of identities such as race, class, and gender, over time and in space. The need to demonstrate intersectionality does not end with interlinkages among identities. It extends to probing the interlocking connections between the local and the global and investigating the intersections between geographies of development and underdevelopment on the one hand and the political economy of multiple identities on the other. Characterized by group and intergroup analyses of social problems and progress, the methodology of stratification economics is holistic. Unlike other holistic methodologies (Street, 1987), however, stratification economics probes entire economic systems and how their parts are interconnected without losing touch with the micro-political economy of the parts, including how their multiple and changing identities are oversimplified and reified as "culture" to offer so-called explanations that are, in many ways, attempts to justify, rather than explain, stratification in Africa.

Here is a political economy that puts the spotlight on structural intersectional compartmentalization, rejects hegemonic discourses that deliberately or negligently categorize effects as causes, and, hence, pursues public policies that can bridge the gulf of wealth and incomes separating diverse groups. This political economy can, of course, do more to decolonize methodologies by borrowing from all fields, not just economics (Smith, 1999); by more strongly embracing dialectics; by considering the intersection, indeed, indivisibility between economy and nature (Brewer et al., 2002; Maathai, 2004) at different scales around the world; and by embracing the richer and better traditions of old institutional economics, including ideas such as cumulative change, which is central to the work of Thorstein Veblen, Gunnar Myrdal, J.K. Galbraith, and K.W. Kapp.

As Charles Gore (2016) argues, a new *paradigm* of development economics is needed. Even if he does not fully elaborate what that means, thanks to Frantz Fanon's admonition to *The Wretched of the Earth* (1961), the struggle for a paradigmatic transformation will not be without vision:

[N]ow is the time to decide to change sides. [235] ... Come, comrades, the European game is finally over, we must look for something else. We can do anything today provided we do not ape Europe, provided we are not obsessed with catching up with Europe. [236] If we want to transform ... into a new Europe ... then let us entrust the destinies of our countries to the Europeans. ... If we want to respond to the expectations of our peoples, we must look elsewhere besides Europe. (Fanon, 1961, 239)

What Fanon means is a total rejection of Western supremacist philosophy of exclusion and compartmentalization. But, as Immanuel Wallerstein (1961) warns, this strategy is not a retreat into hamlet, localist life, but a pursuit of new multi-scalar social relations based on self-determination, sovereignty, equal rights, and equality of race, not just politically but also socioeconomically. Voting rights, which are currently denied to the "Wretched of the Earth" in international circles where the "veto" is the monopoly of the strong and mighty, constitute an epic example of modern fascism in the world system that must be named and shamed. Past humiliating social relations (some, as degrading as servitude for three centuries under colonialism/extended slavery) and raw robbery for even longer periods must be ameliorated through *multi-scalar* reparatory justice (Beckles, 2013); not aid, free, or fair trade, and certainly not the blind faith put in other individual, entrepreneurial options advocated by many such as Hernando de Soto (2000) and Dambisa Moyo (2009).

With the scale of implosion in the core shaking the foundations of Western civilization, stratification, institutional, and (Georgist) property economics provide the hybridized blend of what is called **A Political Economy Approach** for a new beginning. It is also from this tripartite combination that the book takes its name, *Property, Institutions, and Social Stratification in Africa*.

This integrative and holistic method is a better foundation than the alternative fragmentary traditions because it leads to fruitful avenues of data, including primary data that I have collected myself, a reinterpretation of existing data collected by others or produced by institutions such as the courts, and the systematization of fragmentary data. Of course, Africa is wide, diverse, and complex, but its various parts have commonalities too. Being intersectional also means that I can accept that African countries are both diverse and similar (see Crenshaw, 1989). In grappling with this complexity, I have greatly benefited from being the editor-in-chief of the *African Review of Economics and Finance*. Working with bright Africans in the last ten years to develop a better context for the data I have had to study has been a privilege in this regard.

Concepts such as land, space, and rent also take particular meanings in this experience and approach. Land does not take the neoclassical meaning of mere substitutable capital, which can be replaced in the process of production. Neither is land considered synonymous with the exertion of labor on land. Rather, following Africanist conceptions of land developed by, among others, S. K. B. Asante (1975) and H. W. O. Okoth-Ogendo (2003), land is what has been given by nature. The price of this "land" is "rent," which can arise from monopolizing land (monopoly rent), from location or fertility with the potential to give monopoly power to landlords (absolute rent), or from fertility, location, or some investment in land (differential rent), as discussed in more depth elsewhere (Harvey, 1973/2009; Markusen, 1978; Haila, 2016). The combination of these ideas about rent gives rise to other conceptions of rent such as the rents that arise from speculating on money and currency. In this sense, I adapt conceptions of rent from George, Marx, and Proudhon. What makes the conception more Georgist is not the categories but, rather, the tendency of rents to increase in the development process; not reduce with time, as suggested in some Marxist frameworks.

These rents are everywhere, of course. However, they generate different types of social relations, depending on the spaces where they are produced, including urban, rural, or peri-urban, local, national, international, regional, and global. This "spatial perspective" is, however, quite distinct from Akin Mabogunje's approach (see Mabogunje, 1980), which treats the "urban," and the "rural," as quite distinct. Instead, in this book, the two are dialectically interlinked and space is a crosscutting framework. International trade (Chapter 5) is spatialized, as are energy, economic growth (Chapter 6), and human capital (Chapter 4) processes.

More fundamentally, in analysing spatial inequality, my approach contrasts with that of neoclassical urban economics which suggests that spatial racism is temporary and, hence, disappears in the process of economic development. Or, that, if spatial racism persists, it is simply because of human capital differences, individual choices (Glaeser, 2011; Glaeser et al., 2014), or the result of culture. These explanations are captured in the so-called "laws of cultural dominance" (Downs, 1976, pp. 198–201) or "a general theory of 'tipping'" (Schelling, 1971, pp. 143, 181–186) in which, beyond a certain tipping point, the hitherto dominant culture (e.g., white) moves out or flees from its old space to give way to the growing culture of, say, blacks which has increased beyond the tipping point. These explanations are not only static, they are also abstracted from institutional or processes of systemic urban racism and, hence, deny or underplay the colonial and colonizing racism in urban Africa patterned after years of slavery and built into the urban fabric of cities on the continent.

To analyze spatial stratification, my approach is similar to, but quite distinct from, the work of the leading black urban sociologist, William Julius Wilson (see, for example, 1987, 1992, 2009). The similarities center on the recognition of systemic discrimination against Africans. However, unlike Wilson, whose approach emphasizes *intragroup* inequality as fundamental to explaining *intergroup* inequality, although he recognizes the systemic nature of the latter (for a more systematic analysis of Wilson's approach of what is called "the underclass" and its roots in the "split labor market theory," see Turner, 2010, pp. 10–11), I emphasize intergroup stratification as a product of institutions in the world's prevailing economic system. Specifically, I draw on queueing theory, which locates spatial inequality in the firm, or transnational corporations, the family, and the local labour market (Browne et al., 2003). I also draw on landed property and rent (Connolly, 2014). I too acknowledge intragroup inequality, but, much like intergroup stratification, it can be better explained by reference to the production, appropriation, and control of rents as well as the institutions that underpin the global world system. As a sociologist, Wilson's careful analysis of the family is rich with sociological and political economic insights. However, he limits his analysis of discrimination routes to biases against African men. My approach, in contrast, takes discrimination as crosscutting, afflicting both women and men and indeed all genders (see Crenshaw, 1989), albeit in distinct and intersectional ways.

It is on the basis of this approach that the book argues that instead of regenerative and inclusive development, the existing system transfers rents from producers – and reproducers – to absentee landlords, a process whose intensification, although widely recommended, is only likely to accentuate existing stratification, impede attempts to address it, and hide the structural processes in plain sight.

Although quite modest, systematically demonstrating this argument is important because it has serious implications. For example, if upheld, the polarizing debate between Vivek Chibber (2013) and some of the proponents of Southern theory could, I suggest, be resolved because this approach redefines matters of priority and explanation. In this sense, the idealist case for Southern theory (for a broad discussion of the various types of Southern theory, see, for example, Connell, 2004) is less compelling. Indeed, if upheld, it should follow that Africa's under development cannot simply be about shifting gears from one goal to another or even changing a development paradigm (Gore, 2016), which, although better than changing goals, is still idealist. Rather, like Walter Rodney's conception of development (see Rodney, 1972, pp. 3–29), my argument implies that development must be seen as a reorganization of how production, distribution, and their rewards are shared both internally and internationally, indeed globally. However, unlike Rodney, that reorganization can look down at what R. T. Ely, the great land economist, called "the ground under our feet."

## THE BOOK: AIMS, PARADIGM, AND ARGUMENTS

This book seeks to apply but also to advance stratification economics. Using multiple sources of data, the book tries to develop a distinctive stratification economics approach that brings together ideas in (original) institutional economics (such as absentee ownership, cumulative causation, and fictitious commodity), Georgist land economics (especially the notion of "rent"), and Marxist economics (such as exploitation of labor). Together, these concepts help to escape the prison of "culture," the binary tension between culture and structure, and, more fundamentally, simplistic explanations of inequality within Africa and between Africa and the rest of the world.

In developing stratification economics as a new and fruitful tradition in political economy, I reconstruct Figure 1.1 by replacing the notion that forms of capital are substitutes with the idea that they are, in fact, complements. So, reversing the depletion and degradation of natural resources must be central to the process of development. Growth, then, is important if it nourishes the environment and redistributes the wealth within the community of nations. Destructive production that displaces certain groups must be seen as problematic, while structural redistribution must be seen as a useful way to grow.

In this reconstruction, my idea of "human capital" is non-neoclassical, but Weberian and institutional. So, the approach under discussion is more akin to structural-based social change and human development generated from the redesign of institutions. Unlike the neoclassical framework of human capital that asserts that only credentials, good health, and experience matter, in this conception of human capital, the entire gamut of social provisioning and its historical formation and foundations matter in ways that intersect with institutions such as ethnicity, race, gender, and class on the one hand, and the wider global system, on the other. I accept the notion of physical capital subject to three modifications.

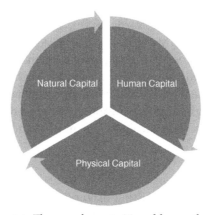

Figure 1.1 The complementarities of forms of capital

First, I recognize the contribution of Africans to its development in both historical times and the present (Rodney, 1972/2011). Second, I note that physical capital, developed for capitalist interests, has also generated and worsened processes of dispossession in a process that Myrdal (1944) once regarded as "circular and cumulative causation." Third, this "combined and cumulative" process (to use Veblen's expression, see Obeng-Odoom, 2018) of developing capital has transferred rents from producers to nonproducers (adapting some of the ideas of Georgist land economics; see George, 1879/ 2006). So, the development of physical capital is not always benign but can be a major contributor to what Fanon (1961) called the "compartmentalized" world. My idea of "natural capital" transcends the conventional wisdom of existing and optimal stocks because I include the meaning of land within Indigenous societies from which Karl Polanyi (1944/2001) developed his notion of "fictitious commodity." This reconstruction of the forms of capital and their interactions help me to escape the many zero sum games in mainstream development economics, ranging from the trade-off between growth and ecological problems to the triumph of pursuing growth at the expense of seeking inclusive social change. One concrete way of overcoming these dualisms is by emphasizing the indivisibility of nature and economy within society, as the African Nobelist, Wangara Maathai (Maathai, 2004), famously showed.

## Scale of Analysis

The book develops a multi-scalar analysis. An Africa-wide investigation is important for this purpose, but so is a probe into the experiences of specific cities and regions in countries such as South Africa (Southern Africa), Uganda (East Africa), Egypt (North Africa), and Ghana (West Africa) and their interractions within the global system in a process sometimes called 'globalization'. In this way, the book avoids methodological nationalism, particularism, and broad-brush, grand narrative methodologies commonly utilized in development studies and development economics.

In short, this multi-scalar investigation provides a requiem for development economics and seeks the development of stratification economics.

## Arguments

The book argues that the existing diagnosis and resulting prescriptions presented by mainstream development economics and development studies not only fail to alleviate poverty, but also performatively contribute to creating and maintaining the structures of inequality and poverty. These policies can be credited for helping to drive growth, yet they have simultaneously created inequalities and poverty in incomes and wealth, as well as widespread "ecological destruction" The book seeks to show that the policy emphases have led to imposed dispossession (when minorities have been forced off the land), induced dispossession (where minorities have to vacate their land because of growing rental values), and negotiated dispossession (when land is bought from minorities at low prices). Many minorities have been excluded from the resulting enclaved economic prosperity. Partakers are better off, but they are often exploited as wage laborers and, even among workers, there have been controversial hierarchies (in the oil and gas industry, for example, between how foreign and African workers are treated).

The cumulative and combined result is that the benefits from the mainstream reforms have been minimal and concentrated at best with only limited returns to the public. Even more fundamentally, reforms have cemented the structures of uneven development within Africa and between Africa and the rest of the World. Indeed, there are strong grounds to contend that the singular achievement of the orthodoxy is obfuscating and perpetuating the status quo. If so, the key site of "development" and "development economics," more specifically, should be in the global north; not the schizophrenic experiments in the south for which Esther Duflo, Abhijit Banerjee, and Michael Kremer have been given the 2019 Nobel Prize in Economics.

The book demonstrates that the existing system *transfers* rents from producers – and reproducers – to rentiers and appropriators. The discourse of cultural backwardness/preservation serves to mask these structural processes, while the modernizing and patronizing discourse of Africa doing well in growth terms serves to legitimate the status quo. The mainstream development economics case that fencing off common and communal land through formalization/Westernization and commuting it to private property will bring about greater prosperity, innovation, security, and sustainability for the future is not only logically faulty, but also empirically unverifiable. In contrast, the reverse is demonstrable. The book shows how privatizing land has undermined the vitality of communities and unchained worsening forms of structural inequality.

Unlike others who contend that the idea of privatization does not work at all or has not worked in practice, the book argues that there are contradictions in the idea itself and the implementation of the idea has worked for some, but worsened the prospects of prosperity for the majority. These outcomes constitute a structural part of land reform which, I show, sows the seeds of inequality and dispossession and, hence, becomes part of the problem rather than the solution that it is often portrayed to be. The structural inequality and poverty impelled by land reform hurts those that have a weak class position (e.g., the poor, women, migrants, precarious labor, and marginalized ethnic groups).

As this outcome is inherent in the idea of land reform, and mainstream development economics itself, conditioned on how it is implemented within diverse institutional contexts, and driven by colonial and external forces, the book puts the case for guaranteeing reward for industry, indeed widening the democratic share of labor both private and associated, but contests the creation of individual property in land which, as the book shows, underpins much of the growing inequality in Africa. It is an argument that brings a perspective on inequality – the structural basis of inequality – which the best (selling) books on inequality (e.g., Thomas Piketty's now famous *Capital in the Twenty-First Century*, 2014) have not considered and cultural approaches have continuously overlooked.

In this sense, this work aspires to be similar to Thomas Shapiro's stimulating book, *Toxic Inequality* (2017), although its stronger emphasis on land makes *Property, Institutions, and Social Stratification in Africa* quite distinctive. While economists such as Dr. Babasaheb Ambedkar sought an alternative land reform through state socialism and land nationalization (Jamma & Damji, 2012), and Erica Field persistently has made the case for addressing the "land question" by marketizing land, a large body of work has developed around Elinor Ostrom's "common pool resources." These ideas of the commons perform poorly in terms of

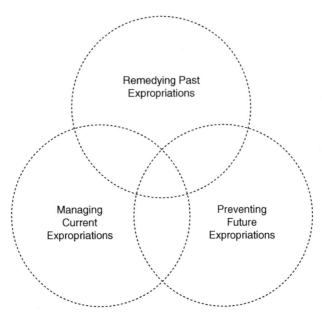

Figure 1.2  Alternative notions of commoning

economic management, end up creating new forms of inequality (e.g., top-down state socialism), or simply ignore the question of justice (e.g., common pool resources) (Obeng-Odoom, 2016c). In turn, these widely held views do not constitute credible alternatives to the dominance of dyadic state-market analyses.

This book, on the other hand, puts the case for alternative commoning. Presented as a diagram in Figure 1.2, this "commoning" can receive direct and decisive public support. So, this commoning is not akin to the *homo suburbius* in the work of Charles Tiebout (Peck, 2011). Rather, it is patterned after the principles of Georgist land economics, which Henry George travelled around the world to publicize (Pullen, 2014).

In *Our Land and Land Policy* (1871), George provided two approaches to ensuring that such commons could be realized. First, for land already taken, taxing the socially created rent would prevent the ongoing problem of privatizing publicly created rent or value (and, hence, the descriptor, 'land value tax'). This policy, however, must go with a related one of untaxing labor because labor is entitled to what she produces, while land is freely given by nature. George's second proposed policy is to prevent ongoing speculative land expropriation and, instead, put an end to the expropriation of land. This approach is different from land nationalization which is grounded in some idea of "equal access to the value of land" dispensed in a top-down, sometimes quite autocratic fashion. Nationalization does not, in principle, challenge the "market society" in the sense that national land leased out to citizens can still be managed along private market logic. It follows that my book entertains the possibility of land used for private purposes, but socially generated "value" must be returned to the society for public use (e.g., public employment programs) and social purposes.

What about trade? The "neoclassical realist perspective," as it is some-times called (Wenar, 2008; Vermar, 2013), sees a potential solution in international trade. In this respect, the argument for trade is couched not so much in terms of comparative advantage in the extractives sector, although that is also important. Instead, the need for international or global "free" trade in oil is usually presented on the grounds that the African state and the institutions in Africa more generally are corrupt. Transnational corporations (TNCs) or international oil companies (IOCs), then, become a preferred institution to govern African commons, espe-cially if these corporations trade with only "democratic" (read neoliberal) regimes, respect local laws, and their own property rights in the commons can be guaranteed by local institutions.

It follows that what is called a "neoclassical realist perspective" is, in fact, a new institutional economics idea of "governance," "good governance," or simply "governance by marketized transnational corporations" (TNCs), characterized as producing "win-win" outcomes. Presumably more experi-enced and better adept at governance, the role of these mineral TNCs and IOCs is governing the commons for the public good through their corpo-rate social responsibility and meeting their mandatory local content requirements. Here, we see the influences of the economics of nudging (through mandatory local content regulations).

Yet, as political economists such as Emmanuel (1972) and Amin (1977) have shown, this approach is bereft of comprehensive analysis centred on inequality. Marxist and some institutionalist alternatives are much better, but they, too, can inspire unhelpful advocacy of (temporary) protectionism (Shepphard, 2012), while so-called "fair trade" usually is unfair (Valiente-Riedl, 2016). These existing alternatives narrowly focus on capital and profits, but what about rents? So, in contrast, this book argues for neither free trade nor fair trade but for the Georgist notion of "true free trade." According to Henry George:

True free trade, in short, requires that the active factor of production, Labor, shall have free access to the passive factor of production, Land. To secure this, all monopoly of land must be broken up, and the equal right of all to the use of the natural elements must be secured by the treatment of the land as the common property in usufruct of the whole people. Thus it is that free trade brings us to the same simple measure as that which we have seen is necessary to emancipate labor from its thraldom and to secure that justice in the distribution of wealth which will make every improvement or reform beneficial to all classes. (George, 1886/1991)

This approach to trade is consistent with Africanist systems of trade. These trade systems are characterised by their common rejection of existing slave-like types of trade, which marginalise and subjugate Africans. Addressing the contradictions in mainstream and alternative trade systems is necessary, but not sufficient. Past problems of expropriation require redress too, raising questions about how to resolve the cumulative problems for the descendants of ex-slaves who have simultaneously suffered years of colonial and imperial expropriation, exclusion, and exploitation. Modern Georgist analyses have been silent on this question, and mainstream ideas in development studies or development economics centered on "helping Africa" through "aid" tend to create conditions for further uneven and dependent development in Africa (Asongu & Nwachukwu, 2017). We know from the stimulating work of Abdallah Zouache, the North African political economist, that both old and new institutional economists have been either patronizing or eugenic on these issues (Zouache, 2017, 2018). So, we need to look elsewhere for inspiration.

African scholars, notably Sir Beckles and William Darity Jr., have respectively developed alternative meso and macro ideas of reparations, reflecting earlier suggestions in that regard by Thomas Sankara (Murrey, 2018). At the meso, Africa-wide level, African countries from which slaves were taken are entitled to reparations based on justice, including – but not limited to – juridical justice. Under international law, slavery against nations was and remains a crime against humanity for which the prescribed remedy is reparation. African-wide institutions such as the African Union can litigate on behalf of Africa, duly supported by regional bodies such as the Economic Community of West African States (see Chapter 8 for details). Aspects of this line of analysis are echoed in "The Abuja Proclamation," "a declaration of the first Abuja Pan-African Conference on reparations for African enslavement, colonization and neo-colonization," which was "sponsored by the Organization of African Unity [OAU, now African Union] and its Reparations Commission" (OAU, 1993, p. 1).

Such reparations, if successfully obtained, would need to be distributed. How to do so is no easy matter. Would reparations be better administered from the Africa-wide or the region-wide African bodies already in existence? It is such a question that highlights the need for macro-national, indeed, transnational analyses of reparations. Building on the experiences of African Americans in the United States, one way to estimate reasonable reparation would be to invoke the spirit of the "40 Acres and a Mule" reform idea. "The 40 acres" would be equal to the present value of land taken from Africans; the "mule" would be the public support, especially where the mule is given in affirmative action (Gates, 2013). The aim would be to publicly acknowledge such wrongs (A), commit to and actually implement repatriation (R), and design the program so well that there will be at least economic closure to the demands on the exploiters (C), although moral claims will forever remain (Darity, 2008). Rooted in justice, it would give no grounds for Western conditionalities which only serve to deepen the structures of inequalities and hence make a bad situation worse. The idea of reparations has a sound economic basis. Although Myrdal's circular and cumulative causation does not draw this policy implication, Oliver Cox's (1945) critique suggests that this is an appropriate policy conclusion.

Whether at the micro, meso, or macro level, the soundness of the specific calculations could be judged by J. R. Commons' notion of "reasonable value." That is, several calculations could be usefully presented by African and other analysts complemented by processes of negotiations to arrive at what is "reasonable."

This reasonableness must, of course, be seen in terms of the combination of reparations for past wrongs and compensation for present and continuing injustices. Indeed, Henry George himself made the point, recognizing the need for correcting past wrongs and the importance to connect such a remedy to present mechanisms of sharing the earth. In his words:

The only one of our prominent men who had any glimmering of what was really necessary to the abolition of slavery was Thaddeus Stevens, but it was only a glimmering. "Forty acres and a mule" would have been a measure of scant justice to the freedman, and it would for a while have given them something of that personal independence which is necessary to freedom. Yet only for a while. In the course of time, and as the pressure of population increased, the forty acres would, with the majority of them, have been mortgaged and the mule sold, and they would soon have been, as now, competitors for a foothold upon the earth and for the means of making a living from it. Such a measure would have given the freedman a fairer start, and for many of them would have postponed the evil day; but that is all. Land being private property, that evil day *must* come. (George, 1883/1981, pp. 157–158; italics in original)

So, reparations must be seen as part of, not apart from, the pursuit of wider present economic reforms. Indeed, present reforms must be linked to the future of the earth, what Adebayo Adedeji (1987) called, "an ecology for economic change" in Africa, or the "search of a theory that links development with the ecology" (p. 6). For Adedeji, this theory must be fundamentally different from the body of ideas that govern Western ecologies in the sense of prioritizing "social justice, equality of opportunity, equitable distribution of income, and the democratization of the development process" (pp. 6–7). Indeed, these concerns must extend to the question of intergenerational equity which, in current analyses, neglect what Henry George (1885) called "the crime of poverty" and how it might be addressed.

Controlling the source of life, of living, land, makes the poor slaves to landlords because people are denied the right to life and living that way. Controlling the values of land makes the wages of the laborer hostage to the wishes of landlords because land rent takes away wages. Incentives for work can be killed in this process, too, although the volume of work itself could progressively decline such that there would be less work in society. Ways of ensuring this reduction include eliminating destructive "work" like war. Often, hunger, disease, crime, and grime stem from the drive to control land. Finally, the power of rent, or of landlords to extract rent, makes them masters over the poor.

Curent and future inequality could be comprehensively addressed in a number of ways. Institutionalizing reparations to address past wrongs and guaranteeing that the fruits of labor are not taxed nor taken away by capitalists in modern times are possible ways of doing so. Taxing land rents – that is, returning to the public what is socially created, and putting these returns to public purposes can be another way. Placing a tax on inherited land/preventing the inheritance of land and the privatization of currently common land could address both both existing and intergeneration poverty/inequality. Prosperity could be guaranteed as incentives for work would be provided, high cost of housing removed, crime reduced, and social protection offered for the downtrodden.

These arguments for the commons and commoning do not seek a return to an idealized *gemenschaft* based on questionable pristine African culture, but rather structurally different African societies grounded in transforming institutions and processes, while replenishing the carrying capacity of the environment.

## THE STRUCTURE OF THE BOOK

The book is divided into three parts, respectively contextualizing the problem under investigation (Part A), showing the limitations of existing explanations and solutions (Part B), and putting the case for alternative analyses and transformations (Part C). Part A is made up of the Introduction and this chapter, "The Foundations for a New Beginning." The next part, B, is made up of five chapters described as follows:

Chapter 2: *Property Economics* The chapter observes that in contemporary political economic analyses of development processes, the "Coase Theorem," especially as popularized in Hernando de Soto's *The Mystery of Capital,* has been one of the most discussed, albeit controversial, frames. De Soto's views – patterned after those of John Locke, Garett Hardin, and Robert Lucas – are shared by economists such as Erica Field.

Although well received by global development agencies such as the World Bank, de Soto's argument positing that a cultural change away from informal institutions toward the creation and institutionalization of individual property in housing and land will revive "dead capital" and enable the poor to emerge from abject poverty has been widely criticized. These criticisms show that (a) the thesis is flawed, (b) the flaw is due to implementational problems, and (c) the practical implications arising from the thesis are largely neutral and will neither improve nor worsen poverty.

While agreeing with the first criticism, this chapter argues that the second critique must be nuanced, and the third is entirely mistaken. Utilizing insights from Joseph Schumpeter, Karl Polanyi, and Henry George, the chapter makes the case that applying de Soto's ideas through policy would be ineffective in curbing urban poverty, and actually serve to simultaneously entrench and augment it. There is merit in de Soto's assumption that the poor possess some economic agency and may, indeed, secure socially beneficial outcomes through pursuing innovative and entrepreneurial endeavors. Yet, his conception of such processes remains largely isolated from broader political economic considerations and so requires more systemic empirical analysis. What does "land reform" actually mean? How has it been carried out? In what ways has land reform met its posited goals in Africa?

Chapter 3: *Land Reform* In responding to the questions raised in Chapter 2, Chapter 3 emphasizes the empirical experiences of land reform in Africa. The focus on empirical outcomes is particularly important because many economists such as Jean-Philippe Platteau and Hanan Jacoby are cautious about such "reform," but the tendency of advocates is to emphasize the importance of land reform for poverty reduction in Africa. However, how reform comes about and evolves, what it is and what it does are situated, not universal, as neoclassical and new institutional economists suggest.

This chapter sheds light on the meaning, evolution, and outcomes of land reform, stretching from the days of land titling which (re)shaped local land markets to contemporary pressures of "land grabs," which can be seen as a logical extension of national land markets. The chapter draws on historical and contemporary socio-legal and political-economic sources of evidence, analyzed within a stratification economics framework. It shows important features of continuity and change in both colonial and postcolonial land reform. While precolonial land tenure relations are misrepresented as entailing no market activities, the concerted effort to introduce "capitalist markets" into the land sector to produce "socially efficient outcomes" has led to results that contradict the posited goals of land reform and, perhaps, worsened the problems the reforms aim to redress.

Chapter 4: *Human Capital* But if so, it is crucial that Chapter 4 highlights and assesses orthodox responses to three remaining questions in development economics, namely: what the role of human capital in the process of economic development is? how this role transforms during a period of resource abundance? and what place education takes in empowering labor to reclaim or transform surplus value? The chapter proposes different responses to all these questions. Accordingly, the case is made to replace the neoclassical concept of "human capital" with "human development" or, even emancipation and to move from theoretical to substantivist analysis of oil, education, and labor relations. In this sense, if there is a need for a concept of human capital at all, then it must be radically different from the predominant neoclassical perspective. Yet, the story of mainstream economists is not thus oriented. Instead, many neoclassicists focus on increasing the quantities of both human and physical capital through trade. So, the next chapter considers another posited explanation: international trade.

Chapter 5: *International Trade* International trade, including trade in crude oil and petroleum products, has been widely encouraged as a mechanism for the development of Africa, and its related environmental disasters in the continent tend to be considered as "accidents." This chapter develops an alternative analysis influenced by the work of Henry George, especially as contained in his books – *Protection or Free Trade* (1886) and *Our Land and Land Policy* (1871). The chapter argues that widespread petroleum "accidents", indeed social costs reflect the addiction to growth and its underpinning monopolistic petro investments by both international oil companies (IOCs) and national petro monopolies across the petroleum value chain. While the private appropriation of commonly generated rent in the petro industry is justified by advocates on grounds of "development," its structural processes generate routine accidents and social costs of displacement, exclusion, and socioecological disasters that cast doubts on the extractivist-based trade regime that is widely praised or questioned on trivial grounds of volatility; not on grounds of serious and widespread socioecological accidents. and social costs of accumulation

Chapter 6: *Economic Growth* Just as the tools of "problematic explanations and solutions" (Part B) require critical reappraisal, so too does the vision of economic growth. Africa's hitherto negative image is now being rapidly replaced by a new persona: "Africa on the rise." Developed mainly from Africa's growth experience, this reimaging of Africa has generated considerable interest even among Africanists concerned that the continent has often been the target of crisis jokes. Even more notably, the rebranding of Africa has gained traction in corridors of power and centers of finance. For this latter group, however, the narrative signals more than a cultural repackaging. It is about confirming that Africa is ripe and ready to host investment, and to open up markets in areas where they did not exist or existed but were not capitalist in form. Either way, however, the "Africa on the rise" narrative achieves a major political and economic goal. Neglecting ethical questions about sustainable jobs, which also means less work, inequality, and ecological crisis, while extolling the virtues of capital accumulation, it extends a particular neoliberal ideology which favors people with market power, not the majority with precarious positions or their relationship with nature.

It is with these arguments that Chapter 6 closes Part B of the book, emphasizing the central theme: that the existing explanations of the African condition are fallacious and their resulting posited solutions are misleading or create even more problems. If so, the question of what alternatives can be developed becomes the logical next step in the book. Chapters 7 and 8 investigate two types of alternatives. The first is socialisms; the second, Africanisms.

Chapter 7: *Socialisms* This chapter critically engages various socialist tactics advocated for the liberation of Africa. Both analytically and in terms of policy, this chapter draws on, but also critiques, Marxist economics. Using examples of land reform and the nationalization of mines and rigs, the chapter shows that the theories might be logically plausible and, indeed, popular among segments of the population involved in uprisings, but they are empirically unverifiable. In particular, they have not succeeded as yet in addressing problems of absentee ownership. The chapter, therefore, questions attempts at wholly embracing these socialisms. Similarly, it cautions against seeking to combine the "best" elements in each of the socialisms. It is possible to draw selectively from these philosophies and synthesize their ideas with other philosophies to help better understand or shape (if possible) the course of some of the ongoing uprisings (which suggest that alternatives are, indeed, needed). However, various Africanisms provide more direct and, perhaps, more relevant foundations for ongoing efforts toward deeper forms of liberation.

Chapter 8: *Africanisms* Based on the policy compass developed in Chapter 7, this chapter analyses recent Africanist developments, that is, continental African initiatives, that seek to push the boundaries for alternatives to both capitalism and socialism. These developments span lower-class and middle-income protests on the streets to middle-income and humanist high-income protests mostly in the law courts in Africa. They seek to change the course of capitalist development not really through socialist revolutions but through a reworking of the institutions of the continent and the world system. The chapter questions many of them, while others are shown to be more promising. Within the so-called prospects are also dangers. Perhaps reworked, the prospects for some of these Africanisms that are neither capitalism nor socialism can, indeed, liberate the continent and address the inequalities that constrain the aspirations of its people.

Conclusion: *Concluding the groundwork for a new political economy of the Global South* The conclusion of the book returns to questions about the appropriate paradigm for studying African political economy. The chapter reemphasizes the case for using a stratification economics approach, presents the arguments developed from this paradigm, and contemplates the various ways in which, on the basis of the study, stratification economics can be developed further to become a new political economy approach for the entire Global South.

# PART II

# PROBLEMATIC EXPLANATIONS AND SOLUTIONS

2

# Property Economics

## INTRODUCTION

Property economics is a highly influential source of cultural explanations of Africa's "backwardness." As the detailed historical account by C. W. Dickermann and her team (1989) has shown, focused on facilitating transactions, property economics has consistently questioned the nature of Africa's land tenure systems, while seeking to justify, to extend, and, indeed, to universalize the idea of private property as it is understood in capitalist economies. For property economists, the explanation of inequality and the prescription for its resolution are held to be fundamentally about property (see, for a review, Christophers, 2018; Domeher et al., 2018).

Since the stereotypical view is that African – indeed all black – property cultures hold back the continent from catching up with the West, the standard property economics prescription is for Africans to let go of their embrace of these cultures (collective systems of land ownership to be precise) in order to enable them succeed in expediting the transition to capitalist social organization (see, for example, Central Land Council, 2013; Deininger & Xia, 2018), which is "the only game in town" (de Soto, 2000, pp. 208–209). So, "Is succeeding at capitalism a cultural thing?" (de Soto, 2000, p. 205). The answer is "no," but only on a crucial condition: "that of making a transition to a market-based capitalist system" (de Soto, 2000, p. 209).

The positive role of well-defined individual property rights in poverty reduction and societal progress has been at the forefront of liberal philosophy and political economy since the debates between William Blackstone and his strident opponent Jeremy Bentham during the late eighteenth century. While Blackstone sought to respect local contexts and histories, Bentham tried to remove them, contending that such traditions were constraining.

In their place, he prepared the grounds for developing a science of property economics rooted in individual rationalism and the natural rights of individuals to private property (Commons, 1924/1925, pp. 371–373). I return to this Benthamite view in Chapter 3, where I show that these principles, as embodied in contemporary property economics, are extensions of John Locke's treatise on property and, more recently, patterned after Garret Hardin's notion of the "Tragedy of the Commons."

For the present chapter, the focus is on explaining the theorization of property by contemporary economists, particularly those working in the tradition of new institutional economics, including Ronald Coase, Armen Alchian, and Harold Demesetz, who emphasized the centrality of individual property rights to achieve a range of political economic outcomes (for a review, see Wiener, 2011). This argument centers on the "Coase Theorem," the idea that well-defined property rights reduce transaction costs to little or nothing and facilitate capitalist property transactions, which, in turn, enable economically lagging areas (such as African countries) to catch up with more prosperous areas (primarily in the West).

While often attributed to Ronald Coase, it is widely accepted that Coase himself did not systematically popularize this frame (see, for example, Lai & Lorne, 2006; Lai & Chua, 2018; Lai & Chau, 2018). Rather, it is the economist, Hernando de Soto, who has most popularized this worldview in Africa. Recipient of the 2017 Global Award for Entrepreneurship Research, Hernando de Soto is not only well-known in the academy but he also is revered in policy and business circles. Martin Andersson and Daniel Waldenström's (2017) systematic assessment of the impact of de Soto's work provides important insights. In the last three decades, de Soto's work has influenced highly visible economists like Milton Friedman and Ronald Coase who have publicly praised de Soto's work. Indeed, de Soto's work also influenced powerful global development organizations such as the World Bank whose *Doing Business Reports* have been inspired by de Soto's books, the *Mystery of Capital* (de Soto, 2000 – hereafter *The Mystery*) and the *The Other Path* (de Soto, 1989).

*The Mystery*, arguably de Soto's most successful work, requires our attention for this reason. In this work, de Soto forcefully refutes critical accounts of the contemporary global political economy, particularly Mike Davis' (2006) *Planet of Slums*. Davis shows the inequalities between the conditions of most people who live in slums and wealthier people in Africa. In contrast, de Soto argues that slums are better characterized as a planet of wealth inhabited by latent entrepreneurs, waiting to become billionaires. For de Soto, the realization of such potential only requires the creation and institutionalization of individual, private property in land and housing. Similar to Muhammad Yunus' widely celebrated idea of microfinance and credit, de Soto's thesis has received local, national, and global praise. It has been quoted as support for public policy and inspired many individual tenure formalization programs in developing countries (Gilbert, 2002, 2012; McFarlane, 2012). For example, Ghana's Minister of Finance and Economic Planning in 2007 reminded the Parliament of Ghana about the commitment of the government to the application of de Soto's ideas. The minister said:

> Mr. Speaker, government believes that a key constraint in the credit delivery chain is the inability of Ghanaians to offer their houses as collateral because of lack of proper legal title. As a result of this unfortunate situation, the vast majority of properties in Ghana have, in the words of the famous economist, Hernando de Soto, become "dead capital." Consequently, government has decided to task the Attorney General and the Ministry of Lands, Forestry and Mines to explore alternative approaches to land titling that would free up this dead capital to support a credit-based economy. (Wiredu, 2007, p. 424, emphasis added)

Simultaneously, however, de Soto's thesis has been widely criticized by many commentators, especially urban scholars and development planners. These concerns range from costly processes of registration; the unwillingness of many banks in developing countries to advance credit facilities based only on the possession of title certificate (Abdulai, 2006; Abdulai & Ochieng, 2017; Domeher et al., 2018) in land and housing; the empirically verified lack of correlation between individual property rights and secure tenure; the correlation between weak individual property rights in land and housing and secure rural and urban land tenure in Africa (Bugri, 2008; Domeher & Abdulai, 2012; Domeher et al., 2018); the lack of systematic research to back de Soto's thesis (Gilbert, 2002, 2012); de Soto's mistakes about the historic role of private landed property rights in America's ascent to the position of a world economic power (Benda-Beckmann, 2003); the tendency to treat "the poor" as an undifferentiated class; and the conflation of different types of property rights in land and housing (Benda-Beckmann, 2003).

Most of these criticisms, thus, frame the error in de Soto's thesis as primarily procedural or definitional which, consequently, undermines the feasibility of implementing his ideas in practice. In turn, they suggest that by correcting his problems of definition or improving legal institutions to enforce property rights, it would be possible to overcome the challenges of *The Mystery*.

While not "incorrect" per se, this panoply of concerns ignores the important political-economic issue of the evolution of poverty and inequality levels. It is, therefore, important to look at whether inequality and poverty worsen or improve over time under the conditions envisaged by de Soto. Existing studies (e.g., Home & Lim, 2004; Elamin, 2018) arguing, for example, that the application of de Soto's thesis creates extra costs for the poor who try to register their urban land and real estate, do not address the issue. Additional empirical analysis is needed to investigate what the effect of titling has been on poverty and inequality in Africa.

In the meantime, conceptual answers can be found in the work of Joseph Schumpeter, Henry George, and Karl Polanyi. The three – who have worked, respectively, on innovation and entrepreneurship as drivers of economic development, on the role of economic rent in economic development, and on the role of "fictitious commodities" and the "double movement" in shaping the dynamics of capitalist economic development – bear directly on de Soto's claims.

While on the surface, the work of Joseph Schumpeter may be taken as confirming de Soto's thesis, that of Henry George and Karl Polanyi demonstrate that de Soto's thesis is fundamentally flawed. A critical analysis and synthesis of these seemingly differing conclusions, however, reveals that applying de Soto's ideas through policy would be ineffective in curbing urban poverty, and actually serve to simultaneously entrench and augment it. Moreover, while de Soto's assumption that the poor possess some economic agency is sound and may, indeed, secure socially beneficial outcomes through pursuing innovative and entrepreneurial endeavors, his conception of such processes remains largely individualistic and abstracted from broader political economic considerations.

The rest of this chapter is divided into four sections. The next provides a "big picture" analysis of *The Mystery* from the perspectives of Schumpeter, Polanyi, and George. Following that, the chapter zooms in on the specific postulates in *The Mystery*, related to the nature of property, capital and capital accumulation, while the subsequent section briefly evaluates existing empirical evidence related to de Soto's thesis. Finally, concluding remarks highlight the key impediments to *The Mystery*.

## The Mystery of Schumpeter's Ideas on Innovation and Entrepreneurship?

Schumpeter's ideas on innovation and entrepreneurship provide a useful framework to examine the claims in *The Mystery* because they recognize the creative force of the entrepreneur. His concepts have a direct bearing on de Soto's postulation of "dead capital," how it can be revived, and how it can be used to liberate the poor from the shackles of poverty. Schumpeter argued that innovation – the process of combining old things in new ways, using new ways to produce old things, and improving existing ways of doing old things – is the principal driver of economic development, enabled in part, through the availability of credit to support entrepreneurs (Schumpeter, [1912] 2003, 1928, 1947, 1954). To him, even without a change in the noneconomic, the economic could change, mainly because of the activities of the entrepreneur – defined as the agent who does "new things or . . . things that are already being done in a new way (innovation)" (Schumpeter, 1947, p. 151, brackets in original).

While Schumpeter's concept of innovation is explained mainly in terms of firms (Schumpeter, 1928, p. 381), it may be deemed consistent with de Soto's idea that poor people (or, "firms," in Schumpeterian political economy) have agency and can be resourceful entrepreneurs. Furthermore, it may be used to explain why poor entrepreneurs may be constrained by a lack of access to credit or suffer from insecure land tenure, as argued by de Soto. Indeed, it may be argued that de Soto's emphasis that addressing poverty must centre on the economy of the poor is quite similar to Schumpeter's idea of "development of the economy from within" ([1912] 2003, p. 66). Likewise, the emphasis on credit in de Soto's analysis of economic development and Schumpeter's argument that "[c]redit-creation is the method by which the putting to new uses of existing means of production is brought about" (1928, p. 382) may be said to be analogous.

However, a scrutiny of the substance of Schumpeter's oeuvre shows that it differs fundamentally from de Soto's analysis of economic development, in terms of methodology, diagnosis, and proposed solutions. Methodologically, while Schumpeter argued that innovation and entrepreneurship can flourish under either capitalism or socialism (1947, p. 151), de Soto (2011) insists that it is capitalism alone that can create the necessary conditions of entrepreneurialism. Furthermore, for de Soto, geography, time, and history count for little or nothing, but Schumpeter paid careful attention to such factors in explaining economic development. Indeed, he insisted that an appreciation of history, theory, statistics, and economic sociology is cardinal to any economic analysis (Courvisanos & Mackenzie, 2011). So, the lack of convergence in the levels of technological capacity between Africa and the rest of the world is not reducible to an absence of mimicry of Western institutions. Rather, it is seen as a function of and contributor to wider political economic inequalities between Africa and the rest (Evangelista, 2018). Schumpeter's approach is holistic, eclectic, and hermeneutic, while de Soto's is narrow, selective, and positivist.

In Schumpeter's words:

> On the one hand ... [my] approach is concerned with the concrete course of development in a particular time and at particular locations, with changes in industrial organization, in methods of production and quantities produced, in technology and welfare, the emergence of certain new industries, and the decline of others. On the other hand ... [I approach economic analysis by looking at] how and by what process ... concrete changes occur ... [and] is it possible to recognize regularities in the way that everything new arises? And if so, can these regularities be formulated in a general way? (Schumpeter, [1912] 2003, p. 63)

De Soto reduces the problem of economic development to the absence of individual property in land and housing characterized by the lack of possession of title certificates. In contrast, Schumpeter argued that creative response is contingent. He paid particular attention to three defining factors; namely, quality of personnel available in a society, the relative quality of personnel in particular sectors of the society, and the general patterns of behavior that are socially and historically constructed (Schumpeter, 1947). Schumpeter considered the capitalist order to be unstable and marked by dispossession. In a process that Schumpeter called "creative destruction" (1954, p. 81–86), he argued that capitalism tends to create and destroy existing structures, and thereby advances one interest while diminishing the interest of others. In contrast, de Soto sees a harmonious, win-win dynamic in capitalism.

In terms of diagnosis, Schumpeter looked at economic development mainly as the process by which the economy propels itself through innovation to expansion ([1912] 2003, p. 67). This process is sandwiched between two others, namely the dynamic mixing of economic variables in a stable condition ("circular flow") and a tendency for impediments to innovation and hence development to arise in the process of economic development. It is these three processes of circular flow, economic development, and the impediments to development that collectively constitute Schumpeter's Theory of Economic Development (Elliot, 1983, p. 279–280). So, Schumpeter's theory was more sophisticated and better considered than the obtuse economic development diagnosis made by de Soto.

Regarding prognosis, Schumpeter forcefully argued that capitalism cannot survive its own internal contradictions. To him, with the success of capitalism comes a destruction of the social institutions that support it. He argued that the capitalist order cannot be stable, as people tend toward profit maximization and begin to resist being subordinated (Schumpeter, 1928, 1954, p. 417–418). In turn, Schumpeter resisted the market failure criterion as the sole basis for state funding of science, technology, and innovation in the process of development which, in the case of de Soto, would be based on nothing other than giving property titles to the poor (for a general discussion, see Joseph & Johnston, 1985). Socialism, Schumpeter indeed argued, is the alternative and one that is workable (1928, 1954, p. 61).

De Soto, on the other hand, looks at the capitalist order as stable and perpetual, while socialism is conceived of as a fundamentally unworkable system (2000, 2004). The positive, asocial, and "stable" view of capitalism advocated by de Soto can be found in the World Bank's policies on "sustainable rural and urban development" or what Carlos Oya (2011, 2012) has called neopopulism. The Bank's policies tout neo-NGO progressive credentials, but they are built on restrictive neoclassical economic assumptions such as the rational man and naturally created free markets. While this orientation is not unrelated to the research approach adopted by the World Bank, the trinity of research approach, advocacy, and policy are not necessarily consistent either. As with *The Mystery*, the Bank's policies on urban development and poverty reduction extend neoliberal thinking, which promises to address world poverty through market solutions. This neoliberal view assumes that poor people are rational; that they are profit maximizing; and that creating private property in land and housing removes high transaction cost and promotes efficient markets. In turn, well-functioning markets address the problem of missing information and pave the way for credit supply and development (Oya, 2007, 2011, 2012).

From Schumpeter's perspective, however, this reading of the process of economic development by de Soto and like-minded world development institutions such as the World Bank is problematic because it misrepresents and oversimplifies the process of economic development. Even more problematic and worrying, as Karl Polanyi and Henry George suggest, is the effect of de Soto's ideas on the state of inequality and poverty levels.

### Karl Polanyi, Henry George and the Demystification of *The Mystery*. . .

Karl Polanyi and Henry George are two leading heterodox political economists who paid careful and substantial attention to the role of land in the process of economic development, so it is also important to consider the claims contained in *The Mystery* from their perspectives.

According to Polanyi ([1944] 2001) and George ([1879] 2006, 1881, 1898), individuation and commodification of land tend to cause poverty, inequality, and social distress. This diagnosis has nothing to do with the "creating barriers for the poor" argument, which is typically used by development practitioners when analyzing the work of de Soto (see Home & Lim, 2004), important as that is. Rather, it relates to the annexation of land, itself a free gift of nature, and subsequent attempts to exclude others from its use.

Polanyi argues that land is a "fictitious commodity" because it is not produced for market exchange. Rather, it is a free gift of nature. Given that land is not a commodity, it does not easily follow the dictates of demand and supply, forces that, according to neoclassical economists, govern commodities (goods and services created by human exertion for exchange). In turn, wherever there has been an attempt to enclose or annex the commons, inequality tends to worsen (Polanyi, [1944] 2001). Thus, even if various real estate finance schemes (e.g., Real Estate Investment Trust and secondary mortgage markets) are used as temporary fixes to bureaucratically "distribute" land and housing, Polanyi suggests that individuation and commodification of land as advocated by de Soto tend to worsen inequality and poverty in the long run. To Polanyi, the "land economy" is "embedded" in society; that is, it is considered as part a wider socioecological system. So, tearing land away from that system by subjecting it to impersonal forces of demand and supply, or what Joy Paton (2010, p. 81) calls "anonymous market system," usually causes massive social deprivations because that commodification deprives people of their livelihoods and social identity.

What about the effect of already individualized and privatized land on inequality and poverty levels? George's contribution to the political economy of land looks at the process in which already privatized land attains value and how that value is distributed among different social classes ([1879] 2006). George argued that it is investment in the society as a whole, speculation, population growth, and general advance of the society that drive up the value of land. He contended that the activities of landlords do not typically add any extra value to land. By definition, landlords "own" land; their "(in)activity" does not add value to it (George, 1881, 1898). While landlords can invest in land and their investment can increase its value, land values tend to rise because of factors unrelated to/in addition to the personal investment of landlords. Yet, the total increase in the value of land "after all the expenses of production that are resolvable into compensation for the exertion of individual labor are paid" (George, 1898, p. 150) tends to be captured by landlords alone as *produit net* or economic rent (pp. 150–151). In time, the capture of rent from the production process eats into the rewards of labor and capital. Thus, for George, individuation of land not only creates inequality at the base but also shrinks workers' wages and capitalists' money capital. George regarded this dynamic as a leakage from the production process that tends to inhibit the process of capital accumulation. He recommended a tax on economic rent to address the problem.

The analyses of Karl Polanyi and Henry George turn the prediction of *The Mystery* on its head because they fundamentally challenge its assumption of the benefits to be derived from supporting land enclosures and private property in land and housing. It might be argued that privatizing and registering individual property is not against the Georgist analysis because George advocated land tax. That is, de Soto's work can be seen as enhancing the assessment and collection of land tax because the administration of taxation is greatly enhanced by the creation of land and property registers. However, this interpretation of George's political economy would be wrong because it did not require land tax for revenue assessment and collection for its own sake, but mainly as a system to redistribute unearned income.

To Polanyi and George, the way to address urban poverty is first and foremost to communize land, not commodify it. Polanyi left his analysis at that level and did not show how to move from the present to his ideal. Rather, he indicated the various ways in which the ideal might be realized: "[t]his may happen in a great variety of ways, democratic and aristocratic, constitutionalist and authoritarian, perhaps even in a fashion yet utterly unforeseen" (Polanyi, [1944] 2001, p. 259).

George, in contrast, was more categorical. He considered mechanisms such as efficient government and government regulation; and argued that they are ineffective because they tend to be inefficient and lend themselves to abuse by corrupt officials. Also, they do not address systemic problems (George, [1879] 2006, pp. 165–179). George's favoured strategy was to tax economic rent, or land value, first to "neutralize" the unfair advantage of landlords and then to distribute the resulting revenue via investment in social services (Stilwell & Jordan, 2004; Stilwell, 2011, 2019). To him, the institution of land value tax has the advantage of discouraging speculation: it is hard to avoid and easy to collect. Unlike other taxes, it is not a disincentive to work because it is not a tax on what labor creates; rather it is a tax on the wrongful appropriation of nature (George, [1879] 2006, pp. 180–191). Polanyi and George were not against all private property.

Polanyi wrote of shifting "industrial civilisation" into a "nonmarketing basis" ([1944] 2001, p. 258), whereas George advocated rewards for human exertion ([1879] 2006). What they both opposed was the commodification of land. They contended that it was unjust to apply the principle of property – "to every produce; the producer" (George, 1898, p. 461–464) to land because land is a fictitious commodity (Polanyi, [1944] 2001). This argument about property and how it relates to capital, and capital accumulation is fundamental to grasping the systemic problems in *The Mystery*, so it requires further illustration.

## Conceptual Challenge: Property, Capital, and Capital Accumulation

While de Soto seems to be following the liberal perspective that the law is the source of property or that necessity leads to property, as, respectively, argued by Jeremy Bentham and Blackstone (see Wiener, 2011, for review), George and Polanyi argued otherwise. To them, property in land everywhere arises from conquests and coercion, leading to the concentration of land in the hands of the army, tribal chiefs, and the class of priests in a process mediated by lawyers (George, [1879] 2006, p. 205). The unifying factor in all these processes is compulsion, intimidation, and pressure – by a privileged class (Polanyi, [1944] 2001, p. 37), not necessity as de Soto argues. The detailed historical processes through which private property in land entered global political economic discussions are contained in Marx's *Capital* (1990, p. 877–895). Polanyi ([1944] 2001, p. 37) regards the processes as "a revolution of the rich against the poor."

De Soto also sees property mainly as a reified relationship between human beings and things, namely between individuals, on the one hand, and houses and land, on the other. This view is pervasive, even among leading property theorists today. Consider the following statement by the eminent property scholar couple Franz von Benda-Beckmann and Keebet von Benda-Beckmann and their colleague, Melanie G. Wiber: "property concerns the organisation and legitimation of rights and obligations with respect to *goods* that are regarded as valuable" (Benda-Beckmann et al., 2009, p. 2; italics added). The view of property as a relationship between individulas and things tends to feed into other understandings of property as well. For instance, the legal definition of property (emphasizing rights) tends to stress a relationship between the rights of owners, lessees, and realty. The bundle of rights metaphor is typically used to organize the many rights involved in this asocial relationship (Benda-Beckmann et al., 2009, pp. 16–19).

However, from a political-economic perspective, property constitutes a social relationship, first and foremost, among human beings. Cast differently, it is a social relationship between production agents (Milonakis & Meramveliotakis, 2013; Bromley, 2019, pp. 221–223). The social construction of property view, as opposed to the asocial and commodified view of property taken by de Soto and other neoclassical economists, places the consideration of class and power and hence social stratification at the center of urban poverty analysis.

Integral to that analysis is how to conceptualize the role of capital and the process by which it accumulates. De Soto argues that capital is mainly two things; namely, an asset and the potential of that asset to produce further goods and services (de Soto, 2000, p. 34). Of the dual meaning of capital, his preference is the latter. In his words, "capital is not the accumulated stock of assets but the *potential* it holds to deploy new production" (de Soto, 2000, p. 35; italics in original). George ([1879] 2006) and Polanyi ([1944] 2001) admit this general Smithian view of capital, but they also stress its social construction. That is, they see capital as a social relationship between classes and how that relationship shapes, constrains, and interacts with forces of power, exploitation, and expropriation.

To de Soto, the process of accumulation turns on the hinges of capital. He argues that "[c]apital was to be the magic that would enhance productivity and create surplus value" (de Soto, 2000, p. 35). This framing leads him to extol the virtues of capital without considering the contribution of labor. From a Polanyian–Georgist perspective, however, the active force or source of production is labor, not capital. It was the exertion of labor on land that led to the creation of capital. It is the continuous exertion of labor that creates surplus. Therefore, the thinking that, somehow, capital a priori created labor and its power is misleading. While capital appropriated the tools of labor in the first place (Marx, [1867]1990, pp. 56–57), labor, in the words of George (1898, p. 414), is always the "initiatory factor" in production.

According to George ([1879] 2006), every capital is the accumulation of someone else's exertion of labor. Thus, to George, the suggestion that surplus is gained from capital is akin to placing "the product before the producer" ([1879] 2006, p. 41) or, in common parlance, placing the cart before the horse. George does not suggest that capital is not important. Indeed, capital shapes the form and can limit the efficiency or even productiveness of industry (George [1879] 2006, p. 47). Also, capital can help labor more effectively and appropriately use land or nature, while also aiding the development of a division of labor for increased production (George [1879] 2006, pp. 46–47). However, admitting that capital plays this role is not the same as saying that capital creates surplus, as claimed by de Soto.

Thus, however one looks – from the perspective of either Schumpeter, Polanyi, or George – *The Mystery* is not only an ineffective strategy for addressing poverty but also a contributor to increasing deprivations and socioeconomic differentiation. Implementing *The Mystery* tends to empower one class against others; disrobes land and labor of their "social covering"; and diverts attention from structural causes of poverty.

### Real World Effects of the de Soto Thesis

So far, the demystification of *The Mystery*, based on insights from Schumpeter, Polanyi, and George, has been mainly theoretical. Equal attention to empirical evidence is necessary to complement the analysis, but not possible in this chapter. Furthermore, as already noted, the argument made in this chapter departs from existing perspectives on de Soto's work that typically use a binary framework, looking at whether de Soto's thesis works or fails. So, empirical studies cast in this chapter's way of seeing have not been conducted.

Briefly, however, it is possible to tease out lessons from some recent related empirical studies in developing countries. Doing so requires addressing a set of three related questions; namely, whether (1) there has been the creation of individual property in land, evidenced by the mystification/registration of individual land rights; (2) the mystification has led to increase in land values partly because of title registration but also as a result of other factors such as urbanization and speculation; and (3) the "unearned income" is not clawed back for redistribution. If the answer to all three questions is in the affirmative, then relative poverty or inequality should tend to rise, not decline, as claimed in *The Mystery*.

Turning to the brief empirical exercise, it is important to first clarify how widespread is the support for title registration. Many global institutions, including the World Bank and the Commonwealth Association of Surveying and Land Economy, support the wave of formalization and regularization (Dickerman et al., 1989; Obeng-Odoom and McDermott, 2018). Next, there is formidable evidence of increases in land values following registration (see Besley, 1995; Felder & Nishio, 1998; Koo, 2011; Manirakiza, 2014; Goodfellow, 2017) – sometimes as high as 23.5 per cent (Lanjouw & Levy, 2002) – general public investment in urban society (Benefield, 2009, Debrezion et al., 2007; Côté-Roy and Moser, 2019), and speculation (Hui et al., 2010). Then, there is the third and final test: are the increases in land value, less the cost of landlords' expenses, taxed for redistribution? UN-HABITAT (2009, 2011) studies and other local cases studies (e.g., Boamah et al., 2012a, 2012b; Goodfellow, 2017) provide evidence that the social, political, and institutional arrangements in the Third World do not easily make it possible to cream off unearned income from the increases in land value for the purpose of redistribution or investment in social services. The reasons for this state of affairs are numerous. They range from poor infrastructural facilities to collect property taxes, the lack of land-based tax regimes (UN-HABITAT, 2008a) to conflict of interest (Goodfellow, 2017).

Consequently, the increases in land values, following registration, urbanization, speculation, and public investment in land, are captured by private individuals/landlords. Given that the answers to our three-stage test are all in the affirmative, it follows that inequality must rise. UN-HABITAT's (2008b) "Harmonious Cities" details growing inequality and uneven urban development typified by social polarization and unequal access and control of land. It shows that inequality has set in motion a cycle of further inequality. Cities, UN-HABITAT notes, are prospering but neither equitably nor sustainably. Thus, Glaeser may declare a contemporary *Triumph of the City* (2011), but UN-HABITAT data show that the urban experience is more akin to the interpretations of Schumpeter, Polanyi, and George that emphasize social dysfunction and stratification. Implementing the ideas in *The Mystery* is analogous with instituting inequality, which UN-HABITAT (2008b) and many others (e.g., Gittings, 2010; Stilwell, 2019) demonstrate, not only causes moral discontent but also constitutes a brake on economic development and absolute poverty reduction efforts.

Inequality drives social conflict, reduces happiness, and contributes substantially to both crime and grime. Of course, there are other sources of inequality, such as the effect of winning a lottery, so growing urban inequality or increasing relative poverty cannot all be ascribed to the application of *The Mystery*. However, the interrelated empirical evidence showing the growing popularity of *The Mystery* and its application, spikes in land values, inability to redistribute those increases, and rising urban inequality may be taken as vindicating the position of Schumpeter, Polanyi, and George.

De Soto's argument about the agency of poor people and the possible use of entrepreneurship for social ends is borne out in some slum communities in the Third World. Some studies (e.g., UN-HABITAT, 2003; Owusu et al., 2008; Anyidoho and Steel, 2016) show that slums are not altogether places of despair. Through innovation and entrepreneurship, a number of dwellers have connected to global markets and, as a result, the social conditions of some of them have improved (see Grant & Oteng-Ababio, 2012; Anyidoho and Steel, 2016). The "entrepreneurial slum," as McFarlane (2012) has recently called the slums in de Soto's work, however, thrives on complex social networks, institutions, and relations, and even then, under difficult circumstances, that lead to different and differentiated experiences (Obeng-Odoom, 2011). Labor, as with land, is a "fictitious commodity" (Polanyi, [1944] 2001). They had neither the properties of goods and services made in the market, nor are their uses governed solely by universal commodity laws. Rather, the community, the state, and, indeed, the society in which they are located, as a whole, shape their nature and character (Paton, 2010; Levitt, 2017). In other words, even "the entrepreneurial slum" is embedded in complex socioeconomic and political relationships.

In practice, the poor witness and experience what Polanyi called "double movement": markets are extended on the one hand, while formal and informal institutions are created and encouraged to ensure that markets survive (Paton, 2010, p. 85; Levitt, 2017). Thus, while finding that de Soto's assumption that the poor possess some economic agency is sound and may, indeed, secure socially beneficial outcomes through pursuing innovative and entrepreneurial endeavors, de Soto's conception of such processes remains largely individualist and detached from broader political economic considerations. Similarly, while in some cases (see Singh & Huang, 2011), there is evidence of an inverse correlation between stronger property rights in land, on the one hand, and poverty and inequality levels, on the other, the relationship holds only when property is socialized. It follows that the assumptions and predictions in *The Mystery* are not only simplistic, but also misleading.

## CONCLUSION

By utilizing insights from Schumpeter, Polanyi, and George, this chapter has made the case that de Soto's ideas are not only grounded in highly problematic assumptions about the nature of political economic processes, but also that their implementation through policy would be ineffective in curbing urban poverty and actually serve to simultaneously entrench and augment it. The analyses demonstrate that, while de Soto's assumption that the poor possess some economic agency is sound and may, indeed, improve their social conditions through pursuing innovative and entrepreneurial endeavors, his analysis of such processes ignores broader political economic considerations. The source of the flaw in *The Mystery* is structural. Regarding capital only as stock for increasing further wealth, rather than as social and class relations, suggesting that the capital-accumulation process is powered at the origin by capital without considering the collective contribution of labor in developing tools and conceptualizing property as a relationship between individuals and landed property, rather than principally as a social relation, lead to a highly asocial analysis of urban poverty and social stratification. Contrary to suggestions by critics that the policy implications of *The Mystery* are neutral, or that *The Mystery* simply does not work in practice, its application in the form of development and urban policy is analogous with institutionalizing inequality and poverty, and wider questions of social stratification while diverting attention from root causes.

The next chapter places the work of de Soto in the context of a wider debate on land reform in Africa.

3

# Land Reform

## INTRODUCTION

Land reform has reemerged as a focus of attention in discussions about inequality in Africa. In his contribution to the *Cambridge Journal of Regions, Economy and Society*, Howard Stein (2011) discusses how, although most World Bank economists were explicit about seeking efficiency gains from land reform, at the implicit level, their emphasis was on using land reform to address inequality. Reforming land tenure can address inequality because, according to these economists, the prevailing forms of land administration were biased in favor of elites who undeservedly captured rents. In this sense, land reform was aimed at removing state-driven distortions that created advantages for only a few groups of people. Catherine Boone's (2018) more recent review makes similar comments, as do many other studies about the historical importance of land in economic analysis (Arndt, 1987, pp. 102–104; Atkins, 1988; Stilwell & Jordan, 2004; Todaro & Smith, 2006, pp. 428–440; Foldvary, 2008). Together with the current global interest in searching for explanations of inequality (see, for example, Piketty, 2014; O'Donell, 2015), the focus on land reform should require no further justification.

In this case for equity in the distribution of both income and wealth, women's empowerment has become a major focus (Food and Agricultural Organisation, 2002, pp. 25–27; Chu, 2011, pp. 36–38). The UN-HABITAT has been one of the global institutions committed to using land as a vehicle for gender equality and economic development. In 2006, for instance, a conference in Bagamoyo, Tanzania, which was jointly organized by the Commonwealth Association of Surveying and Land Economy (CASLE), the United Nations Human Settlements Program (UN-HABITAT), and the African Real Estate Society (AfRES), sought to "propose the way forward on poverty alleviation through sustainable land management and administration" (CASLE, 2007). It was in that same year that the Global Land Tool Network, a partnership between the UN-HABITAT, Swedish International Development Cooperation Agency (Sida), the Norwegian Ministry of Foreign Affairs, and the World Bank, was formed. All these efforts are aimed at enhancing economic development through securing and promoting equal land rights for both genders, but especially women (see SDGs 1, 2, 5, 11, and 15). Economists and sociologists alike stress the desirability of secure land tenure for human development (Kerekes & Williamson, 2010; Kelly et al., 2019), with the World Bank in general and World Bank economists in particular (see Collins and Mitchell, 2018), leading the others to contend that land reform provides a reliable route for addressing inequality – in terms of income, wealth, race, and gender.

However, whether the specific land reform favored in development economics can close inter-group disparities in wealth and income has been the subject of bitter controversy. Two views are prevalent. The dominant position is that held by most neoclassical economists who, starting in the 1970s in particular, put a strong case for Coasian individual land rights system over and above rights held by the state and collectives widely popularized by de Soto as a way of guaranteeing security of tenure. This system was held to be superior to the alternative public or collective system of land tenure (as discussed in Chapter 2). In the 1980s, critics, however, pointed out that the Manichean analysis of individual versus state rights was not satisfactory. It could be possible, the argument went, that secure individual rights would not ensure the redress of marginalization. Indeed, critics contended that focusing on group rights was, instead, a surer path to progress. Attempts to synthesize these views have been along two main lines (Lea, 2008, pp. 31–49): the first (strongly developed by Will Kymlicka) posits that both rights can coexist, while the other, notably argued by David Lea, sees that there is a tendency for the two to coalesce.

This chapter revisits these polarized views by examining the nature, practices, and outcomes of the land tenure systems in Africa in the light of recent debates about "land grabbing." However, the approach used in this chapter is methodologically distinct from existing research, including studies published in leading journals such as *Journal of Agrarian Change*, *Journal of Peasant Studies*, and *Development and Change* (see Table 3.1). The more Marxist-oriented research tends to be focused on land at the global level, while law-oriented research is cast in national terms. Microeconomists are more concerned with household-level economics to the neglect of multi-scalar analyses that draw on law, economics, and

Table 3.1 *Reconceptualizing research on land*

|  | Local | National | Regional | Global |
|---|---|---|---|---|
| Research on land microeconomics |  |  |  |  |
| Research on the macroeconomics of land |  |  |  |  |
| Research on land grabs |  |  |  |  |
| This chapter |  |  |  |  |

political economy more widely (Obeng-Odoom, 2013b, chapter 8; Oya, 2013). In turn, the state of knowledge on Africa's land economy is quite fractured and fragmentary.

As Table 3.1 shows, while existing studies have largely considered "land grabs" as a "new" global-scale phenomenon and, hence, neglected research and debates on tenure security at the local, national, and even regional levels. This chapter, in contrast, takes the view that, as the case for land reform always included the development of a global land market (see, for example, World Bank, 2003a), articulated with local, national, and regional land markets, the development of such a global land market ought to be seen as part of, not apart from, the analysis of land reform. Indeed, the transformation of land from its use value under customary tenure to emphasize its exchange value in a global political economy and its resulting consequences for society and economy are key concerns in land economics generally and in the land economics of Karl Polanyi and Henry George in particular, as we saw in chapter two.

Consequently, the chapter considers the "land grab" phenomenon and the questions of tenure security and title registration dialectically. Developing an approach in which such land grabs are properly deemed land transactions in a global land market which, according to mainstream economists, can bring about convergence in intergroup inequalities, specific cases are considered. Empirically, four African countries are used to assess the nation-centric claims about land reform, followed by a more "global," that is, Africa-wide, analysis of trade in African land across the world.

Based on this approach, the chapter argues that there are significant gaps between the theories, how they are implemented, and their outcomes in relation to reducing stratification and intergroup inequalities. Indeed, in many cases, land reform has widened these differences, suggesting that, rather than inclusion, land reform has been a path to exclude poorer and weaker groups such as migrant women. Through land reform, a global land market has developed in Africa but, in contrast to the claims by advocates, this market has been a conduit for transferring African wealth to the Global North and elsewhere. Although questions of implementation may blur the lines between what works and what does not, this finding provides strong grounds to be skeptical of theories about African land tenure systems and how they work or should work.

How might this argument be framed in a wider Polanyian framework? A key rallying point in Polanyian thinking is the notion of embeddedness. Polanyi (1944/2001) explains that, while exchange is immemorial, precapitalist exchange was not organized in the "self regulating market." Under feudal and mercantilist systems, there was exchange and barter, along with tribute and tithe to the aristocratic monarchy. However, those markets were accessories of society: they were subordinate to politics, religion, and economy. The implication was that the markets were not capitalist or "self-regulating." Under capitalism, however, the sequence has often been regularly tinkered with and encouraged to change: society has become subordinate to markets. There has been aggressive commodification. Markets have assumed a disproportionate role in society. Markets have been created or recommended for a great number of things, commodities and non-commodities alike.

To Polanyi, commodities are things produced to be bought and sold, so land, labor, and money are *ipso facto* not commodities even though they are marketized in capitalist societies. Thus, for Polanyi, these are fictitious. Land, labor, and money are also fictitious for two other reasons. First of all, they do not obey the laws of demand and supply. That is, while in the event of a drop in price, supply is expected to fall and demand rise to a point when demand and supply meet to establish the equilibrium price, neither land, money, nor labor necessarily behaves in this way. So, they are fictitious commodities. Secondly, they are fictitious because of their strong reliance on institutions – not just markets – to function properly.

Polanyi ([1944] 2001, p. 73) recognized these non-market institutional arrangements as possibly tending to produce a harmonious society. The reverse logic – the market society enamored with what he called "commodity fiction" (p. 76) – is contentious. He argued that this commodity fiction – that attempts to disembed the economy from society, to technicalize it, to remove it from religion, culture, and politics – is the myth around which the capitalist system revolves. The implication of this commodity fiction is to make society an accessory of the market. In turn, society is stripped of its cloth of customary and social protection, becoming exposed to the socioeconomic and political tensions and contradictions, leading to "social dislocation" (p.79). The transfer of rents from producers to rentiers is a key mechanism that underpins this and other structural inequalities and social problems (George, [1879] 2006, p. xv).

While this chapter does not adopt a strict intersectional use of the concepts of embeddedness, disembeddedness (commodification), and social dislocation in Karl Polanyi nor seek to "prove" how Henry George's notion of transferring rent from producers to rentiers produces and reproduces inequality (George, [1879] 2006, p. xv) and, hence, demonstrates the limitations of land reform, students of Polanyi and George can reconstruct the evidence in those terms.

The chapter begins by reviewing the theories that inform the main prescriptions of the two schools of thought on land reform. Next, the chapter looks at the various approaches, practices, and outcomes of land reforms in Ghana, South Africa, Uganda, and Egypt. Then, it teases out lessons from these experiences which might be useful in refining the theories based on which land reforms have been undertaken.

## LAND POLICIES IN AFRICA: INDIVIDUAL RIGHTS VERSUS SOCIAL CAPITAL

To understand the debate about individual and communal land rights and how these rights affect secure tenure and gender relations, it is important to explain the concepts of property, land tenure, and secure tenure.

These notions are often reinterpretations of ideas from philosophers such as John Locke (see, for example, Gibbard, 1976; Judge, 2002; Arnot et al., 2011) and tend to be highly contested (Boydell et al., 2007). Generally, property is seen as a broad term denoting tangible things, relationships, or rights to the use and ownership of those things. It is when "property" is qualified by "real" or "landed" as in "real property" or "landed property" that it becomes narrowly focussed on land and the rights therein. Property rights are, therefore, land rights: certain rights that are exercised over land which, in turn, entail an enforceable duty on others not to interfere with those rights (Cole & Grossman, 2002; Abdulai, 2006; Bromley and Anderson, 2012, pp. 41–42). Land tenure refers to the system of institutions or rules of land ownership, use, and management, and obligations, responsibilities, and constraints on how land is owned and used. It is commonly said to be "secure" if it assures owners that their rights are free from expropriation, encroachment, or forced eviction (Food and Agricultural Organisation, 2002). How to attain these aspirations in a way that is sensitive to gender relations is the subject of bitter controversy.

The two polarized views, focussing on individualism and collectivism, are subsets of the broader natural rights and conventional schools of thought that have historically debated the place of property in economic development (Obeng-Odoom, 2016f).

## INDIVIDUALISM

Individualism, broadly construed, means self-love, selfishness, or a concern for only oneself as opposed to a collective. However, as shown in the previous chapter, in property economics, individualism connotes the idea that it should be possible – indeed desirable – for property rights to be clearly delineated, formally registered, and privately appropriated and sold (Balibar, 2002, p. 299; Bromley, 2019). This idea has strong connections with methodological individualism or the doctrine that all social phenomena can best be construed and explained in individual, rather than collective and structural, terms (for a discussion, see Hodgson, 2007; Bromley, 2019). Thus, the concept may be used to describe individuals who are working together to create, to market, and to sell rights in property to satisfy their own utility but also to diffuse the forces of economic development. In this way, the argument goes, economic convergence between the rich and the poor is assured. As shown in Chapter 2, these claims echo the Coase Theorem in property economics widely popularized by Hernando de Soto.

Individualism is often said to underpin the capitalist system of production. Its origins date as far back as the era of the enclosure movements when common lands were fenced off to become private lands. As a system, which has been the focus of extensive discussion, the essential argument for individual property rights is, therefore, well documented (see Dobb, 1963; Haila, 2016; Christophers, 2019). Proponents of that system claim that, unless a bundle of rights can be privately owned by individuals, they would have little incentive to put it to the highest and best use or little interest in ensuring that it is used sustainably. From this perspective, people are driven mainly by self-interest, which, in turn, spurs them on to be productive. According to this view, communal property rights are inefficient because, not having any private or individual interest in a resource, people are likely to become irresponsible and act in ways that injure the common good or what Garrett Hardin (1968) called a "tragedy of the commons." By this idea, Hardin argued that commonly held land is open to abuse and overuse not only because of overpopulation but also because of self-interest that characterizes human nature. Privatization is preferable not because it is flawless, but because there is no better alternative to it. Indeed, privatization provides not only efficiency and effectiveness but it is also popularly supported because, without it, common property brings ruin to all. As two advocates of private property rights Alchian and Demsetz (1973, p. 19) put it, "persons who own communal rights will tend to exercise these rights in ways that ignore the full consequences of their actions." That is, collective land tenure systems are inherently insecure.

Land tenure is secure if it ensures equitable access to, distribution, and control of landed resources as well as protection from arbitrary displacement and dislocation from land. Because of the diversity of imageries that secure tenure evokes, there is no one way of guaranteeing it to enhance the living conditions of Africans (Obeng-Odoom & Stilwell, 2013, p. 328). Yet, within the individualist school, it is commonly assumed that formal recording of interest in land to ensure individual trade in the land market "secures" it (see, for example, Ministry of Lands and Forestry, 1999; Kelly et al., 2019).

The idea that individual, rather than group, rights are superior and more conducive to economic development has a long intellectual history coinciding with the rise of the Chicago School of economics in the 1920s who further developed the idea and provided responses to critics (see Jones, 2010; Nik-Khah & van Horn, 2018). The direct application of this idea to land in the developing world, however, gained momentum in the 1990s. Then, as now, the work of Hernando de Soto, the Peruvian economist or the "Messiah of people's capitalism" (Davis, 2006, p. 80), whose work was discussed in detail in Chapter 2, also became highly influential. It promised the developing world a cure to end the problem of insecure tenure. De Soto cannot be said to be the originator of the idea of individual private rights, as applied to land, of course. Before his seminal work (de Soto, 2000) was published, Feder and Feeny (1991) had long argued some of the main ideas often attributed to him, including the argument that individualizing land tenure cures asymmetric information and provides the needed guarantee to obtain security for credit (for a review of the literature on this theme, see Dickermann et al., 1989). Indeed, the so-called debates between the natural rights and conventional schools of property rights have been raging for years. Richard Schlatter (1951), Brett Boyce (2007), and David Lea (2008) have all provided detailed historical accounts of the extent of this pre-de Soto literature. More recently, the *Review of Radical Polical Economics* has published a synthesis of these histories (Obeng-Odoom, 2016f).

However, as Chapter 2 showed, de Soto has been one of the leading advocates of private property rights in land as a way of promoting economic development in the economically weak countries. According to de

Soto (2000), a crucial cause of insecure land rights is the nature of traditional land ownership, particularly its communal nature and lack of documented information. He contrasts the communal nature of land tenure and
the dearth of information in developing countries with the situation in the
developed countries where every parcel of land is formally documented.

For de Soto (2000), not only are communal ownership and a lack of
information recipes for insecurity, they are also impediments to domestic
and national investment. These characteristics, he argues, render the
landed asset of people in developing countries defective because land
cannot be traded or used as collateral for credits. The situation of the
poor, in the view of de Soto (2000), is akin to corporations that cannot issue
bonds or shares. In effect, the asset of the poor is dead capital (de Soto,
2000, p. 5). For these reasons, he advocates a private property rights system
in which land is individually owned, recorded, and commoditized.

The World Bank has independently developed these ideas in its reports,
but, as Allan Gilbert (2012) and others (see Chapter 2) have shown, the
Bank has also been influenced by the work of de Soto. The World Bank has
been championing these views since the 1970s. In its seminal report on
land, *Land Reform* (World Bank, 1975), a strong case was made for the use
of formal title registers, individual tenure, and promoting market exchange
in land. Its lead economist with responsibility for land and development
economics, Klaus Deininger, was later to publish a paper reporting that the
World Bank had changed its views (Deininger & Binswanger, 1999). The
revised World Bank position is stated in its 2003 report, *Land Policy for
Growth and Poverty Reduction* (Deininger, 2003). Like the 1999 paper, the
World Bank stresses its change in orientation, but a critical reading reveals
that the structural argument remains the same or similar: the marketization of land is key for economic development and poverty reduction;
customary land requires recording and state backing to be secure; secure
tenure is given by the state through enforcing formal land rights; women's
rights are better guaranteed by formal rights; more formal tenure is the
only reason credit can be given; customary tenure ought to evolve to
individual tenure in the process of economic development; and land
must be regarded as an "asset" and its exchange encouraged (Deininger,
2003, pp. xvii–xlvi).

Advocates of this view – including Duke University economist, Erica Field
(2004, 2005, 2007) and others from the University of Guelph (Kelly et al., 2019)
– argue that formalized, individual titles to land can be used to access credit
through which the poor can escape the problems of poverty. That is, individual
land rights, properly documented, make land tenure secure, credible, and

tradable. As such, de Soto regards the label, "poor people" as a misnomer: these are "poor businessmen" who would immediately become rich if given formal, individual title to their land (de Soto, 2004, p. 2). Individual property rights would enable houses to have "parallel purpose," beside shelter, because "they can be used to put in motion more production by securing the interests of other parties as 'collateral' for a mortgage, for example, or by assuring the supply of other forms of credit and public utilities" (de Soto, 2000, p. 32). As is usually the case in neoclassical economic theory, gender is not a prominent feature of de Soto's work. However, others have put the theoretical case for how titling and formalization might empower women. Development economists tend to argue that securing women's individual rights and joining them up in, for example, co-operatives would lead to greater efficiency in farming (through, for example, incentivization), welfare and poverty reduction (through, for example, credit), empowerment (for example, through increased confidence arising from obtaining more rights), and eventually equality relative to the position of men in the household and community (Agarwal, 2003; Panda & Agarwal, 2005; Agarwal & Panda, 2007; Agarwal, 2016) or protect women from the complications of discriminatory practices of inheritance (Kelly et al., 2019). Similar positions are commonly taken in the wider development studies literature (see Griffiths, 2000; Jackson, 2003; Whitehead & Tsikata, 2003; Boone, 2018).

The final aspect of the mainstream case for titling is the development of a global land market. Reforms are usually intended to ensure that land markets develop not only at local, national, or even regional scales but also at the global level. As noted by the World Bank in its seminal report on this issue, *Land Policies for Growth and Poverty Reduction*:

> The experience of farm restructuring illustrates that it is impossible to divorce land tenure from broader policy and institutional issues and access to local as well as global markets. Most of the economic benefits of titling have initially been concentrated in urban areas, where credit markets were much faster to emerge than in rural ones. The malfunctioning of rural output and factor markets in a risky environment has in many cases prevented households from leaving former collectives. Improvements in the legal and institutional environment will therefore be critical. To ensure a gradual improvement in the functioning of rural markets, including those for land, establishing a correspondence between land shares and physical property and eliminating implicit and explicit restrictions on land rental will be important. (World Bank, 2003a, p. xxxix)

From this perspective, it is important not just to appeal to global land markets, investment markets at the global level, or national markets as separate, a fragmentation that characterizes research on land transactions (see, for example, Cotula & Pollack, 2012). Rather, in a political economic analysis in the stratification economics tradition, it is important to raise the issue of "articulated land markets," of which one is the global land market. In this network of land markets, national land markets act as a revolving door for land transactions. So, the land markets usher in investors and they create a platform for others to invest in the global land market. Without this simple, but important, emphasis, the concept of "self-regulating market" in Karl Polanyi is meaningless. By this idea of "articulated land markets," the markets are supposed to work at every level, creating a grand system of markets in which markets, through their own logic, reproduce additional markets. In the words of a leading Polanyian political economist, Fred Block:

The self-regulating market of free market theory is postulated to be a tightly coupled system because shifts in preferences and prices are supposed to move quickly from one market to another so as to bring supply and demand back into balance almost instantaneously. In fact, one of the key reasons that free market theorists are suspicious of government regulation of markets is the fear that such actions will impede the ability of markets to ad just quickly to changes in the availability of certain economic inputs. (Block, 2012, p. 31)

To activate this theory, an additional construct of a "property-owning" society in which individuals have the right to freely enter and exit various markets at will is needed. In a property-owning society, these markets, while presented as seeking to alleviate poverty, are, in essence, designed to close the wealth and income gap. Indeed, the theory of inequality behind land reforms is that, the involvement of the state creates unfair advantages for a few. Promoting individual property rights, on the other hand, is likely to remove these problems to create a level playing field. In the words of the World Bank:

In many instances land markets' ability to transfer land, for instance, from inefficient and bankrupt state enterprises to private users, will still not only be beneficial in terms of efficiency, but will also be conducive to the emergence of a reliable and robust financial system. For this reason an efficient system of land administration that minimizes transaction costs is likely to have considerable benefits. (World Bank, 2003a, pp. 97–98)

It is this grand land market that is expected to remove the problems of inequality and bring about intergroup convergence in wealth and incomes and convergence between the social and economic conditions in Africa and the Global North.

## COMMUNITY LAND RIGHTS

The second view about how to ensure secure property rights is strikingly different. Argued by a communitarian school, the characteristic claim is that land reform should revert to a traditional land tenure system. This view is rooted in the concept of social capital that was popularized by James Coleman. Social capital is commonly regarded as the advantages individuals derive from their social networks, for example, made up of clan members. Social capital usually arises from a conglomerate of expectations, obligations, and trust among a group of people (Coleman, 1988). Coleman (1988) argues that it confers several advantages on individuals, such as obtaining information that would otherwise have required more time and cost to get. Norms in networks such as eschewing selfishness in favor of actions that inure to group or network benefit all members of the group.

Rules and taboos in the network free and bind, and liberate the people in the network for their common good, especially if the network is closed such that the activities of each member affect the others and affected members can team up to sanction a member in the group (Coleman, 1988, pp. s105–s106). Social capital is said to be particularly strong in families, especially if the relationship among the members is strong such that human capital can have a positive impact on children's intellectual development (Coleman, 1988, pp. s110–s113). On the basis of this logic of the necessity of noneconomic relationships, some sociologists, anthropologists, and economists have argued that the key to economic development in economically weak countries, such as those in Africa, is to ensure a deepening of networks of trust in the society (Tomer, 2001, p. 1051; Andriani and Christoforou, 2016).

Applied to land tenure, the argument is that traditional forms of tenure that are based on custom is the most effective way to ensure secure tenure. According to communitarians, insecure tenure is the result of two main factors: state-led policies, which ignore traditional values, and individualized property rights, which marginalize rather than empower. Both reasons are counter productive because they lack the pristine African culture of equitable land tenure (see Amanor, 2001, pp. 5–20, for a full discussion).

According to Katz (2000, p. 115), "the existence of social capital can substitute for well-defined property rights ... respect for customary law and viable local institutions, based on sustained interactions among resource users over time, can enforce respect for private property boundaries and regulate exploitation of common property resources." Advocates of communal land rights claim that it is sensitive to gender relations and promotes equality. Here, they sometimes argue in ways that have features common to cultural relativism. That is, they celebrate cultural difference, celebrate viewing women as part of a group, namely, the household, and so not really discriminated against in terms of the land question (Hellum, 1998, pp. 94–105). The more popular "gender" position among communitarians is to accept that women may be discriminated against in a communal land tenure system, but such women are mostly those "alien" to particular settlements. Native women, using their male social capital in the form of networks, can have access to land and get their property rights secured. That is, brothers, husbands, sons, nephews, and brothers-in-law can provide that support that formal, individual institutions may not be able to deliver. From this perspective, customary practices are not simply parasitic (Yngstrom, 2002; Asaaga and Hirons, 2019). Rather, they entail mutual rights and obligations between genders. From this perspective, women are neither subordinate to men nor are their rights simply secondary as claimed by individualists (Gray & Kevane, 1999; Kevane & Gray, 1999).

It is useful to consider how these theories play out in policy discussions about socioeconomic development in Africa. Often, they influence the land reform policies prescribed by international development agencies interested in economic development in Africa. These agencies advocate land reform policies that usually combine the individual property rights paradigm with the communal property view in a plural legal regime where the two systems are mostly interdependent (Griffiths, 1983, 1996; Moore, 1998), at least in the short-run. In the long-run, the policies typically endorse an "evolutionary view" because they aspire for a private property rights regime through the titling and registration of land that was originally "communally" owned. Leading proponents of this approach are the World Bank and the UN-HABITAT and their policies of "land administration" fostered through the creation of land registries and the Global Land Tool Network (GLTN).

The World Bank (2003a, p. 4) explains why individual land rights should be chosen over "community" land rights:

First, to reduce conflicts in land ownership and land use, and provide secure land titles in both urban and rural areas. The land titles would assure security of tenure to land and peaceful possession, facilitating investments in housing, industry, agriculture and services sectors of the economy that will generate employment and economic growth. Second, reforming and modernizing public sector administration and management of land and decentralizing land administration services to the local level structures would rationalize land policies and institutional responsibilities for land administration, and streamline operational practices. Third, facilitating participation of civil society and the private sector would check excesses of public sector management, reduce land transaction costs and promote transparency in the administration and management of both public and private land and self help initiatives for growth and development, building on the cultural heritage of [Africa].

The view that an individualist perspective is the way to ensure secure and equitable land rights has had significant influence in Africa. Is this approach a panacea? It is useful to ascertain whether there is a congruence between theories and implementation and between outcomes and theories. Several detailed country case studies already exist (for example, those contained in the edited volume by Moyo & Yeros, 2005). Therefore, the present chapter does not duplicate this effort. Rather, it seeks to review the evidence from the detailed studies, regarding the extent to which the theories about land tenure reforms are borne out in practice. The analysis, in turn, provides lessons to enrich the debate about land tenure, gender empowerment, and economic development. The principal focus of the chapter is on land reform experiences in Ghana, South Africa, Egypt, and Uganda; four African countries with different land rights histories. Therein lie some possible tensions, relating to ontological, epistemological, and methodological issues: how can we compare countries that differ in terms of their history and institutions?

At the root of these issues is the conception of space. If space is seen as bound and absolutist, these questions of place, scale, and causality arise (Ward, 2010). However, this chapter takes a relational view of space. It is a view that makes a comparative analysis possible. It entails a functionalist, rather than formal, comparison. That is, it does not, for example, formally compare the urban land system in one country to another because "urban land" may mean different things in different countries (Gordon et al., 2007). Rather, it looks at processes and patterns in different countries. This view is grounded in three related principles: first, countries can be perceived as unbounded, related, and interconnected – locally, nationally, and internationally. Second, the urban and rural space and scale evolve, so a rigid conception of scale or space does not help. Third, the wave of globalization means that it is possible to look at different spaces within global processes. The aim of this chapter is not to provide the basis of a theory, but rather to understand how the different countries have responded to global trends of land reform and the outcomes of such experiments. To avoid overgeneralization, the chapter highlights the context of each of the cases, a practice successfully used by other social scientists (see Ward, 2010; Christophers, 2018).

## GHANA

"The term land," N. A. Ollenu began in his magisterial book, *Principles of Customary Land Law in Ghana* (1962, p. 1), "includes the land itself . . ., things on the soil . . ., any estate, interest or right in, to, or over the land or over any of the other things which land denotes, e.g., the right to collect snails, herbs, or to hunt on land." For Ghanaians, "the first basic principle of our [Ghanaian] customary land law is that there is no land in Ghana without an owner" (Ollenu, 1962, p. 4). But this idea of ownership, as well as the notion of owners, is as wide-ranging as the conception of land itself.

Ownership ranges from the paramount interest in land or the allodial title through sub-paramount titles, to essentially perpetual, but still possessory, interests such as usufructuary estates. Other notions of ownership are more temporary, ranging from periodic tenancies to licenses (Ollenu, 1962). Owners of land include the state, traditional authority, individuals, and families (Geary, 1913; Ubink, 2002; Kasanga, 2003; Abdulai and Ochieng, 2017). These owners exchange land in various ways, including through markets, through gifts, and through compulsion with or without compensation (see, for example, Lentz, 2013; Asante and Helbrecht, 2019).

Often characterized by complexity and debates that play out in different arenas (e.g., Avoka, 2009; Ghana News Agency, 2009a, 2009b; Abdulai & Hammond, 2010; Amanor, 2010 Abdulai and Ochieng, 2017). Ghana's land economy is often portrayed as chaotic and labyrinthine. A free-for-all space where population growth compounds the confusion, formal land title registration continues to be advocated as solution for order and for equity because locally devised "short-cuts" such as allocation papers do not meet the full benefits conferred by formal land title registration (Mireku et al., 2016).

Central to this mainstream diagnosis is that Ghana's land economy is in crisis because of the dominance of the customary system which, according to Kasim Kasanga (2003), is about 78 per cent of the national total. Framed in these terms, successive governments have undertaken several changes in land administration, including formulating a National Land Policy (Ministry of Land and Forestry [MLF], 1999). According to the National Land Policy of Ghana (NLP), the government will "undertake tenurial reform process, which documents and recognizes the registration and classification of titles, and speed up title registration to cover all lands throughout Ghana" (MLF, 1999, p. 16).

The reforms included implementing a program for the production of large-scale maps, enacting legislation to require landowners to properly demarcate the boundaries of their land, establishing an Early Warning Mechanism to detect possible areas of dispute, and getting the Chief Justice to establish a special division of the High Court to deal with problems of land (MLF, 1999, pp. 16–17). The vision of the policy is to individualize land rights or, if collective rights are registered, and make such interests in land easily tradable. In order to achieve this vision, the government undertook land reforms in 2003. These reforms were collectively called the Land Administration Project (LAP), comprising four main components that deal with harmonization of land policies, institutional changes, monitoring, and evaluation (see Karikari, 2006; Kudom-Agyemang, 2009; LAP, 2009, for details).

Have these changes made land rights secure? What about intergroup equity: does it remain substantial, have any improvements been made? Several studies, even if there have been some marginal gains (see, for example, Hughes, 2003; Bugri, 2008; Hammond, 2008; Ubink and Quan, 2008; Abdulai, 2010; Ehwi et al., 2018) answer the first question in the negative. Most other studies tend to answer the second question in the negative too by contending that land reform has not made wealth distribution more equitable (see, for example, Sandbrook & Arn, 1977; Howard, 1978; Duncan & Brants, 2004; Austin, 2005; Amanor, 2006; Aryeetey et al., 2007, p. 19; Eagle Group, 2007; Ghana Statistical Service, 2008; Owusu, 2008; Amanor-wilks, 2009; Consultant, 2009; Duncan, 2010; Abdulai and Ochieng, 2017). It is more useful to consider the evidence more systematically.

As of 2003, there were 15,000 land cases pending before the courts in Accra (World Bank, 2003b); 9,214 cases pending before the courts in Kumasi (Crook, 2004); 74 land cases pending before the courts in Bolgatanga, Tamale, and Wa (Abdulai, 2010); and 40 cases pending in Cape Coast (Cashiers' Office, 2010). Overall, there were an estimated 60,000 land cases in Ghana in 2003 (Kasanga, 2003), as against 11,556 land cases in 1999 and 14,964 cases in 2002 (Kotey, 2004). This implies that, between 1999 and 2003, there was a 519 per cent increase in the number of land cases in Ghana. Between 2003 and 2011, only 3,684 cases were resolved (Larbi, 2011). These figures exclude over 770 land disputes that arose between 2003 and 2010, which were resolved through alternative dispute resolution (LAP, 2010). More specific evidence suggests that questions of land conflict have not ameliorated. Indeed, in the case of Cape Coast, for example, the number of cases pending in the high court as of 2008 was 114, an increase of over 100 per cent over 2003 levels (Cashiers' Office, 2010). Between 2010 and 2015, D. K. Bansah (2017) monitored and compiled 63 public complaints published in the media about private security persons ("land guards") recruited to protect the land of their employees. These complaints doubled from nine in 2010 to eighteen in

2014. Indeed, by November 23, 2015 – more than a month before the end of the year – twelve complaints had already been published. These stories show that some land guards commit murder and that others – by wielding deadly weapons – show the potential to commit murder.

The reasons for land disputes can be inferred from the relief sought in the land cases. Between 1961 and 2004, 31 per cent of the reliefs sought were declaration of title, 19 per cent recovery of possession, and 22 per cent related to recovery of possession. Disaggregated further, there was an over 500 per cent rise in the declaration of title relief sought prior to the 1980s (1971–1980) when registration was voluntary, and the post-1980s when registration became compulsory (based on figures made available by Kotey, 2004, p. 98). While the data do not allow for an analysis of the share of disputes that are ethnic, class, or inheritance based, it is probably correct to say that these intermingle in reproducing and sustaining land disputes. Thus, the assumption that chiefs, being the custodians of land, are driven solely by a sense of community good, is shaky.

Some chiefs and other traditional rulers or elders who abuse their role as custodians of land justify their actions on two main grounds. First, they argue that the times have changed: custom is dynamic and no longer means that communal land belongs to the community. Therefore, some chiefs argue that they can sell communal land for their private gain. The second discourse is the understanding of customary land as "royal land." Being leaders of the royal family, some chiefs contend that they have the right to sell communal land for their private gain or the benefit of the royal family (Ubink, 2007; Boamah, 2014a, 2014b; Tieleman and Uitermark, 2019). These discourses and their implementation have made chiefs a wealthy class.

In turn, people have become keenly interested in holding the position of chief (see Sutton, 1984; Hughes, 2003; Tieleman and Uitermark, 2019), a trend that has contributed to protracted conflicts about who can be a chief. In 2009 alone, there were 220 chieftaincy disputes reported at the National House of Chiefs in Ghana (Ghana News Agency, 2010a). There have been some attempts to keep the chieftaincy institution in check. For instance, the Office of the Administrator of Stool Lands Act (OASL) 1994 (Act 481) establishes the Office of the Administrator of Stool Lands to manage stool lands (Kasanga & Kotey, 2001). However, this institution is limited in its mandate. It only manages revenues from ground rents, farm rents, and compensation sums, and royalties from timber and mineral leases granted by chiefs. Between 2005 and 2009, the office disbursed an estimated $52 billion (Ghana News Agency, 2010b). The constitution stipulates that 55 per cent of that amount should be given to local governments, 20 per cent to the traditional authority, and 25 per cent to the stool. The formula implies that 45 per cent of revenue (from these three sources) goes to chiefs and landed elites. They receive their share in addition to payments for leases of land, which they grant to individuals and institutions.

Therefore, the power of chiefs remains intact, in spite of the subtle attempt to control the institution. Indeed, in the *Ghana Bar Association v Attorney General* case, the Supreme Court of Ghana ruled that neither the High Court nor the Court of Appeal has any jurisdiction in chieftaincy matters. The court seemed to be saying that chiefs should be a law unto themselves and that the National House of Chiefs should be the appropriate forum to resolve chieftaincy issues (for an analysis of the case, see Kludze, 1998). So, the state, overall, has ended up further entrenching the class position of a landed elite. In turn, chiefs remain largely unaccountable. An analysis of all land disputes from 1961 to 2004 shows that over 60 per cent of them arise from the multiple sale of land, while the rest includes conflicts between chiefs about who owns what land and disagreements between landlords and tenant farmers. Overall, 67 per cent of plaintiffs are poor farmers (Kotey, 2004). The evidence shows that land policies have not been able to ensure secure tenure of land, as promised. Indeed, it has not succeeded in "protecting the rights of landowners and their descendants from becoming landless," and not succeeded in curbing the incidence of land encroachment and multiple land sales. Consequently, real estate developers now market gated housing estates as a haven for security (Ehwi et al., 2018) – but therein lie problems of (in)equity of access and also of the distribution of wealth given that only the "top 1 per cent" in Ghanaian society can afford this posited "solution" to the problem of widespread insecurity of tenure.

## Equity

People can gain access to land in Ghana, among others, by approaching chiefs, the earth priests, the Lands Commission, families, or individuals, depending on the type of land they seek to acquire. Within the customary setup, access to land is gendered. Under customary land tenure, access to land is contingent on systems of inheritance and lineage. The patrilineal and matrilineal systems are the main types of lineage systems in Ghana.

Under the matrilineal system of inheritance, a father and his children do not belong to the same matrikin. That is, unlike the patrilineal system where children in a marriage inherit the estate of their father if he dies intestate, in the matrilineal system the man's estate goes to his extended family, if he dies intestate. Generally, the estate of the man is inherited, first, according to gender, and second according to seniority. As such, a man who dies without making a will is succeeded by his eldest brother or, in the absence of any surviving brother, the man's eldest nephew. Under customary rules, a man has to provide for the upkeep of his wife and children who, in return, should work for him. However, by working for him, they are not entitled to any share of the property they helped him acquire. All such property goes to the man's nephew or any other more senior male if the man dies intestate. In a matrilineal system, the man's wife obtains no inheritance if he dies intestate. A woman's property goes to her children regardless of the system of inheritance, if she dies intestate (see Ferrara, 2007, for detailed discussion).

Post-2003 land reform tries to correct these biases against women. The Intestate Succession Law, 1985, PNDCL 111 attempts to ensure rights for widows and children in matrilineal and patrilineal systems, who otherwise might not inherit any property had the estate of a man been distributed according to customary law. However, several studies (e.g., Kasanga & Kotey, 2001, p. 13) show that it is the customary system that remains the guide of inheritance *as well as* general access to land. In the Dangme East District of the Greater Accra region, for example, women can only acquire property if they team up with men (Women in Law and Development in Africa [WiLDAF], 2011).

Also, the law deals with inheritance of a spouse, but in Ghana the majority of marriages are polygamous (WiLDAF, 2006, p. 2). In turn, there are many other "spouses" who are not catered for in the law. More seriously, the law is about inheritance, not the rights of spouses during the dissolution of their marriage for reasons other than death. Compensation for wives during a divorce is guaranteed in the superior courts of Ghana only if the wife can prove that she contributed substantial amounts of money to the acquisition of the property, as stipulated in the Matrimonial Causes Act (WiLDAF, 2006).

In spite of this complex picture, the orthodox reading of equitable access to land by women is through ensuring "increased land titles registered by women" (World Bank, 2003b, p. 3). Between 1989 and 2002, sole women constituted only 25 per cent of people who registered title in Accra (the capital city of Ghana), and only 23 per cent of those who registered deeds (Dawuona-Hammond & Minkah-Premo, 2005). From 2008 to 2011, however, 1,683 women registered deeds, with only 359 as "joint owners." Further, 810 titles were registered by women, with only 295 as "joint owners" (Larbi, 2011). While this turn is a major improvement over the previous situation, it does not address how the experience compares with the situation of men. It is telling that most of the women registered *deeds*, not *titles*. Under the *Torrens System* operated in Ghana, it is titles, not deeds, that confer state protection. Registered land is conclusive evidence of ownership; a registered deed is not (Agbosu, 1990, pp. 122–124). In turn, women continue to have an inferior position under the law.

Gender inequality is manifested in the lack of access to and control of land by women (Duncan & Brants, 2004). An estimated 52 per cent of women in agriculture do not have clearly defined rights over the land they cultivate (Eagle Group, 2007), suggesting that control of land is a problem too (see Duncan, 2010). Not surprisingly, in a national survey of 556 people who have experienced the land title registration in Ghana, all the women interviewed rated the impact of title registration as low. According to the consultant (2009, p. xx) who carried out the survey, "the . . . members of women's groups did not recognize any impact across the board, [they] only recognized a 'low' level of impact in the efficiency of the service delivery."

This evidence shows that the challenges of registration are not merely because of limited coverage, lack of institutional capacity to register more land, or logistical limitations, as is often argued (e.g., Mireku et al., 2016; Phanwin and Lambrecht, 2019). No doubt such administrative problems constitute major hoops. Indeed, as R. J. Ehwi and L. A. Asante (2016) have shown, administrative improvements in the Accra Lands Commission reduced the number of months required to register land from thirty-six to three. Yet, the real question to advocates is not efficiency gain in the process of registration but rather how the few people who have registered their land have experienced the posited benefits of security and equity.

On this fundamental issue, the evidence shows the *inherent* ineffectiveness of land reform as a tool for guaranteeing security of tenure. If S. K. B. Asante (1975) is right that what is seen as chaos in Ghana's land economy is, in fact, a struggle between the original trusteeship idea of property and the private property concept that underpins most of the development paradigms in modern Ghana, then it is even more doubtful that land reforms as conceived, designed, and implemented in Ghana can address the deep-seated structures of wealth and income inequalities. As Kimberle Crenshaw (1989, 1991) contends, the emancipation of black women requires intersectional redesign of institutions, but such intersectionality must simultaneously address other political economic forces and prcesses that militate against Africans – not only in the US, or Ghana, but elsewhere in black societies such as South Africa.

## SOUTH AFRICA

Land tenure in the apartheid days was shaped by segregationist policies, which concentrated land in the hands of white people. The 1913 Land Act No.27 and the 1936 Trust and Land Act No. 18 were the main laws that sowed the seeds of discrimination. These Acts effectively reserved 87 per cent of land for whites, coloreds, and Indians, but mostly for whites. Black South Africans, who constituted about 75 per cent of the population, were crowded on the remaining 13 per cent of land. Segregation existed even within this 13 per cent (Fourie, 2000). Blacks who spoke different languages had to live in specific places. These rules were not the only ones that institutionalized land segregation.

The South African Development Trust imposed further restrictive conditions, including a request for blacks to seek permits before they occupied the land. All blacks who owned freehold titles outside the designated 13 per cent were dispossessed of their land. Over 17,000 separate pieces of legislation and instruments were passed to consolidate these policies (Fourie, 2000). Within the 13 per cent of land occupied by blacks, compliant traditional chiefs remained active, generally being used by the apartheid state or the colonial forces to perpetuate unequal land ownership within the customary land system while the authority of "disagreeable" chiefs was undermined by the apartheid state. Where chiefs did not exist, compliant chiefs were created (Ntsebeza, 2005). So, a colonial and colonizing land economy was deliberately produced to transfer rents from the black to the white populations.

The end of apartheid in 1994 also gave birth to a new property economics of how to bring about convergence of wealth and incomes between black South Africans and the white, wealthier South Africans. Surprisingly, this property economics is quite simple. As stated by Ben Cousins (2017), the solution is for the state to "extend the system of title deeds to all South Africans." The basis for this claim is that the inequality of black South Africans arises from living in "communal areas" under backward, unelected chiefs. Indeed, in these communal areas, certain cultures are prevalent: cultures of collectivity which, even if not ingrained, are sustained by property cultures that increase transaction costs (see Chapter 2 for the theoretical case of individualism). So, there is no better way to address the problem than to erase this backward black system and replace it with the cultures of the white South Africans.

This view is quite prominent in South Africa today. Indeed, several attempts have been made, post-apartheid, to remedy the inequities in land management (Cousins, 2017). A land reform program was adopted in 1994 and consolidated in the 1996 Constitution of South Africa. Its primary concern was the correction of "apartheid inequalities" by stressing values of redistribution and restitution. However, since 2000, the values were changed for more market-driven aspirations because the former were deemed not to be conducive for efficient land management. The latter, narrow, market-heavy and so-called efficient approach protects large commercial farm owners (Cross & Hornby, 2002; Sihlongonyane, 2005). Some traces of redistribution are contained in the current system, too, but they are underpinned by the "willing buyer; willing seller" model which dictates that redistribution takes the form of minimal state support of poor people in the form of giving subsidies to purchase land rather than direct state acquisition of large tracts of lands concentrated in few hands.

So, the state now supports profit-making private groups. As such, large numbers of poor people have to pool their resources together to obtain land. This approach is a way by which the state has tendered to support emerging black commercial farmers, rather than the rural poor (Hall, 2004). Furthermore, farm workers commonly do not have secure land rights. Legislations such as the Land Reform (Labour Tenants) Act of 1995 and the Extension of Security of Tenure Act of 1997 have sought to improve the rights of farm workers (Cross & Hornby, 2002; Claasen and Lemke, 2019). However, powerful farm owners have, in practice, denied farm workers these rights, especially the right against the arbitrary eviction of tenants (Cross & Hornby, 2002). Nkuzi Development Association and Sikhula Sonke Union (cited in Makanga, 2009) have estimated that over 1 million black workers have been evicted from farms since 1994.

In protest, Sikhula Sonke, a woman-led farm worker union, and the Women on Farms Project, a farm-worker support organization, demanded, "[t]hey should give the farms to workers and bring in the government so that the farm workers can be shareholders and make them BEE [Black Economic Empowerment Program] farms, prioritize land redistribution for farm workers, especially women farm workers and build the capacity of farm workers, and enable them to own and manage their own farms"(Makanga, 2009, n.p.). In addition to gendered discrimination, to this day, "farm workers employed on commercial farms are among the poorest and most food insecure population groups in South Africa" (Claasen and Lemke, 2019, p. 417) So, over two decades after abolishing apartheid insecure tenure, the reforms are yet to correct the insecurities and inequities they were designed to address. Worse still, several land claims from the apartheid days have not been settled. The 2000 South African Survey revealed that only 41 per cent of all claims lodged with the Commission on the Restitution of Land Rights have been settled (Sihlongonyane, 2005).

It may be argued that the implementation of a program for redress is, itself, important recognition of the existing problems. Indeed, since a majority of the landless people in South Africa were black women, ensuring secure women's rights was a central aim of the land reform and many policies were adopted to achieve that aim (Cross & Hornby, 2002; Cousins, 2016, 2017). Also, there have been several attempts to remove gender-based inequities. Both the Green (1996) and White (1997) Papers of the Department of Land Affairs stress gender issues and warn against discrimination against women with respect to land rights (Jacobs, 1998). In addition, the state has passed the Communal Land Rights Act (2004), which contains explicit provisions about women empowerment and prohibits land rights discrimination against women on the basis of their gender (Cousins, 2007, 2016, 2017).

However, in practice, the reforms have not changed the power structures embedded in custom that impinge negatively on women. There seems to be state support for the customary system and chiefs. The Traditional Leadership and Governance Framework and Communal Land Rights Acts entrench the traditional system. In addition, the role of other institutions, such as land-owning farmers, which co-existed with the chieftaincy system remains largely intact (Ntsebeza, 2005). The reform has been concerned with "macro-national" issues whereas the micro-local and household power structures, which curtail women's land rights, have remained unresolved in practice (Cross & Hornby, 2002; Cousins, 2016, 2017). The land sector agencies, such as the Department of Land Affairs, are commonly overwhelmed by the severity of the problem of gender inequality. Also, some officials do not know how to ensure that women are not marginalized in the reform process. Another obstacle to the gender issue is the rather limited number of civil society organizations that specialize in promoting women's rights to land (Jacobs, 1998; Walker, 1998; Cousins, 2007). These impediments have limited real progress in promoting a gender-sensitive land reform program.

The evidence shows that the land reforms in South Africa have not been as effective as promised. The promised convergence of wealth is yet to take place. Indeed, inter-group inequalities have worsened in a process in which land title registration has become an instrument for reproducing rather than curbing inequalities (Cousins, 2017; Beinart, 2018). Land tenure in South Africa remains insecure and land-based inequality is prevalent. Those who own land have no "peace," as there are recurrent struggles to occupy or invade land (Sihlongonyane, 2005). Over 80 per cent of land is concentrated in the hands of minority white farmers (Toulmin, 2008, p. 13) and the situation of most women, with respect to access to and control of land, has not significantly improved (Cross & Hornby, 2002). As with Ghana, the South African experience shows that, in practice, both individual and collective land tenure systems oversimplify claims of gender-sensitive social and economic development. Indeed, collective and individual theories have a uni-polar understanding of secure tenure as "quiet enjoyment," whereas the South African example shows a more complex picture that goes beyond markets and law. Secure tenure could also be about the redistribution of land. Further, merely changing laws to make women's communal land rights to individual land rights does not substantially improve land-based gender inequalities.

The recent work of Ben Cousins and his team (2017) arrives at similar conclusions (see also Beinart, 2018). The poor, typically black workers in informal economies, are overrepresented in the 60 per cent of the South African population whose land is unrecognized and uncertain. Not only is registration inappropriate for these people, registration is also incapable of delivering its promises of bringing about convergence in inter-group wealth and income. Indeed, registration by decollectivising land and stripping it of its social networks often provides a path for the poor to transfer their wealth to the wealthy and powerful. In this sense, the problems of state incapacity to handle the sheer number of applications to register land if they were to be made and the prohibitive cost of such registration are less serious problems. What is more fundamental is the inability of registration to account for the complexity of property rights for the poor whose economic strategies are not, and cannot, be captured by a system of land reform that is based on entirely different sets of assumptions.

Whether alternatives to this system recognize these fundamental tensions is debatable. Would tolerating a dual track system in which the tenures of the poor exist side-by-side with those of the rich be an effective alternative? What about supporting locally developed alternatives to registration, making the poor leaders in the process of titling, or substantially supporting "social/untitled tenures" (Hornby et al., 2017; Beinart, 2018)? These suggestions are interesting, but they potentially downplay the fundamental problems of land: the power imbalance recurrently entrenched because socially created rents, privately captured by the rich, are used to maintain, indeed to reproduce, superficial discourses and practices of "security of tenure" in ways that obfuscate the land question. The place of land in producing and reproducing political economic stratification in society, then, is poorly appreciated by the prevailing land reforms in South Africa.

The recent *Mary Rahube* issue or the *Mary Rahube and Others* case (no. 101250/2015) issue, resolved at the High Court of the Republic of South Africa (Gauteng Division), exemplifies the superficiality of land titling as land reform.[1] As the Court upheld, title registration is so superficial that it neglects the fact that, under apartheid, black women could not hold property and that the current title procedures simply allow pseudo "property owners" to convert "their land" to private property without systematic investigation into the history of how apartheid land laws bolstered the power of the wealthy, of men, and of stronger races and classes to appropriate land from the weak. In turn, title registration has become a way to hide the structural inequalities that remain at the heart of wealth and income stratification in South Africa today. The Court's decision – to strike down section 2(1) of the Upgrading of Land Tenure Rights Act 112 of 1991 (ULTRA) as constitutionally invalid because it provides, through land title registration, a carte blanc path to legitimize androcentric and white supremacist policies – casts significant doubts about using land titling as a tool for removing or even reducing wealth inequalities between groups.

Even more compelling is the result of the 2018 land audit conducted by the Department of Rural Development and Land Reform. The survey shows

Individuals, companies and trusts own 90 per cent of land in SA, and the state 10 per cent. Of this 90%, individuals own 39%, trusts 31%, companies 25% and community-based organisations 4%, with co-ownership at 1%. In terms of farms and agricultural holdings, 97% of the total agricultural holdings are owned by 7% of landowners. Agricultural land ownership by race: 72% of farms and agricultural holdings are owned by whites, 15% by colored citizens, 5% by Indians, and 4% by Africans" (cited in Ramaphosa, 2018, n.p.)

So, as this case shows, land titling is, if anything, rather, a tool for producing and reproducing intergroup inequality.

## UGANDA

Uganda does not have the same racialized wealth inequalities that characterize South African society. Mostly agrarian, and mostly rural, the more relevant case for titling-based land reform is that it would protect small-scale farmers from predatory activities of the state and guarantee their participation in the market economy (Boone, 2018). Together, title registration would improve their economic well-being and bring greater convergence in wealth and incomes between farmers and wealthy classes in Uganda.

---

[1] The press release and the full judgment can be seen here: www.lhr.org.za/news/2017/press-statement-%E2%80%93-mary-rahube-hedsrine-rahube-others-case-no-1012502015 (accessed 31 July 2018).

How has this system of land reform evolved? A brief history of land tenure in Uganda is needed to understand its present forms and appreciate the nature and effects of recent reforms. According to Mugambwa (2007), this history could be examined along five different time lines. Prior to colonization, land was customarily owned. During British colonial rule, there was a systematic erosion of this form of tenure through the institution of pilot projects on individual land tenure systems because the British colonialists believed that communal land ownership impeded individual enterprise and economic development. After independence, however, such projects were halted. There was a return to "traditional" land tenure with the enactment of the Public Land Act that gave greater recognition to customary law. The reasons for the return were legion. Among them, state officials felt that customary land tenure was more African. Also, the pilot project on individual land tenure was not driving economic development as the British had claimed. Further, independent Uganda professed to be socialist and individual ownership was felt to be an anathema to socialism. In any case, customary land ownership did not mean that individuals could not own land. So, overall, customary land tenure was preferable (Mugambwa, 2007). The fourth phase of the story is the entry of dictator Idi Amin who abolished all forms of communal ownership and vested land in the state. All customary holders had to apply to the state for leases. Amin's policies caused widespread panic and opposition that inhibited the implementation of the full program. The fifth stage relates to when the country became more stable from the mid-1980s. Land reforms were once again put on the government agenda – individual or communal land tenure? The 1995 Constitution recognized both. In addition, leaseholds and *mailo* (quasi freeholds) were recognized. Apart from urban areas and the Kingdom of Buganda, most land is held under customary law (Mugambwa, 2007).

Over 75 per cent of all land in Uganda is customarily owned and is not covered by formal documentation (Busingye, 2002). This system is recognized by the Constitution of Uganda. However, the Uganda Constitutional Commission has recommended that customary ownership should be phased out, not radically, but by "encouragement" because it is anathema to economic development and agricultural modernization. So, the Land Act of 1998 provides room for customary land to be converted to statutory or freehold land but not vice versa (Mugambwa, 2007). One survey of 970 households with over 2000 parcels of land without title showed that over 95 per cent of those who qualified for title documentation want to have regular title (Deininger et al., 2006).

It does not seem that there is a problem of insecure tenure in Uganda as pertains in Ghana where land rights are often the subject of litigation. The overwhelming desire to obtain physical proof of rights does not seem to be a result of a fear of dispossession. Rather, it is the result of the glamorization of reforms, particularly the idea that title certificates would enable holders to obtain credit from banks and increase the economic value of their land through the ease of transferability (see Deininger et al., 2006). It is hard to make any definitive statements about the potency of land reforms in Uganda because of its limited scale. Nonetheless, there is some evidenc (Hunt, 2004) to be pessimistic about the benefits of the reforms. Banks in Uganda, as elsewhere, consider other factors beyond just title before advancing credit. Indeed, in some cases, title may not be needed at all for credit to be given.

Also, under customary land tenure, the predominant tenurial system in Uganda, there is discrimination against women. The constitution is explicit that customary rules apply only when they do not discriminate against any persons. However, in the traditional setup, women are seen as "property" rather than "persons." Since property cannot own property, women tend to be discriminated against in land ownership. This patriarchal system of land administration makes it hard for women's interests in land to be articulated or enforced, although specific provisions such as section 40 of the Land Act of 1998 seek to protect them (Busingye, 2002; Hunt, 2004). The solution, as seen by advocates of the reform, is to give individuals title certificates to land that can be enforced in the law courts.

However, this view has been questioned (see Adoko and Levine, 2009) because the traditional system that pertains in most ethnic groups actually gives more rights to women than the state freehold system. The biases against women within the traditional system arise from a misinterpretation of custom rather than any inherent issues with traditional practices, suggesting that individual and formal rights cannot resolve questions of insecure tenure because the land sector institutions responsible for formalization do not fully understand the customary system (Adoko and Levine, 2009). Formalisation creates its own problems. Indeed, in some cases, lower court judgments are not grounded in evidence. Together with the refusal of the state to enforce some court decisions, a problem that has left many people disillusioned in the some court system, it could be argued that reform could more usefully address these broader issues directly, rather than focus on formalization and individualization, with its many and varied limitations (Adoko & Levine, 2009), including rising fraud and insecurities in Uganda (Wiegratz, 2016).

The evidence from Uganda shows that people embrace reforms for reasons other than bringing about secure tenure. Thus, although not apparently facing problems of insecure tenure, the prospect of using land as a means to obtain credit is driving the process. This trend signals that the individualization of tenure may create a false sense of hope that credit is a panacea for poverty reduction only to open the floodgates of socio-cultural change characterized by fraud (Wigratz, 2016) that worsens social stratification in Uganda.

## EGYPT

The land tenure system in Egypt has undergone three phases of change. Before 1952, a chieftain land tenure system prevailed in Egypt. However, this form of tenure was different from the kind of customary land tenure in Ghana, South Africa, and Uganda because kings controlled the Egyptian state, beginning with the Ottoman Empire. Peasants got from five to eight fedan or acres of land which they controlled and used but whose ownership rested with the state.

This tenurial arrangement was enshrined in the first land law, Ottoman Land Law of 1858. Five different types of land tenure systems existed then but the state had a strong "presence" in the management of all types of land. From 1871 to 1918, a new system called Taboo was effected to enable occupants and workers of state land to buy and own, if they so chose. A number of laws were enacted to modify the land situation, from time to time, but in all cases the monarchy had strong control (El Araby, 2003). This land tenure system benefitted a few landed elite. Only 0.1 per cent of all land owners owned 20 per cent of cultivated land; 199 out of 2,000 large land owners owned 7.3 per cent of land, a significant number of whom received the land from kings for helping in military expeditions. On the other hand, 3 million peasants or fellahin owned only less than 1 acre (fedan) of land. Though the peasants constituted 75 per cent of land owners, they owned only 13 per cent, the rest was owned by absentee landlords (Bush, 2004, p. 11).

In 1952, there was a social revolution to correct general inequalities in society. It tried to correct the three bases of social stratification: wealth (based on land and private industry), family name (the ability to trace one's name to a "great family"), and power (based on proximity to the Khedival authority) (Nelson, 1968, p. 62). The state redistributed land by setting ceilings on how much land could be owned and leased to individuals. Landholdings that were in excess of the ceilings were redistributed to peasants. An estimated 10 per cent of the cultivated area of Egypt was redistributed. The landholdings of a majority of the middle class, whose landholdings ranged from 15 to 20 fedans, were not redistributed. Thus, the program was targeted at the largest "monopolists" (Nelson, 1968, p. 62; for details of the land redistribution, see Margold, 1957). In spite of the limited scope of the land redistribution, the biggest estates of 200 fedans disappeared while the peasants who occupied the lowest ebb of the strata experienced a 74 per cent rise in the size of their parcels of land. Because of this land reform and other social reforms, poverty fell from the 1950 level of 56.1 per cent to 23.8 per cent in 1965 (Bush, 2004, p. 11).

From 1970 to date, however, the values of the social revolution have been shelved. Market liberalization started in 1970 and accelerated in the 1990s when structural adjustment policies were implemented. Currently, the attempts to introduce markets in land and minimize state intervention have become prominent. Under the aegis of USAID, formal titling is being carried out. In addition to the general pro-individualism case discussed in Chapter 2, formalization and titling, its advocates claim, would promote productivity of agriculture and economic growth. With less government control, individuals could buy parcels of land beyond the ceilings that were imposed during the social revolution period. In turn, some individuals accumulated significantly more land than others (Bush, 2004). Even with these changes, relative to the other cases considered in this chapter, Egypt has perhaps the strongest state intervention in the land sector. Indeed urban land is strictly controlled by the central government, governorates, and local government. Strict rules exist on how to sell land and what to do with land. Local governments, the governorates, and the national government all are suppliers of land.

However, red tape and "paper bureaucracy" continue to make access to land and equity a major problem in urban areas and the limited political participation and opaque administration enable the market to corrupt the officials, leading to a land tenure system that is built on patron-client relationships (El Araby, 2003). Historically, this statist power as used in land administration has benefited the urban elite who use their influence to get the undemocratic state to lease land or sell it cheaply to them (Aliston, 1997). It seems that state dictatorship and economic liberalization in the land sector led to several cases of land alienation, especially from the poor, whose economic position seems to have declined after liberalization (Payne et al., 2009). Yet, liberalization did not abate. Indeed, enacting Law 96, which legitimizes the exchange of land (Bush, 2004), signalled an unquestioned faith in markets. This experience shows how an authoritarian state could promote individualization in property rights, which, in turn, leads to opportunities for patronage and absentee ownership. Urban residents in Egypts have long owned land in rural areas, as Jane Rolandson's (1996) classic study of land ownership in Oxyrhynchus city between 30 BC and 3rd AD shows. However, many of such landowners were also farmers and tenants doubling as landowners. Oxyrhynchus city residents were usually relatives of the residents in the neighbouring rural areas who doubled as their tenants. Absentee ownership was rare as was speculation. Consequently, stratification was not as widespread as it is in modern urban Egypt, characterised by speculation and absentee ownership.

More recent post "Arab" – or more specifically, North African – Spring research (Dixon, 2014; Furniss, 2016; Shawkat, 2016; Bayat, 2017) reveals the moral limits of land markets: market-based patronage, and its resulting insecurities, creating an inherently corrupted capitalist land market in which not only the state but also the wealthy and the powerful appropriate prime lands and evict the "99 per cent." The Egyptian uprising of 2011 was a popular rejection of these policies and of these specific capitalist features of Egyptian political economy (Amin, 2011), but it is not clear that, even after the revolution, the society has transformed. If at all, as Amin (2011) suggests, the revolutionary ideals have quickly been mainstreamed. The result is a growing food crisis in Egypt, which the wealthy and their capitalist private firms (e.g., Citadel Capital) supported by the state are seeking to solve by appropriating even more land from a global land market in Africa.

## A GLOBAL LAND MARKET

Since 2007–2008, large tracts of African land have been leased to foreign and local interests for periods sometimes as long as 99 years in a global land market. Indeed, when GRAIN, the global NGO, first reported this surge in large-scale land acquisition in 2008 (Alden Wily, 2012, 2013; Borras & Franco, 2012), the initial estimates given were 2.5 million ha of land. Subsequently, the World Bank updated the figure to 56 million ha around 2010, increasing substantially to. around 71 million ha two years later (International Land Coalition, 2012).

These figures are likely to have been conservative and of indicative value only because a substantial number of land acquisitions around the time were unreported, or were shrouded in secrecy. Furthermore, some of the countries offering parcels of land did no scientific mapping from which categorical claims could be made. In the case of South Sudan, for example, one acquisition was said to be for 600,000 acres in Lainya, but cross-checking shows that the county of Lainya is itself only 340,000 ha in extent (Pearce, 2012, p. 45).

While some of the leased land has since been put to the development of recreation complexes and others to the development of nature reserves, most land-use change has been of four kinds: from food cultivation for local consumption to food cultivation for export; from food to biofuel production; from non-food to food cultivation; and from non-food to biofuel production (Borras & Franco, 2012). According to the International Land Coalition (2012, p. 4), 78 per cent of land leases are used for agricultural production, with biofuel production taking about 75 per cent of the agricultural category. The rest are for mineral extraction, forest conservation, and tourism.

In addition to "physical land," water bodies are also being traded. In Senegal, a 400,000-acre transaction with Saudi Arabia is close to River Senegal, which will be the source of irrigation (Pearce, 2012, p. 33). In South Sudan, the new government seems to be negotiating to send water to Egypt by preparing to allow Egypt to construct a canal to channel water from the Nile around the giant Sudd Swamp, which is the second largest swamp in the world and the site of great wildlife diversity and pasture. The canal will enable the Nile to deliver more water to Egypt, much of which currently evaporates from the swamp during its year-long journey (Pearce, 2012, p. 49). Under international law, host countries must generally undertake to provide water to investors as without water the investors cannot fully benefit from their investment. In turn, governments may be sued if, say, in the process of supplying water to their citizens, they are unable to satisfy international private interests (Pearce, 2012, p. 102–103).

The identity and methods of the traders vary greatly. Countries, state corporations, private interests, missionaries, NGOs, and universities are all involved. International interests dominate, although there are local actors involved in land deals, too. Unlike pre-2007/8 land leases, post 2008 acquisitions have been carried out from within and outside the West, including from countries such as South Korea, Saudi Arabia, and India that have been prominent in land purchases. "Traditional" land traders such as the UK have remained active, too.

Three main methods have been used to obtain land leases; namely, negotiations with central government without consulting local government and local chiefs; with local chiefs without consulting central and local government and local communities; and with central and local government and local elites, including chiefs, but without consulting other elders in the communities. The triggers or factors influencing success and failure of negotiations are mainly religious affinity, whether indigenous title is recognized, national governments' business policies, and level of development (Schoneveld et al., 2011; Pearce, 2012; Maconachie & Fortin, 2013). Also, rich governments improve their chances of seeking land deals by investing in the dilapidated infrastructure of poorer countries in return for land. That is evidently what for a while was going to happen in Kenya where the government of Qatar was to build a billion-dollar port facility in exchange for 100,000 acres of irrigated land on Lamu Island (Pearce, 2012, p. 36).

The role of the global financial institutions, such as the World Bank, is self-serving. Not only does it carry out studies to identify vacant land such as *Rising Global Interest in Farmland: Can It Yield Sustainable and Equitable Benefits?* (World Bank, 2010), at least the International Financial Corporation of the World Bank is itself a trader in the land market (Liberti, 2013, p. 101). Also, they have favored the registration of titles to make it easier to trade in land. On the part of investors, the financial powerhouses have offered huge loans, others have directly invested, and many more have offered guarantee and investment advice. Glossy magazines have been produced and an aggressive campaigns waged. Both seek to encourage the sale and purchase of African land.

## (IN)EQUALITY?

In some cases, the trade in this new global land market has created employment, increased food production, introduced modern equipment in agricultural processes, and increased the circulation of foreign currency in local and national economies. But, to a greater extent, they have displaced large households and populations, created inequality and food insecurity, and dispossessed large sections of the indigenous population of their land (Mwakaje, 2012). However, these social costs, to use KW Kapp's (1950/1971) descriptor, are not equally borne by different groups.

Analysis of outcomes can be done in many ways. One method is to compare the aims and claims of the projects. Another approach is to assess what opportunities had to be given up in order to obtain such outcomes or land use change.

Using these methods to analyze the existing evidence, examples abound of projects that have given less than the claimed benefits. For instance, jatropha companies in the Pru district in Ghana provide 120 low-income jobs (US$50/ month) for 780 ha of land leased out. While employees like their jobs for the security of income flow, they see that it is better as a complement rather than as a substitute (Schoneveld et al., 2011). In Ethiopia, the Daudi Star Agri has employed only about 12 per cent of the number it promised to do. Where some benefits have accrued, in opportunity cost terms, these have been fewer benefits accruing to the people who have lost their land. In Togo, for a lease of 2,700 ha of land for 99 years, Global Greenleaf PLC (Greenleaf Togo) has created only 600 jobs (Stadia Trustees, 2011, p. 2), and "[a]t the plantation site villages . . . their inhabitants are being helped to relocate to the edges of the plantation or to areas set aside for the locals" (Stadia Trustees, 2011, p. 4). Here, even where jobs have been created, as in Ghana, the people have lost control of their labor. That is, they have shifted from being self-employed to being employees.

Further, there is a creeping tendency to squeeze the control of seeds out of the hands of local farmers and hence make them further dependent on agro business capital. According to Greenleaf Global PLC, in Ghana, early maturing breeds of maize (maturing in 110 days) produced by scientists were going to be used by Greenleaf Global, and for the jatropha plantation in Togo, jatropha seeds were sent from Ghana (Greenleaf Global PLC, 2011). The role of Togolese farmers as seedlings cultivators was thus done away with. While the use of genetically modified seeds and imported varieties may be economically efficient, the gradual disempowerment of farmers by making their skills redundant raises important political-economic concerns.

Evidence also abounds of poor labor conditions on the new farms arising from land-use change and dwindling job prospects. In the case of Ghana, for instance, people in the Pru district have got jobs but have failed to obtain leave to enable them to do community work. In Kenya, the agro-missionary entity, Dominion, has failed to give proper medical treatment to workers injured while working (Pearce, 2012). The jobs created on the new farms, especially those for the locals with little education, have a tendency to dwindle in number with time when the jobs for which they are qualified are no longer available, as is openly admitted by agribusinesses in Ghana (Schoneveld et al., 2011).

There are already signs that engineers, scientists, and other high-profile agri-professionals are preferable to common laborers. Most agribusinesses tout the impressive array of professionals on their teams, and local expertise is hardly valued or it is valued up to the point that it no longer yields sufficient business (Pearce, 2012). Related to this is the lack of expertise in host regions and the imported labor from Egypt, especially, but also elsewhere. In one case, a Dubai-based finance group is paying $100 million for one farmer from the USA to develop similar American-type farming in Tanzania (Pearce, 2012, p. 36).

The claims that land-use change brings modernization and food security are equally problematic. Most produce is sent out of the host countries unprocessed. In the few cases of mechanization, this has come at a cost to the environment as large amounts of natural reserves are destroyed, as found by Schoneveld, German, and Nutakor (2011) in Ghana. Also, most food grown locally is exported. For instance, Greenleaf Global PLC (2011) planned exporting 70 per cent of the maize it produced locally.

It is not that investment in land has created no benefits; rather that these have been unevenly distributed and obtained at high social costs (Kapp, 1950/1971). Chiefs in countries where customary law is recognized often directly benefit from land acquisitions. In Ghana, chiefs typically compare the benefits from land deals with how much donation they get from settler farmers. Government officials too benefit, and in some cases government officials are used as consultants by agribusinesses (Schoneveld et al., 2011; Tieleman and Uitemark, 2019). In the Bombali and Tonkolili districts of Sierra Leone, the Swiss firm Bovid Agroenergy has invested in a fifty-year lease of a large lot of 57,000 ha and changed its use from food production to an export-oriented biofuel project. In so doing, it has expedited de-agrarianization forces that have put most small-scale farmers out of work and spat them into agribusiness apparatus making them wage labor. While land trade for biofuel production has given jobs to some individuals, most are only casual labor whose wages are much lower than they were made to believe and many more have been rendered jobless (Maconachie & Fortin, 2013).

Companies and investors earn much more profit, which explains their growing interest in the current model. According to Agri Capital Ltd. (2012), a London-based firm investing in Sierra Leone, there was a 16.2 per cent return on investment in its first year of harvest in January 2011, and a promised 7 per cent increase in land value. Most companies pay little or no taxes. Most of these companies get tax waivers, so governments hardly benefit from tax revenues. Indeed, it seems the government of Ghana exempted Greenleaf PLC from corporate taxes for ten years (Greenleaf Global PLC, 2011). Also, because most of the investors are from countries outside the land-trade area, most of the returns are repatriated to foreign lands. Indeed, in most of the land deals, there are no restrictions on capital flight. In turn, the countries from which the investors originate benefit, while the host countries remain primary producers.

Investors do not benefit equally, of course. Some investors are swindled and obtain little or no reward for the risks they take. An example is the case of Greenleaf Global PLC, which was operating in Ghana and Togo. Investors sunk £8.2 million into land deals with the promise that they would receive a return of about 20 per cent within twelve months when, in fact, no careful prior analysis had been made. Also, the company claimed it had had a bountiful harvest in 2010 and paid huge returns to investors when, in fact, no such thing had ever happened. In the end, the company was rendered insolvent (Insolvency Service, 2012).

The distribution of losses is also uneven. Settler farmers have missed out more than native farmers. For instance, in Ghana, settler farmers are the first targets to lose land. Also, ethnic minorities are left worse off. In Ethiopia, people from the lowlands, historically opposed to the government, lose more of their land than those on the highlands (Makki, 2012). Furthermore, the distribution of losses is gendered. Women in Ghana experience the losses differently to men because land often regarded by men as fallow is used by women to grow some vegetables, so when these fallow lands are traded, women lose out. Given that women do most of the water-fetching, outsiders trading water lengthens the journey time for them. Similarly, the journey time for looking for firewood seems to have lengthened. While private agribusinesses claim that such lengthening was already happening after years of destroying their own environment (Schoneveld et al., 2011; Wisborg, 2012), evidence from Tanzania disputes such claims (Mwakaje, 2012).

Meanwhile, this global land market is widening income and social inequality. By the very nature of the distribution of benefits and losses, people who have are getting more, while the rest are struggling. According to Pearce (2012, p. 78), there is now an "enclave economy" in which land traders and their cronies live in great prosperity, while the others struggle to make ends meet. Social inequality has been linked to poor health, poor food security, crime, grime, and unhappiness. Poverty eventually worsens when these worsen. Indeed, the widespread displacements in these processes illustrate the growing inequality.

Similar concerns apply in Ethiopia (Wayessa & Nygren, 2016; Nygren & Wayessa, 2018), where, until recently (see Wayessa, 2018), the government was pursuing a villagization project in which some 180,000 people would be resettled in areas where, according to the government, social amenities were available. Yet even people with such amenities were relocated, an experience which exposes the overt mission of the project. Not surprisingly, the place of the resettled people is being taken by agro-industries. For the resettled locals, their new locations have worse livelihood conditions than their original homes (Pearce, 2012, p. 11). Thus, starting from a perspective of coming out to "help" the poor of the world get energy or food, this global land market seems to be the cause rather than the cure for this canker.

These empirical examples establish what Brett Christophers (2018) has called 'the new enclosure'. Albeit at a much global level, outcomes of this new enclosure dispute both populist and ideological representations of neoliberal land transactions. It is misleading to contend that land markets have brought no benefits to local populations, but also misleading is the claim that the processes and phenomena of land markets are win-win. What the examples reveal is a clear case of "accumulation by dispossession"

(Harvey, 2003), but also what can be called "accumulation by dislocation." Exploitation and expropriation are commonplace and the so-called benefits are concentrated rather than spread. Actors in a stronger class position have appropriated greater gains The majority of people have had to live with secondary and transitional land rights, and insecurity. Even within the marginalized classes, there is much social stratification along income and wealth lines, as global capital takes advantage of noncapitalist or partially capitalist systems transformed by colonial and neocolonial forces. These differential social costs at the local, national, regional, and global levels reveal land markets as a particular type of market that creates, rather than resolves, inequality.

## LESSONS AND CONCLUSION

What lessons can be learned from the theory, practice, and outcomes of land tenure reforms in Africa? The chapter has discussed rural, urban, and peri-urban land interchangeably. Part of the reason for doing this is that, although there are some cases in Africa where urban land tenure differs from rural land tenure (Chimhowu & Woodhouse, 2006), land tenure systems in most parts of Africa, including the cases under study, do not differ radically according to settlement type. In Kampala, the capital city of Uganda, for example, the city's land tenure system is made up of a combination of customary tenure [*mailo*] (52 per cent), state land (38 per cent), and land owned by individuals and institutions (Giddings, 2009).

Another reason is that what is called "urban land" could be surprisingly hard to define. Is it to be defined according to location, density, or statute (Gordon et al., 2007)? Take South Africa. There, the customary system applies only in "communal areas" which usually are rural areas. However, within those rural areas, there are settlements that are densely populated (Cousins, 2007, 2017) and others that may be classified as urban in other African countries (Department of Economic and Social Affairs, 2009). Also, while it is known that the total land in South Africa is 1,220,813 km$^2$ and that 19.3 per cent of it is owned by the state, it is not clear exactly what share of the total land in South Africa is urban, rural, or peri-urban (Gordon et al., 2007). Given that about 57 per cent of the population in South Africa lives in urban areas (Gordon et al., 2007), it may well be said that customary practices pertain only among the estimated 18 million people (43 per cent of the population) who live in peri-urban and rural areas. In Ghana, it is not whether settlements are "urban" or "rural" that determines the rules of land tenure. Rather the rules of tenure are contingent on whether land is classified as "state," "customary," or "private individual" (see Woodman, 1996). So, while it is admitted that the cases are not altogether the same and, thus, discussing them together is likely to raise methodological problems, using a relational concept of space allows one to focus on the bigger picture, especially the lessons that the experiences of these countries teach us about collective and individual land tenure. Six of these lessons need particular emphasis.

First, as a problem, insecurity of tenure has different meanings. In Ghana, it connotes the multiple sale of land that leads to protracted litigation. However, in South Africa, it means the likelihood of eviction, inequitable land distribution between races, and lack of secure jobs for farm workers. Second, there is nothing inherently egalitarian about a "communal system" of ownership. It is usually biased against women and favors the rich and mighty. This is, on the evidence, the case in Ghana, Uganda, and South Africa. Nevertheless, individualization is no answer. Titles per se do not necessary bring about equality between genders because the inequality faced by women is embedded in social structures, embedded in law, and embedded in the economy.

Third, a statist regime where the machinery of partially democratic government is used to centrally control land administration is not necessarily efficient. It might be effective in controlling urban land use, as the Egyptian case shows, but the absence of channels of accountability makes that model vulnerable to patronage and clientelism. Centralization also tends to create red tape and administrative inertia.

Fourth, individual land ownership overstates its perceived advantages. The lack of credit is not the source of all deprivations; therefore, not all forms of deprivations can be remedied by creating access to credit. Similarly, financial institutions do not necessarily give applicants credit only because they possess title certificates.

Fifth, combining individual and so-called communal system creates a situation where one leads to the demise of the other. A system of reform that extols the virtues of individualized land tenure commonly leads to a demise of the "communal system." Glamorizing individual tenure system such that people without it feel the need to obtain it is likely to lead to a decline in interest in communal land tenure systems. As the Ugandan case study shows, the claim that individualized land tenure opens up credit opportunities may create a situation where people, who otherwise may not have a need for title certificates, crave title certificates, although, in practice, such certificates do not guarantee access to credit or secure tenure.

Sixth, beyond the rhetoric of using reform to improve the material conditions of the poor, reforms benefit people in authority and private capital: some traditional power groups, white settler groups, state officials, and private capital. Decollectivisation does not only reduce transaction costs, it also ensure much smoother transfer of rent from the poor to the rich. These six lessons have implications for the two main theoretical positions that underpin land reforms in most countries in Africa. The "de Soto therapy" is built on assumptions that are simplistic.

Credit does not automatically arise from formalization. More fundamentally, the individualized system wrongly perceives the traditional system as an open-range system with no rules, making it vulnerable to free rider-problems. This reading of customary land ownership is incorrect because there are tribal rules about how people in communities can use and dispose of land. That, however, does not mean that these rules are egalitarian (see also Cotula et al., 2009; Onoma, 2009). The social capital approach, with its assumptions about pristine African culture, misrepresents the day-to-day conflicts in communal land ownership. Chiefs frequently act in ways that enhance their material position and the rules of "social capital" are written to favor some and punish others. Conceptually, those who benefit from these networks, such as the chiefs and tribal leaders, could be said to be gaining from "social capital." Similarly, the patronage in the Egyptian system can be called "social capital," given that it makes it possible for individuals to benefit from noneconomic social networks. Furthermore, the so-called cultural networks are not historicized, so it is not known whether these cultural rules are the result of emic or etic accounts. Tribal leaders reify rules and discourses that put them in powerful positions in order to keep the status quo.

However, more careful analysis of the roots of these customs shows a different picture. In Ghana, for example, a rich historical analysis of the rules of communal land ownership by the historian Jeff Grischow (2008) shows that the historical roots of chieftaincy was one closely related to economic wealth and power. Therefore, from the beginning, people with more resources became chiefs and, in turn, created rules to further entrench their positions. This material basis of political power is often lost on social capitalists, prompting Ben Fine (2010), one of the concept's most outspoken critics, to observe that social capital as a concept is flawed, theoretically and empirically. It could mean anything from clientelism to advantages from familial or old school networks; and fails to account for context, history, power, class, and gender relations.

Both theoretical approaches discussed in this chapter have some strength. The individualized system could be beneficial in terms of its emphasis on establishing clear boundaries and rights to clearly identifiable people. However, contrary to popular perceptions, especially held by people outside the "community," "who owns what" is known in communities. Similarly, while "opaque land tenure system" is a problem, it is usually not the only or main basis for insecure tenure. It is often the biased rules of custom, the abuse of office by its trustees, and their lack of accountability to the people within the community – a dynamic which is a function of the specific history of colonial, neocolonial, and imperial land relations – that underpin the source of insecure and unequal land rights (see Amanor, 2005, 2010; Moyo & Yeros, 2005; Ubink, 2007, 2008).

So, it is not simply the erasure of these supposedly backward customs through the creation of a (global) land market that is a panacea. If anything, it is the reverse: the great transformation in land relations into a fictitious commodities that lead to the social creation, but private appropriation, of rent, as the work of Karl Polanyi and Henry George show respectively.

By analyzing land reform in this historical, empirical, and integrated way, this chapter has shown the grave limitations of mainstream development economics and of its theoretical and policy instruments. As conceived, designed, and implemented, land reform steeped in the Coasian theorem, itself a reflection of the Benthamite natural rights school of property economics, is not, and cannot, be an institution for inclusive African development. Indeed, as the chapter has shown, land reform is, rather, a tool for transferring African wealth to the rest of the world in ways that widen, rather than close, the many fissures of development and underdevelopment.

If the inequalities and social stratification in Africa do not arise from the continent's land tenure system, is human capital a better explanation? Many economists think so, but the nature of their claims and in what ways they are demonstrated in practice require more systematic analysis.

# 4

# Human Capital

## INTRODUCTION

The lack of adequate levels of human capital is promoted and held by development institutions such as the World Bank and many leading development economists to be the cause of Africa's backwardness. Building human capital, then, is posited as a sure path to convergence. Engraved on the World Bank head office in Washington DC is the question, "Why does human capital matter?" The answer, also boldly embossed on the building, is "[i]nvesting in people builds human capital, which strengthens inclusive growth and the competitiveness of nations" Similar answers are given by economists when asked the question, "why isn't the whole world developed?" Richard Easterlin (1981) famously pointed to inadequate human capital, especially in Africa, as the reason; and, in his classic 1961 paper, "Investment in human capital," economics Nobel Laureate Theodore Schultz noted that "[l]aborers ... become capitalists ... from the acquisition of knowledge and skill that have economic value" (1961, p. 3). Professor Schultz further noted that "this knowledge and skill are in great part the product of investment" that ought to be encouraged and studied in economic analysis. Indeed, he argued, "To omit them ... is like trying to explain Soviet ideology without Marx" (p. 3).

Economists since the days of Schultz and even before (Hodgson, 2014) have considered investment in human capital to be crucial to employment and returns. Thus, when Icelandic economist Thorvaldur Gylfason (2001) showed that an oil boom undermines human capital, exponents of mainstream economics seemed to have concluded that the last hope for the poorer countries, rich mainly in resources and encouraged over the years to invest in human capital, had lost the last plot in their quest for economic development. This is particularly so because there has been a long tradition in neoclassical economics that the abundance of and dependence on natural resources is a curse, especially for African countries (Auty, 1993; Karl, 1997; Carmody, 2011). To resolve this confused situation, private or public–private partnerships through local content policies have been recommended and implemented as a way of using the market to ensure that Africa can "catch-up" (Stevenson, 2014; Ovadia, 2016a; Kinyondo and Villanger, 2017).

We should, therefore, expect the following:

(a) that more oil leads to a reduction in both the demand for and supply of education;
(b) that international oil companies (IOCs) or oil transnational corporations (TNCs) single-handedly provide education and experience in ways that prevent oil from undermining human capital formation; and
(c) that the demand for education would (i) turn labor into capitalists, (ii) substantially enhance the conditions of workers, and (iii) bring economic convergence in intergroup inequality internally and internationally.

The chapter re-examines these claims. In doing so, it also ascertains to what extent local content, underpinned by the economics of nudging, can address the human capital problems in Africa. For the latter purpose, the chapter (1) probes the relevant legal instruments to identify the nature of "legal interference in private interests" (Sunstein, 1986), (2) offers a re-appraisal of surveys on or about local content laws (e.g., Darkwah, 2013; Obeng- Odoom, 2014a; Ablo, 2015, 2016, 2017; Panford, 2015, 2017), and (3) provides a synthesis of the previous two data-sets and data sources, some of which have been (a) personally collected in the form of interviews or publicly sourced and systematized from (b) recently published data in academic research (e.g., Darkwah, 2013; Obeng-Odoom, 2014a; Panford, 2014, 2017) and (c) bulletins offered by civil society groups and publicly debated or contested in the media (Behrman et al., 2012; Bob-Milliar and Obeng-Odoom, 2012).

This troika has been previously used by institutional economists seeking to investigate, among other things, the "legal foundations of capitalism" (Commons, 1924/1934a, 1934b) and is well-documented (e.g., Molotch, 1970; Molotch & Lester, 1999; Beamish, 2002; Matthewman, 2012) to be effective in analyses of this kind. In strengthening the analytical foundations of stratification economics, the specific approach utilized is "evolutionary and behavioristic, or rather volitional" (Commons, 1924, p. vii). This approach views the law and legal instruments as part of, rather than apart from, the underlying economic system and connects the ramifications of such laws to society, economy, and environment. The relationships between people and between humans and nature, and how institutions mediate these relationships, are considered in the analysis, unlike mainstream mechanistic economics in which the emphasis is on man–nature relations, and centers on individual and household analysis with little consideration for institutions. According to Commons (1924, p. 387):

> a behavioristic definition of political economy as the subject-matter jointly of the sciences of law, ethics and economics, would not be limited to the traditional mechanics of "production, exchange, distribution and consumption of wealth" which are relations of man to nature, but would include them as secondary, and would be defined as primarily a set of relations of man to man, both national and international.

Distinct from mainstream behavioral economics often utilized in development economics (for a discussion, see Bannerjee & Duflo, 2009, who were awarded the 2019 Nobel Prize in Economics, and Altman, 2009, 2012, 2015, professor of behavioral economics and former president of the Society for the Advancement of Behavioral Economics), this approach is "volitional" or behavioristic because it deals not only with feelings and commodities but also with the future, which is often its starting point (Commons, 1924, pp. 4, 6, 7). The approach centers on rules about transactions and laws (actions between and among people with reference to natural resources) that give rise to rights and duties. Such transactions are formulated around different ideas about value, including psychological (anticipation) value, not only exchange value. A transaction is understood as the product of *real* value (the value of commodities, that is, cost of goods and services produced for the purpose of exchange and consumption), *psychological* value (or expectations of people), and *nominal* value (value established in the market, for example, through haggling rules prescribed by law). This approach, then, helps to understand, to analyze, and to explain commodities, feelings, and transactions – between humans and between humans and nature.

In doing the analysis, I focus first on Ghana and then, through an engagement with the vast amount of work done by Jesse Ovadia culminating in his book, *The Petro-Developmental State in Africa* (Ovadia, 2016a), place my claims within a wider African political economy (Carmody, 2011). Starting with Ghana is important, not only because it is one of Africa's latest entrants into the global league of oil producers but also because the maiden issue of the *Ghanaian Journal of Economics* has specifically called for more studies on education and human capital formation (Alagidede et al., 2013). Besides, while the claim made by Schultz (1961) that labor can become capitalists through education may sound extreme, economists, both academic and professional, place major emphasis on human capital formation and how it tends to be destroyed by resource abundance (see, for example, Gylfason, 2001; Wadho,

2014). These issues remain important to political economists who eschew methodological individualism and embrace methodological holism. Yet, while studies on oil in Ghana have proliferated (see, for example, Gyampo, 2011; Gyimah-Boadi and Prempeh, 2012; Ackah-Baidoo, 2013; Bawole, 2013; Ayelazuno, 2014; Fosu, 2016), those on human capital formation have been few (e.g., Darkwah, 2013; Panford, 2014; Ablo, 2018) and not yet framed in political economic terms – an approach which, as I will advance, not only builds on but also transcends the few relevant studies.

Based on this approach to data collection, interpretation, and analysis, the chapter shows that Africa's experiences with oil can contradict all aspects of the mainstream account of oil boom, human capital, and economic development in the sense that (a) both the demand for and supply of education have dramatically increased during the oil boom, (b) this boom is neither the result of local content alone nor the product of distorted public interventions. Rather, the expansion of education is a function of cumulative institutional forces and processes as well as aspirations for a different reality in the future. In turn, there are strong grounds for demanding – as of right – that the fruits in the oil industry be shared. That is, if the fruits are collectively produced and repro-duced, then they must also be widely socialized and diffused. Yet, (c) invest-ment in "oil education" has not been accompanied by the expected "returns on education" in the sense of establishing congruence between jobs expected and jobs obtained and (d) much of the relatively little employment generated is gendered and precarious work, with annualized wages that are different and differentiated between local and imported labor, creating a labor aristocracy in the workforce that is not necessarily linked to embodied investment in educa-tion and experience as workers of similar experiences and education but different gender, ethnicity, and race are differentially rewarded. These argu-ments, showing contradictions and incoherence in the neoclassical human capital theory, extend the growing literature in the political economy of education, labor, and returns (see, for example, Folbre, 2012, 2014; Dunn, 2014; Bailly, 2016) by attempting an explanation for the enthusiasm about the supply of and demand for education in the context of Africa's vast natural resources.

The rest of the chapter is divided into four sections. After this first introductory section, Section 2 reviews the nature of human capital theory, oil and economic development. Section 3 explains the economics behind the contention that private education and experience is a silver bullet. Section 4 contains empirical analyses in four subsections that successively detail the demand for and supply of education, provides an explanation of this pattern, shows how this trend relates to employment and returns, and investigates the ways in which the analyses in the preceding three subsections are typical or particular.

## SECTION 2: HUMAN CAPITAL THEORY, OIL AND ECONOMIC DEVELOPMENT

Many social scientists and other scholars place considerable importance on education. For example, geographers have had a keen interest in the relationships among learning, innovation and regional economic development, as exemplified in special journal issues with titles such as "From Earning Region to Learning in a Socio-Spatial Context" (Rutten & Boekema, 2012) and "Regions as Knowledge and Innovative Hubs" (De Propris & Hamdouch, 2013). In sociology, Max Weber's tome, *The Protestant Ethic and the Spirit of Capitalism* (1930/2001), marked new directions in the contribution of experience and education to economic development.

Human capital theory in mainstream economics is, however, different. Not only is this distinctive because it is part of the World Bank's agenda and, hence, substantially promoted as part of World Bank mission and vision, neoclassical human capital theory also is integral to the idea that capital formation is crucial in the process of economic development (for a detailed history, see Bailly, 2016). In these respects, neoclassical human capital theory is imbued with far more explanatory and political power than, say, the Weberian and feminist conceptions of human capital, discussed at length by Nancy Folbre in her David Gordon Memorial Lecture (Folbre, 2012). Yet, human capital received emphasis only after years of interpreting capital as *physical* (not human) capital formation. For the poorer countries, the announcement that economists were introducing a new understanding of capital formation as the driver of economic development came at a conference in Addis Ababa in Ethiopia, where Hans Singer noted "The fundamental problem is no longer considered to be the creation of wealth, but rather the *capacity* to create wealth" (cited in Arndt, 1987, p. 60, *emphasis* in original). Principally espoused by mainstream economists, human capital theory received academic prominence through the work of Schultz (1961) and Becker (1962), which, together with that of others, has been synthesized by latter-day economists and taught in the major textbooks on economic development such as *Economic Development* (Todaro & Smith, 2006).

Briefly, the human capital theory of education (as part of marginal productivity theory) holds that the value of education is mainly instrumental and, on its own, brings about major overall returns to the recipients (private benefit) and major returns to the public (social benefit), although it is also accepted that education comes with both direct and indirect benefits. By this theory, higher levels of human capital provide insurance against discrimination by race and ethnicity, as discriminating employers have to pay a wage premium for the preferred ethnic or racial group. With time, the cost of the premium becomes prohibitive, forcing discriminating employers out of the labour market, while non-discriminating employers make more profit, as they incur much lower overall cost of production from paying lower wages. Consequently, all employers are incentivised to be non-discriminating. In terms of gaining employment, therefore, human capital theory gives no room for long-run discrimination (Stilwell, 2019, pp. 80–84). In this theory, discrimination is either endogenous or exogenous. If discrimination persists in the labour market, then, it must be from the privilege food workers; not from employers. If discrimination is exogenous, then, it arises from institutions which create unequal human capital endowments (Dymski, 1985). Investing in education ostensibly leads to higher rates of productivity, better prospects of employment, and higher earnings too. By this theoy, wages are purely a function of education; not any social provisioning process such as collective bargaining, or familial networks (Folbre, 2012).

More controversially, human capital is said to be the missing element that would make the poor "catch up" with the rich. In turn, intergroup inequality and, indeed, interregional/intercontinental inequality, such as the wide gaps between Africa and the rest of the world, must be attributed to inadequate human capital in the poorer regions (Easterlin, 1981; Gylfason, 2012). Accordingly, as Nancy Folbre (2012) emphasizes, work-based productivity and general progress and change in society arise not from collective social organization but, rather, through individual experiences and self-interested individual investment in education.

Clearly, human capital is broader than education. Indeed, Gary Becker's (1962) classic study identified schooling, on-the-job training, medical care, and the acquisition of information as primary examples of investment in "human capital," to which the returns are rewarding employment. However, the relevant aspect of the theory for this chapter is education, which not only helps reduce the number of births and, hence, acts as a brake on population growth (itself a dampener on human capital because it often prevents investment in education, see Gylfason, 2012, pp. 31–32), but also is said to enhance labor and labor power.

Aside from productivity improvement, employment, and economic returns, human capital is also seen as encouraging the quicker embrace of information and communication technology (ICT) and other technology, as well as new ideas for social improvement, better health, and entrepreneurship

(Murphy & Siedschlag, 2013; Bartel et al., 2014). Harvard economist, Edward Glaeser, is one of the most enthusiastic proponents of the contribution of human capital to entrepreneurship, ideas, variety and hence increase in the demand for labor and the growth of cities. For Glaeser, it seems "educated cities" have low levels of unemployment; indeed, education is said to be a predictor and generator of employment, both through entrepreneurship and through firms' demand for labor (Glaeser, 2011; Glaeser et al., 2014). In this sense, investing in human capital is seen as one important way out of poverty and the path to development. Critics, including Anirudh Krishna (see, for example, Krishna, 2008), provide a more skeptical view.

In fairness, even within neoclassical economics and its variants, there is a critical awareness of and sensitivity to intractable issues. For example, in which direction does causation run: is it from education to economic development or from economic development to a more educated population? Lant Pritchett (see, Pritchett, 2001), for example, suggests the later, while Edward Glaeser has tended to suggest the former (Glaeser, 2011; Glaeser et al., 2014). Regardless of these narrow "directional" debates, the consensus within the mainstream is that education plays an instrumental role. This role may come later in the process of economic development, but even if so, it will elevate development to freedom, a much wider conception.

That is evidently the argument made by Amartya Sen, the eminent Noble Prize-winning development economist. In *Development as Freedom* (1999), Sen notes:

I must also briefly discuss another relation which invites a comment, to wit, the relation between the literature on "human capital" and the focus in this work on "human capability" as an expression of freedom. ... At the risk of some over-simplification, it can be said that the literature on human capital tends to concentrate on the agency of human beings in augmenting production possibilities. The perspective of human capability focuses, on the other hand, on the ability – the substantive freedom – of people to lead the lies they have reason to value and to enhance the real choices they have. The two perspectives cannot but be related, since BOTH are concerned with THE ROLE OF HUMAN BEINGS [capitalization added], and in particular with the actual abilities that they ACHIEVE AND ACQUIRE [capitalization added] ... But the yardstick of assessment concentrates on different achievements ... The human capital perspective can – in principle – be defined very broadly to cover both types of valuation, but it is typically defined – by convention – primarily in terms of indirect value: human qualities that can be employed as "capital" in production (in the way physical capital is). In this sense, the narrower view of the human capital approach FITS INTO THE MORE INCLUSIVE PERSPECTIVE OF HUMAN CAPABILITY, WHICH CAN COVER BOTH DIRECT AND INDIRECT CONSEQUENCES OF HUMAN ABILITIES [Sen, 1999, p. 293, capitalization added].

Sen continues:

The two perspectives are, thus, CLOSELY RELATED but distinct. The significant transformation that has occured in recent years in giving greater recognition to the role of "human capital" is helpful for understanding the relevance of the capability perspective. If a person can become more productive in making commodities through better education, better health and so on, it is not unnatural to expect that she can, through these means, also directly achieve more – and have the freedom to achieve more – in leading her life. (Sen, 1999, p. 294, capitalization added)

It can, therefore, be concluded as follows:

(a) Sen's human capability theory is, in fact, instrumentalist much like the neoclassical human capital theory;
(b) Sen's human capability theory gives far more explanatory power to human capital (education, experience, health) than the neoclassical human capital theory; and
(c) Therefore, Sen's human capability theory gives even greater role to human capital, especially in underdeveloped regions, than the neoclassical human capital theory, in "catching up".

Providing training, then, seems to be a free pass to the class of the affluent, especially if, as *The Economist* (2014) magazine puts it, the education is practical, supports the status quo, and can be used directly by capitalist firms. From this view, the arts and humanities, especially obtained from obscure schools, are regarded as liabilities (*The Economist*, 2014). The general case for internships, degrees from prestigious universities, and rankings-based education can be put in this category. Similarly, anything that detracts from human capital formation is considered undesirable.

Thus, the work of the Icelandic economist, Thorvaldur Gylfason (2001) was something of a watershed in mainstream economics, in that he argued that abundance of oil in an economy crowds out the education sector. According to Gylfason (2001), public expenditure on education, years of schooling, and gross secondary school enrolment usually decline with mineral booms. He supported his view that "natural capital" displaces "human capital" with evidence that when countries experience booms, they tend to place a lower premium on education. Even when publicly funded, Gylfason argued, the quality of education may be poor as it is not necessarily demand driven. So, inputs, outputs, and participation in education all suffer after a boom in minerals: natural resources bring risks. One is that too many people become locked in low-skill intensive natural-resource-based industries, including agriculture, and thus fail, through no fault of their own, to advance their own or their children's education and earning power.

Another risk is that the authorities and other inhabitants of resource-rich countries become overconfident and therefore tend to underrate or overlook the need for good economic policies as well as for good education. In other words, nations that believe that natural capital is their most important asset may develop a false sense of security and become negligent about the accumulation of human capital. Indeed, resource-rich nations can live well off their natural resources over extended periods, even with poor economic policies and a weak commitment to education. Awash in easy cash, they may find that education does not pay. Nations without natural resources have a smaller margin for error and are less likely to make this mistake (Gylfason, 2001, p. 858).

Many other economists have subsequently endorsed this theory or been influenced by the study. The Pakistani economist Wagha Ahmed Wadho (2014), based at the Lahore School of Economics, has demonstrated additional mechanisms – such as corruption and rent seeking – and confirmed the central thesis: an oil boom is usually deleterious to human capital formation. Philip Bell (2014), an educationist, has argued in the *Australian Universities' Review* that a minerals industry boom draws students away from universities, demonstrating how universities struggle to attract regional students who prefer to seek well-paid jobs for which no tertiary-level education is required. Similarly, Thomas Measham and David Fleming (2014) argue that coal seam gas areas in Australia witnessed a fall in the number of people with university degrees and an increase in those with vocational certificates between 2001 and 2011.

In North America, Schafft, Glenna, and Green (2014) also link boom and doom in human capital creation, in a paper drawing on the perspectives of school education leaders in Pennsylvania to identify the ramifications of the oil and gas industry for local educational investment and enrolments, and hence future economic development. While a boom puts pressure on education facilities, they question whether it provides incentive for investment in expansion of educational facilities: "These are questions that bear further research, in particular in terms of the ways in which new forms of inequality, insecurity, and social exclusion may accompany rapid economic expansion" (Schafft et al., 2014, p. 401).

This crisis view of natural resources has had a long history in economics. Popularly known as the "Dutch disease," the founding principles of the *methodology* that first led to this conventional thesis are ascribed to John Cairnes, the Australian economist who, in 1857, studied the impact of that country's 1851 gold rush on other sectors of the economy (Bordo, 1975; World Bank, 1988, p. 21). Later, this paradox of abundance was framed around the so-called Gregory Thesis (Murray, 1981) after R. G. Gregory (1976) who showed how a natural resources boom might lead to deindustrialization in Australia. The concept was recalibrated as the Dutch disease by *The Economist* magazine, in an account of deindustrialization experienced in the Netherlands and attributed to dependence on North Sea oil and gas (*The Economist*, 1977).

The work of Max Corden and Peter Neary (1982) deserves lengthy consideration because of its fuller explanation of the Dutch disease. According to these writers, in a resource-rich economy, capital and labor tend to move away from the manufacturing sector to the booming sector, and this movement can, in turn, cripple all other sectors – a process they called "resource movement effect." A "spending effect" sets in when, with the demise or contraction of sectors other than the booming one, prices of goods and services in these non-booming sectors rise as demand outstrips a declining supply. A spending effect can also set in when the sudden inflow of resources increases the purchasing power of some locals who, in turn, demand more of certain services – a process that tends to push up the prices of such services. Either way, relative prices of goods and services increase in the booming economy.

This, in turn, increases the *relative exchange rate*. While this process will not automatically affect the *nominal exchange rate*, it usually does so. The new spending processes lead to the purchase of more local currency, either because foreigners are buying more local currency in order to buy the country's natural resources, or because foreigners are paying the country international currency that is then used to buy local currency. As more local currency is bought, the price or exchange rate of that currency appreciates. A strong currency is good, but not so good for manufactures that are exported because they become uncompetitively expensive in global markets. Similarly, as the country's currency strengthens, it becomes cheaper for people to import more goods, and that too can adversely affect manufacturing as fewer local manufactures are bought (Corden & Neary, 1982; Neary, 1982; Barder, 2006). Most economists who study Africa and other resource-rich but materially poor regions have applied this resource curse view of natural resources (see, for example, Sachs & Warner, 1995; Collier, 2009a, 2009b; Sala-i-Martin & Subramanian, 2012; Tiba, 2019).

### SECTION 3: PRIVATE EDUCATION AND EXPERIENCE AS A SILVER BULLET

The provision of private education and experience, otherwise known as TNC-led supply of "local content," have been widely advocated as Africa's silver bullet to the crisis of natural resources (Ovadia, 2016a), quite extensively discussed in Section 2. Local content entails nudging international oil companies (IOCs) to support the supply of both education and experience to Africans in order to "catch up."

The economics behind this posited panacea is hardly discussed, but probing the nature of "how we see" is a crucial step in analyzing "what we see," whether as part of the problem or a silver bullet. In neoclassical economics, however, paternalism, especially state intervention, is an abomination. On the supply side, paternalism is seen as coercive and inefficient, typically breeding corruption and distorting incentives for firms. The reasons offered against demand-side paternalism are rather different. Consumers' "free" choice is deemed best made by themselves. As Samuelson (1938) famously argued, free choice unmistakably demonstrates consumers' "revealed preference." Since then, neoclassical economic theories have typically reserved three roles for the state, ranging from managing externalities that the market fails to account for or address, through reducing monopoly power of firms, to providing goods and services about which there is severe asymmetric information such that the allocative role of the price mechanism breaks down. These instances are, however, the "exceptions" in neoclassical economics. For the most part, the state should take a minimalist role because the price mechanism in a market economy is capable of ensuring a more efficient allocation of goods and services. Therefore, the state that governs least, governs best (Pressman, 2001, pp. 1104–1105). "Free markets," on the other hand, are seen as the primary mechanism for identifying and fulfilling the preference of human beings, firms, and the environment efficiently and effectively.

One scholar who has offered a sustained challenge to this view is Cass Sunstein, renowned among legal scholars and theorists, so his challenge (Sunstein, 1986; Thaler & Sunstein, 2003; Thaler et al., 2012) must be considered seriously. Sunstein argues that the assumptions of paternalism are false and the mainstream account about how individuals make choices is misconceived. According to him, individuals consistently commit errors in their choices, choices that are hardly rational. In fact, behaviorally, individuals are often in a conundrum between the impulsive doer (*homer economicus*) and strategic planner (*homo economicus*), but it is the former that typically prevails (Leonard, 2008). Individuals are easily influenced by almost everything, so they have no "true preference" per se. As individuals are influenced, and they can be influenced either way, Cass Sunstein argues that "libertarian paternalism" – a "new paternalism" that guarantees choice and still directs individuals to the best choice – is the answer to social problems (Leonard, 2008). Such libertarian paternalism is not coercive but rather encouraging. What it does is to *nudge,* rather than compel, individuals and firms. Realizing that the paternalist – whether public or private – is highly influential, Cass Sunstein's interest is in helping paternalists improve their "choice architecture" or how they make choices to nudge the world in a desirable direction (say choice architects can base their nudging on what the majority of people want). In this sense, individual preferences no longer constitute the sole standard for making judgements about utility. At the economy-wide level, Sunstein hinges his case on more growth, suggesting that nudging is a better motor for growth. Mann and Gairing (2012) have recently shown that Sunstein's arguments have been widely applauded and hence widely cited in favorable terms, even among mainstream economists. Indeed, in 2017, Sunstein's collaborator, Richard Thaler, was given the Nobel Prize in Economics. Thaler would cite his work with Sunstein in his Nobel Lecture as crucial in the development of the theory (see Thaler, 2017).

What makes Sunstein's argument even more interesting is not that it is part of the story of a Nobelist (that is, well-known) or even a challenge to the mainstream – there is no shortage of such (see, for a review, Stilwell, 2012, 2017, 2019). Rather, it is because it is neither Marxian nor Keynesian, the grounds from which most radical challenge of mainstream analysis has come. For Sunstein, "a new paternalism" is *the* ultimate challenge to the economics orthodoxy. It is, therefore, important to study the claims made by Sunstein in their confrontation with mainstream contentions. Much of the research on paternalism focuses on the demand side of nudging, using examples of individual suboptimal consumption and individual decision-making that shows important weaknesses and hence seeks to answer questions about whether interveners do better, whether interveners *can do* better, and under what circumstances interveners can or will do better (see, for a review, Leonard et al., 2000; Mann & Gairing, 2012). Concomitantly, the focus of this chapter, showing that nudging also takes place on the supply side, for example, in labor allocation, helps extend the literature.

Paternalism in the oil industry has to be systematically analyzed. Daniel Yergin's (2009) authoritative book on the history of the oil industry, *The Prize,* is a useful starting point to think through paternalism in the oil industry. The book shows that, historically, bouts of paternalism in the oil industry took the form of compelling oil companies to directly support the economy, setting prices for oil, imposing import quotas, and imposing restrictions on foreign exchange. This type of paternalism was particularly intense during the Great Depression of the 1930s, prompting the international oil companies (IOCs) to reach the "As-Is" or Achnacarry Agreement of cooperation, among others, to defend themselves against control by the nation states. The outbreak of World War II, Yergin (2009) shows, ended this agreement – around the same time that Mexico took the historic step of nationalizing its oil industry. Venezuela, on the other hand, developed quite a different path. In 1945, the socialist party (Acción Democrática, with its origins in Generation of 1928) of Venezuela implemented what can be said to have constituted the first outlines of a local content policy. In this policy, Juan Pablo Pérez Alfonzo, the Minister of Development, supported by President Romulo Betancourt, postulated three key pillars. First, it achieved a 90 per cent indigenization of the industry. Second, the indigenization went with the fifty-fifty principle in which the state captured 50 per cent of the rents accruing to the IOCs. Third, downstream activities (including transport, refinery, and marketing) were developed and also taxed for the benefit of the state to be used for social purposes. However, international imperialism coupled with local neocoloni-alists overthrew the socialist regime in 1948, a move welcomed by the oil industry that accused Alfonzo's group of being communists.

Since then, the oil industry has fought against both outright nationalization and Alfonzo-style local content. Indeed, globally, debate on paternalism in the oil and gas industry was centered around the effectiveness of "energy nation-alism." A recent detailed review of the idea (Peigo & Ruas, 2015) exemplifies these reactions. On the one hand, mainstream economists have condemned it, arguing that historically the oil sector grew because of the absence of any paternalistic behavior by the state. On the other hand, there are those who write more favorably about how paternalistic roles helped steer the develop-ment of the industry. Yet, even such sympathetic writers point to inefficiencies of the producer states and their politics, which makes them unstable and hence unreliable. Partnerships are the more favored in a third strand of the literature in which the more privatization, the better. While it differs in detail from the classic orthodoxy, this partnership strand is essentially similar to the main-stream position of freeing the industry. Indeed, since the twentieth century, there has been heated debate on what caused the 1970s oil crises. Were they the outcome of poor policies or the result of capitalist markets in their best shape? Historians have recently warned that this retrospective reflection is necessary but it is not sufficient to understand the issue of paternalism in the oil industry. At the very least, the reaction to oil is not only derivative from past expectations but also indicative of future expectations (Bösch & Graf, 2014).

In that sense, one important question in the literature has been under what circumstances do oil producer countries nationalize the control of oil resources. This question relates to the upstream (production-related) aspects of the oil industry rather than the midstream (marketing and distribution-related aspects of the industry) or even the downstream (oil products-related) oil sector. As most countries own their oil resources, it is the *control* of such resources that constitutes the main differences among countries (Sarbu, 2014). Of this question, there are two subissues (Obeng-Odoom, 2014c). One is how to control and the other is how much to control. Of the two, it is the latter that has generated more recent interest (Sarbu, 2014): what are the drivers that will make an oil-producing state lean towards either (1) using a national oil company to control oil industry or (2) inviting TNCs that are often foreign based into the extraction of oil (p. 30)? In the literature, five possible reasons have been given for the tendency to nationalize.

Bianca Sarbu (2014) classifies them into the following:

[about the control of oil, namely] the more complex the geological conditions are, the less state control is expected in the upstream sector; The lower the technical capabilities of the NOC [national oil companies] are, the less state control is expected in the upstream sector; The higher the oil prices are, the more state control is expected in the upstream sector; The higher the oil reliance of the oil producing state is, the more state control is expected in the upstream sector; The higher the level of executive constraints is, the more state control is expected in the upstream sector. (Sarbu, 2014, pp. 71–74)

Establishing which of these is the most probable is not easy and is likely contingent on what analytical approaches are used. Sarbu's (2014) study is a case in point. She uses both quantitative and qualitative approaches to determine which factors shape the likelihood of state control. The quantitative approach is a two-limit Tobit model incorporating the dynamic panel fractional estimator. This is supplemented by a case study approach involving the investigation of the experiences of Saudi Arabia and Abu Dhabi, two oil-rich countries with contrasting experiences about the control of oil. She finds that the two methodologies yield different results. On the one hand, the quantitative approach shows that the decision to nationalize is driven by four main factors. One, geology or how the physical and chemical composition of the oil fields enhances or constrains oil extraction. Fields that are easily navigable encourage nationalization. Two, technical know-how or whether by nationalization the state can in fact produce its own oil. Three, trends in international oil prices with an upward trend tending to encourage nationalization. Four, and most importantly, the amount/level of oil reliance with the more reliant nations being more likely to nationalize.

On the other hand, the case studies show that it is the effect of colonialism, the age/experience with oil production, local pressure to nationalize, and the political orientation of national leaders that collectively determine whether oil producers nationalize. It is likely, then, that institutions and local context play a major role, but have to be understood within the global world system. Existing studies have, however, been analytically limited (Sarbu, 2014). Delimited to a focus on producer or consumer countries and sometimes on the relationship between the two and how they are echoed in the operations of IOCs and the role of national oil companies (NOCs), Bianca Sarbu (2014) has argued that such studies would be better off if placed in the historical role of the oil industry, its centrality to capitalism, and its complexity in terms of the various actors involved in the industry. Studying local content policies is one way to respond to such a case.

Existing local content policies differ substantially from the Alfonzo-type local content policies, in terms of their assumptions, how they structure capital–labor relations, and foreign–local relationships (see, for a review, Tordo et al., 2013). In Africa, the adoption of these local content policies and laws was a post-2005 process, arising from years of concerns that the extractive industries were not contributing enough to the continent's economic development and were, in fact, making conditions worse in many mining societies and nations. Local content policies and laws have the firm support of the world development agencies such as the World Bank (Ovadia, 2014). As it did in its well-known report, *The East Asian Miracle: Economic Growth and Public Policy* (World Bank, 1993), the World Bank has a particular way of framing local content strategy generally and explaining its outcomes: presenting it as a market friendly approach (Gore, 1996). In its specific application to the oil industry, local content falls within the idea of libertarian paternalism in the sense that it seeks to avoid the pitfalls of direct control and free markets by nudging the actors towards behaviors that will empower indigenous labor without impairing the fruits of industry. How local content plays out in practice, however, requires more careful study.

Based on the foregoing, we would have to expect the following:

(a) More oil leads to a reduction in both the demand for and supply of education;

(b) IOCs or oil TNCs single-handedly provide education and experience in ways that prevent oil from undermining human capital formation; and

(c) the demand for education would (i) turn labor into capitalists, (ii) substantially enhance the conditions of workers, and (iii) bring economic convergence in intergroup inequality internally and internationally.

## SECTION 4 EMPIRICAL ANALYSIS

### a The Demand and Supply of Education

Since the discovery of oil in commercial quantities in 2007 and the commencement of oil export in 2010, investment in oil-related education in Ghana has increased in a number of ways (Oteng-Adjei, 2011; Darkwah, 2013; Obeng-Odoom, 2014a; Panford, 2014, 2017). Examples are the establishment of new subjects in tertiary institutions, introduction of new programs on oil and gas, provision of new technical educational institutions to offer certificate courses on oil and gas, oil companies' supported expansion of research programs and laboratories on oil and gas, and state support/sponsorship of many national officers to study oil and gas either in the country or overseas. Moreover, the state has obtained a USD38 million-dollar loan facility to build capacity, including "the development of indigenous technical and professional skills needed by the petroleum sector through support to selected educational institutions" (Oteng-Adjei, 2011, p. 2). Furthermore, Ghana National Petroleum Corporation is sponsoring some of its staff to undertake oil and gas educational programs. Civil society groups have also organized many oil and gas seminars and conferences for think tanks and the general public.

These levels of support in the education sector draw on public, private, and public–private initiatives. Consider the oil courses on offer at the Takoradi Technical University. Supported by both the state and the private sector, they provide education in oil extraction. The polytechnic is offering the National Vocational Qualification in oil six-month diploma course valued at USD7,500 per student, from which thirty-two people have graduated. Tullow Oil, a major oil company in the country, invested USD5 million in setting up the course and its facilities, and eight of the graduates were directly sponsored by Modec, a company involved in the oil industry in Ghana. The Kwame Nkrumah University of Science and Technology, also a public tertiary institution, is to graduate 1,270 degree-level and postgraduate students from oil and gas courses in the next five years, while the University of Ghana has advertised for law qualifications in oil and gas and the University of Cape Coast invited applicants for places for Master of Business Administration in oil and gas. Owing to the actual and expected rush for such courses, other universities such as the University of Mines and Technology have invested in staff development by sending academics overseas to train in oil and gas (Panford, 2014, 2017). There are many non-tertiary training institutions, vocational institutes, and learning centers springing up in the country to supply "human capital" to support this young industry (Darkwah, 2013; Obeng-Odoom, 2014a; Panford, 2014, 2017; Ablo, 2018; Ackah et al., 2019). These developments have not reduced the share of government expenditure going to general education in Ghana. Generally, public expenditure on education was 9.1 per cent of gross domestic product (GDP) in 2007 when oil was discovered and increased to 10.1 per cent a year later (Ministry of Education, 2010). According to the 2013 expenditure figures released by the Ministry of Finance and Economic Planning, public funding to the Ministry of Education was 23.8 per cent of the total budget (computed from Ministry of Finance and Economic Planning, 2013 – six years after oil discovery and three years after successful export of oil began). Between 2013 and 2014, there was a 62.5 per cent increase in the public funds allocated to education (Ministry of Finance, 2013b). Table 4.1 contains data on trends in the supply of schools published in *The State of the Ghanaian Economy* (Institute of Statistical, Social and Economic Research (ISSER), 2012). This statistical information provides further evidence of positive investment in education.

Table 4.1 shows that, across all levels – crèche/nursery, kindergarten, primary, junior high school (JHS), and senior high school (SHS) – there has been an overall substantial increase in the supply of education. Both the public and the private sectors have consistently increased the supply of schools since the discovery of oil in 2007. Datasets with the same level of detail for tertiary education are hard to come by. However, there is evidence that there was a 19.7 per cent increase in the number of tertiary students enrolled in Distance Education Programme between 2010/2011 and 2011/2012 (Ministry of Finance and Economic Planning, 2012). Tertiary education has percolated only 9.7 per cent of the population but, aside the fifty-five accredited private tertiary institutions, the supply of public education has increased over the years. As of 2010, there were seven public universities and three institutions considered specialist and tertiary, ten polytechnics, and thirty-eight education training colleges all of which are public (Alagidede et al., 2013). Since 2017, a state policy of providing "Free Senior High School" ("Free SHS") been implemented. The official estimate for the total number of enrolment as a result of making SHS free is 90, 000 students in 2017/2018, doubling to 180, 000/ 181,000 new student enrolments in 2018/2019 (Ofori-Attah, 2019, pp. 33 and 161).There has also been investment in the quality of the education supplied. The state seems to have made some interventions along the lines of infra-structural enhancement of ten technical institutes, two polytechnics, and the College of Technology, while some 200 teachers in technical institutes were supported in continued professional development in 2013 (Ministry of Finance and Economic Planning, 2013a). In 2012, 8,409 pupil teachers were

Table 4.1 *Trends in the supply of schools, Ghana 2007–2011*

| Level | Provider | 2007/8 | 2008/9 | 2009/10 | 2010/11 | % Change, 2007–2011 |
|---|---|---|---|---|---|---|
| Crèche/Nursery | Public | 657 | 770 | 796 | 666 | 1.37 |
| | Private | 2,947 | 3,385 | 3,739 | 4,303 | 46.01 |
| Sub-total | | **3,604.00** | **4,155.00** | **4,535.00** | **4,969.00** | **37.87** |
| Kindergarten | Public | 11,140 | 11,827 | 12,481 | 13,263 | 19.06 |
| | Private | 4,309 | 4,612 | 4,990 | 5,538 | 28.52 |
| Sub-total | | **15,449** | **16,439** | **17,471** | **18,801** | **21.70** |
| Primary | Public | 13,247 | 13,510 | 13,835 | 14,431 | 8.94 |
| | Private | 4,068 | 4,371 | 4,744 | 5,292 | 30.09 |
| Sub-total | | **17,315** | **17,881** | **18,579** | **19,723** | **13.91** |
| JHS | Public | 7,423 | 7,656 | 7,969 | 8,462 | 14.00 |
| | Private | 2,319 | 2,557 | 2,799 | 3,247 | 40.02 |
| Sub-total | | **9,742** | **10,213** | **10,768** | **11,709** | **20.19** |
| SHS | Public | 493 | 493 | 496 | 511 | 3.65 |
| | Private | 207 | 177 | 201 | 209 | 0.97 |
| Sub-total | | **700** | **670** | **697** | **720** | **2.86** |

*Source:* Calculated from Institute of Statistical, Social and Economic Research (ISSER), 2012

sponsored to receive upgraded teacher training in the Untrained Teachers Diploma in Basic Education (Ministry of Finance and Economic Planning, 2012). Furthermore, in 2013/2014, the national state, through the Ministry of Education and Ghana Education Service, organized in-service training, skills improvement, and educational training for 3,086 kindergarten teachers, 13,264 teachers in the primary school, and 6,534 teachers at JHS (Ministry of Finance, 2013b). So, both qualitatively and quantitatively, investment in oil has not impaired the quality and standards of education.

So, from the supply side, Ghana has not followed the part predicted by economic theory. On the demand side, too, the number of students enrolling in education is on the rise, as shown in Table 4.2. Similarly, the ratio of the population enrolling at all pre-tertiary levels is on the rise (Table 4.3). It is often the case that there is a substantial gap between enrolment and completion in Africa, hence the gross enrolment ratio (GER) is said to be a poor measure of education demand. However, in the case of Ghana, the net enrolment ratio (NER), while not as high as the GER, is also largely on the rise. Indeed, between 2008/2009 and 2013/2014, NER at primary level increased marginally from 88.5 to 89.3 per cent (Ministry of Finance and Economic Planning, 2015).

These gains have contributed to economic growth. In 2011, the growth rate in the education subsector was 3.8 per cent but it increased to 6.7 per cent in

Table 4.2  *Trends in the number of people enrolling in education at different levels,*
*2011–2013*

| Level | 2013/2014 | 2014/2015 | 2015/16 | 2016/17 |
|---|---|---|---|---|
| Kindergarten | 22,052 | 23,239 | 22,052 | 23,239 |
| Primary | 22,289 | 23,489 | 22,289 | 23,489 |
| Junior High School | 14,767 | 15,804 | 14,767 | 15,804 |
| Tertiary | 318,607 | 319,659 | - | - |

*Source:* Ministry of Finance, 2015, 2018, Budget Statement and Economic Policy of the Government of Ghana (2016, 2017), Ministry of Finance, Accra

Table 4.3  *Gross enrolment ratio (GER) in Ghana, 2010–2014*

| Level | 2010/11 | 2011/12 | 2012/13 | 2013/2014 |
|---|---|---|---|---|
| Kindergarten | 98.4 | 99.4 | | |
| Primary | 96.4 | 96.5 | 105.0 | 107.0 |
| Junior High School. | 79.6 | 80.6 | | |
| Senior High School | 36.5 | 36.9 | | |

*Sources:* Ministry of Finance, 2012; 2015

2012. In 2013, the targeted growth rate (4.0 per cent) was exceeded (4.6 per cent; Ministry of Finance and Economic Planning, 2013a). So, the investment in education has been worthwhile, in growth terms at least.

How might we make sense of these differences in the economic explanation and the experiences of Ghana? One way is to use the concept of frames. The conceptual metaphor of a frame draws attention to how a phenomenon is seen and in what way it is appreciated (Bohman, 2010). In Ghana, oil and gas education is framed as a prerequisite for success in the industry. Furthermore, the current level of capacity in the field has been framed to be inadequate. With one estimate (Iddrisu, 2014) suggesting that about half the professional workers in the oil and gas industry would have retired by 2017, there have been high expectations that there is going to be substantial demand for oil workers. It is within this context, together with claims of oil courses of beckoning opportunity in the industry (Darkwah, 2013; Pegram et al., 2019), that the boom in education can usefully be framed.

## b  Explaining the Boom in Education

Indeed, what these examples show is that the mineral boom–education nexus is contingent, not categorical. It is not only a case of different institutions and contexts, but also *framing* that can make the difference. Where opportunities and risks in oil are framed as continent on attaining certain educational skills and experiences, the educational institutions, the oil companies, and the government fan this perception by investing in the sector, the media produces images of opportunities linked with education, and people perceive opportunity as linked to attaining educational ends and, hence, are likely to embrace education (Obeng-Odoom, 2014a).

Oil has become an important commodity in Ghana in a short period of time. In 2019, "the benchmark revenue crude oil output" was 63.4 million barrels (Ministry of Finance, 2019, pp. 67-68), although the average production of oil in Ghana per year is 38.73 million barrels (Ministry of Finance and Economic Planning, 2015; budget bullet point 183). Between January and September 2015, the value of crude oil exports was nearly 19 per cent of total merchandise export (Ministry of Finance and Economic Planning, 2015; budget bullet points 61 and 62 Ministry of Finance, 2019, pp. 67–68). Revenues from the resource constitute about 10 per cent of Ghana's GDP and the oil reserves have been considered substantial enough to serve as guarantee to obtain major loans in the international market. The oil industry has contributed to shaping internal social and spatial transformation such as the relationship between the oil city and other regional capitals, the oil city and its peri-urban surroundings, and the internal organization in the oil city itself. Oil has also played a key role in defining new external relations with countries such as Côte d'Ivoire, the United States, the United Kingdom, and, significantly, China, with which Ghana is trading much of its oil reserves in exchange for infrastructural development and developmental loans (Obeng-Odoom, 2014a, 2015a; Phillips et al., 2016).

In theory, this level of importance implies that the recent decline in oil prices globally - from US$ 76 per barrel in the January/ June period of 2018 to US$ 71 pr barrel in the rest of the year (Ofori-Attah, 2019, p. 44). is likely to be felt across the country. As a detailed review of studies on Ghana's oil and gas industry (Obeng-Odoom, 2015a) shows, however, while there has been a reduction in revenue, institutional design (the use of sovereign funds) by the state in response to civil society activism, the futures deals of oil, and the "save some" rather than "spend all" strategy, have provided some protection for the country. In turn, Ghana has not as yet experienced a Dutch disease typically defined in terms of the destruction of the manufacturing sector, currency volatility, and reduction in the investment in social services. This governance of the oil sector is one indication of paternalism in the oil sector. Paternalism in the oil industry in Ghana has been shaped by three key factors: first, Ghana's experiences with mining, especially gold; second, the experiences of other oil-rich countries such as Nigeria; and third, the fear of future oil-related challenges (Arthur & Arthur, 2015). Thus, while the formal policy framework was prepared in 2010 and the law enacted in 2013, the considerations for these were events that had taken place before as well as the anticipation of events that would take place after. Indeed, assessments of activities in Ghana and those of a big regional neighbor, and the international experiences of oil helped shape Ghana's policy and legal frameworks. Ghana has a national oil company, the Ghana National Petroleum Corporation (GNPC), but it came into being not as a nationalization effort, but rather as a state initiative to help look for oil in the country (Obeng-Odoom, 2014a). With the election of the liberal New Patriotic Party government in the early 2000s, the role of GNPC changed from actually exploring for oil to a more market, IOC-facilitatory role – with the tacit endorsement of the World Bank (Phillips et al., 2016).

Since the discovery of oil in commercial quantities in 2007, following the general trend in local content policy-making in Africa, Ghana embarked on this process to get similar benefits. The policy has been neither carefully theorized nor conceptualized, but it provides an extensive 2010 Local Content Framework. According to the framework, "The oil and gas industry is known to contribute significantly to the strong economic growth of countries that produce oil and gas. It is anticipated that the development of the oil and gas industry will be a source of accelerated growth, poverty reduction and general prosperity to the people of Ghana. The active involvement of Ghanaians in the oil and gas development, through local content and participation, has become a major policy issue" (Ministry of Energy, 2010, p. 2). The focus on growth as a bulwark for poverty reduction, "general prosperity," and sustainable development is typical of local government policies around the world: they are grounded in the idea that growth will transform the society (Tordo et al., 2013). In the Ghanaian case, the idea is to create the "enabling environment" (Ministry of Energy, 2010, p. 4) to stimulate the free choice and actions of actors.

In 2011, the Petroleum Commission was set up, among others, to "promote local content and local participation in petroleum activities as prescribed by the Petroleum Exploration and Production Act 1984 (PNDCL 84) and other applicable laws and regulations to strengthen national development" (section 3f, Act 821). The Commission was set up under *The Petroleum Commission Act 2011* (ACT 821) in 2011. It was in 2013 that this effort matured into a binding law called the *Petroleum (Local Content and Local Participation) Regulations, 2013, LI 2204.*

So what does the law say? The Local Content Law in Ghana is one of the most formidable pieces of legal legislations in Africa. It is based on three central pillars: vision, strategy, and monitoring and enforcement. The law envisages the following: employment generation for Ghanaians; capacity development of Ghanaians in the oil industry; making Ghanaian local businesses in the oil industry internationally competitive among others to enhance the economic value or quality of products and services in the oil and gas industry; local retention of some "patents" of ideas generated from local oil industry; and ensuring that international oil companies transfer their technology for the development of the local technological base in the industry. On the demand side, concerns have been raised about whether the specific labor requirements are too ambitious, whether there is enough labor to fill the specialist jobs required, and the possibility of fronting for foreigners (e.g., Darkwah, 2013; Ablo, 2015; 2018; Arthur & Arthur, 2015; Pegram et al., 2019). These issues are particularly pertinent because of the nature of the content of the first schedule (see Table 4.4). As of December 2011, 57 per cent of all employees in the industry were Ghanaians (Arthur & Arthur, 2015), a share that remained the same around mid-2012 (Panford, 2015, 2017). Of this cohort of workers, most worked as "other staff" and technical core staff both onshore and offshore (Ablo, 2012; Obeng-Odoom, 2014a; Panford, 2015). This scorecard makes the concerns raised quite valid.

The supply concerns are rather different. Questions have been asked (Ablo, 2015; Ablo & Overå, 2015) about whether entrepreneurs, especially small-scale ones, can win any favorable contracts given that all the government does about nudging is just that: nudge. Because of this, small-scale suppliers have been struggling to make ends meet. Again, this evidence gives weight to the concerns raised.

Table 4.4 *Legal stipulations of local content in the petroleum industry in Ghana*

| Local Content | Minimum Legal Requirements and Timelines | | |
| --- | --- | --- | --- |
| | From Beginning | Five Years after Commencement | Ten Years after Commencement |
| Goods and Services | 10% | 50% | 60–90% |
| Recruitment and Training | | | |
| (i) Management | 30% | 50–60% | 70–80% |
| (ii) Technical Core Staff | 20% | 50–60% | 70–80% |
| (iii) Other Staff | 80% | 90% | 100% |

*Source:* Adapted from Government of Ghana, 2013 (the First Schedule, L.I. 2204)

Yet, the law provides clear strategies to actualize this vision and even address many of the concerns raised. To enable local employment, the law provides that local expertise, goods, and services (legal, banking, and insurance in particular) are used. Its vision for education is to be attained through making IOCs sponsor Ghanaians for further education in the oil and gas industry, and give Ghanaians opportunities for practical experience. Ghanaian local businesses are to become internationally competitive by making it compulsory for them to be involved in the supply of goods and services to IOCs, while the transfer of technology is to be achieved through the principle that all entities in the oil and gas industry must undertake research and development.

To ascertain the success of the law, there are requirements for monitoring and enforcement, with the Local Committee and the Petroleum Commission as the monitoring agents. Monitoring processes include strict reporting standards with guidelines on what to report and what sorts of information are needed, for what, whom, and why. Also, where entities do not directly meet the legal requirements, they are to provide a clear plan as to how and when the requirements will be meet. The commission is given the power to hear complaints from all, including aggrieved people, and to investigate any information it receives, including the use of Ghanaians to front for IOCs, and to recommend either a fine or a jail term for prosecution of entities that break the law.

Education and training too are witnessing a boom. As a result of nudging, both deeper comprehensive education and vocational training have expanded. Apart from the formal, public institutions involved in training (e.g., Takoradi Technical University, Kwame Nkrumah University of Science and Technology, National Vocational Training Institute), there are many other non-core training institutions that are now involved in training too and/or supporting the training of staff and others through the grant of scholarships. This is evidently the case with the national oil corporation, GNPC, and Tullow, the giant transnational oil company (Panford, 2014, 2015, 2017). There are also many private providers offering various levels of training, some of which are local, such as Oil and Gas Training and Recruitment Centre (Obeng-Odoom, 2014a), and others international, such as WorleyParsons and Harvard Marine Petroleum Training Institute (Darkwah, 2013).

The content of the education offered varies depending on the expertise and focus of the institutions involved. Even within institutions, "petroleum-related education" varies depending on discipline, as Table 4.5 – based on the oil education program of Goodwill International Group in 2012 – indicates. Table 4.5 shows that the content of "petroleum-related education" can be wide-ranging and is open to many points of entry (e.g., business, science, and social sciences). Goodwill International Group has a diversified portfolio of courses offered, as can be seen in Table 4.5, but other institutions are more specialized in the courses they offer. For instance, in Sekondi-Takoradi, the Oil and Gas Training and Recruitment Centre gives courses in oil instrumentation and process monitoring, development, and implementation (Obeng-Odoom, 2014a, pp. 99–100). Similarly, the content of petroleum-related education on offer in the public institutions, such as the Takoradi Technical University (TTU) and the Kwame Nkrumah University of Science and Technology (KNUST), is more specialist, engineering, and science focused. Much of this boom in the supply and diversity in the content of education is uncoordinated (Panford, 2014, 2015, 2017). Yet, unlike research that claims that oil and gas crowds out education (see, for example, Gylfason, 2001, 2011, 2012), the Ghanaian experience has been a case of successful nudge, driven by how opportunities and challenges have been framed in the oil and gas industry. Indeed, one institution alone, the Kwame Nkrumah University of Science and Technology (KNUST), is looking at graduating over 1,000 students in just five years' time (Obeng-Odoom, 2015b).

Much business activity has been rekindled by the law and the actions of both private (TNCs) and public (state institutions) nudgers or choice architects. Resulting from the cumulative influence of these interlocking processes of nudging and framing (Obeng-Odoom, 2015b), at least thirty local industries are now working in the oil and gas local industries in response to the law (Ablo, 2015, 2018). Most are in the form of services such as the recruitment and training of oil and gas workers, the supply of items such as lubricants, equipment in the form of personal protective equipment (e.g., boots and helmets) to the IOCs, and the offer of catering services to the IOCs or more precisely TNCs. Many of the business activities are on a small- and medium-scale basis, typically employing between six and ninety-nine workers.

Most are typically diversified and continue to diversify, a demand-driven response to the preferences of TNCs. They start off by doing one thing and grow into providing more diversified services (Ablo & Overå, 2015). Also, they typically face information constraints and constraints related to their international competiveness but also they struggle with local bureaucratic challenges.

Yet, many are able to capitalize on networks to overcome or mitigate the challenges. Such is evidently the case for many, especially medium-scale companies (employing between thirty and ninety-nine workers) who utilize the opportunities made available to them by the Enterprise Development Centre (EDC), a public–private information-sharing initiative, many,

Table 4.5 *The contents of various oil and gas training programs, 2012*

| Number | Discipline | Modules |
|---|---|---|
| 1 | Accounting and Finance | Petroleum Accounting, Petroleum Economics, Energy Trading and Risk Management, and Taxation and Fiscal Regimes |
| 2 | Marketing | Managing and Understanding the Customer, Retail Management-Customer Care, Personal Selling Management, and Credit Control |
| 3 | Retail | Forecourt Management, Credit Control, Retail Management-Customer Care, and Tanker and Product Management and Safety |
| 4 | Oil and Gas Management/ Commercial | Energy Policy and the Environment, Energy Trading and Risk Management, Oil and Gas Contracts Law, and Petroleum Economics |
| 5 | Purchasing and Supply | Negotiation and Contracts Managements, Supply Chain Management, Procurement Management, and Stores and Inventory Management |
| 6 | Health and Safety | HSE Management System, Confirm Space Entry, Hazardous Materials, Hot Works, Lockout/ Tagout, Permit to Work, Working at Height, Manual Handling, and Mechanical Handling |
| 7 | Environmental Management | Energy Policy and the Environment, Applied Environment, Applied Safety |
| 8 | Human Resource | Essentials of Human Resource Management, Communication Skills, Local Content and Stakeholder Management, and Negotiation and Contracts Management |
| 9 | Project Management | Project Management Strategies, Negotiation and Contracts Management, Project Finance, and Project Team Building |
| 10 | Security and Protection | Intelligence Gathering and Counter Insurgency, Maritime Security and Safety, Conflict Prevention and Resolution, and Stakeholder Management |
| 11 | Media and Communication | Public Relations, Communication Strategies, Energy Policy and the Environment, and Local Content Management |
| 12 | Drilling and Product Technicians | Rig and Drilling Operations for Technicians, Oil and Gas Production Operations for Technicians, Applied Health and Safety, and the Environment |

*Source:* Taken from page 2 of the 2012 Certificate of a graduate of Goodwill International Group Oil and Gas Training in Accra, Ghana

especially medium-scale companies (employing between thirty and ninety-nine workers), benefit from the EDCs to mitigate or overcome the challenges (Ablo, 2015). More established service industries that are members of the Sekondi-Takoradi Chamber of Commerce and Industry (STCCI) also obtain information and networking assistance (Obeng-Odoom, 2015a). Whether doing so results in sustainable jobs, however, warrants more careful analysis.

## c Education, Employment, Returns

One way to take stock of education, employment, and returns is to examine the backward, forward, and combined linkages in the oil and gas industry. Leading institutionalists, namely Albert Hirschman (1958, 1984) and Harold Innis (Watkins, 1963), have successfully utilized this institutional analysis elsewhere. From this perspective, jobs related to backward linkages are those that are generated from input industry and those that are generated from forward linkages arise from the processing of oil, while combined linkages connect or arise from both.

These jobs may be located in three different, but related, areas in the oil industry: upstream, midstream, and downstream. Upstream, on-rig jobs have been reported in Ablo's (2012) survey, but there are far fewer than promised. Besides, they are highly gendered. The high -paying ones have usually gone to men, while women have typically taken cleaning and cooking jobs that are low-paying. Career advancement has also been reported to be much more oblique than expected. In spite of these pressures, the evidence (Darkwah, 2013) shows that more and more people are being trained for such jobs with the effect that "a reserve army of labor" exists to hold down wages on the rig. Midstream transport or support services jobs have also started springing up to provide rig-related equipment, but these are few at this stage, while downstream, oil-product-related jobs are yet to pick up – mainly due to the lack of a petrochemical industry in the country (Obeng-Odoom, 2013e, 2014a, 2015d). Construction jobs are on the rise, but they have accrued to males for the most part, with low-paid positions going to women who struggle to work in the sector (Owusuaa, 2012), raising questions about the neoclassical human capital theory.

Indeed, the processes of obtaining and maintaining jobs in upstream and midstream sectors have been characterized by widespread discrimination. Recruitment firms have been openly biased in favor of certain social groups or, more precisely, ethnic groups. This ethnic-based recruitment process has become institutionalized and entrenched in an environment where oil TNCs retain only particular companies to handle their recruitments (Ablo, 2012). In this sense, the endogenous thesis that if discrimination persists, then it must be because privileged workers perpetuate it (see Dymski, 1985) is not borne out by the Ghanaian experience. Discrimination does not end in the process of recruitment. Systemic bias also characterizes the work relationship between employers and workers, albeit more in the form of racial rather than ethnic discrimination. Schlumberger, a global oil and gas project management service company with subsidiaries in Sekondi-Takoradi, for instance, is reported (Myjoyonline.com, 2014) to be paying expatriate staff rental allowances that are over 106 times higher than that of the local workers on grade 10 of the pay scale, resulting in stratification in the class of oil workers. More systematic research (e.g., Panford, 2017; Ablo, 2018) suggests that these disparities are widespread. Indeed, in a rare insider's account, *In Pursuit of Jubilee: A True Story of the First Major Oil Discovery in Ghana*, George Yaw Owusu (2017), a prominent employee of KOSMOS, provides graphic details of cases when he, a black member of staff, is paid substantially less than white junior members of staff, although far more qualified and far more senior. So, the human capital claim about unequal endowment as explanation (see Dymski, 1985) is questionable.

Table 4.6 shows that this practice is widespread, even if the magnitude is much lower, on average, in the rest of Ghana. Table 4.6 also shows that, although the gap between imported and exported labor has narrowed, on average, imported labor is paid more than twice as much as local labor for similar types of work and similar (or even higher) levels for human capital jobs. So, not only is there racism against minorities, the industry is also characterised by "racial domination", with blacks as a super-exploited class (Dymski, 1985) from both an "inferior race" and "inferiorised country". Both racism and racial domination in the industry, not "irrational", not "temporary", and not merely "superstructural" (see Dymsky, 1985). So, attempts to contest such practices have led to growing reports of discrimination and exploitation of oil workers in Ghana, resulting in protest that, in turn, has led to recriminations in the form of witch-hunting, scapegoating, and victimization of oil workers, especially those prone to unionization, by some oil companies (*Daily Guide*, 2014). More fundamentally, there is significant mismatch between where the jobs are created and areas with the most need for jobs. In turn, oil-related jobs go to people who live outside or are from outside the oil region – where most people have been displaced as fishers, fishmongers, and farmers (Obeng-Odoom, 2014a; Eduful and Hooper, 2019).

These challenges are simultaneously peculiar to oil workers but also similar to the experiences of workers in capitalist workplaces both within Ghana and elsewhere in Africa or the world at large. They are peculiar because many workers who labor on rigs are offshore and hence removed from others onshore. We know from Richard Jeffries' (1978) book – *Class, Power and Ideology in Ghana: The Railwaymen of Sekondi* – that one way workers in Sekondi-Takoradi developed a sense of unity and solidarity was that their friendships deepened in social settings – at work, in the society at large, and at home (Jeffries, 1978, pp. 191–196). It follows that being physically removed from these social institutions make the experiences of oil workers quite different: they simultaneously lack the social support of their families and other workers but it also means that their families do far more caring work at home. That said, the experiences are similar to workers in other capitalist workplaces. For instance, Margaret Peil's classic study – *The Ghanaian Factory Worker: Industrial Man in Africa* (Peil, 1972, p. 21) – showed that "Industrial workers have common problems of unsatisfactory pay and conditions, of unemployment and poor housing."

Clearly, then, libertarian paternalism in the oil sector remains wedded to the same capitalist logic of employing fewer people and exploiting those few – both to maximize profit. It can sound ironic that unemployment can be deemed a good thing, but in neoclassical models, such is a prominent line of reasoning. Here, leaving some people unemployed is seen as strategic to disciplining labor as it helps make the possibility of being sacked real to labor by creating a substantial "reserve army of labor" ready to take over existing employees' jobs (Kalecki, 1945, 1971). It is logically plausible, then, that it is not in the interest of capitalist oil companies to keep employing until the rate of unemployment is zero. Therefore, a private sector solution to the unemployment problem in Ghana is theoretically implausible.

Underemployment, discrimination, and precarious employment are more empirically verifiable in the petroleum industry in Ghana. Graphic details of such contradictions among rig workers in the petroleum industry in Ghana can be found in Ablo's studies (e.g., Ablo, 2012, 2018). Some IOCs terminate contracts with workers without resort to due process. Many "employ" workers without any employment contracts (Ablo & Overå, 2015). Generally, indigenous workers tend to earn less pay, as Table 4.6 shows.

Table 4.6 suggests that, on average, it could take two-to-three years for local labor to earn what imported labor is paid in just one year. In practice, expatriates can be paid 800 per cent higher than the Ghanaian technicians who have the same level of experience. According to one local technician, "We work in the same environment with foreign workers, but we are not entitled to the same conditions of service albeit we are exposed to the same risk in the line of duty" (*Sahara Reporters*, 2014). Expatriate workers also

Table 4.6  *Earnings (US$) in the oil and gas industry in Ghana,*
*2012–2015*

| Salary | 2012 | 2013 | 2014 | 2015 |
|---|---|---|---|---|
| Average for local labor | 40,200 | 40,500 | 55,000 | 52,000 |
| Average for Imported Labor | 139,900 | 121,600 | 118,000 | 115,000 |

*Sources:* Adapted from Hays Recruiting, 2012; 2013; 2015

have better prospects for work advancement than locals (Ablo, 2012, 2018; Obeng-Odoom, 2014a). In seeking to maximize profit, major concerns have been raised over health culture and safety processes in the oil and gas industry (Achaw & Boateng, 2012; Tetteh, 2012). While recent business theories suggest that capitalist oil companies are no longer just about profit making and many are involved in charitable giving through corporate social responsibility in oil-bearing communities (Hilson, 2014; Hilson et al., 2019), without profit maximization, most other "social responsibilities" will not be pursued. Labor exploitation remains the key and primary source of surplus in capitalist production (Marx, 1867/1990; Standing, 2009).

Sekondi-Takoradi, Ghana's oil city, has witnessed significant growth in its economy (Obeng-Odoom, 2014a; Fiave, 2017). The establishment of the Enterprise Development Centre (EDC), while not wholly for people in Sekondi-Takoradi, has contributed to the economic surge. There is much evidence (Ablo & Overå, 2015; Ablo, 2018) that local Sekondi-Takoradi people are involved in the provision of services, others who have lived in Sekondi-Takoradi for most of their lives have benefitted too, and partnerships between people from different cities in Ghana have flourished. However, the focus on driving overall national growth has diverted attention of local content policies from the material conditions of workers. In turn, local content policies make only two distinctions: Ghanaian or foreign.

The relentless pursuit of growth has also turned attention away from growing inequality in the oil city of Sekondi-Takoradi. Such a pursuit has encouraged speculative processes and activities that, while driving growth, engender social inequality (Obeng-Odoom, 2014a; Fiave, 2017). With the influx of investors and oil workers into Sekondi-Takoradi who are willing and able to offer international currency for rental accommodation, landlords have become significantly more well-to-do, while renters have generally become worse off. There has been much physical restructuring of the location of different classes. Some house owners have rented out their houses in first-class neighborhoods and moved to middle-income neighborhoods only to displace those former residents who then move further into the poorer neighborhoods. Such owners-turned-renters are, however, proportionately fewer than those compelled to look for accommodation elsewhere. Still, the outward look of the city is now more clearly class-based with Beach Road being for the wealthy and Anaji and Tanokrom less so (Obeng-Odoom, 2014a; Eduful and Hooper, 2019). For the first time in its socioeconomic history, "oil-led gentrification"(Eduful & Hooper, 2015, 2019) has become commonplace in Sekondi-Takoradi.

Also, accumulation in the city has further polarized the income and asset divide between gender. Contrary to mainstream accounts (Ross, 2008), that suggest that women *choose* to stay away from the oil industry because they are much better off doing so having obtained windfalls from their husbands who work in the industry, in Sekondi-Takoradi, indeed in the oil industry in Ghana more generally, opportunities for women have been significantly less in evidence with oil creating spaces socially constructed as "men's jobs." On the other hand, existing "women's jobs" are being systematically undermined and destroyed as presumably higher order (read, "more masculine") jobs are created (Obeng-Odoom, 2014a, 2016e; Overå, 2017). Such is evidently the case with agrarian jobs in oil-bearing peri-urban communities, where the destruction of female livelihoods has made access to food for families insecure, made it more difficult for children to be educated, and weakened family bonds as men migrate away from their wives and children to look for alternative sources of income (Adusah-Karikari, 2015; Overå, 2017). In turn, detrimental patriarchal structures are reinstated in the place of old and debilitating structures. Outside such processes in peri-urban areas, urban development activities have also displaced women. The redevelopment of Takoradi Market Circle, a trading hub for the oil-bearing region, is a case in point (Amiteye, 2015). Here, the city planners appear to have ignored the voices of women who dominate trading activities. The plan to create more stores (mostly rented by male traders) than stalls (typically occupied by women), for example, is one way that the position of men has been privileged at the expense of women. The links between patriarchy and capitalist urbanism are here given in clear form not only in the devaluation of women's labor but also in the undervaluation of female work.

Indeed, there is a third gendered problem: the neglect of women's care responsibilities in the home, that make it possible for men to work (Folbre, 2012, 2014). These "invisible hands" (Benya, 2015), then, contribute to the oil industry but in the typical androcentric character of the oil industry, this contribution is both unrecognized and undervalued.

Many men have also been made worse off by oil, of course. Indeed, as the local content policy focuses only on the *creation* of local content and not the *destruction* of local content through loss of local farming, fishing, and trading, many victims of this process have been poorly compensated or not compensated at all for their losses (Obeng-Odoom, 2014a). The point is that weaker groups have missed out on the oil boom in ways that the local content law does not anticipate. The contractual terms, institutions, and regulatory regimes are also weak. The majority shareholders – with a combined share of 86.25 per cent – in the national oil resource are international oil companies such as Tullow, Anardako, and Kosmos.

The National Oil Company, the GNPC, has only 13.75 per cent of the oil resource. In theory, it is possible to use the capture of royalties and taxation to rebalance the unequal exchange between the state, indeed Ghanaians, and foreign capital. Yet, in the case of Ghana, this regulatory power has also been surrendered. The state only negotiated to receive 5 per cent of crude oil production in royalties and much less (3 per cent) in royalties from gas (Obeng-Odoom, 2014a, pp. 52–53). Compared to the industry standards globally, Ghana's 5 per cent royalty regime is the smallest, indeed smaller than the sub-Saharan average of 7 per cent (Obeng-Odoom, 2014a, p. 153). There is a requirement for the oil TNCs to pay income tax, but the law practically makes this payment discretionary on the part of the companies because the state has to depend on the say-so of the oil TNCs to report their real taxable income, being the difference between their revenue and their cost of operation. In practice, the companies have typically paid little or no tax as they often declare that they have made zero taxable income (Obeng-Odoom, 2014a).

In addition, the oil TNCs are not required to pay profit tax. Overall, then, Ghana's oil model concedes enormous power to foreign capital – leaving very brittle contractual rights for the state. This experience epitomizes the concession model. In his 1979 classic study on mineral agreements, eminent jurist and scholar S. K. B. Asante (1979) showed the essential features of the concession: the transnational oil company makes equity investment in the oil field and practically assumes sovereignty over the host country and its resource in which the TNC has invested. By so doing, the concession grants "exclusive, extensive and plenary rights to exploit the particular natural resource" (Asante, 1979, p. 338). In addition, the oil TNCs have been granted generous terms on their imports and exports: tax exemptions on the import of equipment and supplies and tax exemptions on oil exports (Panford, 2015, 2017). The total estimate for how much the state is losing from such exemptions is not yet available, but it is known that for only one of such TNCs, the Ghanaian state will be losing USD3.8 billion in tax exemptions over the life of only one oil block (Phillips et al., 2016). Thus, through a combination of law and imperial economic calculations, a "legitimate" basis for economic exploitation has been inscribed.

Setting a limit to the economy and society is the wider environment that reminds us of the embeddedness of economy in society and society in economy (Polanyi, 1944/2001). Panford's (2015, 2017) research shows that the institutions responsible for environmental protection, notably the Environmental Protection Agency, face severe infrastructural challenges that limit its functions. In the Western Region as a whole, there is only one official with the requisite qualification to head a laboratory to ascertain environmental safety in oil and gas installations and operations. To compound the problem, this specialist faces limitations in travelling to carry out inspections, in turn, depending on the oil companies to support his site inspection through giving him "lifts." The real challenge, however, is not so much the administrative concern per se but how it compounds a more systemic challenge: the non-emphasis on the "environment" in the conceptualization of the local content program. In turn, the loss of flora and fauna and fishing stock in the city and the region (Boohene & Peprah, 2011; Hilson, 2014; Adusah-Karikari, 2015) is not seen as undermining local content.

From a more narrow, urban economic development perspective, recent international research in another oil city (Li et al., 2015, p. 317) shows that a philosophy of "production first; living second" is economically and environmentally destructive. Disregarding the environment undermines local content as massive pollution eventually discourages investment into oil cities, forcing city authorities to use "saved up" investment funds to try to clean up the city. More broadly, the environment is an organic part of local livelihoods in Sekondi-Takoradi, so any attack on it is an attack on the people supposedly being helped by local content.

In short, nudging in the petroleum industry in Ghana has worked in directing the economy towards the path of growth. Yet, libertarian paternalism is not just about moulding markets socially. It is also about how private choices are better if they are planned. In turn, libertarian paternalism is analytically analogous to Austrian thinker Friedrich Hayek's idea that the only planning that works is planning for the market (Hayek, 1945). As Thomas Leonard (2008) has pointed out in his review of research on new paternalism, much of the idea can be seen as an attempt to correct market failures. In turn, libertarian paternalism offers a criticism of mainstream economics but not a *critique* of that approach to economic analysis. Nudging leaves the fundamentals of economic growth and how it is helped by individualism and private sector expansion intact. Grounded in a restricted conception of neoliberalism as "free markets," it assumes that the key challenge is to prove that markets are not free after all and cannot be free and that intervention is needed to correct market failures. As Cass Sunstein famously noted, "Indeed, the 'market failure analogy' is the precise one here; the various categories of cognitive distortions present a similar case for collective action" (1986, p. 1140).

This is an important insight, of course, but it is not necessarily sufficient to capture the full challenge that political economy poses to mainstream economics. This challenge is not based on the size of the state but on how the state intervenes and for what ends (Stanford, 2008). It is well-known in political economy that "actually existing neoliberalism" entails intervention or nudging in this sense (see Cahill, 2010, 2014; Cahill & Konings, 2017). What political economists seek is growth with *structural transformation* (Gore, 2007), *systemic* redistribution, social protection, and ecological sustainability with contextual sensitivity (Obeng-Odoom, 2015c). So, at the fundamental level, nudging must be rooted in the idea that the market is typically socially embedded, as argued by Karl Polanyi (1944/2001), and second that the social purposes of nudging are not business-as-usual capitalist processes, but social inclusion and ecological sustainability – ideas that K. W. Kapp developed in his book, *The Social Costs of Private Enterprise* (1950/1971).

### d. The Political Economy of the Petro-Development State in Africa

Still, it is important to probe further. For a continent on which human capital policies have been advocated, designed, and widely implemented, just how typical is the Ghanaian case? Escaping the prison of this single case study is, fortunately, quite straightforward – thanks to the sustained field research conducted, especially that by the Canadian scholar-practitioner, Jesse Salah Ovadia. Ovadia's research is vast, but it can be summarized in six themes, namely: (a) investigating the case for local content, (b) examining how local content policies have been promoted by diverse groups, (c) analyzing how local content has been designed, (d) analyzing how local content has been implemented, (e) probing how local content policies compare across countries, and (f) documenting their overarching outcomes. His fieldwork has centered mostly on Nigeria and Angola, but because over 75 per cent of oil produced in Africa come from these two countries, his findings are particularly important. In any case, he has started doing and publishing research on many other African countries, including Kenya, Liberia, Mozambique, Liberia, and Uganda (see, for example, Ovadia, 2016a).

Ovadia's research has appeared in several publications, including Ovadia (2012, 2013, 2014, 2015, 2016a, 2016b, 2016c) – and these are in top outlets such as *Resources Policy* and *New Political Economy*. He has consolidated and further developed this impressive body of research in his book, *The Petro-Developmental State in Africa: Making Oil Work in Angola, Nigeria and the Gulf of Guinea* (Ovadia, 2016a). Reviewers of the book have praised the breadth and depth of Ovadia's research (see, for example, Mouan, 2016; Adunbi, 2016).More recent research has continued this genre of research (e.g., Graham and Ovadia, 2019).

Where he has not as yet covered an area geographically, there is likely no prevailing oil–human capital and local content program. If there is, as in the case of Tanzania, we have research on which to draw lessons (e.g., Siri Lange and Abel Kinyondo's 2016 work on human capital in Tanzania). Even where Ovadia has geographically studied an area, we have additional research on which to draw to contextualise Ovadia's important work. In this sense, research by Michael Zisuh Ngoasong at the Open University in the UK (see Ngoasong, 2014), the work of Adeolu Adewuyi and Ademola Oyejide (2012) on Nigeria, published in *Resources Policy,* and Sylvia Croese's (2018) study of Angola published in the *International Journal of Urban and Regional Research.*

Overall, the results of these studies on other African countries are strikingly similar to the Ghanaian case. While across Africa, human capital policies in the oil industry have enhanced local content, pursuing human capital has been a path to divergence, not convergence. Discrimination is commonly reported among workers with similar levels of human capital. Oil TNCs or IOCs prefer to recruit white Angolans to black Angolans in Angola. It is not just an internal issue; it is also international. So, the first preference is white, followed by white Angolan, then Angolan of mixed race, then black Angolans (Ovadia, 2012, pp. 405–406). Variations of this racial hierarchy can be found across Africa, where African professionals are paid significantly less than expatriate workers – even when they have similar levels of human capital and do similar amounts of work (see, for example, Ovadia, 2014, 2016a).

Beyond pay, the work conditions for expatriate staff are also substantially better, although the full extent of the difference is unknown because of a new headquarterization, a process in which elite expatriate staff are offered additional incentives at the headquarters without the knowledge of local staff. Indeed, an emerging trend is parallel employment in which there are two HR Managers, one local, the other expatriate. Of the two, the expatriate manager is given more sensitive information, which is not made available to the local manager (Ovadia, 2012; Lange & Kinyondo, 2016). More powerful – but unnamed – parallel positions for expatriates have also been documented in Angola, leading Ovadia (2012) to caption his study, "the dual nature of local content."

More frequently, though, this labor aristocracy is in terms of what Irene Browne and her colleagues (2003) call the structural forces that shape earnings inequality and that have implications for wealth inequalities. These practices, procedures, and norms that characterize work relations in the firm are usually explained by queuing theory. This is the idea that inequalities along the axis of race and gender arise because minorities are at the back of the queue for jobs and hence obtain least-paid jobs. It also explains inequalities in terms of a "filtering down" process in which minorities mainly obtain less desirable jobs that filter down to them. In turn, this theory explains gender/race inequalities as a function of the activities of firms or the urban labor market (Browne et al., 2003).

In Africa, this is not theory: it is reality. Africans are concentrated in the low-paying, low-tier positions at the workplace. Or, even when they are mid-level managers and would like to take decisions that would genuinely empower other Africans – consistent with the human capital policies, their decisions are overridden by more senior white members of staff whose preferences tend to diverge from genuine Africanization (Ovadia, 2012, p. 409). So, not only is the share of expatriates in the general workforce higher, the concentration of Africans, especially black Africans, in the degrading parts of the work process is also much higher and, almost always, decisions of even the more powerful African workers can be vetoed by even more powerful white elites. Based on this evidence, it can be argued that firms create and reinforce racial inequality through their recruitment and labor valuation practices. They cluster minorities in low paid roles (horizontal discrimination), and, arguably, discriminate against minorities by promoting only a few of them or none at all (vertical discrimination), or both. Indeed, those who are promoted have no real power as their decisions are often vetoed by white superiors.

Collusion among oil TNCs or IOCs is commonly reported. Again, in Angola and Tanzania, instead of collaborating with the state, IOCs recurrently work with one another to impede state attempts to get stronger and more meaningful contribution to local content. In turn, whether it is in Mozambique, Kenya, Uganda, Liberia, Nigeria, or Angola, TNCs, in essence, determine what local content to pursue (e.g., Ngoasong, 2014; Ovadia, 2016b). Indeed, in Nigeria, the authorities frequently waive local content requirements when, working in collusion, the oil TNCs claim that they are incapable of meeting requirements.

To its credit, local content has contributed to the growth of several small- and medium-scale industries in Africa (Ovadia, 2016a, 2016b). A 'turn around' might even be proclaimed (Croese, 2018). Yet, this change has come about at high social costs (Kapp, 1950/1971) in terms of displacement, inequalities, and exploitation. Still, there is some positive change, even if it cannot all be attributed to TNCs. Indeed, the Catholic Church in Angola has been credited with helping drive industrial development in the country (Mouan, 2016). Besides, the common strategies of the IOCs to resist further local content (Ngoasong, 2014; Lange & Kinyondo, 2016) show that the drive for local content is diffused: from the state, citizens, and global forces, as well as the fear of past problems and the aspirations for different oil futures – as argued in the case of Ghana.

There has been much collaboration among these small and medium enterprises in terms of sharing tools and ideas, as we see in the case of Nigeria (Adewuyi & Oyejide, 2012). However, the distance between TNCs and local small and medium scale industries appears to be growing. The nature of the commonly adopted TNC approach to local content – as Michael Ngoasong (2014) has detailed in his contribution to *Energy Policy* – replicate the labor hierarchies in the class relations and in the resulting industrial structure in Africa. In terms of class relations, TNCs prefer to work with local industries where the owners are mainly foreigners or staff are foreign educated and frequently both. Their usual justification – disputed, nevertheless, by Adewuyi and Oyejide (2012) and Ngoasong (2014) – is that the African alternatives are not as efficient, that their quality is not as high, or that they do not have the technical expertise to meet the specific needs of the oil TNCs (see, for example, Ovadia, 2012, 2016a; Lange & Kinyondo, 2016), recalling the discredited unequal human capital endowment thesis (see Dymski, 1985).

A finding – recurrently highlighted in the studies – is corruption, elite capture, and patronage. How Ovadia has interpreted this set of findings is controversial in three ways. First, he places far more weight on these issues than his other empirical findings – without giving reasons for doing so. His interviews are not counted or tallied, so he finds interviewees who identify corruption, collusion, structural inequality, racism, inefficiencies, and monopoly. If so, how then does he conclude that it is "mismanagement, inaction on the part of IOCs, and a political context beyond the government's control" (Ovadia, 2012, p. 406), which holds the prospects of local content back? On what basis does he limit the concerns about local content to "legal and institutional frameworks" only (Ovadia, 2016b, p. 20)? Why does he "argue for their inclusion in an overall framework for promoting better natural resource governance in sub-Saharan Africa" (Ovadia, 2014)?

Omolade Adunbi (2016), one of the reviewers of Ovadia's book, identifies this tension when he notes, "The book presents an overly optimistic view of global capitalism" (Adunbi, 2016, p. 342). The reviewer prefers Ovadia to take his research to its logical conclusion: the determinism of corruption.

According to him, "hidden in this narrative of African elite capitalism is the prevalence of elite accumulation that is largely responsible for Angola and Nigeria's underdevelopment after many years of petro-capitalism." If so, the reviewer is correct to wonder "how a change in policy towards creating more spaces of accumulation would change that dramatically."

As the existing studies also show that the degree of these issues depends in part on policy design, the power of the TNCs, and wider issues about the local context, the only way to reconcile the contradictions in Ovadia's otherwise impressive oeuvre is to say that addressing the legal issues and improving "institutions" can make local content truly a silver bullet. That is, there is far more information assymetry in Angola than there is in Nigeria (Ovadia, 2014, 2016a, 2016b, 2016c) and, in Tanzania, the human capital policies are less stringent and less elaborate; indeed, "The Act does not specify any percentages for different categories of staff" to be employed where (Lange & Kinyondo, 2016, p. 1098). So, human capital policies have contributed to the bifurcation of the economy, but if they are properly designed and the local institutions are fixed, local content will become a panacea.

Ovadia's empirical research is rich. It shows that, in spite of widespread – even if varied – implementation of human capital policies in the oil industry, there are major problems of corruption, collusion, structural inequality, structural racism, and monopolistic control of African economies. Part of the reason for these outcomes is, as Ovadia's studies show, a particular common approach adopted by the TNCs in meeting human capital issues and part of the reason relates to the nature of capitalist work processes. Ovadia's interpretation that all these are the result of implementation challenges is unconvincing, but understandable. His work is largely atheoretical and, hence, he struggles to sort out effects from causes and how these two are dialectically interlinked and connected to the global economic system. It is extremely confusing to call for more participation when, in fact, and by his own evidence, the problem is one of control. Nevertheless, Ovadia's work and, indeed, the current wider body of research on human capital reach an overarching consensus: at this epoch in Africa's political economy, human capital policies as designed and implemented have not promoted inclusive African development. Rather, they have worsened intergroup inequality in Africa and further institutionalise the underdevelopment of Africa.

## CONCLUSION

This chapter has problematized the orthodox economics assumptions and claims about three crucial questions in political economy, namely: What is the role of human capital in the process of economic development? How is this role transformed during a period of resource abundance? And what is the place of education in empowering labor to reclaim or transform surplus value in the process of uneven development, underdevelopment, and alternative development? Drawing on recent evidence collected from Ghana personally and field research conducted by others – especially Jesse Ovadia – in the rest of Africa, it has demonstrated that an oil boom does not necessarily lead to an education doom. Both demand for and supply of education have increased substantially in Ghana since it became an oil economy. This deviation from theory can be explained by the idea of "frames," that is, where employment opportunities in the oil and gas industry are *framed* as dependent on obtaining scarce education in oil and gas, the level of interest in and support for education by the public, private, and civil society sectors tend to be high, as is the resulting demand for educational services. Importantly, none of these increases has been at the expense of general education. Rather, the demand for and supply of general education too have increased. There is also evidence that the state invests in quality education.

In spite of these increased levels of education, the ensuing employment levels and returns on employment have been substantially lower than expected and different from what has been predicted by orthodox theory of human capital. Far from workers automatically taking leading roles in the oil industry, the story is more nuanced. Some African workers have benefited, but they have benefited substantially less than foreign workers. Many local workers have missed out, and jobs have gone to areas that have not lost too many workers to the oil industry. Women have remained at the margins of oil work. The concept of human capital in a minerals society embodies many socio-economic contradictions and, if at all, increased education and experience have led to widening, not declining, social stratification in Africa. Accordingly, this particular explanation, centered in human capital theory, could be called into question too. The next typical explanation of inequality between Africa and the rest of the world, international trade, therefore, ought to be considered.

### Notes

1 http://ghanaoilonline.org/.
2 The study has over 1000 citations in Google Scholar (see http://scholar.google.com.au/scholar?hl=en&q=Natural+resources%2C+education%2C+and+economic+development&btnG=&as_sdt=1%2C5&as_sdtp=).
3 Thanks to a lecturer on the program who offered this information.

# 5

## International Trade

### INTRODUCTION

Do the barriers to trade provide a more compelling explanation for Africa's inability to "catch up" and the social stratification on the continent? Many economists think so and, significantly, many African leaders share this view, too. Indeed, on March 21, 2018, most members of the African Union signed the African Continental Free Trade Area (AfCFTA) Agreement. Under this arrangement, African countries are expected to rely even more on transnational corporations (TNCs) as the key stepping stones for global trade and, with it, the redistribution of income between groups and regions (UNCTAD, 2018). The previous chapter considered aspects of this interest in TNCs, and Chapter 8 will revisit AfCFTA in a bit more detail (vision, strategy, and differences and similarities with the current trade regime).

As AfCFTA is a vision of internal African continental trade for the future with little to say about global and international trade, it is crucially important to analyse the current natural-resource–based trade regime, as it is the existing trade structure. Much of that focus is the staple of existing research (see, for example, Mutambara, 2013; Feddersen et al., 2017; Dialga, 2018). So, to date, we do not clearly understand the urban and regional themes of international trade. TNCs are increasingly taking power from the hands of resource-rich urban authorities in Africa, with major implications for the distribution of the urban commons and the sovereignty of African peoples and their territory. This "growing sphere of influence of transnational corporations" (Obeng-Odoom, 2015c, pp. 52–53) is, however, poorly understood. Research on urban governance has grown, of course, but the growing uneven relationship between transnational corporations and urban authorities has received little empirical attention (Obeng-Odoom, 2013b, 2016a; Resnick, 2014a, 2014b; Fuseini,

2016; Croese, 2018). TNCs that engage in extraction and production of fuel and minerals receive some attention, but TNCs involved in the storage and transfer of fuels, as well as the governance of urban retailers of gasoline or petrol, have not.

A key reason is that the standard approaches to studying trade typically consider foreign direct investment as separate from free trade, which, in turn, is separate from urban and regional development (Harris, 1991; Westbrook, 2004, 2017). Such separate treatment of trade in economic theory might have technical justification, but it is devoid of contemporary political-economic relevance. In practice, the power of TNCs blurs the lines between trade – the free exchange of goods and services – and foreign direct investment, often seen as a control of territory. Microeconomic analyses of territorial questions exist in the form of Leontief input-output modeling or, as in some aspects of economic geography and urban economics, as discreet and disconnected foci of analyses.

Theories of "unequal exchange" – regardless of whether or not they were Marxist in orientation – provided simple binaries of "core" and "periphery" or those at the top/bottom of a ladder of development (Harris, 1991). Here, scholars as diverse as Samir Amin and Ha-Joon Chang have used their analyses of exchange to promote protectionism, without considering urban and regional questions and how foreign direct investment (FDIs) and trade need to be analyzed simultaneously.

Appropriating this conceptual apparatus, some mainstream economists such as Michael Lipton have exploited this deficit to promote free trade. By claiming that cities in Africa – like capital – exploit rural areas (or workers in the Marxist schema), such economists have inspired anti-urban sentiments in Africa (Harris, 1991; Westbrook, 2004, 2017). Indeed, to this day, mainstream economists tend to focus on using urban–rural dichotomies as alternatives to class analysis, as they claim that protectionism leads to over-urbanization, as cities in protectionist societies are also the central points of urban favoritism (see, for example, Karayalcin & Yilmazkuday, 2014). In turn, such analyses advocate greater trade.

That is what is canvassed in the "stages of growth" thesis in urban economics. Centered around increasing agglomeration economies, declining transaction costs, and technological advancement, advocates claim that firms become transnational through their autonomous strategies (Stilwell, 1995, pp. 114–117; Obeng-Odoom, 2016b; 2017b). This transnationalism is considered to be a key path for global urban economic development. Oliver Williamson, a leading proponent, won the Nobel Prize in Economics in 2009 for such ideas. So, his work requires attention.

Williamson (1981, 2002, 2009) claims that TNCs arise because of their own internal strategies or innovations that economize on transaction costs. To reduce transaction costs, it is more efficient for a single firm to subsume activities under its own managerial control rather than exchanging services with many smaller entities. TNCs exist not only to seek to make a profit, Williamson argues, but also to govern. For Williamson, TNCs offer an alternative mode of governance that is superior to both the market and the state in terms of what he calls "affirmative economic purposes" that are underpinned by efficiency (Williamson, 1981, pp. 1538; 2002; 2009). While Williamson recognizes that TNCs may sometimes falter, he contends that they are inherently a better mode of governance and hence should neither be regulated nor treated "inhospitably."

Although highly influential, these claims have received limited empirical attention, in Africa, at least. There are vast empirical literatures on TNCs and trade, of course, but they are heavily centered on debates about their relationship with national governments (see, for a thorough discussion, Darity & Davis, 2005; Smith, 2016). Representative work in these debates includes Hardt and Negri (2000, 2004) and Korten (1995, 1999). These books have received much praise, but also significant criticism. In his extensive review of Hardt and Negri's first book, Samir Amin (2005) argued that the authors downplay the power of imperial states in advancing seemingly new forces of transnationalism. Critics of Korten's work show that Korten does not sufficiently analyze the relationship between TNCs and the nation-state. As Susan George (1996) explains, Korten's attempt to resolve unbalanced state–TNC relationships assigns too much power to the TNCs and no role to the state. Kuecker (2006), by contrast, complains that Korten attributes too much power to the state, to the point that it becomes intrusive. So, both proponents and opponents focus on the nation-state or central state, and their solutions can be arranged according to whether they favor more or less intervention by the nation-state.

A major problem with this debate over the role of TNCs vis-à-vis the state is that, much like the ongoing debate over globalization, it ignores key analytical distinctions (see, for example, Clausing, 2019a, 2019b). Existing research and policy analysis ends up recommending a wholesale, one-size-fits-all solution (either socialism or improved capitalism) to every social problem instead of applying different solutions to different conditions. In this case, the missing element is the distinction between TNCs that engage in manufacturing or production of services, on the one hand, and TNCs that control natural resources and public utilities, on the other. Yet, different types of TNCs generate quite distinct social relations (UNCTAD, 2007).

In addition to ignoring different categories of TNC activity, there has been a tendency to ignore the level of government involved in the areas of TNC operations outside the home country. The relationship between TNCs and subnational authority has received much less attention than their negotiations with national governments. Almost the only research of note about local government is research about how cities in the Global North have become global and how those cities in the south are globalizing (Sassen, 1991; Grant, 2009). However, in order to understand how TNCs are affecting the commons in Africa, we must focus attention on the subnational level too because it is increasingly becoming the point at which TNCs are engaging the nation-state. It is in this sense too that David Westbrook (2004, 2017) uses the idea of "the City of Gold." "The essence of the city," writes Westbrook (2017, p. 146), "is that economic integration can be used to create human connections that span spaces in complicated ways not reducible to the nation state."

Westbrook provides "an apology for global capitalism in a time of discontent," to use the subtitle of his book, on the basis that the current version of TNC-dominated capitalism is not perfect, but it was constructed to contest a worse problem: Hitler-type nationalism that was sweeping across the world. Thus, although still problematic, the current global political economy is far superior to protectionism. This "City of Gold," then, must be defended both analytically and politically.

Specifically, this chapter examines (1) publicly available data on the municipal activities of TNCs culled from their own corporate reports; (2) the powers of local governments enshrined in local laws vis-à-vis the protections of TNCs under international law; (3) public opinion of municipal residents as captured in various surveys; (4) the results of scientific studies, including those that test the chemical composition of fuels sold by TNCs; and (5) those studies that subject the exercise of political power to social scientific analyses.

On these bases, it can be argued that, although they are not accountable to any electorate, transnational corporations (TNCs) in Africa play significant roles in planning and governing cities in Africa. TNCs effectively manage important aspects of African life through control of municipal utilities, through the corporate governance of natural resources held by Africans in common, and through ad hoc investment practices that facilitate the private appropriation of socially created rents.

While often overlooked, TNCs also control urban mobility through their supply of second-hand cars and motor bicycles, the building and maintenance of roads, and the export of toxic fuels for use in cities in Africa where alternative public transport is limited and has remained so because of directed and externally imposed "advice." On the one hand, the activities of TNCs are legitimized by arguments that denigrate the capacity of Africans to govern themselves and to manage the development of natural resources without the supervision of European, American, Japanese, or Chinese companies. The patronizing critique begins with a commentary on the actions or failure to act by African states, which is treated as evidence of their incompetence and atavism. Africans are presumed in this way to be immobilized by the "resource curse," according to which an abundance of natural resources leads to government corruption and economic instability.

This diagnosis is followed by the use of terms such as "corporate social responsibility" to describe the ways outsiders should help Africans deal with the "curse" of wealth. This discourse serves as the basis for claims that TNCs are essential in guiding Africans along the appropriate paths of development. On the other hand, TNCs assume "illegitimate authority" (Susan George, 2014). They arrogate to themselves municipal power and ignore what surveys show city residents need. They focus on achieving their own ends and use their legal power to parry complaints about their infringement on the sovereignty of subnational states and divided cities as they engage in environmental pillage. Therefore, like property economics (Chapter 2), land reform (Chapter 3), and human capital (Chapter 4), international trade is also a problematic explanation of social stratification in Africa and provides a misleading solution. The "City of Gold" can be helpful analytically, but it also is politically flawed, as will be shown in the last part of this book.

The rest of the present chapter is divided into four sections. The first places the trade question in a wider perspective, seeking to highlight the key issues in the trade debates in Africa. This scene-setting background is followed by the second section – an analysis of theoretical perspectives to clarify confusion in theoretical issues, to generate specific questions, and to point to data needed to verify key propositions. In the third section, case studies in Africa are analyzed to ascertain in what ways they converge, diverge, or transcend the posited mainstream claims about trade, while, in the final section, the chapter reflects on existing approaches to rein in and transcend the illegitimate authority of TNCs.

THE WIDER CONTEXT OF AFRICA'S TRADE IN THE WORLD
SYSTEM

World trade has been substantial but, as recently as 2016, Africa's share of world exports in merchandise was only 2 per cent (Table 5.1). A decline from the 2013 export share of 3.2 per cent (UNCTAD, 2016, p. 2), this trend signals much wider problems. Indeed, as shown in Table 5.1, across various trade indicators, Africa runs trade deficits, whether in terms of trade in merchandise or in services. Africa's foreign direct investment similarly showed a negative balance in 2016.

Expressed as a share of world trade balance, Africa runs deficits on nearly every indicator (see Table 5.1). The issue is not simply about increasing the volume of exports. Indeed, even in times when the quantum of African exports has risen substantially, the returns from such trade flows have been insubstantial. Africa's trade system can, therefore, be regarded as as an "impoverishing model" (Dialka, 2018).

For some political economists, the solution is to pursue protectionism given the centrality of trade deficits in the growing debt crises on the continent. The size of the debt burden in sub-Sahara Africa alone was $57.5 billion in the 1980s, which meant that, of the $50 billion that the region could obtain from exports, nothing could be retained for social investments because it was barely sufficient to pay off the principal of the loan. The situation worsened in 1987, when the size of the debt increased to $138 billion and the value of exports whittled down to only $35 billion (Danso, 1990). The debt forgiveness of the early 2000s, under the Highly Indebted Poor Countries (HIPC) initiatives, helped to bring temporary relief. However, Africa's debt problem persists and is worsening. From 2010 to 2018, the number of countries unable to service their debts increased by 100 per cent. Between 2013 and the first quarter of 2018, the percentage of sub-Saharan African countries that were at high risk of debt distress increased from 20 to 40 per cent (Giles and Pilling, 2018). Whether protectionism is an answer, however, depends on what explains Africa's growing debt crisis.

The standard explanation for this debt crisis is centered on three themes (see Giles & Pilling, 2018, and the International Monetary Fund, 2018a, 2018b); namely, (a) undisciplined public expenditure that should be addressed through austerity measures and the withdrawal of the state from the public provision of resources, (b) increasing interests rates, and

Table 5.1 *Indicators of trade in the world, 2016*

|  | Trade in Merchandise (in USD, Millions) | | | Trade in Services (in USD, Millions) | | |
|---|---|---|---|---|---|---|
|  | Exports | Imports | Balance | Exports | Imports | Balance |
| World | 15,986,095.00 | 16,150,393.00 | −164,298.00 | 4,879,300.00 | 4,797,410.00 | 81,890.00 |
| Developing Economies | 6,988,373.00 | 6,591,306.00 | 397,067.00 | 1,435,740.00 | 1,817,660.00 | −381,920.00 |
| Africa | 348,528.00 | 493,887.00 | −145,359.00 | 95,720.00 | 144,340.00 | −48,620.00 |
| African Share of World Trade | 2.18 | 3.06 | 88.47 | 1.96 | 3.01 | - 59.37 |

**Foreign Direct Investment (in USD, Millions)**

|  | Outflows | Inflows | Current Balance |
|---|---|---|---|
| World | 1,452,468.00 | 1,746,423.00 | 276,769.00 |
| Developing Economies | 383,429.00 | 646,030.00 | 168,958.00 |
| Africa | 18,173.00 | 59,373.00 | −129,136.00 |
| African Share of World FDI | 1.25 | 3.40 | −46.66 |

*Source:* UNCTAD, 2018, Key indicators by economy, table 6.1, pp. 86–97

Table 5.2 *Public debt in sub-Saharan Africa, 2009–2018*

| | | | Percentage of GDP | | | |
|---|---|---|---|---|---|---|
| Year | Revenue | Expenditure | Gross Debt | Primary Balance | Overall Balance | Interest* Payments |
| 2009 | 13.8 | 17.9 | 24.0 | −3.2 | −4.0 | 0.8 |
| 2010 | 15.2 | 18.8 | 22.3 | −2.8 | −3.6 | 0.8 |
| 2011 | 18.3 | 19.3 | 23.3 | 0.0 | −1.00 | 1.0 |
| 2012 | 16.6 | 17.9 | 23.0 | −0.2 | −1.3 | 1.1 |
| 2013 | 14.9 | 18.1 | 24.4 | −2.0 | −3.2 | 1.2 |
| 2014 | 14.5 | 17.9 | 26.2 | −2.2 | −3.4 | 1.2 |
| 2015 | 12.9 | 17.0 | 31.5 | −2.7 | −4.1 | 1.4 |
| 2016 | 12.2 | 16.7 | 36.7 | −2.8 | −4.5 | 1.7 |
| 2017 | 12.8 | 18.00 | 40.0 | −3.3 | −5.2 | 1.9 |
| 2018 | 13.9 | 18.2 | 42.0 | −2.4 | −4.3 | 1.9 |

* Interest Payments = Primary Balance − Overall Balance
*Source:* Adapted from International Monetary Fund, 2018a, *World Economic and Financial Surveys, Fiscal Monitor,* tables A17–A21

(c) inadequate revenues that must be addressed through increased consumer taxation and, in particular, international trade.

However, the data in Table 5.2 raise questions about the existing canonical interpretations. For example, government revenue has remained nearly stagnant at about 14.0 per cent of GDP between 2009 and 2018. Government expenditure has grown, but only slightly (0.3 per cent between 2009 and 2018). Yet, gross debt has nearly doubled.

So, alternative interpretations are needed. One starting point is to view Africa's debt crises as a function of three interdependent factors; namely, slavery, colonialism, and the international financial system. Like the current crisis that creates the situation in which the surplus value created largely by African workers is appropriated in the form of debt payment, slavery and the system of indentured labor created a revolving door between an illegal trade in subhumans (Africans) and a legal system in which African laborers had to work to secure their freedom, which, itself, was pyrrhic because it was curtailed by colonial enslavement and resource plunder. Thus, colonialism was, in essence, a more legalized slave system in which African labor became controlled and African economies became increasingly dependent on the economies of the slaver-colonizers. The international financial system, a capitalist culmination of these pre-capitalist processes, entrenched a global system of dependency and debt.

This complex story of slavery, colonialism, and financial capitalism on a world scale requires more systematic illustration.

Slavery has provided the framework for how Africa and Africans have been engaged to this day. A system in which Africa and Africans counted for little or nothing, the slave framework cast Africans as providers of free energy for the world and nothing for itself. The world's "Wretched of the Earth," as noted in the introduction of this book, Africans are seen as the cheap labor to be used and abused, their resources to be plundered, their spaces to be utilized for experiments and speculation, and their land to be confiscated without compensation. That was evidently what John Locke's theory of property and slavery taught (see Chapters 2 and 3). As subhumans, Africans could not possess land. Dispossessing Africans of their land was just because the slaver could put the land to better uses, including ensuring the prosperity of slave economies such as England whose economic prosperity was tied to the appropriation of slave land and the use and abuse of slaves (Beckles, 2013, pp. 18–19). In this system, the world was indebted to Africa for its contribution of human labor and energy. The world owed Africa the cost of its resources. The world owed Africa ideas. The world also owed Africa the opportunity cost of enslavement. In a faux repayment, the Global North claimed to officially abolish this slave system. Yet, what it did was to blank out the debt owed to Africa and, in its place, rewrite a new code to enslave Africans and to get them indebted in a new colonial division of labor.

Mainstream analysts try to obfuscate these relationships by appealing to the legal doctrine of "privity" and "remoteness" that confines slavery to a brief *moment* in world history that happened so long ago that its effects are long gone. Advocates of slave-based explanations, on the other hand, point to how Africans have a "living memory" of the relationships (Beckles, 2013, p. 16). Others such as Robbert Maseland, the Dutch mainstream economist, seek to use "rigorous" econometrics and large datasets to prove that even the more recent colonialism is too remote. According to him:

Since independence, African states have followed an institutional and economic development path that is determined less and less by their colonial origins and more by their own characteristics and contemporary environment. Indeed, I show that some geographical and social features of the environment are becoming more prominent determinants of institutional development. (Maseland, 2018, p. 284)

Not only is this account of history and modern political economy logically implausible, the datasets that form the basis of the claims are also discredited (Jerven, 2013, 2015; see also the discussion of this problem in the introductory chapter). More fundamentally, this claim grossly neglects the effects of what Professor Mamadou Koulibaly has called, "the servitude of the colonial pact" or, to use the original title of his book, *Les Servitude du Pacte Colonial* (Koulibaly, 2008). This colonial yoke remains in place but its effects are, arguably, even worse.

Consider the case of the current ex-colonies of France. Most of them are locked in the so-called CFA Franc Zone, which, according to Professor Koulibaly, "represents a state-controlled zone of cooperation with, interestingly, the levers of control based in Paris, from where the priority is the interests of France. The satellite states that are members of this zone are dispersed in West and Central Africa (Koulibaly et al., 2011, n.p.)." This CFA or *Communauté Financière d'Afrique* – French Community of Africa – zone is held together by the Francophone Africa's link to the French currency – the Franc and now the Euro – from colonial times to date. This zone is quite large. In fact it is two zones in one. In the words of Gary Busch (2008):

The first is that of the West African Economic and Monetary Union (WAEMU) which comprises eight West African countries (Benin, Burkina Faso, Guinea-Bissau, Ivory Coast, Mali, Niger, Senegal and Togo). The second is that of the Central African Economic and Monetary Community (CEMAC) which comprises six Central African countries (Cameroon, Central African Republic, Chad, Congo-Brazzaville, Equatorial Guinea and Gabon). This division corresponds to the pre-colonial AOF (Afrique Occidentale Française) and the AEF (Afrique Équatoriale Française), with the exception that Guinea-Bissau was formerly Portuguese and Equatorial Guinea Spanish).

Regardless, it is the French treasury that fixes the convertibility to the Franc and, now, the Euro. In turn, it is France that determines, through currency manipulations, how much trade the countries can do and in what ways such trade will benefit France. The monetary dynamics strongly define this colonial pact, but there are also other aspects of the pact. The following summary is based on extensive research by specialists (Busch, 2008; Koulibaly, 2008; Koulibaly et al., 2011; Lehmann, 2012; Jabbar, 2013):

- France has monopolistic rights over natural resources in the ex-colonies, entailing being the first to be given the chance to buy and ultimately decide, in France, how the resources must be used.
- French companies must, to this day, be given the first option to take on the contracts of any national infrastructure projects and government projects, regardless of their quotes. Only if France is not interested are other bids entertained.

- Ex-colonies must be part of the French monetary zone, which means that to secure so-called "stability"
  o central banks take direction from France
  o the fourteen CFA Zone African countries must keep at least half their national reserves in an "Operations Account" at the French Treasury
  o African countries must borrow their own money at commercial interest rates if they need more of their own reserves (because, according to France, charging this interest rate incetivizes financial dicipline).
  o Even if they are willing to pay the interest rates, the African countries cannot be given more than 20 per cent of the previous year's publicly collected revenues.
  o The money in the operations account is invested by the French Treasury on the French Stock Exchange (in its own name) – but the Africans are not allowed to use their own money that way and although the earning are supposed to be returned to the pool, no systematic accounting is done for the Africans to know what happens to their money.
  o France reserves veto powers to override decisions taken by the various central banks or governors of various central banks in this zone.
- Agreement to keep French military bases that can intervene in national affairs to protect French commercial interests. In essence, a permanent and physical reminder that France will not tolerate any "disobedience." Given that all military equipment must also be obtained from France, this imperial overlord can also prepare for any serious incursion by any disobedient servant.

The effect of these arrangements is to transfer rents from Africa to the Global North through France. Like the slave system, African workers' labor and the labor of other Africans at home and on farms contribute to strengthen the French–EU currency. In turn, France is able to maintain a much stronger economy, among others, through easier access to African markets and the power to enter other markets as well. On these bases, and drawing on the principles of cumulative change as variously developed by the original institutional economists such as Veblen, Myrdal, Galbraith, and Kapp, the so-called diminishing effects of colonialism argued by apologists of the system – including the Dutch economist Robbert Maseland, the white South African politician Helen Zille, and the white American Bruce Gilley of Portland State University – must be dismissed.

The key point is that this colonial system of a "new international division of labor" was *patterned* after the slave framework, so the connexion is not just through living memory (Beckles, 2013): it is living in this reality daily in ways that immortalize past memories. A Lockean system of property, post-slavery colonialism had distinctive characteristics. First, Africa had to consume what it does not produce, produce what it does not consume, and produce in raw form for others to process what it needs to consume but only in degraded forms. Second, prices of the products in which Africa specialized had a tendency to fluctuate widely, while the prices of the manufactures in which the Global North specialized were far more stable and often rising. Third, TNCs, under this system, pay little to no taxes. Fourth, in spite of this uneven terrain that left African countries with little resources, Africa still had to take care of its basic needs and basic social infrastructure, including education, housing, and health, in which centuries of colonialism had underinvested. It was, as Walter Rodney (1972) showed, the postcolonial governments who had to consistently seek to provide very basic infrastructure that did not exist or existed in basic form to facilitate the plunder of African resources. For Africa and Africans, the only way was to borrow.

In this context, the international financial system reinforced these problems by both default and design. Not only is it based on speculation, it is also designed to reinforce these structural inequalities. There is the case of the Francophone African countries and their exploitative relationship with France (Busch, 2008; Koulibaly, 2008, Koulibaly et al., 2011; Lehmann, 2012; Jabbar, 2013), but there are also other channels in which debt is reproduced.

According to Alex Danso (1990), the African countries borrowed because it was quite cheap to do so. But, over time, when the African countries were deeply involved, the rules changed. The USA increased its interest rates and made the terms of trade progressively onerous. The emergence of private banks complicated the picture. In this system, trade by the Global North was dominated by powerful TNCs. The grammar of trade itself – denominating transactions in Euros and dollars – created a huge advantage in favor of those countries where these currencies are printed. As more of these currencies were demanded, their prices rose and it cost the Africans even more to get sufficient currency for this global trade. In this regime, any upward swings push Africa into debt. So, the adoption of floating interest rates that made borrowing more expensive put Africa in a precarious position. The 1973–1974 and 1979–1980 oil crises were cases in point, as they made it more expensive to import petroleum. In turn, the African countries had to borrow more and become, as a consequence, more indebted. Not all the debt comes from supposed necessaries, however. The Global North also sells destructive weapons to Africa, after helping create security "risks" that enable the sale of such ammunition.

A startling aspect of this international financial system is that it enables the creation of credit, facilitates their private appropriation, and encourages most of the loans to be reinvested in the West. This feature of the system is discussed at length in the book *Africa's Odious Debts*, authored by Léonce Ndikumana and James Boyce (2011) and widely reviewed by scholars such as John Weeks (2011), Mfaniseni Fana Sihlongonyane (2012), and Floribert Ngaruko (2015). Thomas Sankara, the revolutionary lender of Burkina Faso, understood odious debt well, including its intimate connection to economic slavery, and neocolonialism, disguised as "financial aid" or "technical assistance" (Murrey, 2018). Starting with credit given under pressure by the executive class of politicians in the Global North who are stakeholders in, and often have considerable power over the global financial system, odious debt tends to enslave the debtor. Whether these elite political leaders in the Global North are part of the global financial system is moot. What is important for our analysis is that by giving out substantial loans when the system knows or should have known that such loans set in place a dynamic of private appropriation, that it does not – procedurally at least – have the endorsement of the public it seeks to serve, and it does not serve the public, then a debt-creating machine can be said to be a consanguine part of the global financial system.

Extractivist in essence, this finance system siphons Africa's resources away from the continent. This capital flight – or the outflow of African resources through private accounts into the West to support Western development – is a public debt to the African peoples. However, the outflows constitute a private gain to the international financial system whose agents include leading politicians in the West and elsewhere. Again, this system recalls the slavery–neocolonialism complex. So, between 1970 and 1996, Africa's debt to certain countries was $178 billion, but its external assets in the same group of countries amounted to $193 billion. In turn, Africa was, strictly speaking, a net creditor to the countries to which it was supposed to be indebted (Ndikumana & Boyce, 2011, p. 9). More recently, "[i]n 2010, developing countries received US$455 billion as inflow from the West in the form of Official Development Assistance…however, lost US$827 billion as outflow to the West in the form of foreign public debt service…and reparation of profits by multinationals" (Yimoview, 2018, p. 186). So, the system creates a complex mosaic of inflows to Africa only to set in place a parallel conduit of outflows in the form of private investments that are paid for by the African public as "public debt." It is this system that the World Trade Organisation (WTO) stands for, although, it tries to make some modest revisions from time to time, reflecting sustained anti free trade campaigns.

Africa's growing debt, then, is partly the result of seeking to correct the infrastructural deficits created from years of colonialism, a system patterned after enslavement. This debt also comes in part because of the import of luxuries, especially cars, and their ancillaries, especially fuel. The debt also arises partly from the purchase of destructive goods such as guns and weapons, partly because of the loss in revenue from both resource TNCs' tax holidays and their evasion of even modest levels of tax, and particularly because of the TNC-based private appropriation of socially generated rents (Obeng-Odoom, 2017b). Indeed, it has been reported that Ghana, for example, loses over 200 million dollars annually in tax revenues due to the nefarious activities of service providers of the petroleum sector in order to evade tax.[1] So, the government's recent celebration of the reduction of the debt burden from 73 per cent (December 2016) to 68.6 per cent (end of September 2017) based on borrowing at lower interest rates as "a sustainable path" (see Ministry of Finance, 2018, p. 29) is questionable. Between 2008 and 2016, debt-to-GDP ratio increased from 32 per cent to 73 per cent. This "risk" led lenders to impose higher interest rates, which, in turn, led to interest payments that consumed 45 per cent of tax revenues and 6.8 per cent of GDP in 2016 (Ministry of Finance, 2018, p. 29).

It seems, then, that the aid/public borrowing route is not just dead; it is a dead end. What we have here is not simply a case of the corruption of aid or the corrupting influences of aid in terms of leading to inflation or dependency, for example, as Dambisa Moyo's (2009) *Dead Aid* argues (Weeks, 2011). *Africa's Odious Debt* is not behaviorial economics, as *Dead Aid* claims. They sit, instead, opposite to each other. The debt problem is the story of structural mechanisms that underpin the global financial system. Floribert Ngaruko (2015, p. 220) sums up the case made by Ndikumana and Boyce clearly:

Specifically, the authors consider four modalities whereby foreign borrowing can be translated into capital flight. The first is that of flight-fuelled foreign borrowing, whereby private wealth holders first move funds into an offshore bank account, and then borrow back the money from the same bank. The second modality is that of debt-driven capital flight. Under this modality, the influx of borrowed money

[1] Reported originally by the *Ghana News Agency* and republished on the official website of the Ghana Chamber of Bulk Oil Distribution Companies https://cbodghana.com/ghana-loses-200-million-over-tax-evasion-in-petroleum-downstream/ under the caption 'Ghana loses $200 million over tax evasion in Petroleum Downstream' (accessed 18 June 2018).

pushes up the value of the domestic currency in the short run while, in the long run, as the stock of debt and the prospect for depreciation of the domestic currency grow, it prompts the concerned elites to send money abroad in hard currency accounts offshore while the value of the local currency is artificially inflated. The third modality is that of flight-driven foreign borrowing, *whereby* capital flight generates demand for replacement funds that are borrowed from foreign lenders. The fourth modality is debt-fuelled capital flight, whereby the beneficiaries of loan-siphoning arrangements such as kickbacks, government contracts, inflated procurement costs, ghost projects, etc. then park part or all of the proceeds in safe havens abroad.

In these circumstances, it is trade, the most fundamental of the debates, that requires further analysis. Its advocacy would seem compelling: rather than borrowing, with all these problems, trade would appear to be a panacea. TNCs, central figures in international trade, have received much attention for that and other reasons – but not in terms of their role in international trade centered at the subnational level where most of today's global trade takes place.

## TRANSNATIONAL CORPORATIONS, TRADE, AND URBAN TRANSFORMATION: THEORETICAL PROPOSITIONS

It is important to understand the posited analytical relationships between TNCs and urban development in theory in order to know which data to seek, how to interpret what we find, and what to reasonably expect in the future. That is why theoretical propositions are needed, why they must precede actual evidence, and why theorizing is preferable to moralizing about TNCs.

## STANDARD ECONOMIC THEORIES

In *The Spatial Economy: Cities, Regions, and International Trade*, Fujita, Krugman, and Venables (1999) provide one way of analyzing TNCs in relation to cities, centered on (1) internal firm investments (such as technological advancements), (2) wider incentives offered by urban and national authorities that lower transaction costs, and (3) urbanization economies that enhance the profits of firms and improve urban conditions. Other orthodox economists offer slightly different versions of how relationships between firms and urban areas evolve. But there is a consensus that (1) TNCs offer a mutually beneficial relationship with cities, (2) firms mainly respond to urban environments and their comparative advantage, and (3) firms do not shape those environments except in ways that benefit urban residents and urban authorities (Obeng-Odoom, 2016b). These theories focus mostly on economic growth, but they predict that such growth translates into equitable urban economic development.

According to Williamson (1981, 2002, 2009) and other proponents of direct investment by TNCs, this "trickle down" leads to global income and wealth convergence, which is what justifies accumulation and concentration of wealth by TNCs. Even though Peter Self (1993) famously warned that when TNCs turn into a "government by the market," they would almost certainly create major social problems, new institutional economics theories predict that such a social arrangement generates more efficient and effective urban governance. In this respect at least, that is in the promotion of free trade, neoclassical economists are similar, as Kimberly Clausing's latest book, *Open: The Progressive Case for Free Trade, Immigration, and Global Capital* (Clausing, 2019), shows.

## NON-MAINSTREAM ANALYSIS: STRUCTURALISM, KEYNESIANISM, AND MARXISM

Structuralist, Keynesian, and Marxist theories are not as optimistic about the benefits of free trade and foreign investment. From these perspecives, free trade tends to be characterized by declining terms of trade and worsening problems of surplus labor. That was evidently the case with Raùl Prebisch's structuralist contribution and the work of others such as Hans Singer (as discussed in Chapter 1), culminating in the famous Prebisch-Singer thesis.

A much broader line of analysis in Keynesian-Marxist thinking is the recognition of differences or, more appropriately, the existence of power imbalances. Joan Robinson, a well-known Keynesian economist, developed this line of analysis in her 1979 classic: *Aspects of Development and Underdevelopment*. According to Robinson (1979/2009), free trade has structural problems. The theory that supports it, comparative advantage, does not adequately reflect reality. The theory assumes equal strength of trading partners. It also assumes similar types of elasticity for different commodities. In practice, African nations have weaker bargaining power. Also, typically, the products from the Africa and the Global South more widely – primary products – are price elastic, whereas the manufactures of the Global North tend to be, generally, price inelastic. Again, the pricing of these two types of goods, generally, is different.

The cost-plus theory, suggesting that the pricing of manufactures reflects cost plus a profit margin, implies that primary goods, the specialty of the Global South, is priced based on the vagaries involved in the interactions between demand and supply. These differences, Robinson argues, translate to diverse levels of bargaining power in trade relations, with the Global North dictating the terms for the Global South. From this perspective, Joan Robinson (1979/2009) argues that a popular response like South–South cooperation is doomed to fail, if it is carried out along the free market (advocated by neoclassicals and centred on markets)/comparative advantage (advocated by classicals and centred on the nation-state) framework. In this line of general Keynesian-institutionalist thinking, protectionism or, at least, protectionism-for-a-while, is, thus, often advocated.

More specific, but broadly consistent, lines of analysis can be found in Marxist urban economics. The two main models in this category are the Holland Model and the Hymer Model. On the continuum of Marxist analyses, the Hymer model is probably more Marxist, as it is far more located in the sphere of production, while the Holland model is more focused on the sphere of circulation. Both production and circulation are, of course, integral to the wider Marxist analysis of "circuits of capital" in "the urban process under capitalism" (Harvey, 1978). So, while quite distinct, the two models are better understood and utilized together. The Holland Model distinguishes between three types of firms: leader, led, and laggard. Leader firms control significant resources and command much power. Led firms are mere followers with significantly less power than the leaders. The laggard firms are the least powerful, the remnants (Stilwell, 1995, pp. 103–117). According to the Holland Model, leaders create core-periphery tendencies, in which led and laggard firms become locked into a fixed relationship with the leader firms.

As an alternative to this proposition, the Hymer Model introduced the idea of vertical and horizontal hierarchies, which are based on power differentials. An analysis of those hierarchies makes it possible to predict how firms transform where they are located rather than simply respond to their location (Stilwell, 1995, pp. 103–117). In a vertical hierarchy, the most routine, boring, poorly paid tasks of production are typically set up in the periphery (poor countries), while management, research, design, innovation, marketing, intellectual property, finance, and other well-remunerated aspects of production are reserved for the core regions (rich countries).

In turn, workers in richer areas are given a chance to develop the most powerful social and technical skills and create broadly relevant learning networks, while the most menial forms of work are assigned to poorer areas or, as is increasingly becoming the case, in the newly industrializing countries, a point that Samir Amin developed systematically in his contribution (Amin, 2005) to the Marxist periodical, the *Monthly Review*. In terms of specialization or horizontal hierarchy, the most environmentally damaging parts of production are located in poorer regions while the most rewarding parts are in the richer areas (Stilwell, 1995, pp. 103–117). TNCs are expected to be incubators of inequalities arising from differential locations and differential treatment of workers and capitalists. Consequently, the solution proposed by critics is to disengage from trade or globalization altogether or to invoke state protective powers (Korten, 1995, 1999; Susan George, 1996).

## NON-MAINSTREAM ANALYSIS: GEORGIST "TRUE FREE TRADE"

Protectionism is simply withdrawal from the world, which is not an option. Henry George offered a critique of protectionism in the late nineteenth century that still has relevance today. But his grounds for doing so, his alternatives to it, and the radical differences between his theory of trade and monopoly-based neoclassical theories, are misunderstood (Boyle, 2015). So, a more systematic treatment of George on TNCs is warranted, especially by carefully engaging his *locus classicus* on the issue, protection or free trade. George ([1886] 1991) rejected protection on grounds that it is a "beggar thy neighbor" policy that creates hostility rather than cooperation among nations. Also, the taxation of goods, as proposed by protectionists, penalizes production and human exertion.

Meanwhile, low taxes on land value result in concentrated land ownership and the private appropriation of socially created value. Although George recognized that protectionism can create jobs in the system that regulates trade, he argued that it is far better to create jobs by removing the encumbrances created by concentrated land ownership. George ([1886] 1991) advocated free trade. Apart from the opportunity free trade gives to obtain a variety of commodities and services at reasonable prices, George advocated free trade as an anti-monopoly measure. His consistent argument was that true free trade was intended to abolish monopoly and ensure fair distribution.

In this sense, George's "free trade" differs markedly from what is regarded as free trade in orthodox economics (Beck, 2012, pp. 972–973). George defined free trade as the removal of all taxes on imports and exports (except for health and safety protections) whether they are intended for revenue generation or for protection of local markets. But since free trade increases net incomes, which translate into higher land prices, true free trade occurs only when the elimination of tariffs coincides with the taxation of the value of land and the removal of taxes on wages. His intention for free trade was to bring about a fair distribution of resources, while encouraging labor to freely initiate, produce, and exchange.

According to George ([1886] 1991, p. 286):

Free trade, in its true meaning, requires not merely the abolition of protection but the sweeping away of all tariffs – the abolition of all restrictions (save those imposed in the interests of public health or morals) on the bringing of things into a country or the carrying of things out of a country. But free trade cannot logically stop with the abolition of custom-houses. It applies as well to domestic as to foreign trade, and in its true sense requires the abolition of all internal taxes that fall on buying, selling, transporting or exchanging, on the making of any transaction or the carrying on of any business, save of course where the motive of the tax is public safety, health or morals.

George's free trade ideas were pro-labor, but not Marxist. Free trade need not reduce wages, take away jobs, or create monopolies. Merely instituting protection without commoning land would generate all these social problems. Continuing his previous discussion, George ([1886] 1991, pp. 289) elaborated:

True free trade, in short, requires that the active factor of production, Labor, shall have free access to the passive factor of production, Land. To secure this, all monopoly of land must be broken up, and the equal right of all to the use of the natural elements must be secured by the treatment of the land as the common property in usufruct of the whole people. Thus it is that free trade brings us to the same simple measure as that which we have seen is necessary to emancipate labor from its thralldom and to secure that justice in the distribution of wealth which will make every improvement or reform beneficial to all classes.

This theory of "true free trade" is based on two principles. According to George ([1886] 1991, p. 280), these maxims are as follows:

I. That all men have equal rights to the use and enjoyment of the elements provided by Nature. II. That each man has an exclusive right to the use and enjoyment of what is produced by his own labor. Yet, equal right to land does not mean what is commonly understood by it: equal parcels of land.

According to George ([1886] 1991, pp. 279–280):

Equal rights to land could *not* be secured by the equal division of land, and in the second place it is not necessary to make land the private property of individuals in order to secure to improvers that safe possession of their improvements that is needed to induce men to make improvements. [emphasis in original]

In this sense, George's defense of free trade is anchored on his central principles: guaranteeing private property in the products of labor – both individually and collectively – and abolishing private property in land through land value taxation. Both are aimed at fair distribution. His advocacy of free trade was, therefore, to enable production rather than to penalize it, to support the liberation of workers, and the destruction of TNC monopolistic control of all natural resources.

As none of these principles underpins the orthodox advocacy of free trade and protection, Henry George's preference for free trade is qualitatively different from the current advocacy of free trade. It is also different from the Ricardian defense of free trade or Adam Smith's arguments for unrestricted exchange. In the words of George ([1886] 1991, pp. 289–290):

> The partial reform miscalled free trade, which consists in the mere abolition of protection – the mere substitution of a revenue tariff for a protective tariff – cannot help the laboring-classes, because it does not touch the fundamental cause of that unjust and unequal distribution which, as we see today, makes "labor a drug and population a nuisance" in the midst of such a plethora of wealth that we talk of over-production. True free trade, on the contrary, leads not only to the largest production of wealth, but to the fairest distribution.

In short, the Georgist theory of trade predicts that when TNCs control the commons, workers must necessarily be exploited, inequality must worsen, and the environment must be polluted and misused. Where there is progress, there will also be poverty. The only solution is to treat natural resources as common property that benefits all citizens and to guarantee that labor receives its full reward. This is the complete opposite of the frequently proposed remedies by critics of TNCs: protection, the retreat from globalization, or moral accusations of evil charged against TNCs. While other posited solutions can be considered, any alternative that disregards the two cardinal principles relating to land and labor is unlikely to be effective.

## THE DED FRAMEWORK: TNCS AND URBAN GOVERNANCE

None of the theories discussed (structuralism, Keynesianism, Marxism, and Georgism) sufficiently account for urban governance or the multiple institutions and institutional settings within which TNCs operate and trade takes place. Propositions about TNCs and urban governance can, however, be integrated by adopting the "DED framework" of decentralization, entrepreneurialism, and democratization (Obeng-Odoom, 2013b, 2017b). DED is simultaneously a way of classifying, interpreting, and evaluating urban governance in terms of its posited pursuit of growth, inclusive urban development, and environmental sustainability. In turn, DED can also offer us clues as to what outcomes to expect as different forms of urban governance are implemented (Fuseini, 2016; Fuseini & Kemp, 2016) with diverse public and popular reactions (Asante and Helbrecht, 2019). Decentralization emphasizes the nature of the state and of its urban governance structure, that is, the level of power held by cities and other local governments. Devolution, deconcentration, or delegation are optional methods of exercising decentralization, with important implications for accountability. For instance, in a highly devolved system in which local governments have strong autonomy and revenue raising powers, TNCs face political responses that are different from those where urban local governments merely exercise functions delegated by the central government. Similarly, democratization and democratic institutions can be expected to shape how firms behave, depending on their nature.

These interactions between cities and TNCs are expected to provide economic growth, inclusive urban development, and progressively lower levels of urban poverty as they provide channels of voice and exit that can contribute to the provision of these outcomes. The presence or absence of a free and diverse press, a variety of civil society groups, and truly representative labor unions are important elements in the way local governments respond to the behavior of TNCs. Also crucial are the actions of courts, security services, traditional authorities, and parliament. Even religious groups can be very influential, especially in oil-rich societies where oil experiences are framed in religious metaphors such as "resource blessing" and "resource curse." Even if we assume that TNCs operate exclusively in the economic sphere, they relate to other forces and actors in the economy, including social and public enterprises, other TNCs, and local private firms.

Due to these and other influences on the firm in international trade, the precise circumstances for the rise and the actual role of TNCs in African urban development are empirical questions. Economic theories – be they of the neoclassical, new institutional, Marxist, or Georgist stock – need to be understood and revised in context, taking account of uneven social relations, including relations between countries and regions (Nwoke, 1984a, 1984b; Collins, 2017). So, what outcomes arise and what options exist for redress or reform are mediated by institutions of decentralization, entrepreneurialism, and democratization.

## TNCs AND THE PROVISION OF MUNICIPAL SERVICES

How TNCs emerge and operate in the urban water sector in francophone West Africa requires primary attention because they can help us better contextualize the theories discussed. The French colonial invasion of Côte d'Ivoire (formerly Ivory Coast) marked the end of treating water as common property in Abidjan. However, independence did not end the private monopolistic ownership of water, which is widely regarded as the "French water model" (Komenan, 2010, p. 2). Urban Côte d'Ivoire has known no other water provider than the inherited French TNC, *Société de Distribution d'Eau de Cote d'Ivoire* (SODECI). Founded in 1959, a year before Ivoirian independence, and being in charge of water provision in Abidjan since then, SODECI has been enabled by state power since 1973 to slowly extend its influence to all urban centers (Traore, 2000). SODECI was created out of the French TNC, *Société d'Aménagement Urbain et Rural* (SAUR).

In her study of "Transnational Corporations in Water Governance," Joyce Valdovinos (2015, p. 126) notes:

> The fourth transnational water company is the French group SAUR. Created in 1933 as the *Société d'Aménagement Urbain et Rural* for the design and operation of water production plants, today this firm serves 18,000,000 people [or 18,000 municipalities] in eight countries. Its development in France began with the signing of a concession contract with the community of Villejoubert and other small French rural communities. From its formation until the 1960s, SAUR established itself as "the authority and preferred partner for rural local authorities and rural development authorities." . . . Focusing on the development of water distribution services and treatment of superficial waters, SAUR created the specialized engineering company Stereau in 1959. A year later, SAUR began its internationalization with the foundation of the firm Sodeci (*Société de Distribution des Eaux de la Côte -d'Ivoire*) for managing an affermage contract in Ivory Coast. This contract marked the beginning of SAUR's presence in Africa, a region that became a priority after the creation of the subsidiary SAUR-Afrique.

Since 1960, SODECI has been a private, foreign monopolist, controlling a common good to which citizens of the Côte d'Ivoire have a human right. Both the emergence and growth of SODECI, driven by the intersectional forces of French and Ivoirian state policies and power, contradict the account by Oliver Williamson (1981, 2002, 2009) that TNCs originate and grow mainly based on internal innovations.

The available evidence of the actual performance of SODECI raises even more questions about the model of water control suggested by the new institutional economics. Between 1988 and 2001, the productivity of SODECI workers increased from 161 connections served per staff to 333. This achievement was possible only because of a strictly imposed policy of 300 meter readings per day per meter reader and eight service connections per day per plumber (Obrist et al., 2006). (In case the implications of that work speed-up are not evident, 300 readings per day required one reading every two minutes for 10 hours of work, without any breaks.) That policy led to widespread staff dissatisfaction about being overworked. Those workers who actually voiced discontent lost their jobs. One high-profile case was the summary dismissal of the general secretary of the National Union of Water Workers (International Trade Union Confederation, 2010). New workers were also hired, but they were few in number. For instance, in spite of the growing number of connections and work in the 1988–2001 period, only 280 additional people were employed (Obrist et al., 2006). So, even if there were efficiency gains under the watch of SODECI, they were obtained at significant costs to workers.

Private natural resource monopolies create structural problems in terms of pricing and misallocation of resources (Gaffney, 2016). That explains why the problems Ivoirians are experiencing with SODECI are structural. Indeed, French economists who have been studying the relative performance of French public and private utility providers in France have reached the conclusion that such property relations are both oppressive and inefficient. In one recent study of 177 French water utilities, not only were private utilities providers found to be inefficient, their performance was also environmentally unfriendly and less efficient than public service providers. As Le Lannier and Porcher (2014, p. 557) summarize their findings:

The results show that utilities under private management are on average more complex to manage. Accounting for environmental variables increases efficiency by 0.1 under private management while it only lifts up efficiency by 0.059 for public management. However, even after having taken environment variables and statistical noise into account, private management remains on average less efficient than public management. Public management has an efficiency score of 0.883 against 0.823 for private management. As a summary, even if the technical efficiency gap is narrowing after correcting for structural differences, it remains significantly positive.

Indeed, in France generally, many municipalities are starting to take direct control in the management of their water resources as the prevailing view is that public management is more efficient, delivers cheaper water to homes, and is more reliable as a water provider. In the lead for this municipal democracy is Paris where, since 2009, the city's mayor led this municipal takeover of water resources, announcing only two years later that municipal ownership of water in Paris had caused the price of water to decline by 8 per cent with the tacit endorsement of the French state (Le Lannier & Porcher, 2014). It is, therefore, the height of hypocrisy and a double standard for the French state to continue to impose a monopolistic private-sector regime in its former colonial outpost.

The quality of water supplied by SODECI is highly regarded, but the quality of water in its subsidiary markets – the market for the resale of water and the market for packaged water – has been called into question. Although resold water is from SODECI, which licenses the practice, the company does not monitor the quality of the transfer equipment in subsidiary markets (Obrist et al., 2006). The quality of water packaged in plastic is of inferior quality to tap water directly supplied by SODECI (CIRES, 2015). Research conducted in the Medical Faculty of the University of Cocody shows that packaged water had too many chemical additives to make it "purer," and that purification paradoxically makes it "impure" and unhygienic (CIRES, 2015).

SODECI does not license the packaged water market, so it is not directly responsible for its quality. However, there are important reasons why the rise of packaged water can be linked to the governance of the water sector by SODECI. First, SODECI's water covers only 56 per cent of households in Abidjan, down from 75 per cent in 2002, before the civil war. The decline in water connections has created the conditions necessary for packaged water to thrive. At one stage, the SODECI-created water market extended neither to the *quartiers sous équipés* (defined by Obrist et al., (2006, p. 321) as neighborhoods with poor facilities) nor in *quartiers précaires* (defined by Obrist et al. (2006, p. 321). As settlements regarded as "illegal" by a foreign monopolist, they were not considered worthy of being supplied water – in their own country.

SODECI's discriminatory policies are not new. Most urban residents know that such practice is a continuation of colonial humiliation of Ivoirians, most of whom did not live in the Plateau and Cocody areas in the historical period. Those areas were regarded as the "European quarter" of Abidjan, where the best municipal services were often concentrated. Areas called the *quartiers populaires* (common neighborhoods) were historically occupied by the Ivoirians. The latter areas were provided with few municipal services, and they are now called Treichville and Adjame, two major informal sites that provide housing and work for the poorer classes in Abidjan (Freund, 2001). When the poor gain access to water, they pay more money for an inferior product. For half the population in poor settlements and a few others in formal settlements but whose water supply from SODECI is unreliable, they have to depend on much-better-off entrepreneurs living in formal settlements. Those entrepreneurs have access to SODECI water, which they resell to the poor at a higher cost. One assessment in the mid-1990s showed that retailers could sell water at prices up to four times higher than what they purchased from SODECI (Appessika, 2003). Realizing that they can cash in on this "market," SODECI started issuing licenses to the water vendors to legitimize their sale of water to poorer neighborhoods (Obrist et al., 2006). In doing so, however, SODECI did not take responsibility for monitoring the quality of resold water.

Small-scale water retailers have to service nearly half (45.7 per cent) of the residents in Abidjan (Appessika, 2003). For investors who want a secure return, this is a promising business, especially since any increases in operational cost from licensing can easily be passed on to poorer neighborhoods. As not much investment has gone into the water sector, coverage by SODECI service is expected to decline in the coming years (World Bank, 2015). SODECI is not investing to keep up with growing demand and the government's investment is minimal, averaging only 0.3 per cent of municipalities' expenses in the last ten years (World Bank, 2015). The current situation in Abidjan is dire, since the private sector will only provide water upon payment, and less than 1 per cent of public expenditure is used for water subsidies. For SODECI, however, this situation is a bonanza: if its costs increase, they are passed on to consumers – the luxury of being a monopolist, and hence a price giver rather than a price taker. The state is, however, under the burden of trying to absorb the price increases.

In turn, the proportion of connections that are subsidized is rising relative to fully paid connections (Johnstone & Wood, 1999). Such contradictions also plague other French-owned monopolies in Côte d'Ivoire. Since the controversial election of France-backed, former-IMF economist Alassane Ouattara in 2010, they have worsened. Married to a French woman, Dominique Folloroux-Ouattara, Ouattara is widely regarded as a pro-French president, unlike his predecessor, Laurent Gbagbo, who, in spite of his problematic use of ethnicity to exclude and to divide, spoke against French domination of the Ivorian economy. As Ademola Araoye (2012, p. 441) has shown in his recent book, *Cote d'Ivoire: The Conundrum of a Still Wretched of the Earth*:

By the sixth month of President Ouattara in office, French companies ... had seized the reins of Ivorian business with contract awards from the Ivorian administration to the tune of over 1,500 million Euros or over 2 billion dollars! These were obviously awarded without international tender or safeguards, including a complete lack of due process and transparency.

Elsewhere in Africa, the activities of TNCs raise even more contradictions. In particular, TNCs in oil exploration, production, and sale of petroleum products direct urban development through their social spending and sale of cars and fuel to urban Africa. So, it is important to probe the activities of TNCs in the planning of urban space in Africa.

## TNCS AND THE PLANNING OF URBAN SPACE

Transnational petroleum companies are increasingly planning urban space in Africa. They do so, apparently, in response to state and local content laws and to satisfy the public relations benefit of visibly promoting corporate social responsibility. Local content laws require transnational corporations to employ a mandatory number or share of citizens, rely on local suppliers of services needed by the TNCs, and use local inputs as far as possible.

Corporate social responsibility (CSR) is rather different from regulation. It is not usually a function of state legislation. Rather, the "responsibility" arises from the self-regulation of transnational corporations. CSR principles appear to show that the role of business is not simply profit making in a modern economy (Hilson, 2014; Hilson et al., 2019). This change in emphasis represents a departure from profit seeking, which Milton Friedman (1970) famously proclaimed was the sole purpose of firms. The new model of business considers the firm as a governance structure (Williamson, 1981). That shift is one of the key differences between neoclassical and new institutional economics (Boettke et al., 2012 Markey-Towles, 2019). For the World Bank, the expansion of CSR arises from its win-win nature (Dartey-Baah et al., 2015). CSR takes on various forms, including the provision of services, the building of development projects, and the building of administrative capacity of national and local governments. Although non-binding, transnational corporations see CSR statements as crucial and hence make public their achievements as they do with local content regulations. Table 5.3 provides information about Tullow Oil, a prominent TNC specializing in the exploration and production of petroleum in Africa.

Table 5.3 suggests that the social spending of Tullow is significant. CSR expenditure is widely presented as a contribution to the UN's defunct Millennium Development Goals (MDGs) and current Sustainable Development Goals (SDGs) (Dartey-Baah et al., 2015; Osei-Kojo and Andrews, 2018). On that basis, Tullow's investment described in Table 5.3 can be considered well-intended. Indeed, as local content requirements fill gaps in national and subnational plans, the contribution of Tullow, Kosmos, and other TNCs that try to meet local content requirements make a positive contribution to African economies. For advocates such as the

Table 5.3 *Social contribution of Tullow Oil in Africa, 2008–2015*

| Year | 2008 | 2009 | 2010 | 2011 | 2012 | 2013 | 2014 | 2015 |
|---|---|---|---|---|---|---|---|---|
| Corporate Social Responsibility ($000s) | 1,846 | 2,054 | 2,578 | 11,569 | 19,914 | 17,402 | 10,639 | 7,537 |
| **Local Content ($million): (Purchases from Local Suppliers by Country)** | | | | | | | | |
| 1.  Ethiopia | | | | | | 14.4 | | |
| 2.  Ghana | | | 194 | | 69.2 | 128.0 | 123.6 | 226.0 |
| 3.  Kenya | | | | | 28.7 | 48.0 | 81.5 | 75.0 |
| 4.  Mauritania | | | | | | 7.0 | | |
| 5.  Uganda | | | 26.8 | | 47.5 | 19.6 | 20.3 | 7.9 |
|    Total Local Content | | | 220.8 | | 145.4 | 217.0 | 225.4 | 308.9 |

*Sources:* Tullow Oil Plc, 2010, p. 65; 2012, p. 75; 2015, p. 31

World Bank, therefore, both local content and corporate social responsibility expenditure can only be good. However, there are always strings attached to subsidies, which means that they tend to serve the interests of donors. Investing in urban mobility is a major channel through which TNCs exercise power over urban development. Some TNCs finance road maintenance, building, or expansion to complement national and semi-urban efforts at road building.

Transnational petroleum companies in Sekondi-Takoradi, Ghana's oil city in the Western Region (WR), for example, funded the rehabilitation of the Shippers' Council Roundabout, a major meeting point of several important roads in the oil city. According to an "anonymous planner" (Anonymous, 2017) with extensive knowledge of the region, there is additional "evidence of substantial investment into road construction by TNCs within the Ellembele District of the WR." Much of the construction of roads and infrastructure in oil and gas cities in Ghana reflects a wider program in Africa of Chinese-built infrastructure in exchange for resources, so it is not restricted to Sekondi-Takoradi or Ellembele. Indeed, Mark Lamont (2013, p. 154) has described in detail Chinese-constructed highways in Kenya seeking to help in the transport of oil from South Sudan to the northern parts of Kenya to refine and then export. It is commonplace in Africa for the Chinese state, working with the Chinese TNC Sinopec International Petroleum Corporation and others, to engage in barter trade with African states. In this trade, China is contracted to build roads and other infrastructure paid for with African oil (Odoom, 2015; Siu, 2019).

Such investments have been widely hailed as crucial for Africa. Among other things, they seek to bridge the infrastructure gap in Africa. In addition, they appear to resolve the inability to finance infrastructure deficits due to financial constraints. They also reduce transaction costs, paving the way for business to flourish (Obeng-Odoom 2014b, pp. 172–173; 2015b). TNCs not only finance and build roads; they fill them with cars and motorcycles, which, in turn, they fuel. What requires emphasis is that the cars that get exported to Africa are secondhand (Obeng-Odoom, 2014b, 2015b) as are the motorcycles, usually from China and Japan (Lamont, 2013). The fuels are typically dirty, and there are overlaps between the TNCs that support the building of roads, those that supply cars, and those that fuel the cars. The French company Total, for example, is a TNC involved in exploration, production, and retailing of petroleum products (upstream, midstream, and downstream) (Public Eye, 2016). What it does in one stream is connected to what it stands to gain in another stream. Oil producing TNCs are slowly changing their monopoly structures. According to Public Eye (2016, p. 30):

ExxonMobil was the first major to pull out [of the retail fuel market], closely followed by the other American giant Chevron in 2008. Chevron, which remained present in South Africa and Egypt, sold around one thousand petrol stations to an African consortium composed of Cote d'Ivoire's state-owned Petroci and a Nigerian group called MRS. In 2010, BP and Shell sold most of their sub-Saharan networks, too. Total remains the single exception, increasing its retail market share across the continent.

In 2005, the French company bought ExxonMobil's network of petrol stations in fourteen African countries. Oil trading TNCs, particularly Vitol, Trafigura, Mercuria, and Gunvor together with Shell and Puma Energy, Addax and Oryx Group, and Lynx Energy, have created an African-wide network to supply diesel and gasoline to cities in Africa. These fuels are supplied from European ports located in Amsterdam, Rotterdam, and Antwerp (ARA zone) and American (US Gulf) sources – to African countries (Public Eye, 2016, pp. 83–87). The geography of the ARA zone facilitates the sale of ingredients from, or the hiring of, facilities from the United Kingdom, Russia, and the Baltic Zone to prepare the fuels (Public Eye, 2016, p. 6). Africa imports substantial shares of its fuel from ARA. Indeed, as Public Eye (2016, p. 5) shows, 50 per cent of the imported fuel to West Africa is from the ARA zone. Most of the traders involved in supplying fuel are Swiss companies, a fact that escapes the public because they trade by other names at the pump level, as shown in Table 5.4.

Table 5.4 *Major Swiss companies and their multiple identities*

| Swiss Trading Company | Retail Arm | Petrol Station Brand | Countries |
|---|---|---|---|
| Trafigura | Puma Energy | Pumangol | Angola |
| | | Gazelle Trading | Benin |
| | | Puma | Republic of the Congo, Côte d'Ivoire |
| | | UBI | Ghana |
| Vitol | Vivo Energy | Shell | Côte d'Ivoire, Ghana, Mali, Senegal |
| Addax and Oryx Group | Oryx Energies | Oryx | Benin, Mali, Zambia |
| Lynx Energy | X-Oil | X-Oil | Republic of the Congo |

*Source:* Public Eye, 2016, p. 51

The Swiss companies listed in Table 5.4 are leaders in terms of the number of African countries where they operate (see column 4) and the amount of oil that they supply to Africa, but there are other notable traders too. In 2014, for example, Glencore, Litasco, Sahara Energy, Mecuria, Gunvor (Clearlake), Orion, Trafigura (Delaney), and Trafigura – leading Swiss TNCs – owned 61 per cent of the fuels exported from the ARA zone, while the rest of the TNCs such as Total (7 per cent) and BP Amoco (9 per cent), respectively from France and Britain, exported the rest of the fuels to Africa (Public Eye, 2016, p. 86).

## LIMITS TO TNC SOCIAL SPENDING

The social spending of TNCs raises several questions. Most spending subsumed under the category of corporate social responsibility (CSR) is poorly aligned with national goals, even if TNCs try to articulate their CSR within the UN Millennium Development Goals and Sustainable Development Goals (Dartey-Baah et al., 2015). In many cases, CSR spending is superficial. Surveys by Justice Bawole (2013), Abigail Hilson (2014), and Tina Adusah-Karikari (2015), looking at how TNCs are perceived in oil-bearing communities in Ghana, show that most people feel that there is no genuine, long-term real interest in improving community livelihoods. Real engagement with communities is lacking and is fleeting (Hilson, 2014; Hilson et al., 2019).

Local content spending does better because, by definition, it is based on the idea that the state can use legislation to nudge transnational petroleum companies to provide what the state considers useful (Obeng-Odoom, 2016c). Nevertheless, what the state claims is useful is not necessarily what is actually needed by the people (Obeng-Odoom, 2016c). Local content in practice can face many contradictions. For instance, as shown in Chapter 4, it is a local content requirement in Ghana for transnational petroleum corporations to develop business capacity through the Enterprise Development Center (EDC) but, as Austin Ablo (2015, p. 320) concludes after a comprehensive study, few small companies benefit:

The EDC facilitates interaction between local entrepreneurs, officials of state institutions and foreign oil companies, which enhances local entrepreneurs' knowledge of the oil and gas sector and provides enterprises with an entry point. However, it is argued that only a few well-established medium to large-scale Ghanaian enterprises are able to take advantage of the opportunities provided by the EDC project to expand their operations. The majority of relatively new and small businesses are still unable to gain entry.

More fundamentally, TNCs are using their CSR and local-content spending to plan urban space and hence become a parallel local government. They do so by directly funding the planning process, training local government staff, providing local governments with logistical support, and embarking on public education, thereby replacing the voice of local and national governments. Planning and implementation are the preserve of local governments, but TNCs increasingly appropriate such functions and powers. For example, in Ghana, Local Government Act 462 gives the responsibility and powers of planning urban space to local governments. But this function and the related powers of executing them are increasingly being taken over by TNCs. The disparity between local government and TNCs in local planning is evident in the Western Region of Ghana. Relative to the national government, the Sekondi-Takoradi Metropolitan Assembly (STMA), the local government in the oil-bearing region, receives little investment, but the Spatial Plan of Sekondi-Takoradi is funded by petroleum TNCs (Obeng-Odoom, 2013c, p. 236; 2014a; Fiave, 2017).

Doing so gives the TNCs considerable power over local economic activities and the local government. TNCs substantially determine which local companies obtain the contracts they offer under local content laws. Usually, it is local companies that have experience serving TNCs that are more likely to receive additional contracts (Ablo, 2017). When they do, that sets in motion what Gunnar Myrdal (1944, p. 76) called the "cumulative causation" of inequality.

His specific point of reference was the economic backwardness of African American communities in the United States, but the same principle applies here.

Cumulative causation makes the privileged companies stronger and the companies lacking in contacts with the TNCs weaker. In the political sphere too, there are similar imbalances. One planner, who experienced this power imbalance firsthand, noted that:

> In the Western Region for example, the spatial plans prepared for the six coastal districts were not handed over to the respective local authorities. Rather they have remained with the TNCs serving as a blueprint for their CSR activities. I only secured a copy for myself through a friend who works with the Consultant in Accra. Even the Spatial Plan being adopted by STMA is a draft version. (Anonymous, 2017)

Similarly, Tullow Oil offers training and support to local government staff in Uganda (see Tullow Oil Plc., 2015). In São Tomé e Príncipe, training programs have been given by oil companies. These levels of support appear innocuous; indeed, they tend to be presented as marks of good partnership between TNCs and local governments. However, as Gisa Weszkalnys (2009, pp. 686–687) notes of such "partnerships" in São Tomé & Príncipe:

> Oil companies, for their part, have begun to maintain security of access by cultivating "partnerships" with local governments, politicians, and gatekeepers through deposits, donations, and other favors.

Indeed, even the offer of general information to community members by TNCs raises serious questions. As is well known in "corporate communication and economic theory" (Lah et al., 2016), corporate communication is designed to reduce risk, to protect the reputation of the firm, enhance profit, and enable the firm to blend into the society.

Research in Uganda, Ghana, and Nigeria shows that the TNCs in oil production do their utmost to project a positive image in the society (Behrman et al., 2012). In Kenya, oil TNCs host large public meetings with communities to discuss issues about their livelihoods and community development. By doing so, the TNCs are taking over an institution – *barazas* – previously utilized by local governments to consult with communities. In turn, oil offices have become the go-to places for urban residents to seek redress about services, to get information about jobs, and to seek recognition (Enns & Bersaglio, 2015, pp. 85–86). Similar inverted authority has been reported in Uganda, Nigeria, and Chad where citizens direct their needs, fears, and hope to transnational oil corporations such as Tullow (United

Kingdom), Total (France), CNOOC (China), and Shell (United Kingdom), while local governments remain mere spectators (Van Alstine et al., 2014). The articulation of the rights of citizens, then, is increasingly being directed at the oil TNCs, not urban governments.

Yet, the typical TNC is not seeking to advance the public good but rather to reduce its transaction costs, and, hence, to enhance its own profit. It may also aspire to project the power of its country of origin. Chinese TNCs are a case in point. They explicitly set out to use their urban infrastructure projects to express China's rise as a global power (Amoah, 2014). Indeed, in the infrastructure development projects under discussion, Chinese TNCs determine who is to be employed and under what conditions, which inputs to use and in what proportions (Lamont, 2013; Odoom, 2015; Obeng-Odoom, 2015a). The contracts are not put to competitive tendering processes, as required by laws such as the Public Procurement Act of Ghana, which provides a public competitive bidding procedure for public projects. Indeed, some of the contracts also contain clauses that undermine national laws. The corporation, as J.K. Galbraith (1977) noted, is, indeed, a major source of uncertainty. Together with growing amount of debt and the many insecurity about China, for example, the TNC-trade-FDI nexus is marked by significant uncertainty (Siu, 2019).

Also, as discussed in Chapter 4, under the Local Content Law of Ghana, oil TNCs are required to ensure that, at the start of operations, Ghanaians must constitute 30 per cent, 20 per cent, and 80 per cent, respectively, of management, technical, and other staff, but in the SINOPEC loan agreement, the TNC pushed for and obtained a clause that ensures that, across the board, significantly more Chinese labor (60 per cent) is employed. The Chinese executives have justified the situation by claiming that, because of "Ghanaian culture," Ghanaian workers are not employable and that Chinese work harder. By using the racist argument that Ghanaians are lazy, the Chinese companies limit the number of Ghanaians employed (Lamont, 2013; Odoom, 2015; Obeng-Odoom, 2015a). This experience raises questions about the conditions of labor employed by TNCs and the more fundamental question about whether more work is socio-ecologically desirable.

Oil workers are paid quite well. What is often overlooked is that much oil-related employment is casual, poorly covered by contracts, and weakly unionized. Oil workers can be summarily dismissed. There is a labor aristocracy among oil workers in Africa, characterized by substantial pay differences. Such hierarchies are based on race, even if the labor, its quality, and its training are analogous. In turn, foreign workers can be paid multiple times higher than African labor (Ablo, 2012; Obeng-Odoom, 2016d; see Chapter 4).

Chinese construction firms, to which contracts are given to develop road infrastructure financed from oil revenues, typically employ Chinese labor and few locals. The recruitment of the local labor is mostly on a casual basis to strengthen the ability of companies to discipline workers (Obeng-Odoom, 2014b, 2015a). The "roads for prosperity program" is, therefore, a recipe for unbalanced growth that helps the Chinese economy, but not the local economy in Ghana. Part of the problem lies with the absence of forward or backward linkages, an idea developed by Albert Hirschman (1958) to describe the added employment and production created when local businesses buy goods and services within a community and then promote the creation of new businesses opportunities that spin off from the original ones. Instead, all of the linkages are created in China, leaving only the hollow shell of development in Ghana. As a result, the condition of workers is not as sanguine as widely perceived. Indeed, as Lamont (2013) shows, even after the construction of roads, the Chinese play a significant role in ensuring that the roads are used by supplying secondhand motorbikes. What are the consequences of these contradictions for inequality and (un)sustainability as social costs (Kapp, 1950/1971)?

## CONSEQUENCES FOR INEQUALITY AND SUSTAINABILITY

Clearly, many urban planners in Africa have improved their skills as a result of the activities of oil TNCs – and will continue to benefit from TNCs. As one anonymous planner (Anonymous, 2017) pointed out about TNCs in Ghana: "Tullow reserves a minimum of 10 slots for public servants on its annual scholarship program for Ghanaians." Many locals have obtained education and skills from TNCs. Education facilities and laboratories have been established and equipped through TNCs (Darkwah, 2013; Heilbrunn, 2014; Panford, 2014, 2015, 2017).

Indeed, it has even been argued that Luanda has become a "turnaround city in Africa" in terms of generating socially useful infrastructure, jobs, and revenues for the city authorities all because of the activities of TNCs and their resulting revenues to the state (Croese, 2016, 2018). Many other oil cities in Africa have been transformed. Ablo (2016) gives details about Ghana, and Uetela and Obeng-Odoom (2015) provide a case study of Mozambique. However, the situation is far more complex, if we examine these benefits in terms of relative and opportunity costs – the potential development that did not take place.

To take Ghana as an example, various budget statements, together with the work of J. R. Heilbrunn (2014), suggest that the revenues from oil constitute around 10 per cent of GDP. What we need to know is whether the added income stays in Ghana to promote further development or leaks out to create prosperity in other countries. To determine that we need to ascertain the GDP to GNI gap. A positive value (>0) indicates that net income is lost to the rest of the world through profits, interests, and dividends (Cypher & Dietz, 2004, pp. 31–34). So, in Table 5.5, if GDP minus GNI is positive, outflows from Ghana through TNC activities are much less than inflows into Ghana.

The final column of Table 5.5 suggests that, at least in the case of Ghana, over the period 2009–2015, GDP per capita exceeded GNI per capita by $27. Thus, more income actually leaves Ghana as profits, interests, and dividends than is received as remittances by Ghanaians working abroad.

Incomes aside, very little of the petroleum produced on the African continent is consumed on the continent. Most of it "leaks" into productive use elsewhere. This situation is paradoxical because the continent needs fuel badly. Indeed, between 2000 and 2020, the demand for fuel is expected to double (Public Eye, 2016, p. 30). African countries such as Ghana, Nigeria, and Senegal have refinery infrastructure to produce petroleum by-products locally, but the refineries lack sufficient capacity to refine all of the gasoline and diesel demanded by African consumers and businesses. Because of the bottlenecks in the local production of refined petroleum products, Africa imports fossil fuel from oil traders that profit by buying, refining, and reselling bad-quality fuel at a high price (Public Eye, 2016, p. 50).

However, lack of refining capacity is a minor problem compared to the inability of Africans to retain the oil drilled on African soil for the development of Africa. Although investment in this latent potential to meet the demands of African nations for refined oil products would support local expertise, create jobs, and provide clean fuel, external advice informed by mainstream theories of comparative advantage and the wider politics of neoliberalism discourages the retention of petroleum for development of

Table 5.5 *Per capita GDP (current USD) and GNI (current USD)*

| Year | 2009 | 2010 | 2011 | 2012 | 2013 | 2014 | 2015 | 2009–2015 |
|---|---|---|---|---|---|---|---|---|
| GDP/Capita | 1,096 | 1,323 | 1,587 | 1,642 | 1,827 | 1,442 | 1,370 | 10,287 |
| GNI/Capita | 1,210 | 1,260 | 1,410 | 1,570 | 1,740 | 1,590 | 1,480 | 10,260 |
| Difference | –114 | 63 | 177 | 72 | 67 | –148 | –90 | 27 |

*Source:* World Bank (2017)

Africa. In 2014, as Public Eye (2016, p. 82) shows, West Africa "exported 213.9 million tons of crude oil (while importing 0.2 million tons of crude oil) and imported 18.6 million tons of [refined] products (while exporting 6.5 million tons)." These numbers reveal that Africa continues to serve the same function it did during the colonial era: a source of raw materials to be used for the development of other countries, not for indigenous development.

### RISING INEQUALITY IN CITIES

There is dramatic rise in inequality in cities in Africa in general, but in particular in TNC-dominated and resource-rich cities in Africa. These cities have simultaneously become incubators of internal inequality as well as inequality between internal actors and transnational agents, as exemplified in the case of Port-Gentil in Gabon (Yates, 2014). In Abidjan, the Gini coefficient of 0.5 for income indicates that a wide disparity of incomes exists within the city, much wider than other Ivorian cities with a Gini coefficient of 0.4 (Obeng-Odoom, 2017b). Income metrics aside, inequality can also be seen in terms of municipal service delivery. Again, the levels of inequality differ between regional capitals and other cities and between primary and secondary cities, as the 2014 *The State of African Cities* report (UN-HABITAT, 2014) shows.

In the past, mainstream economists glorified inequality, contending that it was either temporary, needed for efficiency, or acted as an incentive for growth. That has changed, but they contend that the key problem with inequality is that it chokes off growth. In fact, inequality strangles the health of people, undermines social cohesion, creates uncertainties, and reduces the prospects of reaching a consensus on ecological sustainability (Galbraith, 1977; Lewis, 1985; Obi, 2009; Wilkinson & Pickett, 2010, 2018; Stilwell, 2017, 2019; Obeng-Odoom, 2019). As inequality tends to breed further inequality, this problem generates a race to destruction. In cities in Africa, exposure to inequality – through personal contact, visual images, and media accounts – shapes people's attitudes and, indeed, offends people as gross injustice (McLennan, 2016). The growing inequality on the continent today is now quite obvious, spurring popular protest, which Adam Branch and Zachariah Mampilly (2015) have recently described in their book, *Africa Uprising*.

The analysis of inequality by mainstream economists warrants attention. Arne Bigsten (2016, p. 4) summarizes the elements creating inequality in African cities today:

We have thus identified four different types of determinants of changes in the production structure. These are changes in the factor endowment of the economy, changes in goods prices, technical progress and changes in the level of distortions/ interventions/international integration. When seeking to explain inequality and its change, these are key economic factors.

By this claim, Bigsten contends that inequality changes as the payment for different factors of production or sectors of production changes. Thus, in the African case, the relationships of importance are between the formal, capital-intensive sector and the informal, traditional sector, and between the small-scale agricultural and large-scale plantation economies. In the small-scale agriculture sector, incomes are likely to be low compared to incomes in the formal, capital-intensive sectors. By the logic offered by Bigsten, inequality should reduce when every worker in Africa joins the formal sector. This claim ignores exploitation in the process of production and the tendency that the productivity of the formal sector has historically been gained directly at the expense of small-scale farm operators who have been displaced from their land. Thus, the standard development process has created the very poverty it now proposes to overcome.

Another standard economic view posits that inequality in cities is the result of overpopulation either (1) because it intensifies the scarcity of land and increases the labor-land ratio, or (2) because of the "urbanization of poverty" – the movement of the poor from rural areas to cities in the mistaken expectation that they will be better off (Obeng-Odoom, 2010, 2017b). This analysis fails to consider the possibility that the causal relationship is the reverse – namely, that poverty and landlessness have been the major factors causing the growth of population (Remoff, 2016).

Another explanation of urban inequality centers on human capital and how the development of technology now better benefits the most capable workers, leaving behind those with no education or those with outdated education. This is the so-called Tinbergen Model, but the concept of human capital has long roots, going back to the work of Gary Becker and Theodore Schultz and, in contemporary times, to the Harvard urban economist, Edward Glaeser (Darity & Williams, 1985; Hodgson, 2014).

Population-based analysis naturalizes social inequality by blaming the victims. Human capital analysis has the same effect by diverting attention away from the activities of TNCs, when, in fact, TNCs are complicit in the production, maintenance, and extension of inequality. As monopolists, TNCs are usually price givers, their activities are price determining, and they often increase prices to enhance their own profits, even if, as in the case of SODECI, the state attempts to counteract some of the price increases. Even where TNCs are oligopolists – as in the case of oil TNCs – they have a strong effect on determining windfalls and the capture of rents, with little regard to their average cost of production.

## OTHER WAYS TNCs CONTRIBUTE TO INEQUALITY AND ENVIRONMENTAL POLLUTION

There are other ways in which TNCs create inequalities. Investment in urban infrastructure is one leading channel, as Mark Lamont (2013, p. 154) notes in his analysis of the LAPSSET Corridor Project (Lamu Port–South Sudan–Ethiopia Transit), which is "aimed at linking and transporting Sudan's considerable oil reserves to refineries located on Kenya's northern coast and outwards onto the oceanic shipping lanes of the western Indian Ocean and China's industrial southern coast." These sorts of infrastructure projects increase the profits of established businesses doing long-distance trade, but they also displace vulnerable groups and do nothing to help the poor urban neighborhoods that need better transportation. In that way, infrastructure supported by TNCs widens the income gap in many countries. Supporting the planning process and financing urban infrastructure development help TNCs skew the content of plans. Both processes favor TNCs in obtaining road-building contracts (Lamont, 2013; Odoom, 2015). Many oil cities in Africa are increasingly being planned to support the oil companies. For example, in Sekondi-Takoradi, the Spatial Plan makes the success of oil capital central to the success of the city (Obeng-Odoom, 2013c; Fiave, 2017). Research in Sekondi-Takoradi shows that low-income residents are neglected or actually removed at the request of oil TNCs (Obeng-Odoom, 2014a, ch. 5; Fiave, 2017). Hotel owners, landlords, and others in the city privilege workers of TNCs over others, reserving rooms and rental units for the relatively rich workers of TNCs.

Also, attention in public discourse is slowly shifting toward TNCs as the bastions of successful planning and service delivery (Obeng-Odoom, 2014b). Although these TNCs report these activities as a positive contribution, there is a danger that they can easily co-opt the planning process either because local planners feel favorably disposed to them or because the companies actually influence the process.

In Port-Gentil, the oil city of Gabon, Douglas Yates (2014) shows that Elf-Gabon/Total has built roads to connect its investments, such as oil wells and plantations, to its offices (such as the Boulevard Elf-Gabon) and to separate the housing of white French expatriates from ordinary

Gabonese residences. These roads, then, became symbols of both physical separation and inequality in terms of the provision of municipal services, as there were marked differences in the quality of services received in the two parts of Port-Gentil. Indeed, the process of developing housing for French workers displaced many local residents who, as a result, had to live in less desirable places. These oil houses or "concessions," notably La Grand Concession, were gated communities for mostly French workers and very highly placed black Gabonese.

Surrounding them were the quarters of casual and contract workers of the companies. Dubbed "architectural apartheid" (Yates, 2014, p. 170), this spatiality symbolizes the urban interventions of TNCs in Africa. Overall, cities in Africa have grown more and more unequal. The drivers are complex, but the major ones are the monopolistic and oligopolistic structures analyzed here and the differing trends of work-related practices. Socially created rent is privately appropriated by CEOs and expatriate workers, especially male workers as they stand to take more senior roles (UNCTAD, 2007; Obeng-Odoom, 2014b, 2016a). Ordinary workers have numerous grievances against the TNCs and against migrant workers, although there is little basis for the criticism of these internal migrants (Ablo, 2012; Obeng-Odoom, 2014c, 2016a). Potential workers, especially those who have undertaken specific oil and gas education, are disappointed as they have to rely on unstable market forces, based on the logic of demand and supply, for employment, which is unlikely to be forthcoming. So, they lose their meager investment by doing further courses that neither guarantee nor secure jobs in the oil and gas sector (Darkwah, 2013; Panford, 2014, 2015).

The environment also suffers in many ways. There is the well-known – albeit sometimes contested – issue of oil spillage, resulting in the death of animals and plants and hence the loss of biodiversity (Hilson, 2014). But, there is also the less recognized, but potentially even more damaging, practice of TNCs knowingly dumping toxic fuels in urban centers in Africa. These practices are mainly carried out by traders in the downstream (retail) parts of the industry. As cities in Africa become bigger and more populated, so too does the concentration of toxic chemicals in the air. Africa's megacities – Lagos and Dakar – are much smaller than Beijing in China, but they are much more polluted (Public Eye, 2016, p. 5). The TNCs involved in exporting and importing contaminated oil can be vastly different, but they may also be the same. Shell, for instance, plays both roles in different parts of Africa. Sometimes, they may sell refined oil products, but they are hugely expensive and hence create the conditions in which polluting fuels are purchased. Imported fuels are harmful to human life.

Indeed, 80 per cent of all diesel that the Swiss traders and others export from ARA to Africa are 100 times more sulphurous than what is permitted in Europe (Public Eye, 2016, p. 5). The fuels also contain aromatics and benzene, whose use is barred in European and American markets because they are harmful (Public Eye, 2016, p. 6). Fuels sold in Africa are prepared through the blending of waste products from companies in Europe and the United States with cheap chemical ingredients. They have been proven to be harmful to humans: at least 25,000 people will die prematurely in Africa as a result by 2030, and 100,000 will die by 2050 (Public Eye, 2016, p. 6). In Kenya, for example, the costs associated with pollution-related diseases exceed $1 billion (US dollars) (Public Eye, 2016, p. 10). These fuels are corrosive and hence they also destroy car engines (Public Eye, 2016, p. 21). These practices amount to taking high-grade resources from Africa, and spitting back degraded and polluting oils.

This evidence clearly shows that reliance on corporate monopolies, oligopolies, local content rules, or social responsibility principles creates social costs (Kapp, 1950/1971). Although the intentions of some TNC managers may be good, there are structural reasons why powerful companies continue to exploit and cause damage to countries in Africa. Similarly, depending on foreign direct investment leads to deleterious consequences.

TNCs are able to co-opt the planning process and privatize the urban commons. In theory, we expect that, in urban governance as DED, there are opportunities for voice and exit mechanisms to address these limitations, but do those mechanisms work? Can TNCs be made accountable to their host countries?

## LIMITED ACCOUNTABILITIES

Although TNCs engaged in extracting resources from Africa may increase national income, at least in the short run, we must ask whether they benefit Africans in the long run. Since they repatriate most of the rents and leave little petroleum in Africa that might be used as the basis of internal development, it is not clear that the ledger is balanced. In order to truly be a benefit for Africans, TNCs would need to be accountable to Africans. How might that be possible? Specifically, how might Africans dissent from the actions of TNCs operating on their soil? Voting is one way to voice disagreement. But, as TNCs are not elected, elections as a means of controlling them is limited. Using the courts of law, the legislature, and popular pressure through public opinion and civil society activism are additional mechanisms of accountability. The media can be used to investigate the actions of TNCs, especially if uncensored. How these mechanisms work in practice requires some analysis. In African courts, many TNCs have legal protections. They tend to invoke the law to avoid accountability for what they do.

For instance, in terms of selling toxic fuel to Africans, they do not technically breach the law because they sell fuels that, although they know are harmful, do not violate local laws. Indeed, they recalibrate the amount of poison whenever nations change their regulations (Public Eye, 2016). But even when they clearly are answerable, they invoke international law for protection. In the well-known *Tsatsu Tsikata v. Republic of Ghana* case, Tsatsu Tsikata, a key actor in the discovery of oil in Ghana, was charged with willfully causing financial loss to the state. A potential witness in the case was the International Finance Corporation (IFC), which was founded on the vision of the oil magnate, John D. Rockefeller (IFC, 2016, p. 27). Although Tsatsu Tsikata argued in court that he wanted IFC to testify, the latter invoked immunity from domestic court processes under international law, and, hence, refused to answer questions in the Ghanaian courts. Tsikata was jailed in 2008, but he always maintained that the IFC's refusal to testify was a major reason for his loss (Obeng-Odoon, 2014a). While the Supreme Court of Ghana held in 2011 that the IFC as a legal entity was accountable to Ghanaian law, it also noted that the employees of the IFC are immune to Ghanaian law (Benson, 2011).

Nigerians found a way around this problem. Their laws insisted that all TNCs be incorporated under Nigerian law. In that case, TNCs in Nigeria become fully subject to Nigerian Law. That is a double-edged sword. TNCs found guilty can plead independence from the parent company (Amao, 2008). Indeed, even if Nigerian courts found the TNCs culpable, compensation would be limited, as would real enforcement (Abusharaf, 1999). Such were the issues in a recent case in which Royal Dutch Shell was sued in London by two Nigerian oil communities, the Bille and Ogale groups. According to the British representative of the communities and media reports, the suit was taken to the London court because it is easier for the oil company to influence local courts in Nigeria and, even if they fail to do so, the Nigerian state is less likely to be able to enforce judgment against the company (*Reuters*, 2017).

Yet, the bigger principle in pursuing a Nigerian case in a British court is that Royal Dutch Shell Company, headquartered in the United Kingdom, is directly responsible for the polluting activities of its subsidiary company in Nigeria called Shell Petroleum Development Company of Nigeria (SPDC), meaning that two – not one – defendants would be pursued: SPDC in Nigeria and Royal Dutch Shell Company in the United Kingdom. As it turned out, the British judge ruled that SPDC is an entirely separate entity from Royal Dutch Shell, the parent company of SPDC (Schaps & George, 2017). It follows that, in this case at least, a major TNC is using organizational structure not only or even mainly for transaction-cost economizing, as Oliver Williamson argues, but rather as a legal strategy for antisocial activities of destroying the environment and the livelihoods of entire communities – without taking responsibility.

More fundamentally, it follows that the actions of former colonial states support their TNCs to relegitimate control over former colonial territories. As a case in point, President Trump signed a bill to repeal Section 1504 of the Dodd-Frank Act, which required TNCs from the United States to disclose their financial payments to states in Africa, especially, and the purpose of those payments (Guillén, 2017; Lynn, 2011). That provision in the Dodd-Frank Act was passed in response to public demands for TNCs to be more accountable. With its repeal, US-based TNCs can now freely seek to pursue their self-interest without being accountable to citizens either at home or abroad. Following a recent US Supreme Court decision in *Jam V. International Financial Corporation*, if resources could be found by victims, however, they could sue TNCs and world development agencies such as the World Bank in American courts. Actually taking on these TNCs, however, is going to be challenging, given the vested interest of the US state in its TNCs as well as the World Bank in which the US state is a major shareholder.

The resort to the many international agreements and codes about TNCs provides yet another channel to seek accountability. The difficulty, as many legal scholars have shown, is that most of these documents are not legally binding, many TNCs are not signatories, and even when they are binding and apply to certain TNCs, they do not deal with the relevant issues (Amao, 2008; Ekhator, 2016). Most codes and agreements deal with transparency and similar issues, not questions of accountability. The media could, in principle, be a powerful check on the power of TNCs. In practice, as a major study (Behrman et al., 2012) in Nigeria, Uganda, and Ghana shows, transnational petroleum companies pay for favorable stories to be published or unfavorable ones to be censored. When they do not seek to compromise professional journalistic standards, they deliberately feed journalists press releases that romanticize the activities of oil TNCs.

In *The New Media Monopoly*, Ben Bagdikian (2004), the leading thinker on the political economy of the media, shows that what is happening in Africa is, in fact, global. The oil industry dedicates a substantial portion of its budget to creating a positive image of itself and fighting negative media coverage. Indeed, with increasing media monopoly – which in the United States means only five media companies controls most of the news in the country – Ben Bagdikian shows that oil companies are increasingly becoming shareholders of media businesses. In turn, not only do oil companies dominate the media with positive news or attack negative news, they are now increasingly becoming employers of journalists as major shareholders in the media industry.

New media or social media can be an alternative but, in most of Africa, the technology is limited to the most well-resourced and hence is not democratic. Indeed, globally, African internet usage is merely a dependent revolution on corporate technological power in the Global North (Murphy & Carmody, 2015; Gyampo, 2017). While these new media outlets are potentially very important, the lack of checks and balances on their reporting make them vulnerable to manipulation. Therefore, they have the capacity to mislead the unsuspecting public. Both traditional and new media outlets have few journalists with the experience, training, and competence to cover technical oil matters. Often, they are not nuanced in their approach and hence focus solely on accounts of the "resource curse."

These types of stories serve to draw attention away from more fundamental contradictions and asymmetries of power between host countries and the TNCs that extract oil. These dynamics make it easy to manipulate public opinion through media, movies, and magazines. But even when journalists get their stories right, they struggle to take on the sheer power of TNCs and their legal arsenal in the courts. TNCs, then, in essence, have only partial accountability but great power, including the power to dictate the pace of urban development against the wishes of the people. The international media can, in theory, be supportive but, in practice, they tend to toe the line of TNCs from the countries where they are located. Thus, in 2009, when Gabonese in Port-Gentil protested the domination of the Gabon economy by the French oil giant, Total, the media simply reported Total's version of events. The media made it seem that Total was a reasonable company, which faced the challenge of rioting by Africans, a view that portrayed the French as victims (Yates, 2014). More recent research (Laine, 2019) confirms that the French media has remained pro-bank, pro-capital, and pro-France.

Many of these tensions and contradictions persist because of the trans-national nature of TNCs. Transnationalism does not just mean TNCs work in different countries but it also means they are structured in different ways. So, even though they bear the names of the countries in which they operate, their structures are split around the world. The oil company "Total Gabon" operating in Gabon is headquartered in Paris, France. Tullow Oil Ghana working in Ghana is headquartered in London. Kosmos Ghana operates from Hamilton, in the United Kingdom. Anadarko in Ghana is headquartered in The Woodlands, Texas, USA. Hess Ghana is headquartered in New York. Eni Ghana is located in Rome, Italy (Obeng-Odoom, 2014a, pp. 51–52; Yates, 2014). Of course, there are the national and local oil companies headquartered locally but they are less powerful than the TNCs.

## CONCLUSION

International trade continues to be advocated as an escape route out of debt but also in its own terms as a path for the convergence of wealth and incomes across the world. As a path of escape, unfettered free trade is promoted on the basis that it is a way to earn more and to create trade surplus in Africa, while protectionism is seen as an antidote to the loss of foreign currency, a trigger for industrial development or the development of infant industry, and a path to free the continent of debt. In itself, trade can be the road to improved economic governance and a way to satisfy various needs and wants.

However, as this chapter has shown, the reality of trade is more complex. The debt problem is far greater than trade can effectively handle. This is not a story of financial indiscipline, native corruption, or even lack of due diligence. Protectionism sounds like a good antithesis, but it neglects the roots of the current trade regime and their resulting contribution to social stratification and socially stratifying trade.

Debt has been written into the very foundations of the continent as a political economic relation. Stretching from slavery (in which John Locke heavily invested both as a philosopher justifying slavery and a slave-investor trading in slaves) through Lockean colonialism to neocolonial neoliberalism and imperialism, the debts that the Global North owes to Africa – in terms of property, income, and human energy appropriated – have been conveniently forgotten. Africa's indebtedness is recurrently emphasized, but the deliberate production of this debt through the global financial system is almost always underemphasized. Corporate power, particularly in the extractive sectors of the economy, substantially creates and recreates urban space in Africa for corporate advantage, while conveniently ignoring the structural roots of the debt crises on the continent, creating environmental crises, and reproducing new forms of social stratification.

The analysis in Chapter 5 enables us to see how rents generated in Africa to which Africans make the most contribution are transferred to the Global North. In this process, international trade is, indeed, a mechanism for creating – not containing – social stratification. Viewed this way, it is easier to understand how the African commons is being disrupted by regimes of power imposed from outside. Mainstream economics theories fructify transnational corporations (TNCs), claiming that they merely operate in cities but do not shape them. They are presumed to be engines of growth that function in the background, never interfering in the domestic affairs of the countries where they operate. Marxist theories of TNCs recognize that they are often malign sources of social and economic inequality, but those theories lead to nonviable solutions such as avoiding trade or withdrawing from globalization.

Alternatives are needed, of course, but should they be driven by growth centricism? Is the vision of growth-based approach to addressing social stratification that underpins the mainstream case benign, neutral, or destructive? Is economic growth or the lack thereof an appropriate vision? Such questions will form the basis of the discussion in the next chapter.

# 6

# Economic Growth

## INTRODUCTION

The resurgence of economic growth in Africa in recent times stirred a worldwide interest in Africa. Isaac Abotebuno Akolgo (2018a) recently characterized this state of affairs in the *Review of African Political Economy* as "Afro-Euphoria." Once proclaimed "hopeless" by *The Economist*, Africa is now regarded as a "hopeful" continent, incidentally by the same magazine. But why not? Until recently, the GDP figures in Africa were impressive. Between 2002 and 2007, GDP growth in sub-Saharan Africa doubled to an average of 6.2 per cent (Fosu, 2010). This record towered above the average European figure of 3 per cent. Libya even grew by more than 100 per cent in 2012 only. Globally, about half of the top ten fastest growing economies in 2012 were in Africa (Fioramonti, 2014). This image of a fast-growing Africa was stitched on everything Africa, with the February 2014 edition of *Highlife* declaring Lagos as the world's fourth largest fashion city.

The growth mantra was frequently discussed in the international media, such as BBC, and by the world leaders when they mounted international platforms. This optimism was not limited to non-Africans: some African scholars (e.g., Twineyo-Kamugisha, 2012), political parties, leaders, and institutions were similarly jubilant (Obeng-Odoom, 2013e). With interest in growth heightened and African economies regarded as "lions on the move" (McKinsey Global Institute, 2010), economic growth became synonymous with Africa itself.

Now that this growth has stagnated or even declined and demands for long-term deep institutional matters, rather than short-term markers of progress, are being forcefully made (Nega & Schneider, 2016; Mahali et al., 2018), it is timely to reflect on neoclassical-based economic growth itself as a vision, its implications for the material conditions of life, and the wider case for a growth-based approach to bridging intergroup inequality in Africa. Specifically, this chapter considers whether the well-being of Africans improved with the growth of their countries' economies by 1, 2, 3, or even 100 per cent. This discussion is also timely because the European Union's (EU) Africa-EU Policy is fundamentally centred on Africa's growth prospects and growth engineering as a path for peace, security, and inclusive development (European Union, 2019). Much like the OECD (see Schmelzer, 2016), and the United Nations' advocacy of growth in its SDGs and Paris agreement (Northrop, 2017), therefore, economic growth has been promoted as a global master key for the poorer regions to "catch up".

For orthodox economists, the connexion between growth and well-being is straightforward. In theory, an expanding economy typified by more market-based production cannot be attended with unemployment. That understanding earned Gerard Debreu a Nobel Prize in Economic Sciences in 1983, except that when journalists wanted to ask Professor Debreu questions about real-life conditions when he was visiting Australia, the great economist declined to comment. Apparently, Debreu's economics could only be analyzed within his rigorous general equilibrium mathematical models.[1]

That notable real-world challenge to orthodox economics happened in the 1980s, but continuing research and publications by social economists, including those in the *Forum for Social Economics* (Spiegler & Milberg, 2013; Nega & Schneider, 2016), demonstrate that the schism between the world of mainstream economists and the real world remains, arising not only from methodological deficits, but also from ontological and epistemological ones. The work of de La Grandville and Solow (2009) is one example where orthodox economists contend that the economic growth–wellbeing nexus is axiomatic. Henning (2013), Jerven (2013), and Kappel (2014) show that Africa's growth is unsustainable or that the statistical information is unreliable. Others, especially Alude Mahali and colleagues (2018), have argued that growth itself does not capture the deeper issues of well-being in the Global South.

However, the logic of growth itself has gone unchallenged, except in a few cases (e.g., Fioramonti, 2013). Other structural analyses of growth have looked outside the African continent, however. Among them are three classics, namely Baran (1957), Mishan (1967), and Waring (1988). More recent analyses have recognized the need to do similar studies for Africa and

---

[1] This information comes from a discussion with an Australian social economist who was closer to this historic incident than the present author.

the Global South more generally, especially in the light of increasing neoliberalism as a political-economic project (see, for example, Milonakis, 2012; Nega & Schneider, 2016; Akolgo, 2018a, 2018b).

But what is the implication of such a deeper engagement for analysis? The claims that Africa's growth has increased the number of people in the middle-income brackets is a case in point. The African Development Bank, which popularized this concept in recent times, "uses an absolute definition of per capita daily consumption of $2–$20 in 2005 PPP US dollars to characterize the middle class in Africa" (African Development Bank, 2011, p. 2). Based on this conceptualization, the African Development Bank claims that there is convergence of income and possible convergence of wealth within, across, and between Africa and the rest of the world. In their own words:

Strong economic growth in the past two decades has helped reduce poverty in Africa and increased the size of the middle class. By 2010, the middle class had risen to 34% of Africa's population – or nearly 350 million people – up from about 126 million or 27% in 1980, 27% in 1990 and about 220 million people or 27% in 2000. This represents a growth rate of 3.1% in the middle class population over the period 1980 to 2010, compared with a growth rate of 2.6% in the continent's overall population over the same period. About 60% of Africa's middle class, approximately 180 million people, remain barely out of the poor category. They are in a vulnerable position and face the constant possibility of dropping back into the poor category in the event of any exogenous shocks. (Africa Development Bank, 2011, p. 1)

A superficial engagement with this growth account emphasizes data problems or whether the estimates are good enough. A more structural analysis questions the political economy of growth itself, looking at its social foundations as well as its economic and ecological implications (Scharrer et al., 2018). Rebecca Rasch's (2017) paper, "Measuring the middle class in middle-income countries," in the *Forum for Social Economics* discusses the methodological issue more broadly. Should income measures (e.g., absolute, relative, or hybrid) be used, as mainstream economists suggest? According to Rasch (2017), even after controlling for population and purchasing power parity, income measures are inadequate. Many other variables affect the measurement, including the initial distribution of income in the country and household size. Wider socioeconomic measures are important, of course, but they are no panacea. We need to know what is happening in our cities, including changing ways of life and their institutional foundations, what is happening to our environment, and institutional transformations which shape what is happening in the world generally (Neubert and Stoll, 2018; Stoll, 2018). Without this wider conceptual and, indeed, ontological rethinking, we risk rolling back social interventions merely because Africa is rising or because Africa is now a "middle-income" continent. So:

Using strictly income-based measures obscures the fact that a significant percentage of the fabled, emerging middle class in some middle-income countries is still highly undereducated, are not in professional/managerial positions and therefore lack the credentials to upgrade their relative positions in the global economy. Incorporating socio-economic indicators, such as occupation and education, allow for a more complete understanding of the characteristics of these new middle class households and highlight their continued vulnerability. (Rasch, 2017, p. 335)

Therefore, a more comprehensive political economy approach is needed. Using this political economy of growth approach, this chapter shows that the reimaging of Africa in growth terms is not only a reflection of Africa's growth record but also creating "confidence in the market" by confirming that Africa is ripe and ready to host investment and to open up markets in areas where they did not exist or existed but were not capitalist in form. Either way, however, the "Africa on the rise" narrative – indeed all growth praises showered on Africa – achieve a major political and economic goal. Neglecting ethical questions about sustainable jobs, indeed working less, inequality, and ecological crisis, while extolling the virtues of capital accumulation, it extends a particular neoliberal ideology that favors people with market power, not the majority with precarious positions or their relationship with nature. Economic growth, then, must also be regarded as a problematic explanation. Like its tools of commodifying land (Chapters 2 and 3), labor (Chapter 4), and the environment (Chapter 5), mainstream approaches to economic growth must be fundamentally rejected.

The rest of the chapter is divided into four sections. *Poverty, Distribution, and Jobs* examines the connexion between growth and how its effects are distributed. *Spatial Mismatch* examines the urban experience in Africa, while *Ecological Costs of Accumulation,* the third section, analyzes the socioecological footprint of Africa's growth experience. Finally, the last section, *Underlying Causes and Impacts*, shifts the analysis from description to explaining the fundamental causes of the relationships established in the first three sections.

## POVERTY, DISTRIBUTION, AND JOBS

In the previous chapters, we saw that, for mainstream economists, we should expect improvement in poverty, distribution, and jobs when the economy grows. With more growth, we often hear, the poor would benefit, the jobless would find work, and the world would become more equal, cities more liveable, and the environment more sustainable (see also Dollar & Kraay, 2002; Dollar et al., 2016). Of this "growthmania," Ezra Mishan (1967, p. 3) famously observed that, "like a national flag and a national airline, a national plan for economic growth is deemed an essential item in the paraphernalia of every new nation state." For much mainstream economics work, Africa's growth record complies with the expectations of economic theory. There are strong connections and causations between economic growth and the rest: economic growth in Africa is powering precipitous declines in poverty levels on the continent, closing the income inequality gap, and will usher Africa into the promised land: achieving the Millennium Development Goals (Pinkovskiy & Sala-i-Martin, 2014).

To Young (2012), households in Africa are better off today because of economic growth. Increasing economic growth has powered tremendous achievements in education and quality housing, improved the ownership of assets and enhanced the quality of health in Africa. Although Africa remains poor, growth has produced a "miraculous achievement" in transforming the continent (p. 732). So, policymakers will do well to continue in the path of more growth (see also Dollar et al., 2016).

However, upon a closer scrutiny of the data used and the statistical techniques employed for this view, serious questions begin to emerge. Setting aside the generalizing analyses that gloss over the different and differentiating characteristics of Africa as a continent, Harttgen, Klasen, and Vollmer (2013) and Rodrik (2014), among many others (e.g., Devarajan, 2013), questioned the "growth miracle" story, pointing to major deficits in the choice of comparable income data with some taken from national accounts and others compiled from international sources, inherent conceptual biases, and the deficiencies in the econometric models. So, while the work of Young (2012) and Pinkovskiy and Sala-i-Martin (2014) claim a "growth miracle" and a perfect timing for Africa's growth and resulting ramifications, the overall effect of the challenges revealed by Harttgen et al. (2013) and Rodrik (2014) is that these studies do not provide accurate context-specific analysis of the African experience and, for Devarajan (2013), undermine national capacity to collect local and context-specific data. There is also the issue of poor data quality, which, as discussed in the introduction to this book, Morten Jerven (2015) has demonstrated.

In fairness to some of these scholars (e.g., Young, 2012, pp. 699–700), however, they do acknowledge the many limitations in their approach and stress how their conclusion can be valid mainly on the basis of certain "unreal" assumptions. In real life, however, the situation is more complex.

Table 6.1 *Current trends in growth, poverty, inequality, and unemployment, ca. 2010–2017*

| Country | Growth Trend | Poverty Trend | Inequality Trend | Unemployment Trend |
|---|---|---|---|---|
| Mauritius | ↑ | ↓ | ↓ | ↓ |
| Botswana | ↑ | ↓ | ↑ | ↓ |
| Nigeria | ↑ | ↑ | ↑ | ↑ |
| South Africa | ↑ | ↔ | ↑ | ↑ |
| Zambia | ↑ | ↑ | ↑ | ↑ |

*Sources:* Distilled from Jean-Yves & Verdier-Chouchane, 2010; Kent & Ikgopoleng, 2011; Enweremadu, 2013; Chibuye, 2014; Simatele et al., 2015; Motengwe & Alagidede, 2017

The relationship between a growing economy and well-being is contingent. If growth is inclusive, ecologically sustainable, and quality job creating, it offers stronger grounds to be optimistic. That is evidently what is happening in Mauritius and Botswana, as can be seen in Table 6.1. In both countries, growth has come with falling unemployment and poverty levels and, at least in the case of Mauritius, with declining income inequality. Decisive social interventions and programs have been aggressively pursued in both countries. Like education, the cost of housing is low and the environment clean. Mark Twain once called Mauritius "heaven." In the last few years, it has been called "paradise" (*Highlife*, 2014). The same sanguine picture cannot be painted of growing African economies such as Nigeria, South Africa, and Zambia, to give only three examples. While these countries have experienced considerable growth, levels of poverty continue to rise or, in the case of South Africa, remain nearly the same or declining but at a declining or very slow rate (Barros & Gupta, 2017). Inequality has worsened in all these countries.

The South African case requires particular emphasis. Not only is it the world's most unequal society (Barros & Gupta, 2017, p. 19), it is also becoming one of the world's most polluted countries. Growth is a major cause of this twin pattern. As Chris Motengwe and Paul Alagidede (2017) have shown, if high levels of inequality shape South African growth, then growth itself also patterns environmental pollution, as it is so inextricably linked to ecologically devastating carbon dioxide emissions that only a change in track in South Africa can save the situation.

Zambia has increasing levels of poverty, although it is among the fastest-growing countries in Africa. Indeed, as Simatele and his colleagues note,

"Overall, output growth has averaged 6.2 per cent a year since 2003, about half a percentage point more than for sub-Saharan Africa as a whole." The trend is likely to continue, with forecasts putting annual GDP growth rates at 7.5 as the lowest possible band (Simatele et al., 2015, p. 6). In Nigeria, poverty levels have been rising, reaching some 61 per cent in 2012. Indeed, Nigeria is sometimes regarded as the biggest economy in Africa, occasionally overtaking South Africa, the historically biggest economy in terms of economic growth (Muhammad et al., 2017). Yet, like South Africa, this growth record masks serious and worsening economic inequality. In addition, Nigeria struggles with major oil-driven socio-ecological crises. Violence has declined in the Niger Delta area and Shell Petroleum has ceased operations in Ogoniland, but the environmental crises have remained and worsened in some cases (Bassey, 2012; Okechukwu et al., 2012). The growth-based story of "Africa on the rise" is problematic in giving little or no emphasis to quality jobs and, indeed, in extolling values of more and more work for growth – without recognizing the right to quality work, to rest, and , indeed to relax. The "Africa on the rise" logic also generates spatial mismatch.

## SPATIAL MISMATCH

The growth mantra says little or nothing about rural and urban life in Africa, although given the rate at which urban population is growing we need to understand the urban, spatial, and regional aspects of growth and well-being. In an article on *Economist Online*, published October 2, 2012, and titled "The urbanisation trap," *The Economist* observed, "As a general rule, when people move to work in cities, it is synonymous with economic growth and the more people do the first, the more countries are offered the second." Cities in Africa, it argued, do not live up to this expectation, so the urban population must be very unproductive or, put crudely, lazy. This view about cities being production engines and the process of urbanization being an effort to crank the engines of cities is faulty on many grounds.

It misunderstands the nature of urbanization and migration in Africa – a continent experiencing considerable urban–urban migration, secondary–primary city migration, and even urban–rural migration. There is also region–region migration, international migration, and cyclical migration on the continent. Much migration is temporary, although there is permanent migration within Africa too. Each of these dynamics has its peculiarities, although there are important similarities too (see, for example, Ozkul & Obeng-Odoom, 2013; Obeng-Odoom, 2016a). Again, the growth mantra overlooks the institutionalization of capitalist processes intended to keep certain regions underdeveloped, consigning and compelling indigenes of these regions to become a backward "labor reserve," as we see in colonial and dependent urbanization between Northern and Southern Ghana, demonstrated in K. B. Dickson's (1968) classic work and in more recent research (Songsore, 2011; Obeng-Odoom, 2017b). So, to assume that cities arise because of only or mainly economic factors, one set (poverty and disease) pushing and another set (economic prosperity) pulling, is conceptually problematic.

Setting aside the faux claim about the lack of connexion between urbanization and urban economic growth, which exists in much of urban life in Africa (Njoh, 2003; Turok & McGranahan, 2013) – something the World Bank (2009) has been forced to accept after much prevarication for ages – it is simplistic to assume that the urban population in Africa is unproductive.

The UN-HABITAT (2003) offered detailed information about high levels of productivity, creativity, and innovation in various slums in Africa. More recent studies are consistent and further bring to light the activities of well-organized labor groups in slums in cities such as Accra (Farouk & Owusu, 2012; Smiley, 2017; Paller, 2019; Stacey, 2019), Dar es Salaam (Hooper & Ortolano, 2012; Dana et al., 2019), various cities in Namibia (Muller & Mbanga, 2012), and Nairobi (Lines & Makau, 2018). Slums have extreme conditions too, of course, but that is the point: growth tells us little or nothing about the complexities and varieties of urban and rural life. In fact, as in these examples, growth emphasis can misinform. As an aggregate measure, the GDP does not show any spatial differences. While city authorities in Johannesburg, Durban, and Cape Town compile urban-level GDP figures (UN-HABITAT, 2010), growth can tell us just that: growth.

Questions of complexity, such as informal economies and how they operate, are overlooked, as the case studies highlighted in this chapter illustrate. There are other urban and regional dynamics that the "Africa on the rise" story hides. Take the case of Ghana, for example. Franklin Obeng-Odoom (2014a) shows that, with oil, Ghana was growing around 14 per cent but without oil the country had a growth rate of about 7 per cent in 2011. So, the economy was doing really well and the economic managers of the country consistently made this point. However, this story does not show important ethical problems of widening inequality between the oil city and other cities in Ghana, inequality between classes within the city, inequality between in-migrants and natives, and inequality between genders – a very important concern because the current oil-generated jobs are concentrated in male-dominated sectors of the economy and the emergent entrepreneurship in the city is highly gendered

(Overå, 2017). Yet, by the dominant growth account, Ghana too is rising – regardless of whether women in its oil city count for little or nothing.

Unfortunately, this growth-based view is what is influencing urban governance in Africa. In theory, as shown in Chapter 5, urban governance is a broad-based process, drawing on a cluster of ideas from decentralization, entrepreneurialism, and democratization; that is, governing cities not only by markets and the state but also by other actors (Obeng-Odoom, 2013a, 2016b, 2017a, 2017b; Asante and Helbrecht, 2019). In practice, urban governance in Africa has come to represent a pro-market state working in cahoots with international real estate firms, property development consultants and global architectural firms. Together, these actors create "urban fantasies," which are new cities or satellite cities with structures and form that mimic the architecture in Dubai and Shanghai. Such imported plans have little or no local-level input. They tend to supplant the public mandate of national planning authorities. In Rwanda, Kigali is expected to be replaced by a new city whose plans were accepted by the Rwandese Parliament in 2008. Such plans exist in Addis Ababa, Accra, and Nairobi. Their urban function is to inspire business confidence and to "decongest" already crowded cities (Watson, 2013; Clote-Roy and Moser, 2019; Moser, 2019). It is not accurate, however, to regard actually existing urban governance as completely silencing local voices (Bhan, 2014; Clote-Roy and Moser, 2019; Moser, 2019). In urban Ghana, for instance, city residents have resorted to the use of the media, especially phone-in programs, to hold the state to account (Selormey, 2013). Local and international civil society organizations such as Ghana Federation of the Urban Poor are actively involved in grassroots organization. Through the collection and presentation of data on people working in informal economies and settlements, politicians are beginning to be more careful in ordering evictions (Farouk & Owusu, 2012; Paller, 2019; Stacey, 2019). In South Africa, Community Organization Resource Centre in Cape Town works with the poor and have together developed a program of enumeration to deter massive eviction, and it also tries to fight with the poor through the law courts. In Nigeria, Health of Mother Earth Foundation strongly criticizes poor urban governance processes and outcomes. So, urban governance is market dominated but this market power is not going unchallenged.

Nevertheless, marketized urban governance has brought about many failings in urban development. While slum prevalence has declined by some 7 per cent in North Africa and by 5 per cent in sub-Saharan Africa, congestion in cities and increases in income poverty (UN-HABITAT, 2013) and inequalities (UN-HABITAT, 2010) loom. Food security is a problem as is food sovereignty. Emissions from private second-hand cars are increasing as is

Table 6.2 *Spillage in Ivoirian waters, 1981–1991*

| Year | Location | Proximate Cause | Extent of Spillage |
|---|---|---|---|
| 1981 | Lagoon ebries | Human failure at the oil/ water separation unit | >1000 tons of oil |
| 1988 | Offshore buoy | Rupture of a connection line linking a tanker and a buoy | 700 m$^3$ of oil |
| 1990 | Offshore buoy | The same as the 1988 accident but involving a different tanker | 500 m$^3$ of oil |
| October 1991 | Sea | A pipeline from the buoy to the refinery developed a hole leading to leakage | Between 1,500 m$^3$ and 2000 m$^3$ of oil |
| December 1991 | Sea | Disconnect of floating hose linking the buoy to the tanker | 400 m$^3$ |

*Source:* Bender et al., 1993, p. 33

the number of car-related deaths (World Health Organization, 2013), and urban waste (Selormey, 2013; Grant et al., 2019), be it electronic or plastic, is increasing. Indeed, the price for economic growth in ecological terms is particularly heavy.

## ECOLOGICAL COSTS OF ACCUMULATION

Relatively few places in the world would beat West Africa in terms of the socioecological price it has had to pay for accumulation. This price is in terms of major oil accidents and pollution of various kinds. In West African countries where oil drilling is offshore, the effects of such costs are particularly high. Tables 6.2 and 6.3 are portraits of oil spillage and oil accidents in Côte d'Ivoire and Ghana.

Systemic production of inequality, social conflict, and, more fundamentally, ecological crises (see, for example, Mishan, 1967, pp. 36–38) are some of the insidious effects of economic growth, with "petroleum accidents" as one of the most discussed manifestations. Even before actual drilling started in Ghana in 2010, there had been twelve near misses and five incidents in December 2009. For example, in 2009 alone, there were thirty-four accidents and sixty-one near misses (Tetteh, 2012, pp. 32–33). Table 6.3 provides details of additional accidents in the country between 2010 and 2017.

Table 6.3 *A portrait of accidents in Ghana, 2010–2017*

| Sector | Accidents | Key Companies Perceived to Be Involved | Sources |
|---|---|---|---|
| Upstream | Spillage of 706 barrels of toxic substances into the sea | KOSMOS (TNC) | KOSMOS (2010) |
| | The infestation of *sargassum*[2], that threatens marine and fish life | Tullow (TNC) | Ackah-Baidoo (2013) |
| | Spillage of petroleum tar that damages fishing nets of local fishers | The Jubilee Partners | Panford (2017, pp. 148–149) |
| Midstream | Spillage of industrial waste into the surrounding environments | Tema Oil Refinery (National Oil Refinery) | Tetteh (2012) Sarkodie, Agyapong, Larbi, and Owusu-Ansah (2014) |
| Downstream | Environmentally polluting fuels; 93 per cent of which are 100 times higher in sulphur content than what is permissible in Europe and the USA | Various American and British petro TNCs (notably, Vitol and Trafigura) exporting oil from European ports such as Amsterdam, Rotterdam, and Antwerp and American ports. | Public Eye (2016, see in particular, pp. 5, 77; and chapter) |
| | Fumes from fuel stations that directly affect the health of workers | Total (TNC), Shell (TNC), GOIL (National Oil Marketing Company), etc. | Ansah & Mintah (2012) |
| | Fuel Station explosions in Sekondi-Takoradi and Accra. Car accidents, totalling at least 325 in only two years (2010–2011, the period for which data can be found) in Sekondi-Takoradi ("Oil City") alone | GOIL (National Oil Marketing Company) | Obeng-Odoom (2015c) |

[2] These are free-floating seaweeds that often ingest heavy metals and can, in turn, be used to determining heavy metal pollution through a chemical composition analysis (for more detailed description, see Ackah-Baidoo, 2013; Addico & deGraft-Johnson, 2016).

Compared to Nigeria, where oil accidents are far more widespread and much better known (for a discussion, see Sam et al., 2017), these accidents are modest. However, it is crucial to stress that Nigeria is a mature oil producer whose experiences with oil outpace Ghana's by over five decades. Yet, what this portrait of accidents in Tables 6.2 and 6.3 establishes is the foundation for analyzing causes and impacts *across the oil value chain* (in contrast to the typical upstream-centric analyses of the Nigerian case), investigating the independence and interdependence of the various parts of the chain, and probing their underpinning institutional form.

## Underlying Causes and Impacts

Since drilling began in Ghana, there have been even more accidents. As Table 6.3 shows, apart from the spillage by KOSMOS, the *sargassum* problem has taken on a different form. Historically, *sargassum* has been common in the Cape Three Points area and in other rock shores in Ghana (see, for example, Gauld & Buchanan, 1959, p. 121). Indeed, as far back as 1956 and hence before the modern history of oil drilling, the issue had generated much discussion among marine scientists (see, for example, Gauld & Buchanan, 1959). So, the discussion on oil drilling and the presence of *sargassum* in the oil-bearing communities (Hilson, 2014; Obeng-Odoom, 2014a; Owusu, 2017; Panford, 2017) and wider environmental impacts of oil can be considered evident.

It is the complexity of the environmental problems and their cascading effects on the environment and society that require more sustained analysis. Generally, the impact of oil accidents can be classified as "those related to worker safety; toxicological effects on workers, visitors, and community members; mental health effects from social and economic disruption . . . and ecosystem effects that have consequences for human health" (Goldstein et al., 2011, p. 1334). In the Ghanaian case, Table 6.4 provides an overview of the types of pollution, how and where they usually arise, and a note on some of their effects on society and economy.

Air pollution is a major problem. At the midstream, growing accidents at the Tema Oil Refinery (TOR), both in terms of worker accidents on the floor of the refinery and environmental pollution (Tetteh, 2012, p. 27; Table 6.4), raise important concerns. As one study revealed, "Treated effluent from the refinery showed high levels of COD [Chemical Oxygen Demand], BOD [Biological Oxygen Demand], TDS [Total Dissolved Solids] as well as conductivity which were unsatisfactory"(Sarkodie et al., 2014, p. 90). Emissions from cars constitute, perhaps, the most visible form

Table 6.4 *Accidents and environmental pollution in Ghana*

| Type | Conveyor Belts | Sector | Some Effects |
| --- | --- | --- | --- |
| Air pollution | Gas flaring; explosion of fuel stations; emissions from cars, refinery, and transportation of oil | Downstream/ midstream | Hearing problems, loss of plant life, respiratory problems |
| Ocean pollution | Spillage of oil and chemicals for processing oil; use of strong lights and noise pollution | Upstream | Loss of fish life, whale deaths, and loss of livelihoods |
| Land pollution | Seepage/spillage from cars/fuel stations/explosion; spillage during the process of transporting oil; spillage in the process of refining oil | Midstream/ downstream | Loss of biodiversity, loss of livelihoods |

*Source:* Author's depiction

of pollution in Ghana. On average, some 35,000 cars are imported into the country per year (Obeng-Odoom, 2013b, pp. 90–91). Motorcycles are also becoming a major import item. In a period of only eighteen months, 8,918 motor vehicles, including 991 motorcycles, were registered in Sekondi-Takoradi, Ghana's oil city (Obeng-Odoom, 2015c). Mostly old, these motor vehicles also run on fuel that is high on hazardous sulphur content (Public Eye, 2016). In Accra, the toxic element emitted from car fuels – particulate matter – is five times higher than in London, although there are more cars in London (Public Eye, 2016). The resulting deaths or deterioration of the quality of life of victims and their families have been well documented by the World Health Organisation and various other scientific studies (for a review, see Obeng-Odoom, 2013d, 2015c, 2017b).

Ocean pollution is a major issue too. Indeed, by broadening the discussion this way, it is easier to navigate the complexity of causes and effects. For example, the real issues are whether the nutritional content of *sargassum* in the area has worsened since oil drilling began and, if so, in what ways this oil-induced *sargassum* has further worsened environmental problems. Toxicological and nutritional analyses by scientists (Addico & deGraft-Johnson, 2016) show that *sargassum* has become more poisonous. According to the study, "Indiscriminate domestic and industrial wastes disposal, oil and gas activities, mining and high shipping traffic may have contributed to the heavy metal concentrations in the seaweeds" (Addico &

deGraft-Johnson, 2016, p. 2184). The concentrations of heavy metals are highest in the oil zone: Cape Three Points, a finding that is consistent with studies in other extractive zones in the world (Addico & deGraft-Johnson, 2016, p. 2190). So, the evidence is clearly that the industry is a strong contributor to environmental pillage in the country. Such environmental pollution has devastating health effects. According to the scientists who conducted the study, "Most heavy metals, especially arsenic and lead are carcinogenic and are capable of causing skin, lung, liver and bladder cancers and miscarriages" (Addico & deGraft-Johnson, 2016, p. 2184; see Table 6.4).

Land pollution is a particularly important issue, especially if oil drilling is onshore (Sam et al., 2017). In the case of Ghana's offshore industry, the land-based impacts of the industry have often been linked to the expansion of economic activities and their effects on agricultural land. For instance, using remote sensing and GIS methods, a recent study showed that

the expansion of the Takoradi harbor as part of the ERP has been a major contributing factor to the massive land use/cover change that has occurred in the metropolis since the 1980s. It has also shown that loss of agricultural lands to the purpose of expanding urban related activities such as settlements and commercial areas has continued since the discovery of oil. With the constantly increasing population, further encroachment of urban areas into agricultural land space will be inevitable, especially under the current dispensation where expansion of urban activities is unplanned. (Acheampong et al., 2018, p. 384)

Establishing the quality of land itself, whether built or agricultural, however, requires studying the effect of fuel station operations and accidents in the downstream sector on workers but also on land. In an interview with 114 pump attendants who work for Allied Oil (23), GOIL (32), Shell Ghana (29), and Total Petroleum (30) in the Central and Western Regions of Ghana, Edward Ansah and Joseph Mintah (2012) showed that 60 per cent of respondents noted that the OMCs provide and enforce safety policies and 57 per cent reported that the OMCs provide health facilities. Where most OMCs seem to be failing is in their ability to provide personal protective equipment. In turn, petrol attendants are typically exposed to the risks of inhaling hazardous carcinogenic petroleum fuels and vehicular fumes. On this issue, at least, employees of TNCs appear to be slightly better off, as companies such as Shell and Total tend to provide a bit more protection than the local GOIL. The reason is that these TNCs face some pressure from their international associations and tend to be keener on at least being seen as compliant (Ansah & Mintah, 2012). Studies such as Badu's (2015) show that, in addition to the negative effects on workers, such accidents also cause land pollution, endangering agricultural activities as well as plant and animal lives.

Similar effects arise from like processes elsewhere in Africa. In Lagos, the situation is even worse: the particulate matter content of the air Lagosians breathe in is thirteen times more than what Londoners are accustomed to (Public Eye, 2016). The reason is not that poor quality fuel is made in Accra or in Lagos. Rather, some of the world's most polluting fuels mixed in Europe are sold in Accra and Lagos. In turn, between 2009 and 2012, some 70 per cent of the urban population in Africa experienced worsening air quality, a share much higher than anywhere in the world (Public Eye, 2016).

## CONCLUSION

This chapter is a modest effort, limited in two important ways. First, it does not generate new data to enrich the debate. Also, while some issues such as development and environment, economic growth and distribution of wealth, and economic polarization are global in nature, the analysis is limited to Africa, making the scale of the contribution narrow.

Yet, this chapter offers a timely critical perspective on the "Africa is on the rise" discourse that hides more than it reveals. It is silent on quality jobs and working less, silent on ethical matters of distribution, and silent on ecological problems pervasive on the continent. This framing of Africa continues to shape the nature of the external interest in Africa, but is says little or nothing about spatial matters, provides a misleading framework for the complexities in the vast informal economies in Africa, and throws Africa's doors wide open for external plunder, often euphemistically described as "investment." While a few commentators may wish simply to tell good stories about Africa to reverse the negative publicity of the continent, this effort can be and often is compromised. Good storytelling has been co-opted or conscripted into a narrative about Africa for sale. The GDP discourse is, therefore, an effective political tool to excite markets about Africa. It works well in urban and regional contexts to encourage and stimulate the interest of leadership in Africa to open up markets, promote the marketization of countries in Africa, and construct buildings that mark the land and cityscape of market societies.

Thus, the neoliberal discourse that prioritizes and hence celebrates the resurgence of growth in the Global South, as in "Africa rising," for example, and subordinates the environment and society to the obsession for profit-led growth, creates and sustains ecological injustice in the Global Periphery. This dynamic survives by deflecting attention away from the ecological consequences of growth. Its deliberate attempt to delink growth from the crisis of economy, of society, and of the environment serves to perpetuate the myth of economic growth by protecting growth as sacred.

In short, these accidents – indeed social costs (Kapp, 1950/1971) more widely – have occurred because of the drive to maximize profit, to cut costs, to produce more with less and at high speed, and to prioritize profits over environment and society. With profit-led growth a first and primary commitment, the incidents detailed in Tables 6.1 to 6.4 are hardly "accidents." They are predictable, so, the rise in upstream incidents and accidents is hardly surprising. These environmental disasters make the oil and gas industry in Africa one of the most hazardous in the world. Highlighting the business opportunities that Africa can offer as well as Africa's rising economic growth, but sweeping under the carpet the continent's telling market contradictions, either implicitly or explicitly serves as an important ideological purpose. So, without de-emphasizing growth and re-emphasizing broader ideals and ideas of well-being, Africa will be pushed into a growth egress and its economies may be said to be doing really well, but not its peoples, their environment, or their relationship with nature.

Yet, given the current political-economic track on which Africa is travelling, this change in direction is impossible. Alternatives to the current vision of economic growth are urgently needed.

# PART III

# ALTERNATIVES

# 7

# Socialisms

## REVOLT

Socialism is one alternative. Although pronounced "dead" at the end of the twentieth century when its struggle with capitalism was formally ended with the former being forced to surrender to the later (Fukuyama, 1992), the persistent and worsening maladies of capitalism as a system must lead to further discussion of various types of socialism, or, put differently, socialisms. Founded on the premise that nothing substantially good can come from capitalism, a system based on exploitation, wage theft, burn out, rent theft, plunder, and ecological crises on a world scale, socialism promises a link between a more *social* world and the good society. Two of its defining features are the redistribution of land and the nationalization of industry. Does this cluster of options constitute a firmer and more reliable path to inclusive African development in a more equitable world?

On March 17, 2009, a three-month-long struggle by the people of Madagascar against their government's decision to alienate 1.3 million hectares of land to Daewoo Logistic Corporation of South Korea for a maize and palm oil farm for a period of ninety-nine years ended in a popular-based military coup that toppled the presidency of Marc Ravalomanana (Evers et al., 2013; Vinciguerra, 2013). This revolt is not isolated. The uprising in North Africa, dramatized by the self-immolation of Mohamed Bouazizi, a street trader in Tunisia on December 17, 2010, is often widely discussed, but the uprising in Africa does not in North Africa. Similar movements happened elsewhere in Africa. For example, in West Africa, Burkinabes torched their National Assembly in Ouagadougou on October 30, 2014 to end historical injustices, growing social stratification, and continuing oppression. As *Africa Uprising: Popular Protest and Political Change* (2015), a stimulating book written by Adama Branch and Zachariah Mampilly, makes clear, like the whirlwinds that broke loose the chains of slavery and pushed out colonizers from the continent, Africa is now embroiled in popular-based revolts. Indeed, more recently, additional protests have been documented in *Urban Revolt* (Ngwane et al., 2017), in *A Certain Amount of Madness* (Murrey, 2018), and on the streets of Khartoum in 2019.

Prominent African Marxists, including Samir Amin, read the uprisings as signaling a slow march to socialism (see, for example, Amin, 2011, 2014). Interviews with the protesters, analyses of their identities and interests, and longitudinal ethnographic studies of how their motives evolve (see, for example, Branch & Mampilly, 2015; Ngwane et al., 2017; and Asante & Helbrecht, 2018; Murrey, 2018) paint a more complex intergroup picture.

This evidence raises the following questions: what do the protestors demand, and could such demands be met both politically and analytically by Marxist socialism? If not, what do these uprisings imply? The evidence suggests (i) that the demonstrators do not seek socialism, and (ii) that the putative link between a turn to socialism and the good society is not assured. Indeed, such socialist practices can – and often do – complicate social stratification; and (iii) that even if it is granted that the uprisings signal the onslaught of socialisms arising, it is questionable whether the socialism of the physical redistribution of land, the socialism of the nationalization of mines and rigs, and the socialism of protectionism/delinking – the usual demands of Marxist-socialists – are viable alternatives in Africa Today.

Zimbabwe's land reform, in fact, succeeded in improving the livelihoods of low-income farmers, creating, in the process, a small class of "middle-income farmers," and reducing the concentration of land in the hands of white, large-scale commercial farmers. However, it is doubtful that equal physical parcels of land would bring about equity in land ownership and broader inclusive development, when various parcels have wide and differing rents and land value. The continuing problem of absentee ownership connotes not just design problems but points to more fundamental issues about the socialism of land reform. Indeed, as the activities of national corporations that operate like capitalist transnational corporations show, it is questionable that nationalization in and of itself is a sufficient alternative to capitalism. Besides, if capitalism is the enemy, then the social alternatives must be partial: Africa's struggles with stratification are not only the product of capitalism, they are also a function of pre-capitalist contradictions, including years of slavery.

In this sense, Africa's debt problems cannot be discussed only within the brief capitalist epoch. As shown in Chapter 5, protectionism now and trading later when African economies are more "mature" or can take advantage of the prevailing conditions, something Samir Amin (2011, 2014) calls "delinking," could lead to even more stratification as land continues to be commodified in this alternative trading system.

Overall, while the Marxist critique of capitalism has been relentless and long-standing, especially in its rejection of capitalism and imperialism, its analytical reach can be extended and its policy and political alternatives can be reoriented. This critical engagement with Marxist socialisms is developed, together with other versions of socialism, in the next four sections. Starting with Marxist agrarian political economy, the chapter next discusses imperialism and anti-imperialism, land reform, and nationalization.

## AGRARIAN POLITICAL ECONOMY

Although the stereotypical view of Marxist economics is that it involves economic development through class struggle between workers and capitalists, recent archival research by Don Munro has established that Marx continually wrote about the three factors of production – land, labor, and capital – from his earliest writings to his last (Munro, 2013, pp. 223–226). By "land," Marx meant all the elements of nature or the environment below the surface of the earth (such as minerals), the nature that existed on the surface of the earth (including soil, vegetation, and water), and the airspace above the surface of the earth. In his early writings, Marx stressed that at all times throughout human history, whether in communal, feudal, capitalist, or socialized societies and economies, human life can only exist if human labor-power is combined with land (natural resources), often with the use of tools and equipment, to produce the food, clothing, buildings, and other necessities of life – and a surplus product (resources made by labor) was also needed to maintain (or reproduce) the organization of the government of the society. In feudal Europe, landlords held land (soil, forests, other vegetation, mines, water, rivers, among others) as their own property and labor (peasants and serfs) applied their labor-power and their tools to the land to produce a living for themselves on condition that they also produced a surplus that they were required to give to the landlord in the form of rent (Munro, 2013, pp. 223–226).

In capitalism, the extraction of surplus-value took a new form: here, capitalists owned the tools, equipment, and finance (capital) rather than land and, to survive, workers sell hours of their labor-power to the capitalists, only part of which is remunerated with wages (their value), and the capitalist keeps the unpaid hours of labor-power (the surplus value) for themselves (Munro, 2013, pp. 223–226). Marx wrote extensively about

land in *Grundrisse* (Marx, 1939/1993), in Volume 3 of *Capital* (Marx, 1894/
1991), and in *Theories of Surplus Value* (Marx, 1863/2000), as he clarified
how, in capitalist economies, land owners capture some of the surplus
value created by labor and appropriated by capitalists. His arguments are
technical and apply core theoretical concepts (such as capital and labor) to
explain where rent – the seeming property of land – comes from (Munro,
2013, pp. 223–226). For the topic of land grabbing, Marx's discussion of
differential and, in particular, absolute rent gives deep insight into the
process and resulting dynamics of the phenomenon.

In Volume 3 of *Capital*, Marx gives a detailed analysis of how land
captures surplus value in the form of "rent." Marx identified three types of
rent and the process whereby landowners acquire this rent from capitalists
(or labor) in return for the use of the land that is the property of the
landowner for a limited period. He distinguishes between three ways that
the owners of land, in a capitalist economy, can capture differential rent 1,
differential rent 2, and absolute rent. Differential rent 1 is the form of rent
that is captured by landowners when equal amounts of capital (such as
machinery, mining equipment, tools, and infrastructure) are applied to
lands of differing quality (location, mineral richness, and fertility) by labor.
Differential rent 2 is the type of rent that is captured when different amounts
of capital are applied to lands of the same quality by labor. In both cases, if
the product (for example, oil, minerals, forest products, or agriculture) is
sold in a competitive market, then much of the extra surplus value applied by
labor on the low quality land is transferred (through the price of the product)
to the capitalist who produced the same product on the higher quality land –
and this surplus surplus-value (or super profit) is captured as higher rent by
the owner of the higher quality land (Munro, 2013, pp. 223–226).

The mechanism for the creation and appropriation of absolute rent is
very different, and arguably of more relevance to explain land grabs.
Volume 3 of *Capital* and *Theories of Surplus Value* gives a detailed explanation of absolute rent. In essence, absolute rent arises when capitalists
shift their capital out of some sectors of the economy (say construction,
manufacturing, or finance) into land-based sectors (such as agribusiness,
bioenergy, or tourism). If the new capital is transferred onto land where
such investment already exists, then there is a case of differential rent 2
being created (as different amounts of capital are applied to similar quality
land). However, if the capital is invested in new land then the landowner
will charge a one-off, quantity of rent (absolute rent) for the capitalist to have
access to the new land (Munro, 2013, pp. 223–226). These ideas have much
relevance for analyzing competition, investment, capital formation, and

differential impacts but their application in Africa has only been in the mining (Nwoke, 1984a, 1984b) and oil (Bougrine, 2006; Obeng-Odoom, 2014a, 2014b) sectors. As well as explaining the economic processes whereby the surplus-value produced by workers and captured by capitalists can be distributed to landowners, we learn from Munro (2013, pp. 223–226) that Marx also wrote at length about the political processes whereby the land-owners, capitalist, and working classes struggle against one another to establish new legal, political, and military institutions and organizations that would protect their interests. *Class Struggles in France, 1848–1850* (Marx, 1850/2010) and *The Eighteenth Brumaire of Louis Bonaparte* (Marx, 1963), for example, focus on the conflicts and alliances between the landowning class and the capitalist class (of England and Europe) and the destruction of the legal rights of the peasant and related groups to have access to feudal land and their forced transformation into the emerging working class, and the conflict between these three classes as they restructured the institutions of feudal property into privatized property, destroyed communal cultures and promoted cultures of consumption, undermined the power base of labor and established the legitimacy of capital, and replaced feudal forms of government with capitalist-centered forms of government.

For Marx, the transformation of feudal societies into capitalist societies was not a rational, smooth, or evolutionary process but one based on the application of force, where there was dispossession of peasants and the removal of their access to land, their being forced to become the new industrial working class, the revolutions within nations, and the wars between nations that were needed to establish the new societies and states that would privilege the interests of capital over those of labor and the environment (land). As Munro (2013, pp. 223–226) notes, these legal, political, cultural, and institutional transformations of one form of society into capitalist societies are directly relevant to the social and political processes that – unless counteracted – not only facilitate land grabs in Africa but establish the conditions to spread capitalist requirements of privatization and commercialization into other non-landed sectors.

Many researchers have taken Marx's insights into the use of land and extended them to different locations and different eras. One area where this process or reconstruction has been most prominent is agrarian political economy or political economy devoted to agrarian questions that examines the social relations of land and how it plays out in the process of socio-economic and political development (Bernstein, 2010). Most critical political economists equate Marx's land analysis to the "agrarian question" (Akram-Lodhi & Kay, 2010a, p. 179). Indeed, most eminent agrarian political economists pose the agrarian question in mainly Marxist terms. Consider T. J. Byres' (1995, p. 569) formulation of the agrarian question:

In its broadest meaning, the agrarian question may be defined as the continuing existence in the countryside of poor countries of substantive obstacles to an unleashing of the forces capable of generating economic development, both inside and outside agriculture. It represents a failure of accumulation to proceed adequately in the countryside – that impinging powerfully upon the town; an intimately related failure of class formation in the countryside, appropriate to that accumulation; and a failure of the state to mediate successfully those transitions, which we may encapsulate as the agrarian transition.

While Byres (1995) acknowledges that there are some non-Marxist frames of the agrarian question, he suggests the dominance of Marxian frameworks, as can further be seen in the orientation of the papers published in *Journal of Agrarian Change* and *Journal of Peasant Studies*, two leading outlets for research on agrarian political economy. These approaches, broadly constituting "the historical materialist analytical framework" (Akram-Lodhi & Kay, 2010a, p. 179), have been extensively discussed by Akram-Lodhi and Kay (2010a, 2010b), so they are discussed only briefly here.

Marxist agrarian political economic analysis tends to pay attention to the interconnections between the origin of capitalism, its effect on precapitalist social and land relations, and how these connections, in turn, affect continuing transformation of the countryside and implications for towns and cities. Marx himself was interested in how capitalism could be transcended by the class of proletariat. Specifically, he was interested in the nexus between precapitalist agriculture and large scale, agrarian capital. Transition is, therefore, of major interest in a Marxist framework. For that reason, Marx thought that precapitalist forms of labor were only transient and the peasant class would be absorbed into modern capitalist agriculture. This orientation, however, does not necessarily mean that Marx saw the small-scale farmer as a hindrance to capitalism (Akram-Lodhi & Kay, 2010a, 2010b).

In short, the classic Marxian framework stresses how agricultural producers were dispatched and thrown off their land, expropriated of the means of production, and spat out into the industrial sector where they survive by selling their labor. In the process, both propertied and propertyless classes are formed. While the former gains considerable power, the latter class develops an unequal relation with capital either as dispossessed or as subsumed as wage labor, a cohort with further social differentiation. The process here described by Marx was meant to be historically specific and contingent rather than formulaic or teleological.

Unfortunately, while Marx himself based his work on careful class analysis, drawing scientifically on empirical evidence and warning of the need to eschew hasty generalizations (Akram-Lodhi & Kay, 2010a, 2010b), not all his followers have heeded this caution. Food regime analysis is one important but quite problematic Marxian strand that has received such criticism, and other criticisms, including the denial of agency by food regime analysis (see, for example, Arce & Marsden, 1993; Lewonth & Levins, 2007).

Other readings and adaptations of Marxist agrarian political economy try to avoid these problems. For instance, Henry Bernstein's work is insulated from some of the criticisms of food regime analysis. Bernstein's analysis is grounded sometimes in case studies in India and frames the agrarian question in a way that goes beyond food. His approach looks more carefully at "who owns what, who does what, who gets what, and what do they do with it" (Bernstein, 2010, p. 22). It challenges grand intellectual holisms and binaries such as "big is bad, small is beautiful" (Bernstein, 2010, p. 11). Bernstein (2010) understands Marxist analysis to entail acknowledging differences but takes as given that capitalism is a world system. He has explored how the capitalist order works in diverse countries and regions (see, for example, Bernstein, 2005) and has been very influential in Marxist agrarian thought.

Indeed, about ten years ago, Bernstein joined a team of Marxist agrarian political economists to try to fill a gap in some Marxist analyses that place primary focus on labor and capital while acknowledging landowners only perfunctorily. The team was led by Sam Moyo and Paris Yeros and culminated in the book *Reclaiming the Land* (2005), in which they focused specifically on peasants and landowners in specific regions and areas. This angle too constitutes a strand in Marxist agrarian thought. The interest is in dynamics of socioeconomic change at the country side but also within the rural–urban linkages. Its focus has been on the Global South where key questions include the role of structural adjustment policies in the unmaking or remaking of the peasantry and to elevate issues of politics within peasant movements (Moyo & Yeros, 2005, pp. 2–3).

Accordingly, African Marxist intellectuals have tried to adapt this central framework. The specific focus on rent analysis has become increasingly marginal, while more emphasis has been placed on wider agrarian reforms such as changes in production techniques and alterations to the ways in which property and social relations are produced and reproduced through institutions. This differentiation of concepts, of emphases, and of political tactics (see Amin, 2012), as well as the focus on the rights of farm workers and how they intersect with land rights, significantly extend the classical Marxian framework.

Committed to the analytical Marxist tradition, these methodologies have been novel in their insistence on empirical research and the need to go beyond headline claims about failure or success (see, for example, Moyo et al., 2000; Moyo & Yeros, 2005; Moyo, 2011; Scoones et al., 2011; Moyo, 2018). Among the leading centers for such research is the Sam Moyo African Institute of Agrarian Studies (AIAS), which both does empirical work and is involved in rethinking imperialism, as well as mobilizing for land redistribution.

## REDISTRIBUTING THE LAND

Following the analytical groundwork in agrarian political economy, redistri-buting the land is commonly demanded by Marxists in Africa. Indeed, the journal, *Agrarian South*, explicitly seeks this specific alternative program:

> The agrarian question today is a question of wrestling global agriculture, land and other natural resources from the predatory logic of monopoly – finance capital, and of submitting them to the logic of autonomous, egalitarian, democratic industrial and sustainable development, for the benefit of all the peoples of the world. (The Editors, *Agrarian South* inaugural Editorial, 2012, pp. 1–2)

Redistributing the land has also been a recurrent demand by Africans around the world, including African Americans who demanded "40 Acres and a Mule" (Darity, 2008; Gates, 2013), a variant of this program, discussed in the Introduction of this book. Although regarded as populist, this demand is based on careful alternative economic analyses. Before his sudden death, Sam Moyo provided a detailed overview (Moyo, 2018), so what follows is only an attempt to paraphrase a more nuanced discussion. Two approaches are common, as can be seen in the debates by Archie Mafeje and Sam Moyo. One view (led by Mafeje) was that the land question is dominant in settler colonies of Africa where over 60 per cent of the land was alienated and hence the case of reclaiming the land is directly made. For this view, land tenure in non-settler societies is more egalitarian and hence can be supported as nonexploitative and, instead, nurturing of the use of one's labor for one's own use or the use of kith and kin.

An alternative view is that the land question prevails in the non-settler societies as well. In this alternative view, the influence of colonialism is not simply the physical concentration of land, but also the restructuring of production in ways that continue to privilege the colonizer. So, land individuation, the promotion of certain export crops, and the increasing role that land plays in processes of neoliberalization must all lead to the contention that non-settler societies in Africa also face the land question. With growing land grabbing as earlier discussed, the lines between these two views have increasingly become blurred – even if the property relations being produced with the growing commodification of land are not as unequal as those in, for example, apartheid relations.

Many countries in Africa experiment with land distribution. In the 1980s, for example, Thomas Sankara of Burkina Faso rolled out a land distribution programme (Murrey, 2018). Zimbabwe is the quintessential example of modern-day land redistribution programs in Africa. Although widely regarded as a failure, the empirical evidence, as shown in Table 7.1, points to important successes.

Additional qualitative evidence (e.g., Moyo et al., 2000; Moyo, 2011; Scoones et al., 2011) suggests that, in spite of implementation challenges

Table 7.1 *Land holdings by farm type, 1980–2010*

|  | 1980 | | 2000 | | 2010 | |
|---|---|---|---|---|---|---|
| | Farms/households (thousands) | | | | | |
| | 000s | % | 000s | % | 000s | % |
| Peasantry | 700.00 | 98.00 | 1,125.00 | 99.00 | 1,321.00 | 98.00 |
| Middle farms | 8.50 | 1.00 | 8.5 | 1.00 | 30.9 | 2.00 |
| Large farms | 5.40 | 1.00 | 4.96 | 0.4 | 1.37 | 0.10 |
| Agro-estates | 0.30 | 0.10 | 0.30 | 0.02 | 0.25 | 0.02 |
| | Area held (ha, thousands) | | | | | |
| | Ha | % | ha | % | ha | % |
| Peasantry | 16,400 | 49 | 20,067 | 61 | 25,826 | 79 |
| Middle farms | 1,400.00 | 4.00 | 1,400.00 | 4.00 | 4,400.00 | 13.00 |
| Large farms | 13,000.00 | 39.00 | 8,691.60 | 27.00 | 1,156.90 | 4.00 |
| Agro-estates | 2,567.00 | 8.00 | 2,567.00 | 8.00 | 1,494.60 | 5.00 |
| | Average farm size (ha) | | | | | |
| Peasantry | 23 | | 18 | | 20 | |
| Middle farms | 165 | | 165 | | 142 | |
| Large farms | 2,407.00 | | 1,754.00 | | 844.00 | |
| Agro-estates | 8,672.00 | | 8,672.00 | | 6,051.00 | |

*Source:* Moyo, 2011, table 1, p. 262

and important neglected issues such as the rights of farm workers, the land distribution program was quite successful. As Table 7.1 shows, the program created a small class of "middle-income farmers," and reduced the concentration of land in the hands of white, large-scale commercial farmers. Indeed, the sharp reduction of land concentration and the attempt to contain monopolistic land structures that privileged white farmers and penalized black peasants can be counted as one of the successes of the program. From this perspective, the problem of Zimbabwe, then, cannot all be pinned on a failed land reform, whatever that means. More compelling explanations can, however, be found in the imposition of imperial sanctions and the trigger of economic aggression against Zimbabwe.

Still, it is questionable that physically redistributing land would bring about wider redistribution. Consider the problem of absentee ownership. The land redistribution program correctly identified problems of land concentration, land speculation and absentee landownership. While it has been argued that redistributing such land to black farm managers would not cause mismanagement because the white farm owners were absentee anyway (Moyo, 1998), it is questionable whether the members of this new class of black landowners themselves did not create a new class of absentee owners. Indeed so widespread is absentee ownership now that, as recent research (Chiweshe, 2017) shows, both in *Fungai Chaeruika vs. Heather Guild* (appeal) and in *Heather Guild vs. Fungai Chaeruika* (first trial case), the courts in Zimbabwe were consistent and decisive that black beneficiaries were becoming the new absentee land owners and that, whether black or white, absentee ownership was not acceptable Characterised by underinvestment and mismanagement at a time when using the land for sustainable livelihoods is crucially the Zimbabwean courts have tried to address the problems of absentee ownership by redistributing land from blacks to whites.

There is no denial that black farmers – especially women – struggled with structural insecurity of tenure, but land redistribution failed to address what Thorsten Veblen (1923/2009) famously regarded as one of the most serious problems in modern capitalism: absentee ownership (see Chapter 3 on a similar issue in Egypt). Indeed, even bigger than Veblenian absentee ownership is the problem Henry George identified: how such absenteeism is yoked together with speculation, the social generation but private appropriation of land rents, and social inequality. Georgists (e.g., Gaffney, 2009; Haila, 2016) have always argued that physically redistributing land cannot be a solution because those who have small parcels of land but benefit from higher rents and value will evidently be better off than those with equal or even larger tracts of land but who extract lower or no rents. The question then, is rent inequality, not really inequality in physical amounts of land, although the two can also be interlinked. In this sense, the revers land redistribution by the Zimbabwean courts is similarly problematic.

There have been additional land reforms, including titling for presumed security, and proposals by Marxists for the reforms to take into account farm workers' rights. Yet, intersectional problems of race, gender, and class – mediated by rent – have not, as yet, received as much attention. Indeed, this question of rent is almost missing in the work of the leading thinkers on the Zimbabwe land question, but, in the wider question of nationalizing the mines and the rigs, at least, the early Marxists from Africa (see, for example, Nwoke, 1984a, 1984b) gave it serious consideration it, together with imperialism.

## IMPERIALISM

As a concept, imperialism is quite slippery. The old notions of imperialism offered by thinkers such as Lenin were organically linked to colonialism and the thirst for continuing profit. Later conceptions, such as those offered by Rosa Luxemburg, suggesting that without external markets capitalism would falter, were notably criticized by the African Marxist political economist Samir Amin as too simplistic and not very attentive to imperialism itself. To Amin (1977, pp. 108–109), imperialism means more than the expansion of capitalism, and it is distinctive for intensifying uneven development. It generates a labor aristocracy in the center and leads to the erosion of backward areas at the periphery constituted by small- and medium-scale economic activities that are not competitive. It is typified by the ascent of monopoly capital in the core areas of the world system and the suppression of weaker classes at the periphery. This classical definition is offered by other Marxists, too. They are tied to notions of globalization and internationalization, as pointed out in a special commentary in the *Review of African Political Economy* (Bush & Szeftel, 1999). So, there is a strong connection with global expansion of capitalism. But imperialism is not just about capitalism expanding on a global scale. It is, instead, about domination of foreign control (see Smith, 2016). The "foreign" in the hegemonic process can be by the state or other supranational bodies. There are those who contend that the state has withered due to globalization and hence imperialism is mainly by other political economic actors such as transnational corporations.

A second view positions US power as imperialist and focuses greatly on American expansionism and Zionism. A third holds that imperialism remains mainly in the domain of interstate conflict and rivalry (Dunn, 2009, pp. 306–317). This third view is currently the most dominant and is styled as the new imperialism literature (Robinson, 2007). David Harvey is a chief advocate of it, emphasizing in his book, *The New Imperialism* (Harvey, 2003), interstate rivalry and how this leads to domination. It has a ring of the classical core–periphery analysis to it and it powerfully shows change and continuity in imperialist processes by highlighting the continuity of "primitive accumulation" in "accumulation by dispossession." Yet its artificial separation of politics from economics and the placing of one sphere as economic and the other as political have drawn sharp criticism (Brenner, 2006; Robinson, 2007; Dunn, 2009).

To Robinson (2007), contemporary imperialism is broader and multi-pronged. It is certainly capitalism on a world scale, but the domination is by multiple actors in different class fractions both within and outside the territory of domination. Power here is diffused rather than wielded mainly by the nation-state or the transnational corporation. Similarly, the boundaries, if any, between the economy and the polity are blurred. There is a codependence and each sphere has elements of the other while the two are also fused together. But the hallmarks of imperialism remain ever evident despite the substantial changes in the form or the process. These are empire building, territorial expansion, the alloy of faraway markets previously unarticulated to centers of power, and domination of the weak by the strong classes within an expanding but highly exploitative world system that is frequently portrayed as good for the exploited. Messianic features often imbue the imperialist self-belief in being on a form of holy mission for the good of all (Dunn, 2009, pp. 121–127; Stilwell, 2012, pp. xviii), although the source of the right to embark on such a pilgrimage of honor is not made explicit.

This epoch of imperialism in Africa is a third type, rather different from the two earlier versions recently analyzed by Zack-Williams (2013) for the *Review of African Political Economy*. According to Zack-Williams, the first epoch (1875–1945) covered the period of colonialism and fits of independence, and the second epoch was typified by imperialism without by a formal colonizer (late 1940s to the end of the 1990s). The present imperial process (2000–) is therefore distinct from the old forms of imperialism.

However, like earlier forms of imperialism, the contemporary iteration is resisted by struggles of various kinds, some in the form of revolts, others in the form of alternative production in ways that challenge the prevailing ideas (Moyo and Yeros, 2005; Moyo, 2018), not all of which are in the nature of social movements. Nationalizing, or delinking, is one such act of resistance.

## NATIONALIZING, DELINKING

Many Marxists take the view that nationalization is a panacea or, at least, a much better alternative to unfettered marketization monopoly capital. In turn, they seek economic nationalism in the form of either greater protectionism or the nationalization of oil industries. In *Naija Marxisms: Revolutionary Thought in Nigeria*, Adam Mayer (2016) provides a detailed account of the nuances of the work of Marxists in Nigeria where some of the continent's leading Marxists are based. The work of most of these scholars is focused on Nigeria, but it is has been flourishing even if it is unknown to the Western world.

Africa-wide, Marxist analysts have produced world-class research on Marxist alternatives, but this body of work has deliberately been ignored (Mayer, 2016; Collins, 2017). A leading scholar in this genre is C. N. Nwoke (see Collins, 2017, for a critical celebration of Nwoke's work). For Nwoke (1984a, 1984b, 1990, 1991, 1995, 2007, 2013a, 2013b; Collins, 2017), the Global North and the Global South are locked together in a tight world system. The fate of these two, the Global South as the exporter of its own mineral riches and the Global North as the consumer of the fruits of the South, is locked together in a world system in which the gains from this "trade" are skewed in favour of the North. There is, in fact, a distribution of benefits from the South to the North in a process that is sanctioned militarily either directly or indirectly by the countries from which the TNCs have emerged. With legal discourses of the sanctity of contracts as a cudgel, unfavorable initial contracts between TNCs and African states to the effect that TNCs owned the minerals that they "found" flourished. Because such contracts were deemed sacrosanct, no changes were warranted and before Africa's own eyes, TNCs literally siphoned African minerals from the continent to Europe and elsewhere in the advanced capitalist regions. The outcome of this maldistribution, Nwoke argued, is the underdevelopment of the Global South and the unjust enrichment of the North. But, as observed, a related outcome of the imbalance is environmental crisis. The outcome of this maldistribution, Nwoke argued, is the underdevelopment of the Global South and the unjust enrichment of the North. But, as Nwoke (2016) has more recently observed, a related outcome of the imbalance is environmental crisis.

Nwoke (1984a, 1984b, 2013a, 2013b) offers a tripartite solution. First, how this problem is analyzed ought to change. The bargaining model, drawing on the contribution of Vernom, is his focus of critique. Because this model holds that, after a certain time, power automatically shifts from TNCs to host nations, this framework seeks to justify poor terms for the South for the "initial period," which could be as long as a generation. Since the TNCs expect the risk of losing it all later, they try to gain it all quickly. Third world nations, on the other hand, do not question these contracts; in part because they buy into the discourse that if they destroy the sanctity of contracts they also destroy the prospects of doing business with the West and in part because they expect that in the not-too-distant future it will be their turn. As Nwoke shows, this "future" never really comes because the uneven relationship between TNCs and host nation government reflects the wider uneven asymmetries of power. TNCs from France working in the Côte d'Ivoire reflect both the historic unequal relationship between a colonizer and a subjugated state and the uneven power relations between a capitalist powerful country and a subordinated peripheral or weaker country. It is within this constellation of power that the contract is formulated. Also, the bargaining model is vague. In its reference to "gains" it conflates a wide variety of returns that arise from diverse forces and processes. Rents, in particular, arising from "unearned" processes get mixed up with profits that arise from industry and innovation. Without untangling these forces, TNCs become ever more powerful, tending to monopolists and oligopolists through the continuous appropriation of both what is legitimately theirs and what is not and being protected by both contract documents and the constellation of powers, including those in their own countries.

On the basis of this critique, Nwoke (1984a, 1984b, 1986, 2013a, 2013b) offers his second solution in terms of an alternative way to think about TNCs and mining. He favors a Marxist rent analysis because it at least puts the focus of "gains" on rents and its various components as well as power relations. Specifically, Nwoke focuses on "absolute rent," which he equates to monopoly rent, arising from the power to control the oil industry and differential rent arising from the quality of the ores of the Global South. The analyst using this framework must seek – even if imprecisely – try to establish what rent arises from the process, take that away from TNCs, and give back to them their fair share in the form of normal profits.

It is the logical consequences of this analysis that constitute Nwoke's third methodological stance. To capture differential rent, the Global South must be the owners of its own mines. As landowners, all such differential rent will go to them. Absolute rent can be but is not necessarily a consequence of capturing differential rent. To capture that one too, governments in the Third World must form associations and cartels. In this way, they can shape and control the industry, the price of ore, and hence extract absolute rent. This program, which Nwoke (1986) called "economic nationalism," also includes training the talents of the South, breaking the technological dependence of the South on the North, and employing nationals to run the mining sector.

These suggestions are profound, but is ownership structure alone enough to prevent the problems that Nwoke correctly identifies? Edward Ansah and Joseph Mintah (2012) interviewed workers of both types of organization and concluded that, as the logic is similar, these organizations are similarly exploitative. In other words, nationalization in itself cannot address other structural problems when the state is wedded to the idea of growth forever.

Delinking is a similarly spirited alternative. Indeed, it entails nationalization of monopolies or the socialization of the economy as something inherently good but also as a major step toward bringing a unity between political and economic democracy. Yet delinking also has important unique features. Advocated by arguably the most well-known African Marxist, Samir Amin, it has been articulated clearly in books such as *Delinking* (1990) and *The World We Wish to See* (2008). Amin also gave several public lectures and interviews about this idea[1]; likewise, there have been many reviews published in various outlets (see, for example, Pieterse, 1994; Egan, 2011, Zhang, 2013; Kenji, 2018). Delinking has three parts: critique, political alternative, and strategy. The critique arises from the dependency theoretic argument that, through it being linked to the Global North, Africa, in particular, has become not only dependent but also exploited. Amin typically goes back to colonialism and makes his way to the present to show these forms of compelled dependency and the various forms of exploitation.

In Africa, Samir Amin has been the greatest thinker on these issues of delinking and other similarly alternative socialisms. His persistence and energy from the days when he published in tome – *Accumulation on a World Scale: A Critique of the Theory of Underdevelopment* (Amin, 1974) – to his last publications, made him a towering Marxist not simply adopting Marxist socialism but adapting Marxist thought to develop alternative socialisms for Africa. Nevertheless, his delinking alternative is not systematically linked to environment, to the conditions of workers of different gender and races, or to urban and regional development. He recognizes it, but he points to the need for others to link it to his and other analysts' contentions. Of course, he discusses inequality – but not inequality cumulatively developed through slave/indentured labor

---

[1] See various Youtube lectures and interviews: https://www.youtube.com/watch?v=F07FgOx7FVc; https://www.youtube.com/watch?v=s1whGpS2OUU; https://www.youtube.com/watch?v=TIp3hWCCRzc (accessed 9 September 2018).

systems. Amin does not consider whether his alternatives are mutually reinforcing or whether some undermine others. For instance, in what ways are demands for the recognitions of land rights married to questions about industrialization? How, for example, can we see the polycentric world Amin proposes when the diversity of interests are conflictual and not complementary (see also Kenji, 2018) in practical terms? Amin provides no systematic responses or demonstration. Thus, although his critique is compelling, his socialist alternatives require further analysis. Samir Amin (2011, 2014) himself acknowledged that he was making an *input* into broader paths. He insists that no one student can provide an answer; indeed, that it is the Africans themselves who have to develop the alternative. This way of formulating a vision for Africa must be accurate because social problems require *social*, not individual, responses.

## CONCLUSION

Socialisms provide clear and developed alternative paths for Africa to consider. Marxist-inspired policies discussed in this chapter might be questioned by some as centered on system-conforming rather than system-transcending socialisms. Yet this dichotomy is forced. The alternatives covered in this chapter seek to transform the capitalist system from within. In this regard, anti-imperialism is not merely empty talk. Although "talking anti-imperialism" is good in itself, it also provides a framework for autonomous action. Small-scale agriculture is not only important as an idea: it could serve the material needs of people well, as the example of Zimbabwe shows. Whether twenty-first century Africa can, in its entirely and complexity, be liberated through such agrarian strategies is, however, controversial.

Land redistribution and nationalization can work for some time, but it is questionable whether it can eliminate absentee ownership. More fundamentally, physical distribution of land, without any reference to the value of land, can be a vehicle for equity but only for a short while. Also, the record of national oil companies in Africa in relation to the needs of labor, the economy, and the environment (see also previous chapters on trade and economic growth) makes it imperative to ask whether the prevailing socialisms are the most viable alternatives now and in the future.

*Agrarian South* was founded to try to update these Marxist-socialist frameworks (The Editors, 2012). It sought to do so by redefining the "agrarian question." It claimed that, analytically, the agrarian question can be explained as an approach that recognizes the centrality of land, its relations, and mobilization to the global emancipation of the oppressed and the centrality of land reform for progress and prosperity. The agrarian question has evolved in both spatial and temporal terms. In spatial terms, its coverage, analytically at least, has expanded from the Global North to the Global South. Temporally, its emphases have expanded from industrialization (nineteenth century), through national liberation (twentieth century), to monopoly-finance (twenty-first century). In its more contemporary forms, the agrarian question places significant emphasis on gender and ecology. Politically, the agrarian question grapples with seeking a unity among various forms of political organizations, including rural-based movements, urban trade unions, and others within as well as across borders.

While significantly wider than the classic scope for socialisms, these new formulations retain their capital-centered core as well as their emphasis on the physical redistribution of land. They neglect land *rent*, a major source of stratification. In *Democracy and Socialism,* Marx Hirsch discusses "the outcome of socialism" as "the unconscious growth of social structures" (Hirsch, 1966, pp. 261–263). To say that land and, in particular, land rent is key in the story of stratification, however, is to agree with K. W. Kapp that "the process of causation is complex and circular and, as such, has a tendency to become cumulative" (Kapp, 1950/1971, p. xvii).

That is, causation tends to change form because it exists over a long period of time during which one factor acts on another, which, in turn, depends on another factor in the process and so on. Thus initial pollution from an oil rig takes on different levels of toxicity because the pollutant mixes up with other pollutants in the environment, which, in turn, mix up with other chemicals over time. In turn, the resulting malady is an aggregate just as the environment in which it occurs is also an aggregate. It is these circular and dynamic interdependencies that generate or shape the cumulative effects of social costs.

Clearly, capitalism must be changed, but it is not just capitalism that must be challenged. Neither is the problem just colonialism or just imperialism. Rather, it is conditions of cumulative causation that stretch from precapitalist slavery logics to date and the ongoing concretization of institutions such as rent that ought to be fundamentally addressed. Although Marxists claim rent to be important, somehow they tend not to systematically consider its socialisation in their alternatives. However, as this chapter suggests, this missing link can be better developed to explain – and ultimately transcend – social problems discussed at length in Chapter 1. How to do so cannot be abstract and removed from the African context. Clearly, then, it is not just socialisms, but Africanisms that need to be considered even more carefully.

# 8

## Africanisms

Marxist-inspired socialism tends to be built on the widely repeated idea that it is either "socialism or barbarism," which is the left's version of the right-wing motto: "There is no alternative (TINA)". However, neither socialism nor neoliberalism is acceptable, especially when barbarism is clearly not the preserve of only capitalism but also socialism. It was in this context, that Max Hirsch wrote in *Democracy versus Socialism* (Hirsch, 1966), that an alternative path is needed that is not just mutations of socialism and capitalism such as dictatorships, developmental states, or Nordic welfare models.

The interest in Africanisms can be understood within this context. Certainly that is how George Padmore saw the principal challenge when he wrote his classic book, *Pan-Africanism or Communism?* The Coming Struggle for Africa (Padmore, 1956). In more recent times, Rita Kiki Edozie's book, *"Pan" Africa Rising* (Edozie, 2017) can be mentioned as providing a critical defence that there are alternatives to both capitalism and socialism. That such alternatives are needed is quite straightforward to justify.

Africa's underdevelopment is the product of cumulative change, a concept that many institutionalists have adopted to explain transformation (Veblen, Myrdal, Galbraith, and Kapp, as examples). To complicate the picture, the African condition is also the outcome of ongoing contradictions and exploitation whether through trade, through debt, or through land reforms of various kinds.

Addressing these challenges must entail several changes. A key step is breaking cartels and monopolies, especially ones that control natural resources in Africa. By dismantling those forces of economic concentration, systematically building social states, institutionalizing compensation mechanisms to address past wrongs, and treating land as common property, it should be possible to overcome Africa's uneven relationship with TNCs. This strategy cannot be easily utilized without a struggle because

236

previous attempts have sometimes led to military action by former colonizers and current neocolonial imperialists. However, evidence from Africa, including the literature on "Africa uprising" (Branch & Mampilly, 2015; Murrey, 2018), suggests that it can succeed.

Africanisms, or African socialisms, is the umbrella descriptor of these strategies. The idea does not have one meaning, so it is not necessarily coherent except in terms of rejecting both capitalism and socialism and seeking to draw on institutions that have long been considered African or are often appropriated as such because they are consistent with other institutions in Africa. Analytical coherence is not necessarily the vision of these Africanisms, which are, in any case, articulated by a wide range of thinkers with diverse experiences and backgrounds. Rather, Africanisms strive to use this rich diversity to practically address the pressing challenges of Africa without falling into the traps of market dictatorship experienced under both competitive and monopoly capitalism. Africanisms also reject the top-down colonial and colonizing approach of socialisms. According to the African historian, Emmanuel Akyeampong of Harvard University:

The term had multiple meanings, and its advocates were quick to stress that they were not communist, and some said they were not even Marxist. ... African socialism was a search for an indigenous model of economic development for a generation that was justifiably ambivalent about capitalism, but wary of being put in the communist camp ... Importantly, advocates of African socialism often proposed bold and transformative visions for their countries. (Akyeampong, 2018, p. 69)

Many leading Africans have sought to revive these Africanisms and many more call for at least revisiting the strategies. According to Akyeampong (2018, p. 69), "these visions might be worth revisiting, devoid of the paradigm of socialism." The call for a revival of Africanisms also has a popular basis. Indeed, the 2014 insurrection populaire in Burkina Faso appealed directly to the Africanism of Thomas Sankara when it removed Blaise Campaore from office after twenty-seven years of dictatorship (Murrey, 2018). While successfully resisting the attempt by Campaore's private army to stage a coup to reinstate him, a second insurrection populaire, again inspired by the spirit of Sanakarism, was staged (Zeilig, 2017). The repudiation of the labels of "capitalism" and "socialism" is both philosophical and pragmatic. Philosophically, these two world paradigms and economic systems struggle to appreciate the nuances of African economies.

Much like Western civilization and Western thought, the rationalism on which these two systems are based is structurally Manichean and inherently incapable of embracing complexity. The rejection of existing labels and of being labelled is pragmatic in the sense that it facilitates learning and using what works regardless of whether it is socialist or capitalist; labels that speak of purist ideals and academic purity that are rather too abstract for the urgent challenge of African liberation.

On the similarities between Africanisms and socialisms, Africanists reject the contention that the former is patterned after the latter. If there are overlaps, the argument goes, it is rather socialisms that seek to mimic Africanisms, while still devaluing African experiences and value systems by failing to acknowledge them (Mohan, 1966). Indeed, it has been forcefully argued that Marx borrowed heavily from Africanists and African systems – without acknowledging his debts. Pan-African scholars (see Hossein, 2016, 2017) also have carefully shown a black economic tradition that is quite distinct from the capitalism rebuked by Marx as well as the monopoly and financialized capitalisms challenged by leading African Marxist scholars such as Samir Amin.

Thus, the overlaps between Africanisms, on the one hand, and socialisms/ capitalisms on the other must be "the African paradigm in Capital" (Agozino, 2014), "Black Marxism," or "the Black Radical Tradition" (Robinson, 1983/ 2000). In its current form, this "New Pan African Economics" (Edozie, 2017) is a range of approaches to pursuing economic emancipation and maintaining economic self-sufficiency centered on Afrocentric philosophies and cultures that craft an eclectic and dynamic third way to both capitalism and socialism. As a contrasting Afrocentric response to neoliberal Africa rising narratives, including human capital (see Chapter 4 of this book), Afri-capitalism, and Ubuntu business models of Africanism emphasize indigenization not just of the people involved in the business (what local content policies try to do in oil capitalism, see Chapter 4), but also the infusion of a philosophy of pan-Africanism in business. Indeed, by seeking equality of both opportunity and outcome, this pan-African economics styles itself as quite distinct and new (Edozie, 2017).

If so, it cannot be equated to "black capitalism." The latter, contradictory philosophy is simply a capitalist strategy for bringing liberation to the masses – much like Hernando de Soto's well-known idea of property-owning society discussed in Chapter 2. Black businesses, whether they serve just black people or the wider society, in this philosophy, must also be exploitative – much like capitalism itself. Even if this system is not exploitative of local black labor, it must be exploitative or endorse the exploitation of labor, including black labor, elsewhere in the world system (Boggs, 1969; Turner, 2010). It is precisely for these reasons that, even if new forms of Afri-capitalism are not quite the same as black capitalism, it is more empowering to emphasize the philosophies of old pan-Africanism, the challenge of the current and past economic systems of oppression, and the pursuit of new agendas for liberation, including true African trade systems, as discussed in Chapter 5.

This reconstruction must entail social change in how resources are owned, distributed, and maintained. Stratification economists (e.g., Bogan & Darity, 2008; Gĩthĩnji, 2015; Hamilton et al., 2015; Paul et al., 2018) can try to do so while infusing new strategies such as employment programs (e.g., Bogan & Darity, 2008; Hamilton et al., 2015; Paul et al., 2017, 2018) to both reinvigorate and transcend historical struggles. Such an engagement could revalorize old, resilient African practices of autonomy and sharing (e.g., Hossein, 2016, 2017), including the philosophy of burkindlum: which emphasises active rejection of all injustices, embracing a spirit of sacrifice for the marginalised, and the proactive pursuit of social inclusion by rethinking old approach to inclusive development (Sore, 2018, pp. 231–235). In doing so, they are critical because they call into question some of the old Africanisms such as strategies based on the problematic suggestions that ethnic identities are innate or biologically constructed (e.g., Gĩthĩnji, 2015). These Africanisms may be indigenous, but they are not backward-looking. Rather, as Rita Edozie (2017) suggests, they show how a new modernity could be created by Africans, although this agency continues to be shaped by the structure of the world system, with which Africanisms contend and try to rewrite.

The central contention in this chapter is that strategies from within show considerable potential, but they are also significantly limited by historical burdens and continuing forces of discrimination and underdevelopment shaped by the combined experiences of historical and contemporary forces within the global system. The rest of the chapter focuses on the political economy of (a) addressing past expropriations, (b) managing current expropriations, and (c) preventing future expropriations. Among the forces that could drive these changes is the role of protests. As a counter hegemonic force, the role of popular pressure, however, must be seen alongside other sources of change and inertia such that, even within the state, there could be tensions and contradictions between the government and the courts.

## ADDRESSING PAST EXPROPRIATIONS

Addressing past expropriations need not be violent, as it is often thought. Indeed it does not even have to be hostile or confrontational. Under international law, slavery was a crime against humanity. The idea that it was not a crime at the time it was committed is factually wrong. At the time of slavery there was massive protest by leading philosophers. In the parliaments of Britain, for example, the illegality of this criminal institution was recurrently discussed. Likewise, the idea that there was indigenous slavery is not sufficient reason for not calling slavery a crime. Indigenous slavery did not regard Africans as subhumans. Rather, slaves could become members of the royalty. In many international cases of slavery, in fact, the Africans were participants under duress (see Konadu, 2015). Consequently, Sir Beckles' (2013) lifetime treatise that Africa is owed debts by the world powers is compelling. Going to the International Criminal Court can provide one way of seeking justice by demanding these reparations.

For this purpose, it is possible to estimate the boundaries of the reparations program. William Darity, Jr.'s (2008) proposal to reengage the "40 Acres and a Mule" desideratum requires serious attention. Apology rather than the hollow expressions of regret is what is needed. Regret does not carry legal power or obligations; apology does because it gives legal grounds to press charges of crimes against humanity (Beckles, 2013). These charges would need to entail estimating the cost of torture and violence. On technical grounds, both settler and non-settler African countries could be compensated for their dispossession by paying them the present value of rent accruing to that land until now. Africans are also entitled to the "mule" or, in today's terms, public support. This support must be, as explained in Chapter 1, measure up to J. R. Commons' standard of "reasonable value." Several calculations can usefully be presented by African and other analysts complemented by processes of negotiations to arrive at what is "reasonable" to the courts. The payment of reparations must be unconditional but steps need to be taken to institute mechanisms to prevent further torture. The courts can be used to address the mechanism for payment. Genuine cooperation would require parliaments around the world to provide the laws that would create the foundations for legal action.

Reparations for financial aggression against Africa would take a rather different form. Such repayments would seek to recognize that, on the one hand, trading in Western currency has done disproportionate damage to African economies, which have been left, in the case of Francophone African countries, for example, highly indebted. On the other hand, trade and currency exchange, in particular, have significantly enhanced the value of Western currencies (Chapter 5). In this global gamble, the weaker African economies and currencies have been the net losers.

It has long been recognized that this system is inequitable, but the range of solutions on offer does not include reparations. James Tobin, for instance, proposed what is now called the "Tobin tax." In more recent times, levies of various kinds have been proposed beyond currency taxes on the principle that this pseudo-arbitrage is a problem of globalization generally. In turn, France imposed small and differential levies on the cost of flights. The idea being to use the money for the benefit of those who are made worse off by globalization. Others see such a tax more as an intermediary step for global governance where the revenues accrue not to governments but to global organizations for distribution (see Uemura, 2007, 2012 for more detailed discussion).

What is being proposed here is demanding reparations for currency volatility that has happened mainly because African currencies are vulnerable – their value essentially dependent on the volatility of the euro and the dollar – and the strength of the Western currency is buoyed by landed property transactions in Africa. This type of reparation can have the additional effect of reducing currency gambling that hurts African economies (Kapoor, 2004). Revenues from the Reparations Currency Tax could be managed by the African Union and an African Union Parliament that could distribute the proceeds on collectively agreed bases, including which currencies have been most adversely affected and evaluation of national proposals to use these revenues to bring about economic inclusion and social protection.

Slavery is not the only past wrong. Indeed, the African Union, through "The Abuja Proclamation," has been seeking reparations for "African enslavement, colonization and neo-colonization" (OAU, 1993, p. 1). So, racial discrimination and neocolonial "economic advice" forced on Africans are others. In South Africa, for example, much has been said about land reform as a way to transfer wealth (see Chapter 7), but past wealth accumulation cannot easily be addressed by modern-day land reform. The inheritance of historical wealth/poverty reinforces racial inequalities. So, as research by leading South African scholar, Melanie Walker, suggests, those who inherit greater wealth surge ahead, while those who are born into poverty face significantly more daunting barriers to break the chains that hold them back (Walker, 2015, 2016). Institutional political economists tend to recommend an inheritance tax to transfer some of this wealth back to the state for wider redistribution (Stilwell, 2017, 2019).

Stratification economists have sought to widen this strategy by advocating the use of "baby bonds." According to Darrick Hamilton and William Darity, Jr. (2010, p. 215), these would be funds held

for children in families in the lowest wealth quartile and accessible once the child turns 18 years of age. These individual trusts could grow in federally managed investment accounts with guarantees of at least 1.5–2% annual growth rates. We also would determine eligibility for such a program based upon the net worth position of the child's family rather than their income, e.g. all children whose families fell below the national median for wealth would receive 'baby bonds'.

These public bonds are intended to enable historically marginalized Africans to mitigate their starting disadvantage. With the "Rhodes Must Fall" uprising in South Africa, there is clearly a case for adapting such proposals there, given "the apartheid regime made sure that it spent almost five to six times more on a white child than it did on a black child" (Baker, 2019b, p. 40). One independent estimate (Wunder, 2019) suggests that a universal child allowance of US$ 9,330 can lift 75 per cent of households with poor children out of poverty.

## MANAGING CURRENT EXPROPRIATIONS

What about managing current expropriation? As pointed out in Chapter 1, the remedy of past wrongs is incomplete without liberation from current expropriations. Indeed, as both wrongs create structures for damaging intergenerational equity and the environment, managing current expropriations must entail an "ecology for economic change" (Adedeji, 1987), and lasting solutions for "the crime of poverty" (George, 1885).

The remedy that I propose to resolve the tension between the need for technical assistance from abroad and the costs of accepting it is to reclaim the African commons for the people. Specifically, I propose that Africans develop policies that can dissolve monopolies, prevent the formation of new monopolies, and diffuse prosperity throughout the economy. By adopting a tax on land values, not only will resource rents be transferred to the public sector, but the corruption that occurs when rents are privatized will be diminished. If there is little left to take, there is also nothing to fight over. Thus, one of the key remedies lies in the development of tax capacity in African countries. If the rents that currently give rise to conflict and exploitation can ever be fully captured by governments in lieu of other taxes, Africans might finally have the chance to develop their countries on their own terms, not based on the dictates of donors.

The key steps for this alternative entail going beyond growth, promoting happiness, sharing the Africa-wide commons, and empowering labor. In what follows, I clarify these steps and also investigate the obstacles to implementing them, concluding that the prospects for change provide stronger grounds than what J. K. Galbraith (1979) called the "equilibrium of poverty."

## Beyond Growth

As a political-economic concept, "beyond growth" can sound ambiguous, but on careful examination, it is a concrete vision and approach to social and ecological economic analysis. Generations of social and ecological economists have devoted much time to its study, theoretically and empirically. It is a "limit to growth" thesis and goes way back to Mishan (1967) and Meadows, Meadows, Randers, and Bahrens (1972). The Meadows Report strongly advocated stabilization, even a reduction of growth, including the highly controversial recommendation of population control, and the cherished democratic ethos of allowing the nation-state and its peoples to determine for themselves "what is produced, how it is produced, and for whom it is produced." "Beyond growth" provides a radical challenge to the mainstream advocacy of bigger and more integrated markets in the name of globalization. One beyond growth advocate was Schumacher (1973) who upheld "Budhist living," that is, minimal consumption, as an example of a beyond growth philosophy. Another beyond growth advocate is Daly (1990) whose notion of "steady-state economics" is now widely used.

Like Schumacher's "Budhist living," steady-state economics is not an Africa-specific argument, but a universal approach. It is based on the view that the ecosystem the economy is in has a limit, even if the solar system is regarded as limitless. According to Daly (2007), as the ecosystem cannot grow beyond its boundaries, it follows that the economic subsystem has constraints too. Beyond these limits, any further economic growth is uneconomic in the sense that it hurts society to grow. While the hierarchies of limits do not work like a wall against which a car will typically crash, but rather like a budget against which one can borrow but at devastating consequences, the limits to growth are real and dire.

The clash in the current capitalist world, Daly notes, is one between two impossibilities: one physical (ever-growing economic growth), the other political (the political challenge to stop economic growth). As the economy is cast within a finite biosphere and growth everlasting will eventually become "uneconomic," the current model is likely to lead to clashes between human activities and natural abilities. "Beyond growth," then, implies reversing the emphasis on growth in economic policy by destressing accumulation and realizing its physical and ecological limits, and Africa can play a part in this process.

One way to commence this trans-growth and transformative journey is to deemphasize GDP stories and emphasize broader measures of well-being such as happiness.

## Promoting Happiness

Gross national happiness as a policy priority is widely associated with Bhutan where, since 1972, the economic managers of the country have focused their efforts at enhancing the happiness of the people of Bhutan – not their material goals. Even prior to 1972 and dating as far back as 1729, the country had a legal code obligating the leaders to make Bhutanese happy. Since the institutionalization of constitutional monarchy in 2008, it is a constitutional duty (Article 9) for every leader of Bhutan to expand the frontiers of happiness in the country. Bhutanese stress spirituality in their conception of happiness, and humility and service are also emphasized, as are sustainability and the concern for material suffering. These ingredients are systematically collected and analyzed by the Centre for Bhutan Studies. The results of happiness analysis serve as the basis of policy in that country (Ura et al., 2012). The Bhutan experience shows, then, that happiness is not just about emotions: it is much broader.

Generally, the ideas behind happiness go beyond continuously aspiring for more money to wider considerations of love, cooperation, sharing quality time with friends and family, having a can-do attitude, good health, empowering education, spirituality, and a harmonious relationship with nature, sometimes to the point of worship. These can be measured, but not in the way orthodox economists propose to do it, which is reductionist and narrow. For instance, Becker observed that "love and other emotional attachments, such as sexual activity or frequent close contact with a particular person, can be considered particular nonmarketable household commodities" (1974, p. 327). This neoclassical economics view of the family is in sharp contrast with Keynes' deep insights on happiness in which he tries to capture "the non-material, the non-optimal, the non(ir)-rational . . . even the ephemeral and sometimes controversially referring to capitalism as a 'spirit'" (cited in Carabelli & Cedrini, 2011, p.337). But, it is symptomatic of neoclassical economics approaches to happiness which, as with other themes in orthodox economics, are narrow, often making little or no use of historical insights and social economics ideas (Carabelli & Cedrini, 2011, p. 337). Psychologists and heterodox happiness economists typically use broader subjective measures such as employing the questions in the Oxford Happiness Inventory. There have been wide endorsements of the existing methodologies across different countries in the world and continuing attempts to improve how this broader measurement can be utilized, and the UN already collects subjective data on happiness (Argyle & Lu, 1990; Schubert, 2012).

The point here is that happiness is weakly linked with simply increasing national income and an incessant aspiration for material progress. Similar trends – weak links between GDP and happiness – can be found in data collected by others. One such dataset can be found in the World Happiness Report (Helliwell et al., 2018), according to which the countries with the most social protection and the lowest levels of inequality are the happiest in the world. These countries are Finland, Norway, Denmark, Iceland, Switzerland, Netherlands, Canada, New Zealand, Sweden, and Australia. Nowhere in the world, not even in the richest countries, is the GDP the dominant contributor to happiness and it is certainly not the sole contributor to levels of happiness; social support, generosity, and freedom to make life choices are also very important, if not more important.

None of these countries is an Eldorado, however. Australia is notorious for continuously keeping black people in the conditions found elsewhere in Africa (Grieves, 2008, 2009; Foley et al., 2013), and these countries do not do as well when ecological concerns are considered in the happiness index. For example, out of 140 countries ranked on the Happy Planet Index, Australia is 105th, Finland is 37th, and Sweden is 61st (New Economics Foundation, 2012, 2016). Worse performers such as USA rank even lower on this measure: 108th. Indeed, to the writers of the reports, if the world were to copy the excessive consumption in the USA in 2008, we would need four more planets to sustain us (New Economics Foundation, 2012).

On the other hand, less militarily powerful countries do much better. Costa Rica, a country where 99 per cent of the electricity is generated from nonrenewable sources, where there is no military spending (because it has abolished its army), and where there is considerable focus on providing social protection, quality healthcare, and pensions, is the highest ranking (New Economics Foundation, 2016). In *Strength Through Peace* (2019), J. E. Lipton and D. P. Barash mount a passionate thesis that the world should learn from Costa Rica, which, while having no bilateral military arrangements with the USA, no affiliation with NATO, and no army has managed to produce the world's happiest, cleanest, and greenest economy.

Yet, Costa Rica has important challenges. Following the analyses of Costa Rican specialists (e.g., van Noorloos, 2014), it can be argued that the country's tax system penalizes its real workers, but also that it is on the path to rewarding absentee owners by increasingly selling off its national wealth – land – to private entrepreneurs. The effect of transferring public wealth which benefits all people to private wealth which is concentrated in the hands of few people is that society becomes more unequal, as people's access to essential services is progressively reduced (Stilwell, 2019, pp. 20–22). Costa Rica, then, could be joining the club of unhappy countires, not because it is poor, but because it is undermining the basis of its social cohesion. As the 2018 Nordic Economic Review (Nordic Council of Ministers, 2018) shows, similar comments can be made about the Nordic countries. Consider the experiences of Finland. Like the rest of the Nordic countries, inequality is rapidly rising in this country.

While the Nordic specialists' contributions to *Nordic Economic Review* focus on income inequality, they point out that the disparities in income arise because of disparities in wealth as well as the effective reduction of wealth taxes, and the higher incidence of taxes on labor. In this sense, an effective fall in capital and wealth tax as against a higher incidence of tax on workers is a key problem and a major challenge (Kettunen, 2019). Within this context, the privatization of land and, hence, of national public wealth in Finnish cities (Hyötyläinen & Haila, 2018) must be a key medium through which the incomes of the "top 1 per cent" have surged, leaving behind the incomes of the rest with little or no wealth. The state reduction or abolition of social policies such as universal basic incomes and universal education for both Finns and others, worsens this problems. With military spending as a percentage of the Finnish GDP becoming similar to that of many members of NATO, Finland too could be on its way to starting a slow but study glide into cold unhappiness.

This body of happiness research provides three lessons for Africa. First Africa can usefully reject the GDP as the sole or main indicator of progress because it turns attention away from the key drivers of happiness and counts activities that polarize Africa and destroy African resources as favorable. Second, policy makers can usefully embrace happiness as one key measure of progress because it better reflects activities that promote inclusive development, punishes the destruction of the environment and expends resources on items such as the military, and puts the case for stronger social and ecological protection in Africa. Third, happiness measures provide alternative pathways for Africa to draw on its own institutions and resources for its emancipation.

## Sharing the Africa-Wide Commons

I previously suggested that the standard remedy offered to counteract the intrusive power of TNCs is either greater regulation or withdrawal from globalization. For example, the UN Office of the High Commissioner on Human Rights (2016, p. 5) is promoting tighter regulations, but only with respect to TNCs and human rights abuses:

Violations of human rights by such entities, for example in the areas of child labor, environmental degradation and decent work and wages, affected marginalized and impoverished groups disproportionately and exacerbated existing human rights concerns. Although human rights abuses are important, "an international legally binding instrument" to implement human rights principles does not fully grapple with the socioeconomic, political, and ecological contradictions I have demonstrated at the subnational level. The G7 CONNEX Initiative recognizes a power imbalance between TNCs and states, but it conceives of this imbalance only in terms of contract negotiations. Hence the name CONNEX: Strengthening Assistance for Complex Contract Negotiations (G7, 2014).

According to the the G7 (2016, n.p.) Guiding Principles of CONNEX:

The G7 Initiative on Strengthening Assistance for Complex Contract Negotiations (CONNEX), launched at the G7 Brussels Summit in 2014, aims to provide developing country partners with multi-disciplinary and concrete expertise for negotiating complex commercial contracts, with an initial focus on the extractives sector. The CONNEX Initiative is designed to ensure such complex commercial contracts are well-conceived and well-negotiated for a host country's successful and inclusive development, while protecting interests of the host country and investing companies.

CONNEX is part of the new international economic order in Africa.

In contrast with the old international economic order, it seeks to enhance the sovereignty of countries, free the forces of industry to cooperate with nations, and empower the nation-state to be a partner to TNCs. Table 8.1 describes other approaches and contrasts such new approaches with the old international economic order.

Under the new economic order, the attempt is to gain control of a nation's resources. Africa's leading scholar, S. K. B. Asante (1979, pp. 346–347) stated the test of effective control as follows:

In the transnational investment process, control involves the exercise of decision-making powers in such vital operational and managerial matters as budget, expansion and development programs, appointment of top management, pricing, marketing, declaration of dividends, borrowing, reorganization, procurement of equipment, and the integration of the undertaking with the developmental objectives of the host countries.

Thus, the proper test of the viability of any new arrangement purporting to vest control in the host government is: Does the restructuring effectively transfer the power to make or influence the critical decisions on these

Table 8.1 *Options on regulating and controlling TNCs*

| | |
|---|---|
| **Old Economic Order** | |
| Concessions | Power of operation, management, and control are centered fully on TNCs |
| **New Economic Order** | |
| Nationalization | Power of operation, management, and control are centered fully on the state |
| Joint Ventures | Public–private partnerships (PPPs) in which power is shared between the state and TNCs |
| Service Contracts | Service contracts insist that the state is owner and the TNCs are service providers only |
| Technical Assistance | Arrangements in which the TNCs are seen primarily as contractors, bearing no or very little cost of risks. In practice, they tend to give operational control to TNCs. |
| Production-Sharing Agreements | Contractual agreement in which the state is deemed co-manager of extractions. In practice, operations management are left in the hands of the TNCs. |
| Local Content | A form of PPP in which the state nudges TNCs to indigenize |

*Source:* Adapted from Asante (1979)

specific matters at both the board and management levels? This is an exacting test, but it does not end there. Asante (1979) suggests that control also means taking over management, restructuring the fiscal regime to be able to direct TNCs to reinvest their profit in the resources sector, and being able to galvanize and mobilize scattered Indigenous shareholders in times of need.

None of the mechanisms in Table 8.1 satisfies the test. Often, TNCs reserve veto power in their agreements with resource nations. Others classify their shares or the shares of the state in ways that disadvantage the voting power of the state. Local shareholders can also be so scattered that it is difficult to mobilize them to effectively control TNCs and the resource sector. But even when these barriers are not present, there is an imbalance in technical expertise. If people loyal to the nation-state lack expertise in operations and management, public control becomes a Herculean task (Asante, 1979). Is the question, then, how to restructure the state?

## Restructuring the State

Stratification economists typically support a stronger role for the state. In developing policy proposals for stratification economists, William Darity, Jr, Darrick Hamilton, and Mark Paul (see, for example, Paul et al., 2017,

2018) have forcefully put the case for guaranteeing full state employment by giving work to the unemployed and the working poor, indeed to everybody. Described as the "federal job guarantee," such an institution would create jobs that could remove income poverty and, with it, income-related social problems. Crucially, the initiative could also remove the threat of unemployment (Darity & Hamilton, 2012). This proposal advances the present focus on universal basic income by reinvoking a long tradition of Keynesian and institutional political economics.

Because stratification economists have not, as yet, clarified these analytical bases, it is important to provide them here, drawing on what could be called, perhaps controversially, "Keynesian institutional economics" (cf. post-Keynesian theory, see Harcourt & Kriesler, 2015; Halevi et al., 2016; Dow, 2017), and on other better-known institutional economics traditions that have been demonstrated to offer greater analytical and policy coherence (Bromley and Anderson, 2012). The English economist John Maynard Keynes, contended that, without state intervention in economic activity, a capitalist economy is unlikely to attain full employment because different actors are involved in the different aspects of economic activity – such as production, distribution, and consumption – at different times. As such, the state should intervene in economic activity in ways that would ensure effective demand and full employment, through the multiplier effects of investment (Keynes, 1973, pp. 245–254).

According to Keynes (1973, p. 378), "I conceive, therefore, that a somewhat comprehensive socialization of investment will prove the only means of securing an approximation to full employment; though this need not exclude all manner of compromises and of devices by which public authority will cooperate with private initiative." Consistent with this view but contrary to the view of neoclassical economists that the state should break up monopolies, John Kenneth Galbraith (1956), a leading institutional political economist, argued that the role of the state should be to neutralize the power of corporations. This view is the countervailing power of the state that he developed in his early writings, emphasizing the power by the state to counterbalance the original power of monopolies.

Galbraith (1956, p. 138) did not see monopoly as necessarily bad for economic activity if regulated rather than destroyed. Countervailing power of the state is not anti-competition per se. It is regulated competition via the exercise of another power, from an opposite direction. Galbraith (1956, p. 138) was of the view that if countervailing power fails to prevent monopolies from serving only the interest of the rich and other strong groups, government can seek to destroy their original power. In his later work, having moved away from the notion of countervailing power to a focus on inherent power imbalance – as in his books *Economics and the Public Purpose* (Galbraith, 1973) and *The Affluent Society* (Galbraith, 1998) – Galbraith put more emphasis on the need to try to constrain corporate power.

That, nevertheless, does not mean that Keynesian and institutional political economists support an unlimited role for the state. As noted by Keynes (1973, p. 378), "But beyond this, no obvious case is made out for a system of State Socialism which would embrace most of the economic life of the community. It is not the ownership of the instruments of production which it is important for the state to assume." Galbraith (1956, p. 152) cautioned against the danger of countervailing power assuming a career of its own.

Generally, both stratification and institutional political economists contend that the state is a player, not an umpire. Consider the developmental state approach. Advocated by political economists such as Ha-Joon Chang (2002, 2003), this view of the state assumes that it has a well-developed bureaucracy that could be used to enhance socioeconomic development. The developmental state contrasts with a predatory state (a state apparatus used for the exclusive benefit of a few political elites) and an intermediate state (a concept of the state that lies between the predatory and developmental state with a fragile bureaucracy). The developmental state is interventionist. It is not completely insulated from the influence of economic power or the machinations of political elites. However, there seems to be some division of labor among these interest groups and the state, with the political elites dictating the pace for the long-term direction of the society and the bureaucracy (Martinussen, 1997, pp. 238–239).

While there is clearly a bigger role for the state without necessarily the cautious view of institutional political economists, the institutionalist view of the state is quite distinct from a "statist view" in which the state controls the means of production. In the institutional economics approach, the state can invest in such a way that it can create full employment because profit making is not its main motive. Furthermore, the public sector can distribute jobs more equally across cities and regions. Of course, the public sector could be inefficient and some public officers may be corrupt. But, these tendencies, including the issue of lack of accountability, are neither exclusive to the public sector (see Chapter 5 on international trade), nor exclusive to Africa.

As shown in *Governance for Pro-Poor Urban Development: Lessons from Ghana* (Obeng-Odoom, 2013a), private sector inefficiencies and corrupted practices are widespread, perhaps much more than the public sector corruption excoriated, especially by public-choice economists and new institutional economists who write on Africa (see also, Owusu-Ansah et. al., 2018). On the other side, it is well-known that corruption is endemic even in the "successful" developmental state of South Korea. Corruption itself is such a poor explanation of the process of social change that it can be found in varying degrees in every society. Today, in the so-called less-corrupted countries, inequality is on the rise and, regardless of which party is in power, the problem persists. It is these dynamics that Henry George observed in his own society:

The people, of course, continue to vote; but the people are losing their power. Money and organisation tell more and more in elections. In some sections bribery has become chronic, and numbers of voters expect regularly to sell their votes. In some sections large employers regularly bulldoze their hands into voting as *they* wish. (George, [1883] 1981, p. 16; emphasis in original)

These dynamics continue today around the world, especially in the United States (see the special issue of *The Forum for Social Economics*, 2018, on this theme, volume XLVII, issue 2; and Chapter 5). In other words, corruption is usually a symptom. But even if it is the springboard for other social problems, it is a second-generation cause. The focus must be on restructuring the revolving door that transfers rents from Africa to the rest of the world.

The state is important in this sense. In theory, the public sector can boost employment by subsidizing the consumption of necessities to improve effective demand, which, in turn, can create more jobs. Also, following Keynes, the public sector can invest in the real sector of the economy, such as construction of socially useful projects, to create jobs (Kalecki, 1945). This proposal is different from using the public sector as an employer of last resort (ELR) because, unlike the ELR model, public-sector-led job creation does not employ only to correct market failures. Also, unlike the ELR model, which employs people and pays them wages which are close to the minimum wage, the public-sector-led approach can be more accountable and, hence, made to pay decent wages for decent work (excluding fighting in needless wars or making weapons of mass destruction).

If we assume that the public sector is willing to take up this challenge of creating sustainable jobs, an outstanding issue is the financial ability to do so. In the Ghanaian case, it has been argued that such funding could, at least partly, come from land-value taxation and rent tax (Obeng-Odoom, 2014a). In any case, much like other concerns, the issue of funding is a criticism, not a critique.

Fundamental critique comes from the work of Marxist political economists who contend that the state is an instrument of capital and, therefore,
exists only for the capitalist class. In this regard, the state performs two
important roles to enhance the accumulation of capital. First, it provides
ingredients such as communication and transportation services to support
the accumulation process. Second, it provides or supports the institutions
to contain social conflicts that may derail capital accumulation.

It is these roles that James O'Connor (1973) referred to, respectively, as
"accumulation function" and "legitimisation function." Any or both of
these functions may produce outcomes that are favorable to other classes
(Pickvance, 1995, p. 253). However, such an outcome would not mean that
the state intended positive outcomes for any class, apart from the capitalist
class. Modern political economists are also interested in the role of the state
in the economy. They acknowledge that the state can be an instrument for
the dominant class. However, in a democracy, the state needs broader
"consensus" among the populace than that offered by the capitalist class.
Hence, the state is viewed not only as an avenue for oppression but as
a forum of struggle between the various classes or fractions of classes. As
such, the state may sometimes make concessions to enhance "legitimation"
and secure the conditions for reproduction of the political, economic, and
social order (Herbert-Cheshire & Lawrence, 2002; Pressman, 2001). In this
sense, the state can secure the conditions of democratic control for workers
in the oil and gas industry, for example. The question is, if, as Henry
George showed, there is both individual and associated interest in the
work of labor, should workers not have a say in the control of their
associated labor (Obeng-Odoom 2016c)?

## Restructuring Work

What stratification economic seeks is inclusive economies. So, it is not just
work, not even "decent" work, but just work that they propose (for
a discussion, see Lafargue, 1904; Paul et al., 2017, 2018). To realize this
ambition would entail both generalized just distribution of work outside
the workplace, but also workplace democracy, which is quite distinct from
mainstream demands for worker participation. In *Radical Democracy*,
Douglas Lummis (1996, p. 142) clarifies that "the democratization of
work entails more than just some formal arrangement – the nationalization
of industry, the owning of stock by workers, or the like. It entails all of the
changes in management, scale, machinery, speed [. . .]." Table 8.2, based on
the analysis of Christopher Gunn (2011), provides a detailed comparison

Table 8.2 *From participation to democratic control of work*

| <<<<<Participation (Weak) >>>>> >>>>> | | | >>Democratic Control (Strong) | |
| --- | --- | --- | --- | --- |
| (a) Purpose of participation | Inform workforce | Consult with workforce | Share decision with workforce | Enable decision by workforce |
| (b) Voting power | Minority of workers | Equal number of workers and managers | Majority of workers | All and only workers |
| (c) Topics for action by workers | Administrative | Administrative and technical | Admin, technical, financial | Financial, management, |
| (d) Economic and financial role | Negotiating compensation | Negotiating compensation and work conditions | Determining compensation and work conditions | Determining reinvestment of surplus |
| (e) Allocation of surplus | Voice in defining surplus | Representative vote in allocation of surplus | Shared vote in allocation of surplus | Determination of surplus allocation |

*Source:* Adapted from Gunn, 2011, p. 319

between the mainstream idea of participation and the democratic control of work being advocated in this chapter.

The arguments for workplace democracy need not be Marxist to be accepted. Indeed, Georgists make the same argument that the product of labor must belong to labor. From that Georgist perspective, the rents from land can more directly be taxed. Taxing rent has been established to be one way to address not just inequality but also systemic inequality (Obeng-Odoom, 2014a, 2014b). Accordingly, it is a useful approach to institutionalize systemic redistribution if the state will invest the resulting revenues in social protection, in compensation, and in socioeconomic and ecological processes.

Reindustrialization in diversified industries can serve the purpose of increasing the employment base of cities, with implications for the rest of the African nations. With employment along quota lines, such that there are reserved places of work at all levels for indigenes (who have lived, for example, in oil cities and contributed to their growth and they or their descendants will continue to live in the twin city after the age of oil), and industry democracy, the analyzed problems of exploitation and discrimination, can be mitigated, as can the possible problem of recriminations from those who live in oil cities, especially those whose livelihoods have been impaired by the oil industry and those who will continue to live in the city after the depletion of oil and gas.

Capacity development in the industry can go on, but it has to be consistent with democratic paternalism. In this sense, education should not merely be seen as "human capital" development, as in mainstream economics, but as broad-based human empowerment (Obeng-Odoom, 2015b). That entails worker education on worker-controlled industrial processes. Based on a long history of such education in the continent, with teachers, facilities, and logistics germane to this empowering approach to education, the focus is not so much learning how to respect the boss but mostly on ways workers can associate their labor for collective production, management, and control of the workplace. Rather than see oil as "resource" to be exploited for production and profit, this education will emphasize that oil, and land more generally, is not apart from humans but part of them in nature. As stewards of this system, it is human and ecological needs rather than profit that serve as the organizing logic.

None of these ideas can be captured within the mainstream economics concept of human capital, which not only fails to draw attention to the conditions of workers but it also legitimizes these conditions by foreclosing the effort to find answers. As noted by Henry George ([1879] 2006), a single highly educated person among a society of illiterate people can increase her or his wage because of education, but as the general level of education rises to that person's level, the special advantages accruing must pale. George argued that the wages of educated labor tend to decline as a proportion of the surplus produced in society, as increasing rent extracted from land and minerals leak into the coffers of landlords, leaving only proportionately small amount for labor. From a Marxist perspective, surplus value is created.

However considered, education, then, must be broadly understood not as "capital" but as empowerment. In turn, the content of education, especially economics education, must be empowering, socially, economically, materially, even spiritually. After a penetrating analysis to show the "mis-education" of Africans, Carter Godwin Woodson made the following observation (1990/1933, p. 66):

It seems only a reasonable proposition, then, that, if under the present system which produced our leadership . . . we have gone backward toward serfdom or have at least been kept from advancing to real freedom, it is high time to develop another sort of leadership with a different educational system.

For Brazilian political economist Paulo Freire (1970), and his idea of a Pedagogy of the Oppressed, education must make central a critical understanding of how capitalism seeks to subordinate labor and dissipate land and natural resources. It must utilize local experiences of labor to conscientize and to empower, or, in general parlance, to dialogue with people to develop their own consciousness. As a Marxist-based approach that emphasizes problem- and praxis-based education, the ideas of historical process and transition are crucial, as is the philosophy of capitalism as a world and integrated system. So, "oil experiences" can only be part of a broader process of global fossil capitalism and though worker experiences will differ and, indeed, are different and differentiated across space and time and between races and genders, they are also connected to a global struggle for all workers.

This broad economic democracy will have to possess both hindsight and foresight to prevent future expropriations.

## PREVENTING FUTURE EXPROPRIATIONS

The issues under consideration are both systemic and structural. To prevent future recurrence, it is important to reflect briefly on how much of a slave a society will become if its common land is privately appropriated:

> To drop a man in the middle of the Atlantic Ocean and tell him he is at liberty to walk ashore, would not be more bitter irony than to place a man where all the land is appropriated as the property of other people and to tell him that he is a free man, at liberty to work for himself and to enjoy his own earnings. (George, [1883] 1981, p. 99)

Georgist policies offer three interrelated solutions to prevent future expropriations. The aim of these policies is to dissolve monopolies, prevent the formation of new monopolies, and diffuse prosperity throughout the economy. Dissolving monopolies can entail the appointment of local managers to occupy the leadership of the TNCs in an effort to indigenize TNCs and return the commons to local control. Since TNCs are hydra-headed, with dozens or hundreds of subsidiaries, this sort of transfer of control could require a united effort by many nations acting in concert to regain control of their own resources. However, a mere transfer of power within a framework that treats land as a private commodity would not be adequate.

African appointees to head natural resource companies will need to consider land in ways that prevent the formation of new monopolies, including preventing the inheritance of accumulated land or the imposition of an African inheritance tax (see George, 1885). A locally controlled monopoly is only slightly better than one controlled by a foreign company. Adopting a tax on land value to capture any socially created value will remove the incentive to monopolize windfalls and discourage speculative investors. An oil tax does not discourage investment as the resource lobby often claims. In Australia, for example, at least two decades of implementing aspects of a Petroleum Resource Rent Tax (PRRT) has rather expanded revenues. An average of A$2.7 billion per year has been added to the public purse. So, Georgists have been proved right, providing a basis for reworking the PRRT along the lines recently proposed (Murray, 2017).

Once a system is in place to capture the economic rents of natural resources, the public can benefit. The revenue from an African Petroleum Resource Rent Tax (APRRT) could be used in a way to diffuse prosperity. This could be done in two ways: by direct transfers to citizens or by expenditure on public goods. As an example of the first method, Alaska has been distributing a portion of the state's oil revenues directly to citizens since 1982 (Erickson & Groh, 2012; Groh & Erickson, 2012). The second method is the more traditional one of investing in social infrastructure (education, health, and accommodation) and physical infrastructure (water supply, rail transport, public bus systems, public bicycles, and public parks). Both methods disperse wealth that was collected by the state on behalf of its citizens.

## Tackling the Root Causes of Pollution and Accidents

To overcome the fundamental problems in the existing policies, political economists offer at least three alternatives: nationalization, total abandonment of the oil industry, and active civil society leadership within existing property relations in the oil industry (see, for example, Nwoke, 1984a, 1984b, 1986; Bassey, 2012; Mhango, 2018).

Nationalization is a possibility, but what is its utility when the operations of national companies are patterned after transnational accumulation practices as this chapter has shown? What about abandoning fossil altogether and promoting biofuels? This approach is clearly radical in the sense that it seeks to exterminate the entire oil industry. But to what extent is it feasible and how confident can we be in its alternatives of biofuel investment with so much displacement, pollution, and wage and rent theft widely discussed in the land-grab literature? Civil society involvement is important, of course, but even then, citizens and activists need a vision based on alternatives that, at the very least, avoid the contradictions of the present policies or policy proposals, can prevent the strident recurrence of accidents, and are logically plausible.

These desiderata are not easy to achieve but, if incessant accumulation is the driving dynamic behind these accidents, the country would need to look elsewhere for a start. Three possibilities can be considered. First, it could ban the importation of second-hand cars that are harmful to the environment, ban the importation of luxury goods which merely increase the import bill without adding much to the real economy, and increase the provision of safe, affordable, and convenient public transport. These steps could lead to restructuring cities in Africa beyond fossil-fuel-dominated urbanism.

Second, the continent could reduce expenditure on petroleum products by (a) producing them internally and (b) supporting small-scale, locally run biofuel plant farms with extension officers and guaranteed markets. This second strategy draws on well-established import substitution strategies that are not full-blown protectionist programs. Rather, they bring out not often well-expressed ecological strategies embedded in import substitution programs. In turn, they have the potential to make the economy not just self-reliant (see Chang, 2002, 2003, for such import substitution industrialization arguments), but also self-sustaining (in ways not often envisaged by import substitution theorists). Again, the effect of these programs would be to leash, indeed tame and domesticate, the wild forces of accumulation which, when unleashed, tend to cause accidents.

Third, Africa could increase state-to-state trade, including bartering. These interrelated processes would also bring in more income through improving the balance of payment account. They could create more green and clean jobs that are not exploitative (because they are not for profit and many people will work for themselves). Slow growth of this form will also help poverty reduction because the tendency for dispossession of land and private appropriative of socially created rent would be destroyed. More importantly, they will contribute to turning off what Harvey Molotch (1974) famously called "the growth machine": the spark for the flames and fiery accidents.

Many of these ideas might be dismissed as pipe dreams or pie-in-the-sky solutions. Specifically, critics might contend that second-hand cars need not be a problem if the proper repairs or adjustments are made. Indeed, it might be argued that using catalytic converters can address the problem of second-hand cars and that the problem is rather users that do not care or make the needed changes.

However, this criticism places considerable faith in the power of technology to address the ecological crises when, in fact, as I discuss in *Reconstructing Urban Economics* (Obeng-Odoom, 2016d), such technological fixes create a well-documented "Jevons Paradox," the situation in which more technology makes the situation worse as it encourages the use of even more motorization. Not only can a ban reduce the import bill of the country, it can also decrease the number of cars that emit poisonous fumes into the environment (see also Obeng-Odoom, 2015c). Public transportation, including the use of public trains, would rely less on a growing chain of fuel stations and slow down the rate at which the heart of accumulation beats, a crucial precursor to confronting the obstacles to African liberation.

## OBSTACLES

### Weak Tax Capacity in Africa

The strategy proposed is not without its difficulties. In much of Africa, the state's capacity to impose taxation is weak. Colonialism, with its arbitrary amalgamation of groups, led to fragmentary states. That, coupled with the activities of powerful TNCs and years of aggressive neoliberalism, has undermined the African state. All of those factors tilt the balance of power away from the state. As a result, the state in Africa has been left severely handicapped. There are other limits on tax capacity. Logistical constraints are a well-known problem, as are legal constraints, both locally and globally.

The World Trade Organization has rules that block certain forms of taxation of TNCs. Other external agencies put pressure on states in Africa to completely change tax laws to create a good business environment. The residue of colonial planning, with its top-down approach, has not helped. Many citizens do not support the payment of a tax, as the state seldom communicates with them regarding policies of tax collection nor the uses to which a tax is put (Boamah et al., 2012a, 2012b). Competition between the central and local state, especially where the various states are run by different parties and socio-ethnic groups, is another barrier (Obeng-Odoom, 2017a). Then there is the recurrent issue of the database for what land belongs where in the large informal economies of land, although unlike taxes on wages, land taxes do not simply vanish in informal economies. The more crucial obstacle is that propertied classes tend to resist any attempt to improve the capacity of the state to perform its social roles.

## Continuing Interference from Colonial and Neo-colonial Powers

At the level of state structure too, there are important obstacles. Local governments were set up as instruments of co-option, rather than as vehicles of urban and regional transformation (Obeng-Odoom, 2013b). They were intended to deflect attention away from how central governments and states gain power and maintain it, as well as provide an avenue for direct state control. Merely being involved in local activities was intended to make people feel that they were effectively participating in governance and hence effectively part of the system.

Neo-colonial forces continue to preserve the status quo by removing African leaders who try to fundamentally change the system. The removal of Laurent Gbagbo of Côte d'Ivoire in 2011 is an example. Although widely seen as an African leader refusing to accept the results of an election, the Ivorian case is also a story of continuing French intervention in Côte D'Ivoire and of how any attempt to break its monopoly leads to local "crisis." As Ademola Araoye (2012, p. 10) notes:

These intermestic forces are explicitly implicated in the Ivorian crisis. A defining and distinguishing attribute of each of the contending political forces is where it stands in relation to the France problematique in Cote d'Ivoire, indeed in Francophone Africa. The Ivorian state ultimately is an instrument to project the interest of whichever of the internal contesting forces and their transnational allies succeeds in appropriating it. It is also an instrument of France to advance its economic as well as strategic interests.

In Port-Gentil, Gabon, the French built a military base near the shanty-towns where they perceived the most discontent to be. This strategic location enabled the speedy deployment of the army to suppress dissent (Yates, 2014). In short, the structures for bureaucratic resistance are well organized.

## The Property Alliance

The power of the landed and propertied interests in Africa is not easily defeated. It could trigger a reaction very likely to be supported by the oil TNCs. Importantly, neoliberal organizations such as the World Trade Organisation, the US Agency for International Development, the US

Military, the World Bank, and the International Monetary Fund are likely to oppose these changes.

Imperial nations such as France are likely to react badly. France and its top officers recognize their dependence on Africa. For example, the then Director of the IMF, Christine Laggard, has noted that, as of 2010, "The Bank of the States of Central Africa, for instance, places almost 90 per cent of their reserves in the French National Bank" (cited in Lehmann, 2012) Also, Jean Boissonat of the currency committee of the French National Bank famously noted that "approximately half a million Frenchmen in Paris receive their means of survival from the Franc Zone" (cited in Lehmann, 2012). France benefits from African oil, African markets, and African gold reserves. France benefits mightily from interest payments that Africans pay to France for borrowing its own money! Therefore, reworking this system is likely to lead to major struggles, including attempts to topple national leaders through "coups" and "civil wars," planned in, supported by, or executed by France and its allies.

The analysis of Gary Busch (2013) shows that the 2011 civil conflict in Côte d'Ivoire is a case in point. In the lead-up to the conflict, the popularly elected government of Laurent Gbagbo had started reforms to reduce the dominance of French business interests in the oil and gas industry in the country. Two developments were particularly significant. First, Gbagbo rejected an offer to sell off the national oil refinery, the Société Ivoirienne de Raffinage, to Paris-backed representatives of Total-Elf. Selling the national asset would not only have depleted Ivorian capital assets, it would also have made the country even more dependent on France and its transnational oil company, Total-Elf, which would have had the power to control the Ivorian economy through fuel-pricing policy.

So, Gbagbo's refusal to sell the refinery was in the interest of Côte d'Ivoire, but clearly against the interest of international capital and the former colonizer. Second, Gbagbo's government was approached to renew the contract of the French-backed Société d'Aménagement Urbain et Rural (SAUR), which was in charge of the Companie Eléctricité Ivoirienne, the national electricity provider. However, Gbagbo's government refused to do so, indicating that the country would go into the open market to seek a competent operator that would give more value for Ivorian money, pay more taxes, and offer more affordable services. Again, this decision was in the interest of Côte d'Ivoire but, as Busch (2013) shows, infuriated the French authorities. Unable to stand the defiance of a former colony, Paris threw its support behind the rebellion against Gbagbo's government, which was finally toppled in 2011. Thomas Sankara of Burkina Faso suffered a similar fate when he challenged French interest, leading to his assassination and the toppling of his government (Murrey, 2018). Busch's analysis may be contested, of course – as could Murrey's – for there are many interpretations of every conflict. However, precisely for this reason, his account demonstrates that conflicts related to oil and gas cannot simply be attributed to "African failings" or some "natural resource traps" as per mainstream accounts.

## PROSPECTS

However, there are also counteracting, anti-imperial forces that create the conditions for possible success. One counteracting development is the consummation of the African Continental Free Trade Area (AfCFTA) program. Its advantages are less about the boost to GDP of US$3 trillion; rather, they relate more to the 52 per cent increase in cross-Africa trade by 2022 (UNCTAD, 2018). A revised program, among others, to reorient the continent from "growth" fetish, to emphasize the redress of social stratification and ecological pillage, and to put a much stronger focus on commonizing African land, including resources such as oil, of course, would be much more promising. Agreeing on the need for changing the paralyzing trade structure could be similarly propitious, as would addressing any labour practices that could remind Africans of the enslavement of their ancestors.

Anti-imperialism may come in the form of alternative forms of agriculture that part company with the capitalist logic. It may also take the form of overt protest against the advancement of the reaches of capitalism. A hybrid of both can also take place; that is, resistance to agri-capitalist forms of land use and the use of land for noncapitalist farming.

Regarding organizing agriculture in an anti-imperialist way, smallholder farming has gained great popularity in recent times. In this agricultural form, farmers decide what to produce and for whom – a system widely regarded as eco-friendly. In Africa, there is a collection of examples about how smallholder farming in urban areas generates decent income and food to support large numbers of families with small plots (Obeng-Odoom, 2013c). This is not just an African practice. In Asia and Latin America such evidence abounds too.

However, the most popular of such farming types is organized by the global peasant movement La Vía Campesina, formed in 1993. According to eminent political economist Walden Bello (2007, p. 4), "La Via Campesina is probably the most effective of these movements of people." Its central vision is fighting for "food sovereignty" – a broader concept than food security – that entails looking at food as a human right, not just as an aspiration, discouraging fast and junk food, and encouraging a return to common land in which people have use rights in the commons rather than owning them as "property." The project challenges individualism and seeks to speak truth to power by advocating humanism and communalism (Desmarais, 2007; Riddell, 2009). La Via Campesina embodies a transnational peasant struggle. Indeed, the name in Spanish means "Peasant way" or "Peasant Road" (Desmarais, 2007, p. 8).

Other forms of anti-capitalist struggles exist in the form of overt protests or local attempts to use violence to protect land. At present, conflict has been reported between natives and settler communities. In the Pru district in Ghana, minor confrontations between settlers and natives have been reported. There was violence also in the Greenleaf area in Juapong, Ghana, where one laborer was shot dead on April 3, 2012, for trying to clear land for jatropha cultivation when that land was the subject of a long dispute between the chief and another person (Thornycroft, 2012). In South Sudan, there was a public meeting at which residents in the sub-county of Mukaya decided to reject one lease made by so-called influential people who had acted without addressing community concerns (Pearce, 2012, p. 46). In Juba, in the same country, the mobilization of Indigenous lands rights claims continues to be used as a shield to parry attempts at appropriating land for "development" (Badiey, 2013).

Elsewhere, youth groups have reportedly been prepared for armed attack in Gambella, Ethiopia. Conflicts have been reported between the Anuak and the more privileged highlanders; between the Anuak and the government; and between the government, the highlanders, and the Anuak over struggles concerning land. In one case, some 420 people were killed (Pearce 2012, p. 9–16). New research (Wayessa, 2018) shows that these protests have forced the state to dramatically reduce the disposal of land and in many cases has halted it.

In another case in Agogo in Ghana, local residents have expressed much concern about the nature of the land transactions, including the lack of broad-based consultations. In April 2010, a demonstration by the residents became slightly violent, and when police were called in there was shooting in which fourteen people were wounded. Another demonstration was started in 2011 to protest against the dispossession of land (Wisborg, 2012). In Dipale in Ghana, the local people have resisted by abstaining from sharing local knowledge about how to prevent fires, or by not helping quench fires when they start in a region that is very prone to such problems (Yaro & Tsikata, 2013).

Anti-capitalist shifts toward constitutional political economy are also notable. These range from challenging capitalist land investments in Africa's supreme courts (see, for example, Obeng-Odoom & Gyampo, 2017) to the mobilization of lawyers to join others to protest casino capitalism in Africa (Gould, 2006). Indeed, many middle class street protests have entailed the active participation of lawyers. These protests, in general, have been quite successful. They are prospects not so much because they are "new" (see also Branch & Mampilly, 2015). They are not (Abedi, 2018). The judicialization of political economy was a commonly utilized tactic in the independence era, leading to coalitions such as the Aborigines' Rights Protection Society. What is regarded as a "prospect" here, then, is their potency in history and their demonstrated potential today.

These anti-imperialist responses, to be sure, are not only local or localized. Instead, they are getting increasingly regionalized. In 2010, there was the Kolongo Appeal made by peasant groups in Mali who organized local resistance to land grabs. Subsequently, there was the Dakar Appeal which led to a global conference of peasants in Mali in 2011 that ended with a "commitment to resist land-grabbing by all means possible, to support all those who fight land-grabs, and to put pressure on national governments and international institutions to fulfill their obligations to ensure and uphold the rights of peoples" (Nyeleni Declaration 2011, p. 2).

Internationally, many leading French statesmen (e.g., the late Jacques Chiraq and Jean Luc Mélenon) have openly demanded that France abandons its neocolonial interference in Africa. European institutions, including the European Council, have also heaped pressure on France to vacate African soil. And the call for an African–European Peace and Reconciliation Commission to investigate the many past and continuing sins of France seems to be gaining momentum (Busch, 2013). The concrete effect of this accumulation of pressure can be seen in the recent "amnesty" given by the current president of Côte d'Ivoire to the wife of Gbagbo who, like Gbagbo, was a political prisoner.

Increasing awareness that when the US military is deployed to the Global South apparently to protect "American interests," what is happening is that a public institution, the army, is in fact being used to protect the private transnational investments can create outrage and reenergize another Occupy America, this time with a direct demand for the military to stay at home (Gaffney, 2018). The Global South in the United States – here defined as communities of color – have shown that they can stand up against militarized forces as unarmed civilians and when these protests join with "Africa uprising" for a different world, they can be a powerful countervailing force (Branch & Mampilly, 2015, pp. 207–208). Already, US power is slowly weakening in many parts of the Global South (Bello, 2007). The historical lessons of the defeat of colonial and imperial interventions from the decolonization days, including successful military challenge by Ethiopia to Italian imperialism and Haiti to French imperial advances, and the more recent defeat of the US by Vietnam bring form to what Giovanni Arrighi (2007, p. 158) has called the myth of American invincibility.

Internally, the current political regime seeks to take steps toward making Ghana, indeed the entire Global South, self-sufficient in what it calls "Beyond Aid."[1] Like elsewhere in the Global South such as in India (where a cashless economy is being pursued to force the poor to pay taxes), it is doing so by seeking to "formalize" the economy. Ordinary workers in informal economies who are alleged to be escaping the payment of taxes are the primary target to generate internal resources. However, it could potentially achieve much better results by pursuing the proposed alternatives.

Elsewhere in the Global South, bold leaders have been able to pursue similar alternatives. For instance, in Ecuador, Rafael Correa pursued Aslow growth agenda for eight years with popular support (Galárraga & Frelson, 2017). In Ghana, similar levels of support can be found among both the lay and the learned. In her contribution to Africa, the anthropologist Gabriel Klaeger (2013a, 2013b) documents, indeed endorses, organized protests against accidents (sometimes involving road blocks and the burning of tires), while several public surveys (Obeng-Odoom, 2015b) show strong public support for the alternatives discussed. In *Africa Uprising*, Adam Branch and Zachariah Mampilly (2015) provide detailed analyses of popular protests in Africa more widely for political and economic change along the lines of the alternatives discussed. Occupy Nigeria, for example, arose explicitly to demand better, more public use of oil resources. And Trevor Ngwane, Luke Sinwell, and Immanuel Ness's (2017) book, *Urban Revolt*, documents movements against evictions, corporate power, and general marginalization throughout the Global South.

Internationally, there is much pressure on governments that provide support for transnational corporations to withdraw their support or rather support the South for a truly global attempt to protect the environment.

---

[1] N. A. D. Akufo-Addo. (2018). Address by the President of the Republic, Nana Addo Dankwa Akufo-Addo, on the Occasion of Ghana's 61st Independence Day Celebration, at the Independence Square. http://presidency.gov.gh/index.php/briefing-room/speeches/568-address-by-the-president-of-the-republic-nana-addo-dankwa-akufo-addo-on-the-occasion-of-ghana-s-61st-independence-day-celebration-at-the-independence-square (accessed 14 April 2018).

That is evidently what has been happening around the world. Whether in Canada (see, for example, Deneault & Sacher, 2012), in Australia (Ruchira, 2017), or in the United States (Writers for the 99%, 2012), pressure is increasingly building up against the Canadian, Australian, and American states to change their pro-TNC stance that contributes to inertia rather than positive change. Sometimes, when this movement in the North coincides with regime change there, such that progressives take power, the potential for transformation is more immediate. To take one example, New Zealand Prime Minister Jacinda Arden of the Labour Party will no longer grant New Zealand TNCs new offshore oil exploration permits for internal exploration and presumably will not support external explorations by New Zealand TNCs either.[2]

This transnational struggle for another world is particularly effective because they directly confront TNCs, which help maintain the existing problematic system. The dynamism of these TNCs in consolidating their alliances and forming new ones with local and national oil companies shows that only a similarly transnational and dynamic response is going to be effective in transcending the present structure.

Questions could be raised about what share of oil pollution is coming from accidents and the share coming from chronic pollution?

Exact answers are difficult to find, but the issue is not at all about the precise calculations. Rather, what is concerning, is the panoply of the nature and consequences of the broader possible outcomes for which a consensus is developing among a larger community of senior scholars – including Herman Daly and J. B. Cobb, Jr. – who have been studying these issues for years. In their magnum opus *For the Common Good* (1994), Daly and Cobb, Jr. present a voluminous amount of evidence in this genre. Together with the work done by leading organizations such as the Transnational Institute led by Susan George (2014), the totality of the evidence is clearly that these alternatives show promise.

Apart from these clearly superior outcomes, the current state of the nation provides the conditions for introducing this program. The clear evidence that oil TNCs are, at best, only contributors to oil rents leads to the conclusion that a system of oil rent tax can be introduced to socialize oil rents in the country. Also, most of the tax revenues in Ghana come from VAT but, as Francis Andoh (2017) has recently shown, in the last fifteen years, no amount of taxation effort and fiddling of the tax rate has been able

---

[2] E. A. Roy. (2018). "New Zealand bans all new offshore oil exploration as part of 'carbon-neutral future.'" *The Guardian*. April 12.

to generate additional tax revenues beyond 30 per cent of total tax revenue. The reason is that informal economic activities – themselves largely a reflection of growth (Obeng-Odoom, 2011) – cannot be effectively monitored and taxed nor would such taxes be reliable. The current debates within the Ghana Revenue Authority to tax beggars in the informal economy is a clear attempt at looking for "weaker" people.[3]

Conversely, the increasing property values, the expansion of records on property development at the Lands Commission, and the further development of the skill base of land economists in Ghana (who can help work out the land and resource tax due) clearly show that the application of these proposals is possible. Currently underexploited, property taxation generates about 27 per cent (compared to about 30 per cent for VAT) of total tax revenues. Even then, in the oil city of Sekondi-Takoradi, the property tax can help finance about 80 per cent of infrastructural projects (Mabe & Kuusaana, 2016). So, it can finance even more projects, if redesigned, and it can help address the informality problem to which the rent system has contributed. New oil fields can be locally developed under a new philosophy of slow and inclusive growth, and resulting revenues deployed for investment in ecological, social, and public services.

Looking inward connotes indigenization and regionalization. Some critics suggest that natural resources will always plunge Africa into misery, into crisis, into war, and hence imply that no cooperation will be possible (Collier, 2009b). From this perspective, the dispute (Case 23 at ITLOS) between Ghana and Côte d'Ivoire should have become a convenient proof of a "natural resource trap." Set in 1950, the dispute arose after the discovery of oil in 2007 (Banesseh, 2014). Both countries claimed ownership of the disputed area. It was an issue that arose in 2007, leading to several meetings and legislation, particularly on the Ghanaian side but also joint meetings with Côte d'Ivoire. By 2014, there had been about ten joint meetings to try to resolve the issue, but the parties were not successful and had to invite a third party, ITLOS, as an arbiter (Republic of Côte d'Ivoire, 2015; Republic of Ghana, 2015). Many writers on oil would claim this is an "oil problem," a classic case of oil driving crisis. Indeed, Daniel Chirot

---

[3] The debates started with a staff member of the Ghana Revenue Authority (GRA) noting that the GRA would be taxing beggars. A press release by the GRA later contradicted this position, but still suggested that if beggars made enough money to bring their incomes within the taxable income brackets, then they would be taxed. See GRA 2018, "Press Release: GRA to tax street beggars," GRA Press release to all media houses, 30 April 2018. https://kuulpeeps.com/2018/05/kuulpeeps-news-organizers-of-miss-uew-his-facing-the-schools-authorities-over-nudity-on-their-stage/ (accessed 18 June 2018).

(2006, p. 74) specifically predicted that the discovery of oil would fuel conflict, especially within Côte d'Ivoire but with implications for neighboring countries. In Africa, generally, Collier (2009a, 2009b) has been making this case, claiming it is a "natural resource trap," particularly because people are greedy or tend to be aggrieved about not getting enough from oil.

However, the mainstream account overlooks many important cooperative approaches that West Africans have adopted in the past and in contemporary times. Indeed, in the Ghana–Côte d'Ivoire impasse, a peaceful resolution is being pursued under the United Nations Conventions on the Law of the Sea and has persisted to date. At a point, it seemed to have subsided, but it has not. The issue in contest is the methodology for establishing boundaries. The equidistance approach, which the Ghanaian authorities claim is the best under the circumstances, is being challenged by the Ivorians and no progress has been made; hence, the formal arbitration process initiated by the Ghanaian authorities. According to a joint press statement by the Ghana Attorney General and Minister for Justice, the Minister for Energy, and the Chairman of the Boundary Commission, this process is expected to take about three years, or even more, but its outcome would be binding on the parties (Graphic Online, 2014). The arbitration was brought under Part XV and Annex VII of the Law of the Sea Convention and is being heard in the International Tribunal of the Law of the Sea sitting in Hamburg, Germany. The panel was made up of five judges, two of whom were appointed by the contestants, and three mutually appointed. A fuller account can be seen in the written statements of the two parties (see Republic of Côte d'Ivoire, 2015; Republic of Ghana, 2015).

The case has since been determined. No conflicts ensued. Rather, the leaders of the two countries resolved to become, and have since then become, closer. This approach to disagreement contests stereotypes of African conflicts. This experience bears out Cyril Obi's (2009) argument that the "rational choice" school of thought about conflict in Africa is misleading as it is monocausal; fails to see that most so-called African conflicts have transnational, often Euro–American drivers; and ignores intra-Africa cooperation.

What is at issue here is not simply regionalization, however. Often advocated by mainstream economists, who do so from a colonial and colonizing perspective, the case for regionalization entails promoting trade liberalization, trade creation, and scale economies, all of which are intended to achieve economic growth and a dependent economic model (for a discussion of all such approaches, see Robson, 1983, while Auriol &

Biancini, 2015, is a recent example of such mainstream accounts). Such models of regionalization have had low or no transformative effects.

Immanuel Wallenstein ([1961] 2005, pp. 111–128) offers a more detailed account of the limitations of this approach and its resulting regional policies. Briefly, there are at least four reasons. One reason is their mimicry of those forces that have underdeveloped and continue to underdevelop Africa. Another stems from the organization of unity along colonial linguistic patterns: French West Africa, British West Africa, and the like. A third reason is the zero sum contest over whether cooperation should be continent or region focused. Such forces – located inside and outside Africa – guide the world system in a way that is often limiting of possibilities and potentialities of underdeveloped African economies and resource systems. There is even an abstract tension about whether regionalization should be seen as an alliance or a long-term movement. More recently, regionalism has been reduced to a banal interest in neoliberalism, free trade, and economic growth: the same capitalist logic that has led to the underdevelopment of Africa. A key example is *Harmonizing Policies to Transform the Trading Environment: Assessing Regional Integration in Africa VI* (UN ECA, 2013), a mainstream study that advocates regionalism.

In his review of the book, *One Thing Leads to Another: Making the Most of the Commodities Boom in sub-Saharan Africa*, Antonio M. A. Pedro (2014), Director of the United Nations Economic Commission for Africa (ECA), heaps praise on the regionalization for economic growth approach. In fairness to him, he was probably merely echoing what was agreed at the Sixth Joint Annual Meetings of the ECA Conference of African Ministers of Finance, Planning and Economic Development and African Union Conference of Ministers of Economy and Finance in Abidjan, Côte d'Ivoire, held from March 25 to 26, 2013.

The UN Economic Commission for Africa has developed the African Minerals Development Centre. However, like the ECA itself, the emphasis is on all minerals not on the complexities of oil itself. A case in point is the report, Minerals and Africa's Development: The International Study Group Report on Africa's Mineral Regimes (UN ECA, 2011). Fourth, and more fundamentally, they repeat the old vision: national economic growth. Basically, to work toward turning Africa's mineral resources into transforming African countries' experience with economic growth. The contradictions in such processes in today's neoliberal order in Africa where the state is simultaneously supposed to be minimalist, on the one hand, and strong enough to pry open spaces for inter-nation-state integration for growth, on the other, have been much discussed (e.g., Boone, 2007, 2012).

The strategy being advocated in this book is different from all these and hence none of the setbacks should hold cooperation back in the Margin. The cooperation being advocated is specific to oil and gas and has the alternative vision of not just economic growth but a just economic growth, not just policy but a just policy, inclusive social change, and economic linkages (Hirschman, 1958, 1984). Economic coordination and active state involvement to create and redistribute wealth is crucial in this program, but it has to follow direct and decisive community involvement and emancipatory trade unionism.

In turn, decision-making will be more collective under the program being proposed. None of these implies noneconomic engagement or autarky. Isolation is not a choice; what is to be chosen is a new integration with a new vision and from new African paths less travelled. Africans of old have shown that, like lions, they can stand on their own, defying and superseding colonial and racist boundaries. The Governor General of French West Africa in 1930 was shocked at the zeal and drive of French West Africans, as reported by Walter Rodney ([1972] 2011, p. 263). The Governor said,

Each new school that is opened is immediately filled to overflowing . . . At certain places on the Côte d'Ivoire, the villagers pay the teachers out of their own pockets. Our pupils come from distances of 20 to 50 kilometers.

Africa had an advanced civilization and a rich way of life outside the world and Western capitalist order. Indeed, the emphasis on the nation-state today was not the norm: cooperation and integration used to be an important aspect of social and political organization in the Africa of the past. Immanuel Wallenstein ([1961] 2005, pp. 11–26) documents part of this social organization, as do Walter Rodney ([1972] 2011, pp. 33–71) and Frederick Cooper (2014, pp. 38–65) more recently. The intrusion of their systems into the colonial and then compartmentalized world system continue to create significant dangers for the continent but also possibilities. The Africans fought their ways out of centuries of colonialism, through vicious and sustained strategy, and solidarity with those elsewhere who stood with the Africans. There is clear possibility for further decisive steps forward.

Walter Rodney ([1972] 2001, pp. 264–265) gives a rich history of how Africans help their sisters and brothers: how some rich Africans are expected to and some actually do support poorer ones, including how a Somali trader was the first to establish a secondary school in that country, not the colonizer, not Western philanthropy. In short, the West African

Transform Margin provides the possibilities for collective and sustainable self-determination. As Aimé Césaire notes in his *Discourse on Colonialism* (1972, p. 44), to argue Africa is both "ante-capitalist and anti-capitalist" does not mean that the continent is to march backwards into the past. Rather, it is a march forward for a new society. In his words:

> It is not a dead society that we want to revive. We leave that to those who go in for exoticism. Nor is it the present colonial society that we wish to prolong ... It is a new society that we must create with the help of all our brother slaves, a society rich with all the productive power of modern times, warm with all the fraternity of olden days. (Césaire 1972, p. 52)

So, there are possibilities for a new regional approach that revives and adapts that which predated colonial intrusion (see Cooper, 2014). This approach presents possibilities for lasting social change that will generate the autonomy, linkages, and cooperation for alternative economic futures beyond economic growth, economic dependency, and economic subservience.

In this process, the environment must be central. Indeed, in its preliminary verdict, ITLOS (2015, p. 2) notes that both Ghana and Côte d'Ivoire must "act with prudence and caution to prevent serious harm to the marine environment," even if the doom of environmental disaster is yet to descend on the parties. A Regional Pollution Centre can work. It is more useful because pollution is a regional and global problem and, while it may arise locally, it cannot fully be addressed at that scale. Currently, all pollution legislation is national in scope, so they are inadequate. But there are some signs of hope. The Ivorians have the Plan Pollumer, which is a national oil spill plan. The Centre Ivorian Antipollution (CIAPOL) has state-of-the-art equipment and the technical personnel needed for most types of water-based pollution analysis and hence has been proposed as a regional centre for pollution analysis for WATM (Bender et al., 1993). In spite of its many problems, the Environmental Protection Agency (EPA) of Ghana and various pieces of legislation about oil spill in Ghana also offer some hope (Obeng-Odoom, 2014a). In turn, the action-research network, WE-Africa, is calling for "a wellbeing economy in Africa; Africans thriving not rising."[4]

Most of these laws and institutions are national in outlook, so a regional focus will have to be developed. Here, the ECOWAS Centre for Renewable Energy and Energy Efficiency (ECREEE) can be a fulcrum for regionalist

[4] This is taken from the group's official website: http://we-africa.org/.

policy making.[5] Putting in place a regional policy for old and now discredited markets, growth, and efficiency outcomes, however, will not do for
Africa as these visions of Africa have led to empty "Africa on the rise"
discourses expressed in GDP terms but not linked to fulfilling lives
(Obeng-Odoom, 2015a). Linkages too can be created by improving the
capacity and democratizing the management and control of oil refineries in
WATM. International evidence (Huber, 2013, pp. 61–95) shows that, while
settlements around refineries tend to experience ecological and economic
pressures from the processes of refining crude, such locations and workers
in refineries have also been a major force for organizing and demanding
popular management and control of oil processes. This evidence does not
prove that this will happen in the specific case of West Africa, but it signals
such a possibility. Besides, building the capacity of refineries will unleash
a chain reaction and break the colonial model of concentrated
development.

Advantages beyond linkages include self-sufficiency, protection against
the ebbs and flows of oil pricing, and gaining more and cheaper access to
energy. The so-called shale oil revolution has recently reduced American
import of crude oil from African countries such as Nigeria, Angola, and
Algeria. Indeed, since American imports from Africa reached a historic
high of $113 billion in 2008, there has been a downward trend in trade: in
2013, African trade with America was only $50.1 billion. Around the same
time, the total value of trade fell from $141.9 to $85.3 billion being the
lowest since 2005 (Economist Intelligence Unit, 2014, 34). This trend
seems to bear out E. G. Frankel's (2007) famous analysis that oil-rich
regions should be moving away from an economic system that depends
on oil, because alternative energy developments in the West will impact on
the demand for oil. I draw a rather different conclusion for West Africa:
African oil should not be developed for Europe, America, or Asia; African
oil should be used for Indigenous African development.

Energy access reliability and quality are rather low, and poverty levels,
particularly fuel poverty levels, on the continent are substantial. A majority
of the people depend on fuel wood (Brew-Hammond, 2010). Oil products
such as kerosene and LPG form a big part of the energy profile of many
households, especially those in urban centres. In turn, price volatility hits
these households hardest when it occurs. For the majority who cannot
afford these products, fuel wood is the alternative as it is relatively cheap.
Yet, it also contributes to the spectacularly high levels of deforestation in

---

[5] More information about this centre is here: www.ecreee.org/.

West Africa. As noted by Agbanyim (2012, p. 4), from the beginning of the last century to 2008, the use of wood fuel has contributed to a decrease in Ghana's forest from 8.13 million hectares to 1.6 million hectares and Côte d'Ivoire's from 16 million hectares to 6.38 million hectares.

This is not to say, as orthodox scholars often claim, that the poor are to blame for the removal of the forest cover in West Africa. Deforestation in the region has multiple causes, some of which can be traced to colonially inspired commercial farming practices that yielded raw materials for the factories in Europe (Fairhead & Leach, 1998). There is some hope. Côte d'Ivoire has a refinery processing at least 3 million metric tons of crude oil per year. The refinery is based in Abidjan and is the only one in the country. It receives oil transported by sea, at a mooring buoy, which is approximately 1 kilometer off the seacoast. Most of the oil comes from Nigeria, but about 100,000 tons per year is Indigenous, mainly from Espoir (Bender et al., 1993).

In 2004, 35 per cent of the refined products were also sent to Nigeria, with a further 14 per cent to the United States (AfDB and OECD 2006, p. 237). As of 2010, the capacity of the refinery was crumbling, profits falling by 84 per cent between 2008 and 2010. But the state planned to establish another refinery valued at $7 billion in San Pedro, in the Western part of the country (Avery, 2010), which has a port with two quays spanning 736 meters (AfDB and OECD, 2006, pp. 241–242). Further, Côte d'Ivoire has more trained staff in its ministry than other West African countries studied. With such absorptive capacity, the government can consider a medium-term measure to define a regulatory, enforcement, and institutional approach for the sector and begin to identify staff and train them (Matthews, 2014, p. 84). Also, while the government plans to extend this port to the Northern part of the country as the port at Abidjan caters to the needs of 60 per cent of the industries in the country (AfDB and OECD, 2006, pp. 241–242), it is necessary for more work to be done there on both the refinery and the port to enhance the strength of the linkages fostered by the industrial base of the country and improve the distribution of the resulting advantages.

As with Côte d'Ivoire, Ghana has a refinery, the Tema Oil Refinery (TOR), though it currently produces much less than its Ivorian counterparts. It refined and produced 9,616 tonnes of gas in 2007 (Kemausuor et al., 2011). TOR supports the operation of more than 600 industries and their employees in a wide range of sectors, including agriculture, and related sectors. It is on record that this industrial base, small as it is, is the sector with the most linkages to the rest of society (Apeaning &

Thollander, 2013). Both countries can do much better in terms of refining oil. Niger only started commercial oil production and export in 2009, but it is already self-sufficient in terms of refining its own gas supplies. Indeed, Niger is also able to export the surplus of its oil supplies (constituting 65 per cent of all its supplies) to Nigeria (Bazilian et al., 2013). It is not easy for Ghana to achieve the same feat. The infrastructure at the TOR is in poor condition. Indeed, the waste treatment plant is currently dysfunctional, making the refinery incapable of dealing with the treatment of industrial waste. In turn, not only is TOR not functioning properly, but it is also contributing to a public health and environmental disaster (Sarkodie et al., 2014). The policy space is also disjointed with many vague, non-existent, or even conflicting policy signals (Apeaning & Thollander, 2013). Addressing these problems is possible, even if difficult.

Still, substantial changes will be needed in terms of allocating existing oil rents into the refinery sector. Whether a government wedded to the logic of producing more roads is likely to change course requires careful political economic analysis (e.g., Obeng-Odoom, 2015b, 2015c). It seems that it will not be easy to shed this "road-first" policy stance. Yet, given that the recent Afrobarometer Survey shows that on average 70 per cent of the Ghanaian people feel that their government has been "'very ineffective' or 'ineffective' in 'using oil revenues to improve living conditions in the country'" (Centre for Democratic Development, 2014, p. 1), it will be worth considering alternative uses of oil rents.

Developing the refineries in Africa is one important alternative. The prospect of this alternative working is bright, at least because it is internationally known that the high quality of African oil makes it relatively straightforward and affordable to refine. Besides, interviews with local people show much grassroots support for the establishment of local refineries for jobs, but also for the self-esteem of the Africans (Bybee & Johannes, 2014). The advantages of investing in oil refineries in WATM and gaining self-sufficiency in processing oil for the region are legion. Puka and Szulecki (2014, p. 125) note that such regional orientation in policy typically leads to the resolution of the so-called "energy trilemma": energy security, effective and efficient economic performance, and environmental justice.

Apart from the obvious gains of sharing responsibilities and collectively shouldering burdens of energy provision, including export of value-added oil products, the whole continent can benefit from electricity supply and the use of liquefied petroleum gas (LPG) for food production, among others uses (Kemausuor et al., 2011; Bazilian et al., 2013, p. 43). More stable power production is another potential outcome, as is fairer distribution of both access to and control of energy (Obeng-Odoom, 2013a). Clearly then, investment in the oil and gas industry for local self-sufficiency and use is crucial for West Africa to deal with its energy poverty and insecurity.

This program of change must go with another: removing stark inequalities at the roots. Practices about paying expatriate workers wages and salaries that substantially tower above the wages of native labor require decisive reassessment in conjunction with the local oil labor force. Even more crucially, local labor ought to obtain training in managerial and key sectors in addition to the technical but predominantly vocational and lower-level education that abounds now (Panford, 2014; Obeng-Odoom, 2015b). This is particularly important because in West Africa, "[t]he science and economics of oil refining are often left in the hands of expatriates, a situation that does not usually allow for spill-over effects" (Bazilian et al., 2013, p. 45). This was the essence of colonial education: education to support the colonizers' interest, to sustain the capitalist system, to mystify and to reify the West as superior, and to create a culture of imitation of Western processes (Rodney, [1972] 2011). Such management education is enslaving and cannot be considered under "possibilities" for Africa. Rather, the proposal is for a management education in anticipation of a future where the workers and more native labor will rise to take the leadership of the oil and gas industry: a management in the hands of the natives in such a way that the full potential of African managers – not African surrogate capitalists with vision wedded to become the next Europe, America, or Asia – can be realized.

### Evidence of African Autonomous Action and Possibilities for the Future

Recent evidence in Africa, however, gives some hope. The signing of the African Continental Free Trade Area (AfCFTA) Agreement is important for this purpose, even if its continuous commitment to growth and insensitivity to inequality are downsides. The Nigerian courts have ruled that TNCs are subject to local laws. Indeed, as handed down in the *Gbemre v. Shell and Two Others case*, even where local laws are not comprehensive enough, they have accepted that the African Charter on Human and Peoples' Rights is applicable to Nigeria (Amao, 2008). Also, the US Supreme Court has recently ruled in *Jam v IFC* (as discussed in Chapter 5) that TNCs can be prosecuted in US courts for their actions that generate social costs in the Global South. It follows that (1) Africans can unite to set Africa-wide policies that are applicable on home grounds and (2) the courts in Africa can take a more purposive, living, and socially just approach to legal interpretations. In the latter sense, the recent marked departure of the Supreme Court of Ghana from the literalist to the purposive approach to constitutional interpretation is encouraging. Ghana's leading legal scholar and former Supreme Court Judge, Justice Date-Bah (2015), has discussed this in detail.

The aspiration of some states in Africa (e.g., Ghana's) to elect mayors can sharpen competition between them and local governments. At the same time, however, greater downward accountability can provide the basis for creative cooperation among cities and between urban authorities and urban commoners in joint and multiple struggles to govern the city. Sierra Leone – a country with severely limited forms of local governance – offers some lessons. Local governance in the country is based on the principle of direct election of mayors for a single term of four years. To overcome major political differences between the central and local governments, local governments in Makeni, Kenema, Bo, and Freetown have shown that, through local taxation, it is possible to generate substantial local revenues and to limit dependence on central government funding, and hence central government control of how to deliver local services (Jibao & Prichard, 2015).

With all their limitations, elaborate local government systems operate in Ghana, South Africa, and Uganda – all of which are resource states (Obeng-Odoom, 2013b). There is also occasional assertion of decisive central state power. One such utilization of power is the recent concerted effort by Nigeria, Benin, Togo, Ghana, and Côte d'Ivoire in working toward banning toxic fuel exported to their countries by TNCs (The Guardian, 2016). For those cities that, in spite of their shortcomings, try to consistently collect local revenues, over 80 per cent of local activities can be financed that way. In the Sekondi-Takoradi Metropolitan Assembly (STMA), for example, the revenue from property taxes alone funded nearly eight in ten urban infrastructural projects between 2006 and 2013 (Mabe & Kuusaana, 2016). More can be done to increase local revenues to fund the major infrastructural deficit in the metropolis (Owusu & Afutu-Kotey, 2010). More fundamentally, local taxation will need to be explicitly redesigned and implemented as a mechanism for reducing economic inequalities by placing taxes on land rent along with untaxing labor. There is a rent tax in operation, but it is based on contractual rent paid by the occupants of rental housing to landlords.

This rent tax is poorly assessed, being dependent on self-declarations by property owners, and it is only 8 per cent of rental income (Obeng-Odoom,

2014b). There are obligations on TNCs to make royalty payments too. But, in Ghana, royalties are pegged at a mere 5 per cent, much lower than the global average of 7 per cent. Even this rate can be, and often is, further mitigated by transfer pricing. Expatriate workers are exempt from the payment of income tax, but not local labor, thereby institutionalizing a labor aristocracy. The fiscal regime does not include a windfall tax on super-normal profits by TNCs (Obeng-Odoom, 2014a, chapter 8).

The tax system as a whole can be changed to reward effort and discourage speculation and monopoly by shifting the object of taxation to land and away from building costs. As land values in resource-rich cities are rising, a tax on land will increase the revenue to the state, especially if the legislation introducing such a tax does away with the many exemptions granted to TNCs. The income tax can, then, be gradually removed. Removing taxes on labor will enhance its condition and create incentives in all markets. As disposable incomes rise, there will be an increase in local purchases, which in turn will stimulate more economic activity, resulting in a virtuous cycle. The added economic activity will enhance land values, and hence add to the public purse. The process itself will also generate revenue and cultivate experience for a social, Georgist state.

A tax shift also appears consistent with popular demands. Surveys reveal the preferences of urban residents as a guide for public policy. A survey by Wilde, Adams, and English (2013) showed that road construction was one of the three least preferred options of the ten offered for selection. Another survey showed that the residents of Sekondi-Takoradi ranked road building very low, even though road construction is the top priority by TNCs, with government support. A credible survey in Ghana by the Friedrich-Ebert Foundation (2011) shows that public education and public investment in energy are the two top priorities of the youth of Ghana. Energy self-sufficiency was a high priority (Obeng-Odoom, 2015a, 2015b).

Breaking private monopolies and oligopolies can be done by organizing public provision of water supply, oil production, and oil refining at the local, urban level. A network of cities in Africa also collaborates to deliver such services. In doing so, the politics of these new institutions will be such that the public is neither exploited nor excluded.

To emphasize, none of these possibilities are merely a bureaucratic wish list of state-led transformation. There is much popular agency, or politics from below, in which these possibilities are steeped or which ground these options. That is evidently the case across Africa in the Africa uprising, including the more recent experience of Sudanese insurrection. It is also the case when roadblocks are mounted to stop driving altogether or rituals are performed to remove the tendency for accidents to occur on roads. The popular demand for slow speed or anger at overspeeding constitute additional evidence of how ordinary people demand a screeching halt to automobility, a trend that is carefully analyzed in a special issue of *Africa* edited by Gabriel Klaeger (see Klaeger, 2013a, 2013b). Indeed, as the survey evidence I review elsewhere (Obeng-Odoom, 2015b) shows, there is widespread popular rejection of the growing investment in roads in favor of greater sovereignty and economic liberation. If there are possibilities for change, then, these possibilities are, in fact, more popular than bureaucratic.

## Possibilities

The fate of Botswana is usually considered an exemplar for the rest of Africa and proof of the potential for these Africanisms. In his book, *The Silver Bullet*, Georgist economist Fred Harrison (2008, see pp. 41–44) presents Botswana as such. The Matswana state collects more royalties from the TNC, Debeers (which has to pay on production and, hence, pays more revenue to the state), in comparison to other states in Africa that utilize different ways of estimating royalties due. In addition, Botswana extracts a profit tax from DeBeers, an institution that other African countries have struggled to maintain on their books. Compared to Ghana's mere 13 per cent share in the minerals enterprise, Botswana has 50 per cent share in the diamond enterprise, so the state is able to shape the direction of the TNC. Indeed, Botswana also has been able to negotiate for DeBeers to bear a substantial part of any economic declines in the world price of diamonds (Curry, Jr., 1987). In short, the country has developed a mature relationship with a TNC using its rights as a landlord.

In terms of utilization, too, Botswana's experiences are widely praised. By providing for public physical and social infrastructure, the state has succeeded in creating jobs for its people. Even in the private sector, state expenditure has generated employment through forward and backward linkages. Local processing of diamonds has created 3,200 jobs in a country whose total population is only two million people (Biedermann, 2018). In these ways, the state has been able to ensure national economic growth (Curry, Jr, 1987; Valentine, 1993; Harrison, 2008; Gaffney, 2016). This growth has also helped reduce poverty. Table 8.3 shows trends in key economic, social, and ecological indicators.

As Table 8.3 shows, Botswana has been successful on most of the indicators (growth, unemployment, poverty), but it has struggled with

Table 8.3 *Current trends in growth, poverty, inequality, unemployment,
and pollution, ca. 2010–2014*

| Country | Growth Trend | Poverty Trend | Inequality Trend | Unemployment Trend | Per Capital $CO_2$ Emissions |
|---|---|---|---|---|---|
| Mauritius | ↑ | ↓ | ↓ | ↓ | ↓ |
| Botswana | ↑ | ↓ | ↑ | ↓ | ↔ |
| Ghana | ↑ | ↓ | ↑ | ↓ | ↑ |

*Sources:* Adapted from Obeng-Odoom, 2015c, p. 237; UNDP, 2011; 2016

keeping growth inclusive and ecologically sustainable. Through its Income Policy, the state tried to regulate private sector wages to be at the level of public sector wages. It did so quite well through a Wages Policy Committee that regulated wages in the country (Valentine, 1993; Harrison, 2008).

However, its wider policies on social inclusion and social protection as well as the support of informal labor are less successful. Inspired by the advice of the Bretton Woods institutions, the state sought to use "efficiency" rather than "rights" as the guiding principle to distribute its social programs. So, the poor were subjected to a rigorous program of means testing before they qualified for moderate social intervention programs (Ulriksen, 2011). State commitment to the environment is also negligible. Attempts to diversity its economy from mining have largely failed. In turn, as Table 8.3 shows, per capital carbon emissions in Botswana have not improved over the years. Indeed, they could worsen. Botswana continues to have fraught relations with its Indigenous populations and its striving for continuing growth shapes its policy of "subordination and dispossession of the San people" of their land (Good, 2008). Although, as earlier mentioned, Botswana has developed mechanisms for sharing risks with TNCs, its economy is overly dependent on diamonds (Hillbom & Bolt, 2018). These latter policies and problems, however, are neoliberal, not Georgist. The structural nature of its pattern of economic development, inherited from its colonial days, however, suggests that Georgist policies can do better with addressing so-called past problems.

Georgist policies are much more serious in terms of social and ecological interventions and tend to generate much better social and environmental outcomes. In Africa, it is Mauritius whose policies come closest to Georgism. As Table 8.3 suggests, Mauritius scores well on all economic, social, and ecological indicators for this reason. An export-led economy, Mauritius invests substantially in social protection and ecological

Table 8.4 *Social security spending in Botswana and Mauritius, 2001–2010*

| Country | 2001/2 | 2003/4 | 2005/6 | 2007/8 | 2009/10 |
|---|---|---|---|---|---|
| **Botswana, Social Security Spending** | | | | | |
| Pula (Million) | 463 | 384 | 190 | 587 | 553 |
| % Government Expenditure | 3 | 2 | 1 | 2 | 1 |
| % Social Expenditures | 8 | 5 | 2 | 5 | 3 |
| **Mauritius, Social Security Spending** | | | | | |
| Rupees (Million) | 6,698 | 7,887 | 10,305 | 11,745 | |
| % Government Expenditure | 20 | 19 | 21 | 20 | |
| % Social Expenditures | 37 | 37 | 41 | 41 | |

*Source:* Ulriksen, 2011

governance. It deploys a framework of human and environmental rights, not just efficiency. As Table 8.4 shows, the state of Mauritius invests proportionately more of both government and social expenditures on social security spending than Botswana. On average, Mauritius spends about 20 per cent of government expenditure on social security spending compared to a paltry 2 per cent in Botswana. Its labor taxes too are among the lowest in the world. So, again, it is quite Georgist.

Like its investments in society and economy, Mauritius takes its environmental programs very seriously. It taxes oil from cradle to grave, from production to use, and uses the returns to incentivize greener investments. The Maurice Ile Durable (MID) launched in 2008 is a case in point. A tax on fossil fuel, MID has since doubled on coal, liquefied petroleum gas, and other petroleum products. The effect has been to make the price of such products more prohibitive in an attempt to discourage their use. In the case of coal, the price increases has been as high as 9.4 per cent.

Many concerns remain about whether the tax rate is too low, in what ways production can more directly be checked, and whether MID should be developed into a full blown carbon tax or an enhanced emissions trading scheme. These are all questions that have been asked with the intention of improving the environmental record of the country rather than to disparage the country's Georgist credentials.

In the meanwhile, however, Mauritius is a fascinating case study. It has successfully combined economic growth with poverty reduction and a more egalitarian distribution of resources in a cleaner and greener environment, while still open to international trade. It is a country from which other countries in the Global South such as Botswana, but particularly Ghana, can learn.

The power of the landed and propertied interests in Ghana is apt to trigger a reaction very likely to be supported by the oil TNCs. However, as several public surveys (Obeng-Odoom, 2015b, 2015d) show, there is a strong public support for such programs. Experiences from elsewhere in the world clearly illustrate that the implementation of such programs does not wipe out profit arising from genuine effort and innovation. So, after years of implementing an oil tax that captures and returns to the public the aspect of rent contributed by the public, TNCs still find Australia a very attractive business destination. Chadian economists (Gab-Leyba & Laporte, 2016) have also independently arrived at the conclusion that programs of this nature can transform Chadian society by returning to the people of Chad what has been stolen from them by TNCs. These revenues could be used to develop clean fuels refined and used locally. Doing so would lead to the creation of green jobs, insulation against the risks of depending on others for energy security, and, most fundamentally, "prevent 25,000 premature deaths in 2030 and almost 100,000 premature deaths [from oil-related pollution] in 2050" (Public Eye, 2016, p. 6).

Unlike some Marxist programs that demand revolution or nothing, Georgists seek gradual, progressive, and systematic reforms. As Henry George himself showed (see Pullen, 2014; O'Donnell, 2015), public activism and social education can be part of this program of long-term change. Orienting the discourse of oil accidents away from proximate causes, emphasizing tendencies for accidents when the emphasis is on continuing economic growth, putting more pressure on the establishment whenever such accidents occur, and recurrently focusing on the experiences of Botswana and Mauritius centered on new property relations and comprehensive social and ecological protection have shown that fundamental change can be helpful. In short, it is more useful to develop true African free trade as an alternative to existing regimes of protectionism, neoliberal free trade, and humanist fair trade (see also Chapter 5). In these respects, the African Continental Free Trade Area (AfCFTA), the largest free trade area in the world, successfully rejects classical, neoclassical, and Marxist theories of trade and, rather, appeals to non-aligned pan-Africanism as it can more strongly appeal to Africanist systems of trade. In this sense, its advocacy of free trade aspires to be analogous with throwing off the shackles of slavery, colonialism, neocolonialism, illiberalism, and neoliberalism.

However, AfCFTA's exclusive focus on "continental Africa," its disinterest in systemic redistribution, and encouragement of the private appropriation of socially created land rents do not only diminish the scope of "the economic theory of Pan-Africanism" (Fosu, 1999), they also create "progress and poverty," which could undermine the very essence of this Africanist trade regime. AfCFTA, as a new trade order, would not only consolidate structural inequality; it could also metastasise it into a cross-scalar inequality-producing machine with ripple adverse effects for economic, social, and ecological sustainability. What Henry George (1886/ 1991) called "True Free Trade," a new theory, which is based on commoning land for African societies everywhere, and eventually commoning land in other societies, socializing land rent, and active development of non-rentier economies, can more powerfully drive the Pan-African agenda, more effectively address the problems of free trade, and more resolutely decolonize global trade. Such an embrace of Georgism would bring AfCFTA closer to "African systems of commerce" (Konadu, 2009, 2015), further characterized by the total rejection of slave-trade conditions of uneven relationships, slave conditions of work, and slavish commitment to the consumption of injurious commodities such as arms. True African free trade must prioritize human need over property in land or labor, it must shun protectionism, and, instead, promote trade in useful goods and services among Africans all over the world, not just continental Africa. AfCFTA should be seen more as a transit point, not as a destination for Africa.

# Concluding the Groundwork for a New Political Economy of the Global South

What conclusions can be drawn from this study? What lessons can we draw from answers to the questions that motivated this book: namely, what are the patterns and intersectional dimensions of inequality in Africa and across the world? (2) What causes inequality? (3) Why does inequality persist? (4) Why is inequality an important focus for political economic analysis? (5) What can and is being done about inequality and by whom? Now that we have addressed these questions, what lessons and implications can be learnt from our conclusions and arguments for policy and for the study of African economics, indeed for the study of the political economy of the Global South?

This concluding chapter seeks to address these questions by successively recapping the arguments, drawing out their implications for development policy, and reflecting on what the study can contribute to economics. Both development policy and development economics can better recognize and account for the political economic interests that shape the thinking about Africa. In this process, stratification economics provides both a point of departure and a compass for navigating the future. While many obstacles impede the possibilities of change, there are, indeed, countervailing forces that can propel the needed transformation.

## RECAPPING THE ARGUMENTS

Social stratification in the world is widespread and complex. Yet, far more effort has been devoted to the Global North in untangling and redressing it. In seeking to decolonise this uneven knowledge production, which hides social stratification in the Global South, I have focused on Africa - the most marginalised space on earth. In doing so, I have argued that the key concepts of economics used to explain intergroup inequality in Africa and between Africa and the rest of the world raise more questions than answers. Even more unsatisfactory and more dishonorable are their roles in obfuscating the true causes of underdevelopment and creating divisions not only in Africa but also in the Global South more widely. Focusing on monopoly structures and institutions, particularly private property rights established in precapitalist times and nurtured to date, is a more compelling alternative line of analysis. Also more compelling are the possible policy pathways that arise logically from focusing on land, property rights, and other institutions.

These arguments, relating proposals to diagnosis, may sound akin to a *Kicking Away the Ladder* thesis (Chang, 2002), but they are quite distinct. Ha-Joon Chang does not go into the causes of the underdevelopment of the Global South, underdevelopment he takes as given or as a feature of not being allowed to follow the ladder of the West. He holds that the problems of the South cannot be solved by the liberal program. Instead, he proposes protectionist industrialization for growth and a gradual opening up of economies after infant industries can stand on their feet because, as he argues, it is these steps that led the West to where they are now. To catch up, therefore, the South can, and should, usefully ascend the ladder of progress, which, in J. K. Galbraith's *The Nature of Mass Poverty* should entail not just what he called an "industrial escape" (by facilitating industrialization that creates *internal* employment) but also facilitate *external* escape from the continent through emigration (see Galbraith, 1979, chapters 6–8).

The arguments in this book, on the other hand, identify the causes of inequalities as cumulative change in a process in which the Global North has been and continues to be complicit in the conditions of Africa. Not only are they "kicking away the ladder," they have established a system in place to exaggerate the gaps. Growth, industrialization, and protectionism can be – and often are – part of the problem; not solutions. Indeed, if the African countries were to ascend the same ladder that has now been kicked away, the world would be a worse place to live: Africans too would need to enslave other races, or colonize others, rob others, plunder the resources of others, or institutionalise global wage and rent-theft systems as others did, to say nothing of the potential ecological impacts of such strategies.

Analytically, this book takes a step toward – but also beyond – current institutional economics strands of a more radical nature. Compare the book's central treatise with K. W. Kapp's *The Social Costs of Private Enterprise* (1971). Unlike Kapp's *Social Costs*, which points to analytical weaknesses in the state of mainstream economics because it does not take into account the price of growth for the "1 per cent", this book advances the thesis that the cathedrals of development keep Africa in its place by developing an economics that diverts attention from investigations that would liberate the continent. This distraction is important to keep the status quo and to justify the continuing social stratification in Arica and, indeed, between Africa and the rest of the world. In other words, if Kapp advanced an ideational critique, the contention in this book is both ideational and materialist. Or, more precisely, that the ideational "weaknesses" have materialist foundations.

J. K. Galbraith makes that point in his book, *The Nature of Mass Poverty* (1979), where he stresses that development economics was invented to make the West feel good about itself. In this book, that contention is extended to show that the invention of development economics or development policy implicitly and explicitly tries to keep Africa in its place, at the margins. This process of marginalization predates postwar politics of development or the political economy of development economics. There are cumulative, systemic, political-economic interests and reasons why the leaders of development economics and development policy more generally have pursued the ideas that they have chosen, imposed, or negotiated with others. It is not just a "feel good" effect: it is materialist. It is in the interest of France, for example, to develop ideas that deflect attention from its engagement with Francophone Africa.

It follows that the problem with development is not with Africa or with the Global South more generally but rather with the Global North, which leads the mission in propounding theories whose biggest success is diverting attention from critical enquiry to sending Africans and Africanists on a wild goose chase – as the following examples further show.

EXPOSING THE "CULTURE" OF DISTRACTION

### The First Distraction: The Ideology of the Resource Curse Thesis

One of the most influential ways of analyzing resources in Africa is the resource curse thesis. The major strategic significance of this thesis is that it turns attention away from the methods by which TNCs continue to extract economic rents from Africa or invite foreign military assistance to protect their assets. It focuses instead on the presumed deficiencies of Africans in managing their own affairs.

Richard Auty is widely referred to as the person who coined the term "resource curse" (Frankel 2012; Papyrakis 2017; Gilberthorpe and Rajak 2017), and so an examination of his rendition is appropriate to illustrate my point. Auty (1993) sets out to show the failure of the former conventional view that a natural resource endowment helps economies at the beginning of their development process, even if the importance of resources declines over time as other sources of productivity replace raw material extraction. In place of that relatively benign view of natural resource endowments, Auty (1993) sought to show that those endowments impede the development process:

> However, a growing body of evidence suggests that a favorable natural resource endowment may be less beneficial to countries at low- and mid-income levels of development than the conventional wisdom might suppose. Two important pieces of this evidence are the developing countries' postwar industrialization efforts and the performance of the mineral-rich developing countries since the 1960s. The new evidence suggests that not only may resource-rich countries fail to benefit from a favorable endowment, they may actually perform worse than less well-endowed countries. This counter-intuitive outcome is the basis of the resource curse thesis. (Auty, 1993, p. 1)

Auty's concept of a resource curse quickly became part of the new conventional wisdom, being repeated by economists, planners, and politicians, as if it were the final word on the subject. It seemed to a new generation of policy makers as if someone had finally uncovered the explanation for the puzzling congruence of increased wealth and rising poverty. This only seemed like a novel idea because most economists after World War II had forgotten that Henry George ([1879] 1979) explained the paradox in the late nineteenth century.

Auty built his argument on a sleight-of-hand trick. He conflated two quite different meanings of economic rent: resource rents and rents from market distortions. Resource rents were observed as early as the eighteenth century and were considered the unearned gains that came from owning a natural resource that cost less to produce or that yielded more value than equivalent resources. Thus, oil near the surface yields more rent than oil in deep deposits that requires a lot of capital to extract. Auty was certainly familiar with resource rents, but he introduced alongside them a type of rent that was invented in the twentieth century to deflect attention from the original meaning. Rent from a market distortion refers to the increased income that a few beneficiaries receive when government alters the market price of a commodity or service with a tariff or a subsidy. An emphasis on this type of rent derives from market fundamentalism, the belief that market-clearing prices always represent the most efficient price in social terms and that government action that distorts market prices is evil. By conflating these two categories of rent, Auty was making his ideological beliefs seem scientific. Auty (1993) argued that high rents created closed economies with little international trade. What he had in mind in that case was the temporary use of high tariff barriers to enable developing economies to create capital-intensive industries that could eventually become competitive.

This protectionism in the service of an autarkic industrial policy was in sharp contrast to the experience of Taiwan and South Korea, which he presented as successful cases of competitive industrial policy that they had to develop in the absence of a resource endowment. Auty (1993) deemed free trade a blessing, and he declared resource endowments as a curse, even though he really meant that any attempt by government to create an internal market with protectionist policies was a curse:

By the time the larger countries (like China, India, Brazil and Mexico) encountered the AIP (autarkic industrial policy) foreign exchange constraint in the late 1960s (as their primary product exports shrank relative to the size of the rest of the economy) their industrial policy was difficult to reform. This was due to entrenched powerful vested interests that benefited from the rents (returns in excess of normal profits) which were created by the protection of more and more industrial sectors from international competition. (Auty, 1993, p. 2)

Using a skillful conflation of two types of rent, Auty consigned countries with natural resources to failure by arguing against protective tariffs that would create a group of entrenched interests. There was, however, more to Auty's argument than a simple confusion of two types of rent. He also argued that the resource curse was tied to the structure of extractive industries, which made them inherently harmful to the nations where the resources were located. As Auty (1993, p. 3) explained:

Mineral production is strongly capital intensive and employs a very small fraction of the total national workforce with large inputs of capital from foreign sources. Consequently, the mining sector displays marked enclave tendencies. This means that it yields modest local production linkages. [The mining sector] also displays low revenue retention since a large fraction of export earnings flow immediately overseas to service the foreign capital investment.

This abstract argument is meaningless. In the case of a deposit that yields no resource rents, it would be true, since all of the revenue from sales would just cover costs. But TNCs are generally attracted to countries with oil or mineral deposits that yield high rents. Auty simply ignored that fact by defining "rent" in such a way that resource rents simply disappeared. In the normal case of deposits yielding substantial resource rents, one might think that some taxation of those rents could help the nation develop. Not correct, according to Auty (1993, p. 3):

The frequent existence of substantial rents (revenues in excess of production costs and a normal return on capital) on mineral ores can, however, when captured by the government through taxation, destabilize the economy ... The imprudent domestic absorption of mining sector rents is capable of rendering much agricultural and manufacturing activity internationally uncompetitive. This occurs through a process known as "Dutch disease."

The Dutch disease is a relevant concern. If an oil-rich nation allows its economy to be dominated by the sale of oil, the rise in the value of its currency will make the export of other products less attractive in international markets. But there are various actions a government can take to balance the sectors of the economy to overcome the Dutch disease. In any case, the Dutch disease in no way contravenes the rationale for transferring an economic surplus from the private to the public sector.

Nevertheless, Auty convinced economists and development planners that the resource curse is a huge problem and the history of this idea, predating Auty (as shown in Chapter 4) achieved a similar feat: the resource curse is real and must be fought. It might take the form of fiscal indiscipline (wasteful state expenditure of oil revenues), state mismanagement (corruption), or even the pursuit of self-sufficiency or protectionism. But the conclusion was always the same: Africans are not to be trusted with natural resource revenues.

## Another Distraction: The Tragedy of the Commons Thesis

The tragedy of the commons is another distraction. According to the 1990s version of the resource curse, African governments are inherently corrupt and will be further corrupted by income from natural resources. The only solution in this scenario is privatization. An ally in this denigration of the African state was Hardin's (1968) "tragedy of the commons" thesis. His followers regarded Africa as a prototypical case of overpopulation and the unwise use of resources. According to one variant of this overpopulation thesis infused also with human capital logic (which we saw in Chapter 4):

One of the keys to increased prosperity around the world is the persistent trend from short lives in large families to long lives in small families. Birth rates have declined sharply all over the world ... Lower birth rates and reduced population growth enable parents to provide better care for each of their children and thereby to increase their average "quality." Parents can do this by offering each of their children more and better education, health care and other opportunities and amenities that the parents otherwise could not afford ... In many developing countires, especially in sub-Saharan Africa, the decline in birth rates has been disappointingly slow. (Gylfason, 2012, p. 31)

These neo-Malthusians pointed to a new kind of resource curse in relation to common ownership. According to the "tragedy of the commons" idea, when natural resources are held in common they are overused and abused and they lead to pollution and exhaustion. State intervention is not ideal because the state is an inefficient manager.

Thus, ownership of natural resources should be privatized. Here, there is a strong convergence with the idea of the resource curse. If Africans cannot manage their own natural resources properly, then TNCs are needed as a governance structure to solve resource problems (Williamson, 1981, 2002, 2009). The rise of new institutional economics created an intellectual home for economic governance research (Boettke et al., 2012). Ostrom's (1990) emphasis on clear rules of partnership to manage the commons was part of this larger shift. Associated with the focus on management rules was support for the view that the market demands the near-perpetual drilling of oil.

According to the Hartwick Rule, for instance, the managers of a resource-rich economy should invest the returns from natural resources in physical and human capital to lengthen the exhaustibility period and to support society in the post-resource phase (Hartwick, 1977). Milton Friedman's (1957) "permanent income hypothesis" also triggered interest in sovereign wealth funds (Alagidede & Akpoza, 2012; Amoako-Tuffour 2016). The net effect of these intellectual developments was a new insistence that the market signaled more oil to be drilled over a prolonged period. According to Auty (1993, p. 258): "A pragmatic orthodox policy, preferably supported by effective market-conforming intervention, can achieve this."

In the new orthodoxy that rests on laissez faire ideas, the extractive sector becomes the bedrock of a resource economy and typically the bonanza of TNCs (Barkin, 2017). Whereas a global free-trade regime was once justified by the classical notion of comparative advantage, as discussed in Chapter 5, the new rationale for free trade is influenced by neoclassical and new institutional economics ideas of private property that favor the market and the private sector (see Clausing 2019a, 2019b). The classical idea of comparative advantage emphasized the nation-state as the forum for major decision-making, but since the resource curse hypothesis treats states as irresponsible, new actors were needed to fill the gap.

TNCs were increasingly asked to make major decisions about the "global economy," whereas nation-states were expected to limit themselves to "market-conforming interventions," valorized primarily in terms of economic growth (Daly, 2017). So, in his review of Paul Collier's *The Plundered Planet*, Duncan Green (2010) styled Collier's policy recommendation as "drill baby drill." This new framework strongly favored private ownership and management of resources as the only way to overcome the supposed resource curse.

Another factor that has been used to distort perceptions has been the use and abuse of national income data to classify many African nations as suffering from the resource curse. British economist Sir Paul Collier (2009a, 2009b, 2010) advances the view that the African state has been a consistent drag on economic growth and that only greater privatization of the African commons can hold the state in Africa in check. His formula for African success is not for the faint of heart, since saving Africa from itself will require foreign military intervention. This view is consistent with Williamson's (1981, 2002, 2009) idea that TNCs are efficient governance structures that perform much better than the state.

Yet, as Morten Jerven (2013, 2015) has shown, the standard account of Africa's growth and the role of the state is based on questionable data, narrow statistical analysis, and porous historical work. Economic models based on the slow growth of the 1980s and early 1990s in Africa have missed the earlier period of high growth and the rapid development since the mid-1990s. Thus, for example, the statistical techniques and data on which Collier bases his claims of a curse by natural resources and a natural disposition to economic failure and dictatorship are flawed. Analysis based on the resource curse idea has misdirected attention away from the dynamics of the global system and focused instead on the nation-state in isolation as the source of all problems. That is standard orthodoxy in the economic understanding of the state, but it fails to take into account the historically specific pressures facing the state at different junctures, as well as the other institutions with which the state interacts (Klimina, 2018). Often, the state is critically shaped by its interactions with such institutions, operating within particularly land and property rights contexts (Petralla, 1984).

Despite its inability to explain actual historical processes, the resource curse thesis continues to be advanced. As an ideology, the real use of the resource curse thesis is not to clarify social problems but to obfuscate them by diverting attention away from their colonial, neocolonial, and imperial roots. We have seen this ploy before. Rather than face the obvious fact that Irish poverty resulted from British landlordism in Ireland, Thomas Malthus propounded the theory that they were poor because of overpopulation (Remoff, 2016, p. 872–874). In a similar fashion, the resource curse is advanced to justify the view that TNCs are the only institutions that can provide suitable governance structures for Africa. As colonial powers claimed that the inability of Africans to govern themselves justified European control, the resource curse is a diversionary ideology that helps justify the advance of TNCs and to block efforts to regulate and transcend them.

The widespread acceptance of the resource curse thesis has also diverted attention from the desirability of African nations using the economic rent from oil and other natural resources for public purposes. According to the logic of the resource curse, TNCs are doing a favor to African nations by passing the rents along to their shareholders rather than paying a tax to the host nation because any added state revenue would simply cause more corruption. The TNCs make some payments to states, including royalties. However, as Cyrus Bina (1992) shows, the world average of such royalties is 12.5 per cent of the value of oil extracted, whereas the African average is between 5 and 7 per cent. In theory, the TNCs sometimes have leases that include provisions for profit sharing, but actual profit payments are rare since accountants can easily hide profits behind phantom costs (Bina, 1992; Bina & Vo, 2007).

Contracts with TNCs often have exemptions that the TNCs manipulate for a kind of rent arbitrage. That is possible because the contracts are tailored to specific territories. Thus, the laws of many African countries allow TNCs to offset certain costs against rents and, hence, reduce the amount of expected payments to the state.

## A Third Distraction: Human Capital Theory

Other sciences have their theories of human capital. Max Weber, for example, advanced an idea of human capital that would lead to the provision of free public education (Weber, 1920/2019). In *The Souls of Black Folk*, W.E.B. Du Bois (1903/1986) provided a distinctive radical basis to rework black empowerment. These theories offer political canvases on which to concretely rework the material struggles of the marginalized, especially blacks.

Mainstream economics is unique. Its doctrine on human capital does not seek to build. Rather, it seeks to draw attention away from the structures of inequality. To reinvent an idea that applied in its origins to slavery is a painful reminder that mainstream development economics is the enterprise of the slave masters who, in gloating over their supposed enlightened positions, sought to bring about enlightenment to the Africans. This Trojan horse gift, however, recurrently wakes up to do the bidding of the donors: keeping Africa and Africans in their place.

Attempts at addressing this problem have been similarly distracting. Consider the recent proposal by Kaushik Basu of Cornell University to replace human capital with 'focal point' theory. This theory accepts that markets are discriminatory. However, the cause of discrimination is competition itself. Basu (2017) contends that, as employers seek the highest possible levels of profit and, hence, maximum efficiency and competence, they would employ people (white men, for example) endowed with these desirable features. In turn, some groups will always be discriminated against. Basu's (2017) proposed solution is to allow this practice, tax the privileged persons, and use the resulting revenue as 'aid' to those discriminated against. However, this "alternative" is weak in its causal theory, which is abstracted from historical and wider contemporary social relations. Focal point theory also is weak because it could reinforce the perception of black inferiority and white superiority. In this framework, black women are particularly vulnerable, as multiple discrimination converges on them (see Crenshaw, 1989). Affirmative action is not an alternative either because it is based on the narrow "but for" condition discussed in the Introduction. Being the most marginalized in the world means that Africa and Africans do not just struggle against a glass ceiling "but for" which they would "catch up? They are often just subsisting on the the floor or even under the floor and, hence, do not have the luxury of benefiting from band aids called "affirmative action". These distractions must be confronted, whether they relate to physical, to natural, or to human capital. These analyses have implications for stratification economics itself, as an alternative paradigm for political economic research.

### Implications for Future Research in the Global South

The future of the mainstream economics fraternity (including behavioral economics, new institutional economics, Austrian economics, and the economics of the Manchester school) looks shaky because its ideology is misaligned with the aspirations of the majority in the grassroots, and the humanists in the positions of power. It is further weakened by its self-censorship to stop questioning, especially as mainstream economics becomes the official party economics. As Samir Amin once observed, there are no intellectual economists in the World Bank because they have stopped questioning. In his words:

The intellectual is not the technocrat serving the system, but the one who critiques the system. There are no intellectuals at the World Bank. And so the intellectual, or the intelligentsia, is not able to be a civil servant in such institutions. The responsibility of intellectuals is to remain critical of the system. (cited in Aly Dieng & Amin, 2007, p. 1158)

When K. W. Kapp wrote his classic text, *The Social Costs of Private Enterprise* (1950/1971), his key contention was that the underlying framework of mainstream economics – that unfettered competition and investment for profit generate win-win outcomes for environment, economy, and society – was oxymoronic. In contrast, he showed that the process of economic expansion simultaneously generated major social and environmental costs to those who did not benefit from the process of growth. It was a social cost not because it was lower than the benefits from the system but rather because it had been generated as part of the change but not taken into account. These social costs, he contended, could be in the form of accidents, natural resource depletion, and pollution. The system created advantages to a few who did not bear the brunt of its huge disadvantages that were heaped on others who do not share its joys.

*Property, Institutions, and Social Stratification in Africa* makes similar arguments, but in the specific context of development economics and with a stronger emphasis on the nexus between ideational and materialist critique, drawing on stratification economics. The argument is that development economics cannot solve the problems of development, especially as they pertain to Africa. Intergroup inequality has been the principal focus, but inequality is part of – rather than removed from – the wider social costs of development. So, these wider social costs have been elucidated, emphasizing that the more the wheels of change spin, the wider the gaps become for intergroup inequality. That is evidently the case for property economics, land reform, economic growth, and international trade. These are not made for Africa because they make Africa worse off.

Development economics was not meant to be a genuine attempt to understand or to transform Africa for Africans and the Global South. It was created and it continues to be a Western project. What this book has done is to sharpen this critique and to make it more concrete. Mainstream development economics does not provide an effective approach to studying inequality in Africa. Previous criticisms have been useful to show that the field is both Eurocentric and America centric in its concepts and vision of the good society, and that these problems have contributed to worsening social conditions in the poorer nations, especially in Africa. Others have exposed the doublespeak in development economics and in development policy in seeking to "kick away the ladder." However, this book extends this body of work by transcending the premise of the current dissent – including claims that the mainstream's reliance on problematic concepts and unreliable official statistics are the sources of its problems or that the mainstream is limited because it seeks to hide the true path (*national interventions and protectionism*) – to both its central methodology (methodological individualism, methodological nationalism, and transaction costs) and to its ontological position of crude objectivism.

This book has cautioned against the preference for an Indigenous economics that idealizes culture as panacea and other revisionist proposals of today, including the push for a marriage between anthropology and economics. While clearly much stronger on analyzing entire economic systems and, indeed, addressing some of the classical problems in development economics, Marxist and old institutional economics versions of development economics, as alternatives, do not always succeed in probing intergroup inequalities shaped by multiple identities such as race, class, and gender cumulatively developed over the years.

The development of the emergent field of stratification economics, led by black political economists, has been shown to be a more fruitful alternative. This field can better engage the concept of rent, better engage institutional economics, and better engage Georgist land economics – just as rent theorists, institutional economists, and Georgist land economists can draw on stratification economics concepts such as the intersectionality of race, class, gender, on the one hand, and the intersectionality of the local and the global, on the other.

In the march toward a black, indeed a Global South, political economy, the demands by K. W. Kapp (1971, chapter 17) – to return economics to philosophy – and to expand the scope of economic investigation, can be usefully considered. Doing so would entail the fundamental reformulation of concepts such as wealth and value in order to capture social costs. Similarly, such a reformulation would need a stronger embrace of history, original institutional economics, land, and especially rents, emphasizing the intersectional analyses of their gendered, racialized, and class dimensions. Yet, even this more mature stratification economics cannot be a point of arrival. Rather, through a process of continuous questioning, stratification economics – created from the beginning to probe the foundations of the truth about the backwardness of the Global South – can play a leading role as both a point of departure and a compass for the future.

# Bibliography

Abdulai, R. T. (2006). "Is land title registration the answer to insecure and uncertain property rights in Sub-Saharan Africa?" RICS Research paper series 6(6): 1–27.

Abdulai R. T. (2010). *Traditional Landholding Institutions in Sub-Saharan Africa, The Operation of Traditional Landholding Institutions in Sub-Saharan Africa: A Case Study of Ghana.* Saarbrücken, Germany: Lambert Academic Publishing.

Abdulai, R. T., & Hammond, F. (2010). "Landed property market information management and access to finance." *Property Management,* 28(4): 228–244.

Abdulai, R. T., & Ochieng, E.G. (2017). "Land registration and landownership security: An examination of the underpinning principles of land registration." *Property Management,* 35(1): 24–47.

Ablo, A. D. (2012). "Manning the rigs: A study of offshore employment in Ghana's oil industry." MPhil Thesis, Department of Geography, University of Bergen, Bergen, Norway.

Ablo, A. D. (2015). "Local content and participation in Ghana's oil and gas industry: Can enterprise development make a difference?" *Extractive Industries and Society,* 2 (2): 320–327.

Ablo, A. D. (2016). "From local content to local participation: Exploring entrepreneurship in Ghana's oil and gas industry." Ph.D. Thesis, Department of Geography, University of Bergen, Bergen, Norway.

Ablo, A. D. (2017). "The micromechanisms of power in local content requirements and their constraints on Ghanaian SMEs in the oil and gas sector." *Norwegian Journal of Geography.* DOI:10.1080/ 00291951.2017.1299213.

Ablo, A. D. (2018). "Scale, local content and the challenges of Ghanaians employment in the oil and gas industry." *Geoforum,* 96 (November): 181–189.

Ablo, A., & Overå, R. (2015). "Networks, trust and capital mobilisation: Challenges of embedded local entrepreneurial strategies in Ghana's oil and gas industry." *The Journal of Modern African Studies,* 53: 391–413.

Abusharaf, A. (1999). "The legal relationship between multinational oil companies and the Sudan: Problems and prospects." *Journal of African Law,* 43: 18–35.

Acemoglu, D., & Robinson, J. (2012). *Why Nations Fail.* New York: Crown Business, USA.

Acemoglu, D., & Verdier, T., (1998). "Property rights, corruption and the allocation of talent: A general equilibrium approach." *The Economic Journal*, 108(450): 1381–1403.

Achaw, O.-W., & Boateng, E. D. (2012). "Safety practices in the oil and gas industries in Ghana." *International Journal of Development and Sustainability*, 1: 456–465.

Acheampong, M., Yu, Q., Enomah, L.D., Anchang, J., & Eduful, M.(2018). "Land use/ cover change in Ghana's oil city: Assessing the impact of neoliberal economic policies and implications for sustainable development goal number one: A remote sensing and GIS approach." *Land Use Policy*, 73: 373–384.

Ackah-Baidoo, A. (2013). "Fishing in troubled waters: Oil production, seaweed and community-level grievances in the Western Region of Ghana." *Community Development Journal*, 48(3): 406–420.

Ackah, I., Osei, E., Tuokuu, F. X. D., & Bobio, C. (2019). "Oiling the wheels of sub-national development: An overview of development plan implementation in the Western region of Ghana." *The Extractive Industries and Society*, 6(2): 343–357.

Addico, G. N. D., & deGraft-Johnson, K. A. A. (2016). "Preliminary investigation into the chemical composition of the invasive brown seaweed *Sargassum* along the West Coast of Ghana." *African Journal of Biotechnology*, 15(39): 2184–2191.

Adedeji, A. (1987). "An ecology for economic change." *Challenge*, 29(6): 4–8.

Adésínà, J. O. (2012). "Social policy in a mineral-rich economy: The case of Nigeria." In K. Hujo, ed., *Mineral Rents and the Financing of Social Policy: Opportunities and Challenges*. Basingstoke: UNRISD/Palgrave, pp. 285–317.

Adewuyi, A. O., & Oyejide, T. A. (2012). "Determinants of backward linkages of oil and gas industry in the Nigerian economy." *Resources Policy*, 37: 452–460.

Adoko, J., & Levine, S. (2009). "Rural women still have few rights to land in Uganda." *The Guardian Newspaper*, March 26.

Adunbi, O. (2016). "The petro-developmental state in Africa: Making oil work in Angola, Nigeria and the Gulf of Guinea." *The Journal of Modern African Studies*, 55(2): 341–343.

Adusah-Karikari, J. (2015). "Black gold in Ghana: Changing livelihoods for women in communities affected by oil production." *The Extractive Industries and Society*, 2: 24–32.

AfDB and OECD (African Development Bank and Organization for Economic Co-operation and Development). (2006). "Côte d'Ivoire." In *African Economic Outlook 2005–2006*, by AfDB and OECD, 229–244. www.oecd.org/dev/36739479.pdf.

African Development Bank (AfDB). (2011). "The middle of the pyramid: Dynamics of the middle class in Africa." AfDB Policy Brief, April 20, Market Brief. www.afdb.org /fileadmin/uploads/afdb/Documents/Publications/The%20Middle%20of%20the% 20Pyramid_The%20Middle%20of%20the%20Pyramid.pdf (accessed 7 August 2018).

Agarwal, B. (2003). "Gender and land rights revisited: Exploring new prospects via the state, family and market." *Journal of Agrarian Change*, 3(1&2): 184–224.

Agarwal, B. (2016). *Gender Challenges: Property, Family and the State*. Oxford: Oxford University Press.

Agarwal, B. & Panda, P. (2007). "Toward freedom from domestic violence: The neglected obvious." *Journal of Human Development*, 8(3): 359–388.

Agbanyim, O. (2012). "Biogas gets chequered growth." *West Africa Insight*, 3(5): 4–5.

Agbosu, L. (1990). "Land registration in Ghana: Past, present and the future." *Journal of African Law*, 34(2): 104–127.

Agozino, B. (2014). "The Africana paradigm in capital: The debts of Karl Marx to people of African descent." *Review of African Political Economy*, 41(140): 172–84.

Agri Capital Ltd. (2012). *We Harvest: You Profit*. London: Agri Capital Ltd.

Agyeman, J. (2013). *Introducing Just Sustainabilities: Policy, Planning, and Practice*. London: Zed.

Akbulut, B., Adaman, F., & Madra, Y. M. (2015). "The decimation and displacement of development economics." *Development and Change*, 46(4): 733–61.

Akiwumi, F, (2017). "Cultural conundrums in African land governance: Agribusiness in Sierra Leone." *Geography Research Forum*, 37(December): 37–60.

Akolgo, I. A. (2018a). "Afro-euphoria: Is Ghana's economy an exception to the growth paradox?" *Review of African Political Economy*, 45(155): 146–157.

Akolgo, I. A. (2018b). "Agenda 2030 in sub-Saharan Africa: What the Millennium Development Goals' narrative teaches about poverty eradication." *African Review of Economics and Finance*, 10(1): 3–22.

Akram-Lodhi, A. H., & Kay, C. (2010a). "Surveying the agrarian question (part 1): Unearthing foundations, exploring diversity." *The Journal of Peasant Studies*, 37(1): 177–202.

Akram-Lodhi, A. H., & Kay, C. (2010b). "Surveying the agrarian question (part 2): current debates and beyond." *The Journal of Peasant Studies*, 37(2): 255–84.

Akyeampong, E. (2018). "African socialism; or, the search for an indigenous model of economic development?" *Economic History of Developing Regions*, 33 (1): 69–87.

Alagidede, P. (2010). "Editorial." *Journal of Economic Policy Reform* 13(1): 1–2.

Alagidede, P., & Akpoza, A. (2012). "Sovereign wealth funds and oil discovery, lessons for Ghana: An emerging oil exporter." *African Growth Agenda*, 9(4): 7–10.

Alagidede, P., Baah-Boateng, W., & Nketiah-Amponsah, E. (2013). "The Ghanaian economy: An overview." *Ghanaian Journal of Economics*, 1(1): 4–34.

Alchian, A., & Demsetz, H. (1973). "The property right paradigm." *The Journal of Economic History*, 33(1): 16–27.

Alden Wily, L. (2011). "'The law is to blame': The vulnerable status of common property rights in sub-Saharan Africa." *Development and Change*, 42(3): 733–757

Alden Wily, L. (2012). "Looking back to see forward: The legal niceties of land theft in land rushes." *The Journal of Peasant Studies*, 39(3–4): 751–775.

Alden Wily, L. (2013). "Enclosure revisited: Putting the global land rush in historical perspective." In T. Allan, M. Keulertz, S. Sojamo, & J. Warner, eds., *Handbook of Land and Water Grabs in Africa: Foreign Direct Investment and Food and Water Security*. London: Routledge, pp. 11–23.

Aliston, R. (1997). "Review of *landowners and tenants in Roman Egypt: The social relations of agriculture in the oxyrhynchite nome*." *The Classical Review*, 47 (2): 364–365.

Allan, T., Keulertz, M., Sojamo, S., & Jeroen, W., eds. (2013). *Handbook of Land and Water Grabs in Africa*. London: Routledge.

Altman, M. (2009). "Behavioral economics, economic theory and public policy." *Australasian Journal of Economic Education*, 6: 1–55.

Altman, M (2012). *Behavioral Economics For Dummies*. New York: Wiley.

Altman, M., ed. (2015). *Real World Decision Making: An Encyclopedia of Behavioral Economics*. New York: Praeger, ABC-CLIO.

Aly Dieng, A. & Amin, S. (2007). "Reflections: Samir Amin." *Development and Change* 38(6): 1149–1159.

Amanor-wilks, D. (2009). "Land, labour and gendered livelihoods in a 'peasant' and a 'settler' economy." *Feminist Africa*, 12: 31–50.

Amanor, K. (2001). *Land, labour and the family in Southern Ghana: A critique of land policy under neo-liberalisation.* Uppsala: Nordiska Afrikainstitutet.

Amanor, K. (2005). "Night harvesters, forest hoods and saboteurs: Struggles over land expropriation in Ghana." In S. Moyo & P. Yeros (eds.), *Reclaiming the land: The resurgence of rural movements in Africa, Asia and Latin America*, pp. 102–117. London and New York: Zed Books.

Amanor, K. (2006). "Family values, land sales and agricultural commodification in Ghana, at the frontier of land issues." *Montpellier*, 1–13.

Amanor, S. (2010). "Family values, land sales and agricultural commodification in South-Eastern Ghana." *Africa*, 80(1): 104–125.

Amao, Olufemi O. (2008). "Corporate social responsibility, multinational corporations and the law in Nigeria: Controlling multinationals in host states." *Journal of African Law*, 52(1): 89–113.

Amin, S. (1974). *Accumulation on a World Scale: A Critique of the Theory of Underdevelopment.* London and New York: Monthly Review Press.

Amin, S. (1977). *Imperialism and Unequal Development.* London and New York: Monthly Review Press.

Amin, S. (1990). *Delinking: Towards a Polycentric World.* London, NJ: Zed Books.

Amin, S. (2005a). "Review of empire and multitude." *Monthly Review*, 57(6).

Amin, S. (2005b). "India, a great power?." *Monthly Review*, 56(9): 1–12.

Amin, S. (2008). *The World We Wish to See: Revolutionary Objectives in the Twenty-First Century.* London and New York: Monthly Review Press.

Amin, S. (2011). *Global History: A View from the South.* Cape Town, Dakar, Nairobi and Oxford: Pambazuka Press, an imprint of Fahamu.

Amin, S. (2012). "Contemporary imperialism and the Agrarian question." *Agrarian South*, 1(1): 11–26.

Amin, S. (2014). "Understanding the political economy of contemporary Africa." *Africa Development*, XXXIX (1): 15–36.

Amiteye J. (2015). "The proposed re-development of the Takoradi market circle and its likely implications for market traders' access to trading space." Master's Thesis, Department of Geography, University of Bergen, Bergen.

Amoah, L. G. A. (2014). "China, architecture and Ghana's spaces: Concrete signs of a soft Chinese imperium?" *Journal of Asian and African Studies*, 51(2): 238–255.

Anderson, K. B. (2010). *Marx at the Margins: On Nationalism, Ethnicity, and Non-Western Societies*, Chicago: University of Chicago Press.

Andersson, M., & Waldenström, D. (2017). "Hernando de Soto: Recipient of the 2017 Global Award for Entrepreneurship Research." *Small Business Economics*, 49: 721–728.

Andoh, F. K. (2017). "Taxable capacity and effort of Ghana's value-added tax." *African Review of Economics and Finance*, 9(2): 255–284.

Andrew, E. (2012). "Possessive individualism and Locke's doctrine of taxation." *The Good Society*, 21(1): 151–168.

Andriani, L., & Christoforou, A. (2016). "Social capital: A roadmap of theoretical and empirical contributions and limitations." *Journal of Economic Issues*, L(1): 4–22.

Anonymous Planner. (2017). Personal interview with urban planner in Sekondi-Takoradi, Ghana. January 13.

Ansah, E. W., & Mintah, J. K. (2012). "Safety management practices at fuel services stations in central and western regions of Ghana." *Nigerian Journal of Health Education*, 16 (June): 78–89.

Anyidoho, N. A., & Steel, W. F. (2016). "Informal-formal linkages in market and street trading in Accra." *African Review of Economics and Finance*, 8(2): 171–200.

Apeaning, R. W., & Thollander, P. (2013). "Barriers to and driving forces for industrial energy efficiency improvements in African industries: A case study of Ghana's largest industrial area." *Journal of Cleaner Production*, 53(August): 204–213.

Appessika, K. (2003). "Understanding Slums: The Case of Abidjan, Ivory Coast." Submitted as an input to the Global Report on Human Settlements2003. www.ucl.ac.uk/dpu-projects/Global_Report/pdfs/Abidjan.pdf

Araoye, A. (2012). *Cote d'Ivoire: The Conundrum of a Still Wretched of the Earth.* Trenton, NJ: Africa World Press.

Arce, A. & Marsden, T. K. (1993). "The social construction of international food: A new research agenda." *Economic Geography*, 69(3, Part 1): 293–311.

Arestis, P., Charles, A, & Fontana G. (2014). "Identity economics meets financialisation: Gender, race and occupational stratification in the US labour market." *Cambridge Journal of Economics*, 38): 1471–1491.

Argyle, M., & Lu, L. (1990). "The happiness of extraverts." *Personality and Individual*, 11(10): 1011–10117.

Armah, A. K. (1968). *The Beautyful Ones Are Not Yet Born.* Oxford: Heinemann International.

Arndt, W. (1987). *Economic Development: The History of an Idea.* London and Chicago: University of Chicago Press.

Arnot, C., Luckert, M., & Boxall, P. (2011). "What is tenure security? Conceptual implications for empirical analysis." *Land Economics*, 87(2): 297–311.

Arrighi, G. (1991). "World income inequalities and the future of socialism." *New Left Review*, 1(189): 39–65.

Arrighi, G. (2007). *Adam Smith in Beijing: Lineages of the Twenty-First Century.* London: Verso.

Arrighi, G. (2002). "The African crisis: World systemic and regional aspects." *New Left Review* 15(May–June): 5–36.

Arthur, P., & Arthur, E. (2015). "Local content and private sector participation in Ghana's oil industry: An economic and strategic imperative." *Africa Today*, 61: 56–77.

Aryeteey, E., Aryee, J., Ninsin, K., & Tsikata, D. (2007). "The politics of land tenure reform in Ghana: From the crown lands bills to the land administration project." ISSER Technical Publication Series, No.71.

Asaaga, F. A., & Hirons, M. A. (2019). "Windows of opportunity or windows of exclusion? Changing dynamics of tenurial relations in rural Ghana." *Land Use Policy* 87(September): 104042.

Asante, L. A., & Helbrecht, I. (2018). "Seeing through African protest logics: a longitudinal review of continuity and change in protests in Ghana." *Canadian Journal of African Studies / Revue canadienne des études africaines*, 52(2): 159–181.

Asante, L. A., & Helbrecht, I. (2019). "Changing urban governance in Ghana: The role of resistance practices and activism in Kumasi." *Urban Geography*, 40(10): 1568–1595.

Asante, S. K. B. (1975). *Property Law and Social Goals in Ghana, 1844–1966.* Accra: Ghana Universities Press.

Asante, S. K. B. (1979). "Restructuring transnational mineral agreements." *The American Journal of International Law*, 73: 335–371.

Asongu, S. A. & Nwachukwu, J. C. (2017). "Is the threat of foreign aid withdrawal an effective deterrent to political oppression? Evidence from 53 African countries." *Journal of Economic Issues*, LI(1): 201–221.

Atkins, F. (1988). "Land reform: A failure of neoclassical theorization." *World Development*, 16(8): 935–946.

Auriol, E., & Biancini, S. (2015). "Powering up developing countries through integration." *The World Bank Economic Review*, 29(1): 1–40.

Austin, G. (2005). *Labour, Land and Capital in Ghana: From Slavery to Free Labour in Asante, 1807–1956.* New York: University of Rochester Press.

Auty, R. (1993). *Sustaining Development in Mineral Economies: The Resource Curse Thesis.* London: Routledge.

Avery, C. (2010). "Côte d'Ivoire Oil Industry." IAS Group, April. http://iasworldtrade .com/pdf/Cote%20dIvoire%20Oil%20Industry%20Memo.pdf (accessed November 3, 2014).

Avoka, C. (2009). "Meet-the-press statement of the ministry of the interior presented by Hon. Cletus A. Avoka (MP) Min. for the Interior." on 28 July. http://news .peacefmonline.com/meet_the_press/200907/24360.php (accessed 6 December 2009).

Ayelazuno, J. (2014). "Oil wealth and the well-being of the subaltern classes in Sub-Saharan Africa: A critical analysis of the resource curse in Ghana." *Resources Policy*, 40: 66–73.

Ayres, R. U., van den Bergh, J. C. J. M., Lindenberger, D., & Warr, B. (2013). "The underestimated contribution of energy to economic growth." *Structural Change and Economic Dynamics*, 27: 79–88.

Badiey, N. (2013). "The strategic instrumentalization of land tenure in "state-building": The case of Juba, South Sudan." *Africa*, 83(1): 57–77.

Badu, E. (2015). "Determination of hydrocarbon contamination of underground water around fuel filling stations in selected residential areas in the Kumasi Metropolis in the Ashanti Region of Ghana." MSc. Thesis in Environmental Science, KNUST, Kumasi.

Bagdikian, B. (2004). *The New Media Monopoly.* Boston: Beacon Press.

Bailly, F. (2016). "The radical school and the economics of education." *Journal of the History of Economic Thought*, 38(3): 351–369.

Baker, A. (2019a). "South Africa's dividing line." *Time*, May 13: 35–39.

Baker, A. (2019b). "Interview: President Cyril Ramaphosa on fixing South Africa." *Time*, May 13: 40–41.

Balibar, E. (2002). "'Possessive individualism' reversed: from Locke to Derrida." *Constellations*, 9(3): 299–317.

Banerjee, A. V., & Duflo, E. (2009). "The experimental approach to development economics." *Annual Review of Economics*, 1(September): 151–178.

Banfield, E. C. (1976a). *The Unheavenly City*, Boston, Toronto: Little, Brown and Company.

Banesseh, M. A. (2014). "Ghana, Côte d'Ivoire for Arbitration over Maritime Boundary." *Daily Graphic*, September 24. http://graphic.com.gh/news/general-news/31108-ghana-cote-d-ivoire-for-arbitration-over-maritime-boundary.html (accessed October 3, 2014).

Banfield, E. C. (1976b). "Why government cannot solve the urban problem." In H. H. Hochman, ed., *Problems of the Modern Economy: The Urban Economy*. New York: W.W. Norton and Company, pp. 257–272.

Bannerjee, A. V., & Duflo, E. (2009). "The experimental approach to development economics." *The Annual Review of Economics*, 1(September): 151–178.

Bansah, D. K. (2017). "Governance challenges in Sub-Saharan Africa: The case of land guards and land protection in Ghana." Doctor of International Conflict Management Dissertations, School of Conflict Management, Peacebuilding and Development, Kennesaw State University, Kennesaw, Georgia, USA.

Baran, P. A. (1957). *The Political Economy of Growth*. London: Monthly Review.

Barder, O. (2006). "A policy maker's guide to Dutch Disease." Center for Global Development Working Paper 91, July. www.eldis.org/vfile/upload/1/document/0708/DOC14813.pdf.

Barkin, D. (2017). "Violence, inequality and development." *Journal of Australian Political Economy*, 78 (Summer): 115–131.

Barnes, T. (2012). "Review of Marx at the Margins: On nationalism, ethnicity, and non-Western societies." *Journal of Australian Political Economy*, 68(summer): 245–248.

Barros, C. P. & Gupta, R. (2017). "Development, poverty and inequality: A spatial analysis of South African provinces." *The Journal of Developing Areas*, 51(1): 19–32.

Bartel, A. P., Beaulieu, N. D., Phibbs, C. S., et al. (2014). "Human capital and productivity in a team environment: Evidence from the healthcare sector." *American Economic Journal: Applied Economics*, 6(2): 231–259.

Bassey, N. (2012). *To Cook a Continent: Destructive Extraction and the Climate Crisis in Africa*. Cape Town: Pambazuka Press.

Basu, K. (2017). "Discrimination as focal point: Markets and group identity." *Forum for Social Economics*, 46(2): 128–138.

Bauer, P. T. (1971). *Dissent on Development: Studies and Debates in Development Economics*. London: Weidenfeld and Nicolson.

Bawole, J. N. (2013). "Public hearing or 'hearing public'? An evaluation of the participation of local stakeholders in environmental impact of Ghana's Jubilee oil fields. *Environmental Management*, 52(2): 385–397.

Bayat, A. (2017). *Revolution without Revolutionaries: Making Sense of the Arab Spring* Stanford: Stanford University Press.

Bazilian, M., Onyeji, I., Aqrawi, P.-K., Sovacool, B. K., Ofori, E., Kammen, D. M., & de Graaf, T. V. (2013). "Oil, energy poverty and resource dependence in West Africa." *Journal of Energy & Natural Resources Law*, 31(1): 33–53.

Beamish, T. D. (2002). *Silent Spill: The Organization of an Industrial Crisis*. Cambridge, MA: The MIT Press.

Beck, J. H. (2012). "Henry George and immigration." *American Journal of Economics and Sociology*, 71(4): 966–987.

Becker, G. S. (1962). "Investment in human capital: A theoretical analysis." *Journal of Political Economy*, 70(5): 9–49.

Becker, G. S. (1974). "A theory of marriage." In T. W. Schultz, ed., *Economics of the Family: Marriage, Children, and Human Capital*. Chicago: University of Chicago Press, pp. 299–351.

Beckles, H. (2013). *Britain's Black Debt: Reparations Owed the Caribbean for Slavery and Native Genocide*. Kingston: University of the West Indies Press.

Behrman, M., Canonge, J., Purcell, M., & Schiffrin, A. (2012). "Watchdog or lapdog? A look at press coverage of the extractive sector in Nigeria, Ghana and Uganda." *Ecquid Novi: African Journalism Studies*, 33(2): 87–99.

Beinart, W. (2018). "Land untitled." *Journal of Southern African Studies*, 44(2): 365–367.

Bell, P. (2014). "Higher education and the minerals boom: A view from the regions." *Australian Universities' Review*, 56(1): 47–55.

Bello, W. (2007). "Foreword." In A. A. Desmarais, ed., *Globalization and the Power of Peasants: La Vía Campesina*, London: Pluto Press, pp. 3–4.

Benda-Beckmann, F. V. (2003). "Mysteries of capital or mystification of legal property?" *Focaal-European Journal of Anthropology*, 41: 187–191.

Benda-Beckmann, F. V., Benda-Beckmann, K. V., & Wiber, M. G., eds. (2009). *Changing Properties of Property*. New York: Berghahn Books, pp. 1–39.

Bender, K., Jensen,S. K., Ostergàrd, J., & Nogbou, P. (1993). "Oil spill contingency planning in the Ivory Coast." International Oil Spill Conference Proceeding, Tampa, FL, March 29–April 1: 31– 34.

Benefield, D. J. (2009). "Neighborhood amenity packages, property price, and marketing time." *Property Management*, 27(5): 348–370.

Benson, I. (2011). "Tsikata finally wins at Supreme Court." *Ghanaian Chronicle*, January 20. www.modernghana.com/news/313075/tsikata-finally-wins-at-supreme-court.html (accessed 10 November 2019).

Benya, A. (2015). "The invisible hands: Women in Marikana." *Review of African Political Economy*, 42(146): 545–560. DOI:10.1080/03056244.2015.1087394.

Bernstein, H. (2005). "Rural land and conflicts in Sub-Saharan Africa." In S. Moyo & P. Yeros, eds. *Reclaiming the Land: The Resurgence of Rural Movements in Africa, Asia and Latin America*. London: Zed Books, pp.67–101.

Bernstein, H. (2010). *Class Dynamics of Agrarian Change: Initiatives In Critical Agrarian Studies*. Halifax, NS: Fernwood Publishing.

Berry, M. (2013). *The Affluent Society Revisited*. Oxford: Oxford University Press.

Bertrand, M. (2019). "'A cadastre for Mali?' The production of land titles and the challenge of property data on the periphery of Bamako." *Land Use Policy*, 81 (February): 371–381.

Besley, T. (1995). "Property rights and investment incentives: Theory and evidence from Ghana." *Journal of Political Economy*, 103(5): 903–937.

Bhan, G. (2014). "The real lives of urban fantasies." *Environment and Urbanization*, 26: 232–235.

Bharadwaj, K. (1986). *Classical Political Economy and the Rise to Dominace of Supply and Demand Theories*. Calcutta: Universities Press.

Biedermann, Z. (2018). "Africa's dependency curse: The case of Botswana." *ROAPE .NET*, http://roape.net/2018/09/27/africas-dependency-curse-the-case-of-botswana/ (accessed 31 May 2019).

Bigsten, A. (2016). "Determinants of the evolution of inequality in Africa." *Journal of African Economies*: 1–22. doi:10.1093/jae/ejw028.

Bina, C. (1992). "The laws of economic rent and property: Application to the oil industry." *American Journal of Economics and Sociology*, 51(2): 187–203.

Bina, C., & Vo, M. (2007). "OPEC in the epoch of globalization: An event study of global oil prices." *Global Economy Journal*, 7(1): 1–49.

Block, F. (2012). "Contesting markets all the way down." *Journal of Australian Political Economy*, 68(Summer): 27–40.

Boamah, F. (2014a). "How and why chiefs formalise land use in recent times: The politics of land dispossession through biofuels investments in Ghana." *Review of African Political Economy*, 41(141):406–423.

Boamah, F. (2014b). "Imageries of the contested concepts 'land grabbing' and 'land transactions: Implications for biofuels investments in Ghana." *Geoforum*, 54, 324–334.

Boamah, N., Gyimah, C., & Nelson, J. K. B. (2012a). "Challenges to the enforcement of development controls in the Wa municipality." *Habitat International*, 36(1): 136–142.

Boamah, N., Nelson, J. K. B., & Gyimah, C. (2012b). "The impact of land use regulations on residential land values in the Wa municipality, Ghana." *Journal of Housing and the Built Environment*, 27(3): 349–358.

Bob-Milliar, G., & Obeng-Odoom, F. (2012). "The informal economy is an employer, a nuisance, and a goldmine: Multiple representations of and responses to informality in Accra, Ghana." *Urban Anthropology and Studies of Cultural Systems and World Economic Development*, 40(3–4): 263–284.

Boettke, P. J., Fink, A., & Smith, D. J. (2012). "The impact of nobel prize winners in economics: Mainline vs. mainstream economics." *American Journal of Economics and Sociology*, 71(5): 1219–1249.

Boggs J. (1969). "The myth and irrationality of Black capitalism." *Review of Black Political Economy*, 1(1): 27–35.

Bohman, A. (2010). "Framing the water and sanitation challenge: A history of urban water supply and sanitation in Ghana 1909–2005." Unpublished Ph.D. Thesis, Umea University, Umea.

Boohene, R., & Peprah, J. A. (2011). "Women, livelihood and oil and gas discovery in Ghana: An exploratory study of cape three points and surrounding communities." *Journal of Sustainable Development*, 4, 185–195.

Boone, C. (2007). "Africa's new territorial politics: Regionalism and the open economy in Côte d'Ivoire." *African Studies Review*, 50(1): 59–81.

Boone, C. (2012). "Territorial politics and the reach of the state: Unevenness by design." *Revista de Ciencia Política (Santiago) [Journal of Political science]*, 32(3): 623–641.

Boone, C. (2018). "Legal empowerment of the poor through property rights reform: Tensions and trade-offs of land registration and titling in Sub-Saharan Africa." *The Journal of Development Studies*, 55(3): 1–17.

Bordo, M.D. (1975). "John E. Cairnes on the effects of the Australian gold discoveries, 1851–73: An early application of the methodology of positive economics." *History of Political Economy*, 7(3): 337–359.

Borras, S. M. Jr., & Franco, J. C. (2012). "Global land grabbing and trajectories of agrarian change: A preliminary analysis." *Journal of Agrarian Change*, 12(1): 34–59.

Borras, S. M. Jr., Kay, C., Gómez, S., & Wilkinson, J. (2012). "Land grabbing and global capitalist accumulation: Key features in Latin America." *Canadian Journal of Development Studies/Revue canadienne d'études du développement*, 33(4): 402–416.

Bösch, F., & Graf, R. (2014). "Reacting to anticipations: Energy crises and energy policy in the 1970s. An introduction." *Historical Social Research*, 34: 7–21.

Bougrine, H. (2006). "Oil: Profits of the chain keepers." *International Journal of Political Economy*, 35(2): 35–53.

Bourguignon, F. (2016). "How the rich get richer as the poor catch up." *Foreign Affairs*, 95(1): 11–15.

Boushey, H., Delong, J. B., & Steinbaum, M. (2017). After Piketty: *The Agenda for Economics and Inequality*. Cambridge, MA: Harvard University Press.

Boyce, B. (2007). "Property as a natural right and as a conventional right in constitutional law," 29 Loy. L.A. Int'l & Comp. L. Rev. 201 (2007). http://digitalcommons.lmu.edu/ilr/vol29/iss2/2.

Boydell, S., Searle, G., & Small, G. (2007). "The contemporary commons: Understanding competing property rights," State of Australian Cities Conference, Adelaide, Australia, November 2007. In S. Hamnett, ed., *State of Australian Cities (SOAC) Conference*. Adelaide: SOAC, pp. 1087–1096.

Boyle, D. (2015). "Henry George, Jane Jacobs, and Free Trade." *American Journal of Economics and Sociology*, 74(3): 587–599.

Branch, A., & Mampilly, Z. (2015). *Africa Uprising: Popular Protest and Political Change*. London: Zed.

Bratton, M., & van de Walle, N. (1994). "Neopatrimonial regimes and political transitions in Africa." *World Politics*, 46(4): 453–489.

Brenner, R. (2006). "What is, and what is not, imperialism?" *Historical Materialism*, 14 (4): 79–105.

Brew-Hammond, A. (2010). "Energy access in Africa: Challenges ahead." *Energy Policy*, 38(5): 2291–301.

Brewer, R. M., Conrad, C. A., & King, M. C. (2002). "The complexities and potential of theorizing gender, caste, race, and class." *Feminist Economics*, 8(2):3–17.

Bromley, D. (2008). "Formalising property relations in the developing world: The wrong prescription for the wrong malady." *Land Use Policy*, 26: 20–27.

Bromley D. W., 2019, *Possessive Individualism: A Crisis of Capitalism*. New York: Oxford University Press.

Bromley, D. W., & Anderson, G. D. (2012). *Vulnerable People, Vulnerable States: Redefining the Development Challenge*. London and New York: Routledge.

Browne, I., Tigges, L., & Press, J. (2003). "Inequality through labor markets, firms, and families: The intersection of gender and race-ethnicity across three cities." In A. O'Connor, C. Tilly, & L. Bobo, eds., *Urban Inequality: Evidence from Four Cities*. New York: The Russell Sage Foundation, pp. 372–406.

Bryson, P. J. (2011). *The Economics of Henry George: History's Rehabilitation of America's Greatest Early Economist.* New York: Palgrave Macmillan.

Bugri, J. (2008). "The dynamics of tenure security, agricultural production and environmental degradation in Africa: Evidence from stakeholders in north-east Ghana." *Land Use Policy,* 25: 271–285.

Burbidge, D. (2016). "Review of *Africa: Why Economists Get It Wrong.*" *African Affairs,* 156 (460): 574–586.

Busch, G. K. (2013). "The French, the UN and the Ivory Coast." *Pambazuka News,* 628 (May 1). www.pambazuka.net/en/category.php/features/87217.

Bush, R. (2004). "Civil society and the uncivil state land tenure reform in Egypt and the crisis of rural livelihoods." United Nations Research Institute for Social Development. Civil Society and Social Movement Programme paper no. 9, May.

Bush, R. & Szeftel, M. (1999). "Bringing imperialism back in." *Review of African Political Economy,* 80: 165–169.

Busingye, H. (2002). "Customary land tenure reform in Uganda: Lessons for South Africa." Programme for Land and Agrarian Studies (PLAAS), Johannesburg 12–13 August.

Bybee, A. N., & Johannes, E. M. (2014). "Neglected but affected: Voices from the oil-producing regions of Ghana and Uganda." *African Security Review,* 23(2): 132–144.

Byres, T. J. (1995). "Political economy, the agrarian question and the comparative method." *The Journal of Peasant Studies,* 22(4): 561–80.

Cahill, D. (2010). "Actually existing neoliberalism" and the global economic crisis." *Labour & Industry: A Journal of the Social and Economic Relations of Work,* 20: 298–316.

Cahill, D. (2014). *The End of Laissez-Faire? On the Durability of Embedded Neoliberalism.* Cheltenham: Edward Elgar Publishing.

Cahill, D., & Konings, M. (2017). *Neoliberalism.* Cambridge: Polity Press.

Cahill, D., & Stilwell, F. (2008). "The Australian economic boom 1992–?" *Journal of Australian Political Economy,* 61: 5–11.

Carabelli, A., & Cedrini, M. (2011). "The economic problem of happiness: Keynes on happiness and economics." *Forum for Social Economics,* 40: 335–359.

Carmody, P. (2011). *The New Scramble for Africa.* Cambridge: Polity Press.

Cashiers' Office. (2010). "Land cases in Cape Coast." Information made available by the Cashiers' Office (Cape Coast Court Complex). Information taken from case file dockets, process books, and register of land cases, 2000–2009, Cape Coast.

CASLE. (2007). *CASLE Newsletter,* 32, September.

Central Land Council. (2013). "Land reform in the northern territory: Evidence not ideology." Central Land Council, Report prepared in October 2013, Alice Springs, Australia.

Centre for Democratic Development. (2014). "Ghanaians negative on national economy and living conditions." October 22. http://afrobarometer.org/press/ghanaians-negative-national-economyand-.

Césaire, A. (1972). *Discourse on Colonialism.* New York: Monthly Review Press.

Chang, H.-J. (2002). *Kicking away the Ladder: Development Strategy in Historical Perspective.* London: Anthem Press.

Chang, H.-J. (2003). "Kicking away the Ladder." *Oxford Development Studies,* 31: 21–32.

Chibber, V. (2013). *Postcolonial Theory and the Specter of Capital.* London: Verso.

Chibuye, N. (2014). "Interrogating urban poverty lines: The case of Zambia." *Environment and Urbanization.* doi:10.1177/0956247813519047

Chimhowu, A., & Woodhouse, P. (2006). "Customary vs private property rights? Dynamics and trajectories of vernacular land markets in sub-Saharan Africa." *Journal of Agrarian Change,* 6(3): 346–371.

Chirot, D. (2006). "The Debacle in Côte d'Ivoire." *Journal of Democracy,* 17(2): 63–77.

Chiweshe, M. K. (2017). "Zimbabwe's land question in the context of large-scale land based investments." *Geography Research Forum,* 37(December): 13–36.

Chouquer, G. (2012). *The Global Issue of Land Grabbing: Interviews with Charlotte Castan.* Paris: Publi Topex, Presse Edition.

Christophers, B. (2018). *The New Enclosure: The Appropriation of Public Land in Neoliberal Britain.* London and New York: Verso.

Chu, J. (2011). "Gender and 'land grabbing' in sub-Saharan Africa: Women's land: Looking back to the discourses of women's land rights and customary land tenure." *Development,* 54(1): 35–39.

CIRES (Centre Ivoirian de Recherches Economiques et Sociales/IvorianCenter of Economy and Social Research). (2015). "Interview." December. Abidjan, Cote d'Ivoire.

Claasen, N. & Lemke, S. (2019). "Strong ties, weak actors? Social networks and food security among farm workers in South Africa." *Food Security,* 11(2): 417–430.

Clausing, K. (2019a). Open: *The Progressive Case for Free Trade, Immigration, and Global Capital.* Cambridge, MA: Harvard University Press.

Clausing, K. (2019b). "The progressive case against protectionism: How trade and immigration help American workers." *Foreign Affairs,* 98(6): 109–121.

Cobb, C. (2015). "Editor's Introduction: The hidden hand: How foundations shape the course of history." *American Journal of Economics and Sociology,* 74(4): 631–653.

Cole, D., & Grossman, P. (2002). "The meaning of property rights: Law versus economics?" *Land Economics,* 78(3): 317–330.

Coleman, J. (1988). "Social capital in the creation of human capital." *The Journal of Sociology,* 94(Supplement: Organizations and Institutions: Sociological and Economic Approaches to the Analysis of Social Structure): S95–S120.

Collier, P. (2006). "African growth: Why a 'big push'?" *Journal of African Economies,* 00 (AERC Supplement 2): 188–211.

Collier, P. (2007). *The Bottom Billion: Why the Poorest Countries are Failing and What Can Be Done about It.* Oxford: Oxford University Press.

Collier, P. (2009a). *Wars, Guns and Votes: Democracy in Dangerous Places.* London: The Bodley Head.

Collier, P. (2009b). *The Bottom Billion.* Oxford: Oxford University Press.

Collier, P. (2010). *The Plundered Planet.* Oxford: Oxford University Press.

Collier, P. & Venables, A. J. (2012). "Greening Africa? Technologies, endowments and the latecomer effect." *Energy Economics,* 34: S75–S84.

Collins, A. & Mitchell, M. (2018). "Revisiting the World Bank's land law reform agenda in Africa: The promise and perils of customary practices." *Journal of Agrarian Change,* 18: 112–131.

Collins, J. (2017). "Towards a socially significant theory of rent: The contribution of C. N. Nwoke." *Geography Research Forum,* 37(December): 149–165.

Commons, J. R. (1924). *Legal Foundations of Capitalism.* New York: The Macmillan Company.

Commons, J. R. (1924/1925). "Law and economics." *Yale Law Journal*, 34: 371–382.

Commons, J. R. (1934a/2009). *Institutional Economics*. New York: The MacMillan Company.

Commons, J. R. (1934b/2009) *Institutional Economics: Its Place in Political Economy*, vol 2. New Brunswick and London: Transaction Publishers.

Connell, R. (2007). *Southern Theory: The Global Dynamics of Knowledge in Social Science*. Crows Nest, NSW: Allen and Unwin.

Connolly, N. D. B. (2014). *A World More Concrete: Real Estate and the Remaking of Jim Crow South Florida*, Chicago: University of Chicago Press.

Consultant. (2009). "Beneficiary assessment of land registries," LAP, Accra. www .ghanalap.gov.gh/index/.php?linkid=276 (accessed 11 December 2009).

Cooper, F. (2014). *Africa in the World: Capitalism, Empire, Nation-State*. Cambridge: Harvard University Press.

Corden, M. & Neary, P. (1982). "Booming sector and de-industrialisation in a small open economy." *The Economy Journal*, 92(368): 825–848.

Côté-Roy, L., & Moser, S. (2019). "'Does Africa not deserve shiny new cities?' The power of seductive rhetoric around new cities in Africa." *Urban Studies*, 56(12): 2391–2407.

Cotula, L., & Pollack, E. (2012). "The global land rush: what the evidence reveals about scale and geography." IIED Briefing Paper, 2012.

Cotula, L., Vermeulen, S., Leonard, R., & Keeley, J. (2009). *Land Grab or Development Opportunity? Agricultural Investment and International Land Deals in Africa*. London/ Rome: IIED/FAO/IFAD.

Courvisanos, J. & Mackenzie, S. (2011). "Addressing Schumpeter's Plea: Critical Realism in Entrepreneurial History." Victoria, Australia, University of Ballarat, School of Business, Working Paper Series. 003–2011.

Cousins, B. (2007). "More than socially embedded: The distinctive character of 'communal tenure' regimes in South Africa and its implications for land policy." *Journal of Agrarian Change*, 7(3): 281–315.

Cousins, B. (2016). "Land reform in South Africa is failing. Can it be saved?" *Transformation: Critical Perspectives on Southern Africa*, 92: 135–157.

Cousins, B. (2017). "Why title deeds aren't the solution to South Africa's land tenure problem." *The Conversation*, August 14.

Cox, O. C. (1945). "An American dilemma: A mystical approach to the study of race relations." *Journal of Negro Education*, 14(2): 132–148.

Crenshaw, K. (1989). "Demarginalizing the intersection of race and sex: A black feminist critique of antidiscrimination doctrine, feminist theory and antiracist politics." *University of Chicago Legal Forum*, 8(1): 139–167. Available at: https://chica gounbound.uchicago.edu/uclf/vol1989/iss1/8

Crenshaw, K. (1991). "Mapping the margins: Intersectionality, identity politics, and violence against women of color." *Stanford Law Review*, 43(July): 1241–99.

Croese, S. (2016). "Urban governance and turning African cities around: Luanda case study." PASGR Working Paper 018. Nairobi, Kenya: Partnership for African Social and Governance Research.

Croese, S. (2018). "Global urban policymaking in Africa: A view from Angola through the redevelopment of the Bay of Luanda." *International Journal of Urban and Regional Research*, 42(2): 198–209.

Cross, C., & Hornby, D. (2002). "Opportunities and obstacles to women's land access in South Africa." A research report for the Promoting Women's Access to Land CT: Kumarian.

Cui, Z. (2011). "Partial intimations of the coming whole: The Chongqing experiment in light of the theories of Henry George, James Meade, and Antonio Gramsci." *Modern China*, 37(6): 646–660.

Currie-Alder, B. (2016). "The state of development studies: Origins, evolution and prospects." *Canadian Journal of Development Studies / Revue canadienne d'études du développement*, 37(1): 5–26.

Curry, R. L. Jr. (1987). "Poverty and mass unemployment in mineralrich Botswana." *American Journal of Economics and Sociology*, 46(1): 71–86.

Cypher, J. M., & Dietz, J. L. (2004). *The Process of Economic Development*. London: Routledge.

*Daily Guide*. (2014). "Baker Hughes workers demonstrate against victimization." *Daily Guide*, 26 March. www.spyghana.com/baker-hughes-workers-demonstrate-againstvictimization/ (accessed 10 January 2015).

Daly, H. E. (1990). *Steady-State Economics*. Washington, DC: Island Press.

Daly, H. E. (2007). *Ecological Economics and Sustainable Development: Selected Essays of Herman Daly*. Cheltenham: Edward Elgar.

Daly, H. (2017). "Trump's growthism: Its roots in neoclassical economic theory." *Real-World Economics Review*, 78: 86–97.

Daly, H. E & Cobb J. B. Jr., with contributions from C. W. Cobb. (1994). *For the Common Good: Redirecting the Economy toward Community, the Environment, and a Sustainable Future*, 2nd edition. Boston: Beacon Press.

Dana, L-P., Gurău, C., Hoy, F., Ramadani, V., & Alexander, T. (2019). "Success factors and challenges of grassroots innovations: Learning from failure." *Technological Forecasting and Social Change*, https://doi.org/10.1016/j.techfore.2019.03.009

Danso, A. (1990). "The causes and impact of the African debt crisis." *The Review of Black Political Economy*, Summer, 19(1): 5–21.

Darity, W. Jr. (2008). "Forty acres and a mule in the 21st century." *Social Science Quarterly*, 89(3): 656–664. www.neaecon.org/about/.

Darity, W. Jr. (2009). "Stratification economics: Context versus culture and the reparations controversy." *Kansas Law Review*, 57: 795–811.

Darity, W. A. Jr., & Davis L. S. (2005). "Growth, trade, and uneven development." *Cambridge Journal of Economics*, 29(1): 141–170.

Darity, W. Jr., & Hamilton, D. (2012). "Bold policies for economic justice." *Review of Black Political Economy*, 39(1): 79–85.

Darity, W. A. Jr., & Hamilton, D. (2015). "A tour de force in understanding intergroup inequality: An introduction to stratification economics." *The Review of Black Political Economy*, 42(1–2): 1–6.

Darity, W. A. Jr., & Triplett, R. E. (2008). "Ethnicity and economic development." In A. K. Dutt & J. Ros, eds., *International Handbook of Development Economics*, vols. 1 & 2. Cheltenham: Edward Elgar, pp. 267–277.

Darity, W. A. Jr., & Williams, R. M. (1985). "Peddlers forever?: Culture, competition, and discrimination." *The American Economic Review*, 75(2), Papers and Proceedings of the Ninety-Seventh Annual Meeting of the American Economic Association, pp. 256–261.

Darkwah, K. A. (2013). "Keeping hope alive: An analysis of training opportunities for Ghanaian youth in the emerging oil and gas industry in Ghana." *International Development Planning Review*, 35(2): 119–34.

Dartey-Baah, K., Amponsah-Tawiah, K., & Agbeibor, V. (2015). "Corporate social responsibility in Ghana's national development." *Africa Today*, 62(2): 70–93.

Date-Bah, S. K. (2015). *Reflections on the Supreme Court of Ghana*. London: Wildy Simmonds and Hill Publishing.

Davis, M. (2006). *Planet of Slums*. London and New York: Verso.

Dow, G. (2017). "Review essay: The post-keynesian alterantive." *Journal of Australian Political Economy*, No. 80: 221–230.

Dowuona-Hammond, C., & Minkah-Premo, S. (2005). "Report on Review of Studies Conducted on Gender and Land in Ghana and Proposals for Developing Gender Policy on Land Matters," Land Administration Project (LAP)/GTZ, Accra.

de Beauvoir, S. (1949/2010). *The Second Sex*. New York: Vintage Books.

De La Grandville, O., & Solow, R. (2009). *Economic Growth: A Unified Approach*. Cambridge: Cambridge University Press.

De Propris, D.L. & Hamdouch, A. (2013). "Regions as knowledge and innovative hubs." *Regional Studies*, 47(7): 997–1000.

De Soto, H. (1989). *The Other Path: The Invisible Revolution in the Third World*. New York: Harpercollins.

De Soto, H. (2000). *The Mystery of Capital: Why Capitalism Triumphs in the West and Fails Everywhere Else*. New York: Bantam Press.

De Soto, H. (2004). "Bringing capitalism to the masses." *Cato's Letter*, 2(3): 1–8.

De Soto, H. (2011). "This land is your land: A conversation with Hernando de Soto." *World Policy Journal*, 28(summer): 35–40.

de Vroey, M. (1975). "The transition from classical to neoclassical economics: A scientific revolution." *Journal of Economic Issues*, 9(3): 415–439.

Debrezion, G., Pels, E., & Rietveld, P. (2007). "The impact of railway stations on residential and commercial property value: A meta-analysis." *Journal of Real Estate Finance and Economics*, 35: 161–180.

Deininger, K. (2003). *Land Policies for Growth and Poverty Reduction*. Washington, DC: The World Bank.

Deininger, K. & Binswanger, H. (1999). "The evolution of the World Bank's land policy: Principles, experience, and future challenges." *The World Bank Research Observer*, 14 (2): 247–276.

Deininger, K. & Xia, F. (2018). "Assessing the long-term performance of large-scale land transfers: Challenges and opportunities in Malawi's estate sector." *World Development*, 104): 281–296.

Deininger, K., Ayalew, D., & Yamano, T. (2006). "Legal Knowledge and Economic Development: The Case of Land Rights in Uganda." Invited paper prepared for presentation at the International Association of Agricultural Economists Conference, Gold Coast, Australia, August 12–18.

Demsetz, H. (2002). "Toward a theory of property rights II: The competition between private and collective ownership." *The Journal of Legal Studies*, XXXI (June): s653–s672.

Deneault, A., & Sacher, W. (with contributions by Browne, C., Denis, M., & Ducharme, P.). (2012). *Imperial Canada Inc.: Legal Haven of Choice for the World's Mining Industries.* Vancouver: Talonbooks.

Department of Economic and Social Affairs (DESA). (2009).*World urbanization prospects, 2008 revision.* New York: UN.

Desmarais, A. A. (2007). *Globalization and the Power of Peasants: La Vía Campesina,* London: Pluto Press.

Devarajan, S. (2013, October). "Africa's statistical tragedy." *Review of Income and Wealth, Series,* 59: s9–s15.

Dialga, I. (2018). "Changing Africa's impoverishing economic model: Towards a rewarding sustainable specialization model with a new factor of production." *African Review of Economics and Finance,* 10(1): 274–301.

Dickermann, J., Barnes, G., Bruce, J., et al. (1989). "Security of tenure and land registration in Africa: Literature review and synthesis." Land Tenure Center, University of Wisconsin-Madison. Paper, no. 137.

Dickson, K. B. (1968). "Background to the problem of economic development in Northern Ghana." *Annals of the Association of American Geographers,* 58: 686–696.

Diette, T. M., Goldsmith, A. H., Hamilton, D., & Darity, W. Jr. (2015). "Skin shade stratification and the psychological cost of unemployment: Is there a gradient for Black females?" *Review of Black Political Economy,* 42: 155–177.

Dixon, M. (2014). "The land grab, finance capital, and food regime restructuring: The case of Egypt." *Review of African Political Economy,* 41(140): 233–248.

Dobb, M. (1963). *Studies in the Development of Capitalism.* London: Routledge.

Dollar, D., Kleineberg, T., & Kraay, A. (2016). "Growth still is good for the poor." *European Economic Review,* 81(January): 68–85.

Dollar, D. & Kraay, A. (2002). "Growth is good for the poor." *Journal of Economic Growth,* 7: 195–225.

Domeher, D. & Abdulai, R. (2012). "Access to credit in the developing world: Does land registration matter?" *Third World Quarterly* 33(1): 161–175.

Domeher, D., Yeboah, E., & Ellis, F. (2018). "Formal property titles or more? Perspectives from Ghanaian financial institutions." *African Review of Economics and Finance,* 10(1): 243–273.

Dow, A. & Dow, S. (2004). "Economic history and economic theory: The staples approach to economic development." *Cambridge Journal of Economics,* 38: 1339–1353.

Downs, A. (1976). "The future of the American ghettos." In H. M. Hochman, ed., *The Urban Economy: An Introduction to a Current Issue of Public Policy.* New York: W.W. Norton and Company, pp. 195–210.

Du Bois, W. E. B. (1903/1986). *The Souls of Black Folk. New York: Literary Classics of the United States Inc.*

Duchrow, U., & Hinkelammert, F. (2010) *Property for People, Not for Profit: Alternatives to the Global Tyranny of Capital.* London: Zed Books.

Dumont, R. (1966). *False Start in Africa.* New York: Frederick A Praeger.

Duncan, B. (2010). "Cocoa, marriage, labour and land in Ghana: Some matrilineal and patrilineal perspectives." *Africa: The Journal of the International African Institute,* 80 (2): 301–321.

Duncan, B., & Brants, C. (2004). "Access to and control over land from a gender perspective: A study conducted in the volta region of Ghana." Food and Agriculture Organization of the United Nations, Regional Office for Africa SNV Netherlands Development Organisation, Ghana Office Women in Law and Development in Africa, Ghana Office.

Dunn, B. (2009). *Global Political Economy: A Marxist Critique.* London: Pluto Press.

Dunn, B. (2014). "Skills, credentials and their unequal reward in a heterogeneous global political economy." *Journal of Sociology*, 50(3): 349–367.

Dunn, B. (2015). *Neither Free Trade Nor Protection: A Critical Political Economy of Trade Theory and Practice.* Cheltenham, UK: Edward Elgar Publishing.

Dymski, G. (1985). "Introduction (to the special issue on race and class)." *Review of Radical Political Economics*, 17(3): 1–9.

Eagle Group. (2007). *Voices of Women Entrepreneurs in Ghana.* International Finance Corporation, World Bank Group, Washington, DC; and Ministry for Women and Children Affairs, Accra.

Easterlin, R. A. (1981). "Why isn't the whole world developed." *The Journal of Economic History*, 41(1): 1–19.

Economist Intelligence Unit. (2014). *Country Report: Cote d'Ivoire.* London: Economist Intelligence Unit.

Edozie, R. K. (2017). *"Pan" Africa Rising: The Cultural Political Economy of Nigeria's Afri-Capitalism and South Africa's Ubuntu Business.* New York: Palgrave Macmillan.

Eduful, A., & Hooper, M. (2015). "Urban impacts of resource booms: The emergence of oil-led gentrification in Sekondi-Takoradi, Ghana." *Urban Forum*, 26: 283–302.

Eduful, A. K., & Hooper, M. (2019). "Urban migration and housing during resource booms: The case of Sekondi-Takoradi, Ghana." *Habitat International*, 93 (November): 1–10, https://doi.org/10.1016/j.habitatint.2019.102029

Egan, D. (2011). "Review of the world we wish to see: Revolutionary objectives in the twenty-first century." *Journal of the Research Group on Socialism and Democracy Online*, April 10.

Ehwi, R. J., & Asante, L. A. (2016). "Ex-post analysis of land title registration in Ghana since 2008 merger: Accra Lands Commission in perspective." *Sage Open* 6(2): 1–17.

Ehwi, R. J., Tyler, P, & Morrison, N. (2018). "Market-led initiatives to land tenure security in Ghana: Contribution of gated communities." Paper prepared for presentation at the 2018 World Bank Conference on Land and Poverty, The World Bank, Washington DC, March 19–23.

Ekhator, E. O. (2016). "Regulating the activities of oil multinationals in Nigeria: A case for self-regulation?" *Journal of African Law*, 60(1): 1–28

Elamin, Nisrin (2018). "'The miskeet tree doesn't belong here': Shifting land values and the politics of belonging in Um Doum, central Sudan." *Critical African Studies*, 10(1): 67–88, DOI: 10.1080/21681392.2018.1491803

El Araby, M. (2003). "The role of the state in managing urban land supply and prices in Egypt." *Habitat International*, 27: 429–458.

Elahi, K., & Stilwell, F. (2013). "Customary land tenure, neoclassical economics and conceptual bias." *Nuigini Agrisayens*, 5: 28–39.

Elhadary Y. A. E., & Obeng-Odoom, F. (2012). "Conventions, changes and contradictions in land governance in Africa: The story of land grabbing in Sudan and Ghana." *Africa Today*, 59(2): 59–78.

Elliot, J. E. (1983). "Schumpeter and the theory of capitalist economic development." *Journal of Economic Behaviour and Organization*, 4(4): 277–308.

Emeagwali, G. T. (1980). "Explanation in African history." *Journal of the Historical Society of Nigeria*, 10(3): 95–109.

Emmanuel, A. (1972). *Unequal Exchange: A Study of the Imperialism of Trade*. London: Monthly Review Press.

Engels, F. (1884/2010). *Origin of the family, private property, and the state*, marxists.org. www.marxists.org/archive/marx/works/download/pdf/origin_family.pdf (accessed 5 December 2016).

Enns, C., & Bersaglio, B. (2015). "Enclave oil development and the rearticulation of citizenship in Turkana, Kenya: Exploring 'crude citizenship.'" *Geoforum*, 67: 78–88.

Enweremadu, D. U. (2013). "Nigeria as an emerging economy? Making sense of expectations." *South African Journal of International Affairs*, 20(1): 57–77.

Erickson, G., & Groh, C. (2012). "How the APF and the PFD operate: The peculiar mechanics of Alaska's state finances." In K. Widerquist & M. W. Howard, eds. *Alaska's Permanent Fund Dividend. Exploring the Basic Income Guarantee*. New York: Palgrave Macmillan.

European Union (2019). "Africa." Fact Sheets on the European Union – 2019: www .europarl.europa.eu/ftu/pdf/en/FTU_5.6.6.pdf (accessed December 7, 2019).

Evangelista, R. (2018). "Technology and Economic Development: The Schumpeterian Legacy." *Review of Radical Political Economics*, 50(1): 136–153.

Evers, S. J. T. M., Campbell, G., & Lambek, M. (2013). "Land competition and human-environment relations in Madagascar." In S. J. T. M. Evers, G. Campbell, & M. Lambek, eds., *Contest for Land in Madagascar: Environment, Ancestors and Development* (African Social Studies Series; No. 31). Leiden: Brill Academic Publishers, pp. 1–21.

Evers, S. J. T. M., Campbell, G., & Lambek, M., eds. (2013). *Contest for Land in Madagascar: Environment, Ancestors and Development*. Leiden: Brill, pp. 1–20.

Fainstein, S. (2012). "Land value capture and justice." In G.K. Ingram, & Y.-H. Hong, eds. *Value Capture and Land Policies*. Cambridge: Lincoln Institute of Land Policy, pp. 21–40.

Fairhead, J., & Leach, M. (1998). *Reframing Deforestation*. London: Routledge.

Fairhead, J., Leach, M., & Scoones, I. (2012). "Green Grabbing: A new appropriation of nature?" *The Journal of Peasant Studies*, 39(2): 237–261.

Fanon, F. (1961). *The Wretched of the Earth*. New York: Grove Press.

Farouk, B. R., & Owusu, M. (2012). "'If in doubt, count': The role of community-driven enumerations in blocking eviction in Old Fadama Accra." *Environment and Urbanization*, 24: 47–57.

Feddersen, M., Hugo, N., & Ferdi, B. (2017). "Exports, capital formation and economic growth in South Africa." *African Review of Economics and Finance*, 9 (1): 213–244.

Feder, G., & Feeny, D. (1991). "Land tenure and property rights: Theory and implications for development policy." *The World Bank Economic Review*, 5(1): 135–153.

Felder, G., & Nishio, A. (1998). "The benefits of land registration and titling: Economic and social perspectives." *Land Use Policy*, 15(1): 25–43.

Ferrara, E. (2007). "Descent rules and strategic transfers: Evidence from matrilineal groups in Ghana." *Journal of Development Economics*, 83: 280–301.

Fiave, E. R. (2017). "Sekondi-Takoradi as an oil city." *Geography Research Forum*, 37 (December), 61–79.

Field, E. (2004). "Property rights, community public goods, and household time allocation in urban squatter communities: Evidence from Peru." *William and Mary Law Review*, 45(3): 838–887.

Field, E. (2005). "Property rights and investment in urban slums." *Journal of the European Economic Association Papers and Proceedings*, April–May, 3(2–3): 279–290.

Field, E. (2007). "Entitled to work: Urban property rights and labor supply in Peru." *The Quarterly Journal of Economics*, 122(4): 1561–1602.

Fine, B. (2009). "The economics of identity and the identity of economics?" *Cambridge Journal of Economics*, 33: 175–191.

Fine, B. (2010). *Theories of Social Capital: Researchers Behaving Badly*. London: Pluto.

Fine, B. (2019). "In and against orthodoxy: Teaching economics in the neoliberal era." In S. Decker, W. Elsner, & S. Flechtner, eds., *Advancing Pluralism in Teaching Economics: International Perspectives on a Textbook Science*, London: Routledge, pp. 78–94.

Fioramonti, L. (2015). *Gross Domestic Problem: The Politics behind the World's Most Powerful Number*. London: Zed Books.

Fioramonti, L. (2014, February). "Africa rising? Think again." *Perspectives*, 1: 6–9.

Fioramonti, L. (2017). *The World after GDP: Politics, Business and Society in the Post Growth Era*. Cambridge and Massachusetts: Polity Press.

First Energy Capital. (2011). *Playing the West African Transform Margin*. London: First Energy Capital.

Folbre, N. (2012). "The political economy of human capital." *Review of Radical Political Economics*, 44(3): 281–292.

Folbre, N. (2014). "The care economy in Africa: Subsistence production and unpaid care." *Journal of African Economies*, 23: 128–156.

Foldvary, F. E. (2008). "The marginalists who confronted land." *American Journal of Economics and Sociology*, 67(1): 89–117.

Foley, G., Schaap, A., & Howell, E., eds. (2013). *The Aboriginal Tent Embassy: Sovereignty, Black Power, Land Rights and the State*. London: Routledge.

Fondevila, G., & Quintana-Navarrete, M. (2019). "Economic informality as a national project." *Review of Social Economy*, 77(4): 523–554.

Food and Agricultural Organisation (FAO). (2002). "Land tenure and rural development. Rome: FAO land tenure studies for women in communities affected by oil production." *Extractive Industries and Society*, 2(1): 24–32.

Food and Agricultural Organisation (FAO). (2012). *Voluntary Guidelines on the Governance of Tenure*. Rome: FAO.

Fosu, A. (1999). "An economic theory of Pan-Africanism." *The Review of Black Political Economy*, 27(2): 7–12.

Fosu, A. (2010). "Africa's economic future: Learning from the past." CESifo Forum, 11, 62–71. Foundation.

Fosu, A. K. (2016). "Oil and Ghana's economy." In E. Aryeetey & R. Kanbur, eds., *The Economy of Ghana: Sixty Years after Independence*. Oxford:Oxford University Press, pp. 137–175.

Fosu, A., & Gafa, D. (2019). "Natural resources, institutions, and economic development in Africa." *African Review of Economics and Finance*, 11(1): 29–52.

Fourie, C. (2000). "Land and the cadastre in South Africa: Its history and present government policy." Paper presented as a Guest Lecture at the International Institute of Aerospace Survey and Earth Sciences (ITC), Enschede, The Netherlands, 1 November 2000.

Frank, A. G. (1966). "The development of underdevelopment." In K. Rajani, ed., *Paradigms in Economic Development: Classic Perspectives, Critiques and Reflections*, London: M.E.Sharpe, pp. 99–106.

Frankel, E. G. (2007). *Oil and Security: A World beyond Petroleum*. Dordrecht: Springer.

Frankel, J. A. (2012). "The natural resource curse: A survey of diagnoses and some prescriptions." HKS Faculty Research Working Paper Series RWP12–014.

Freire, P. (1970). *Pedagogy of the Oppressed*. New York: Herder & Herder.

Freund, Bill. (2001). "Contrasts in urban segregation: A tale of two African cities, Durban (South Africa) and Abidjan (Côte d'Ivoire). " *Journal of Southern African Studies*, 27(3): 527–546.

Friedman, M. (1957). *A Theory of the Consumption Function*. New Jersey: Princeton University Press.

Friedman, M. (1970). "The social responsibility of business is to increase its profits." New York Times Magazine, September 13.

Friedrich-Ebert Foundation. (2011). *Youth and Oil and Gas: Governance in Ghana Nationwide Survey*. Accra: Friedrich-Ebert Foundation.

Fujita, M., Krugman, P., & Venables, A. J. (1999).*The Spatial Economy: Cities, Regions and International Trade*. Cambridge: The MIT Press.

Fukuyama, F. (1992). *The End of History and the Last Man*. New York: The Free Press.

Fukuyama, F. (2013). "What is governance?" *Governance: An International Journal of Policy, Administration, and Institutions*, 26(3): 347–368.

Furniss, J. (2016). "Postrevolutionary land encroachments in Cairso: Rhizomatic urban space making and the line of flight from illegality." *Singapore Journal of Tropical Geography*, 37: 310–329.

Fuseini, I. & Kemp, J. (2016). "Characterising urban growth in Tamale, Ghana: An analysis of urban governance response in infrastructure and service provision." *Habitat International*, 56: 109–123.

G7. (2014). "Fact Sheet." G7-CONNEX Initiative (Initiative Strengthening Assistance for Complex Contract Negotiations). June 17. Brussels: European Union. http://eu-un.europa.eu/g7-launches-new-initiative-connex-%  C2%96-fair-contracts-can-boost-development/ or www. bmz.de/en/zentrales_downloadarchiv/Presse/CONNEX_Fact_Sheet.pdf.

G7. (2016). "CONNEX Guiding Principles Towards Sustainable Development."

Gab-Leyba, G. D., & Laporte, B. (2016). "Oil contracts, progressive taxation, and government take in the context of uncertainty in the context of crude oil prices: The case of Chad." *The Journal of Energy and Development*, 41(1&2): 253–278.

Gaffney, M. (1994). "Neo-classical economics as a stratagem against Henry George." In F. Harrison, ed., *The Corruption of Economics*. London: Shepheard-Walwyn Publishing, pp. 29–164.

Gaffney, M. (2009). *After the Crash: Designing a Depression-Free Economy*. London: Wiley-Blackwell.

Gaffney, M. (2016). "Nature, economy, and equity: Sacred water, profane markets." *American Journal of Economics and Sociology*, 75(5): 1064–1231.

Gaffney, M. (2018). "Corporate power and expansive U.S. military policy." *American Journal of Economics and Sociology*, 77(2): 331–417.

Galárraga, M. C. V., & Frelson, W. S. (2017). "Ecuador: Mineral policy." In G. Tiess et al., eds., *Encyclopedia of Mineral and Energy Policy*. Germany: Springe, pp. 1–8.

Galbraith J. K. (1958/1998). *The Affluent Society*. New York: Houghton Milfflin Harcourt.

Galbraith, J. (1956). *American Capitalism: The Concept of Countervailing Power*, revised edition. Cambridge: The Riverside Press.

Galbraith, J. (1964). *Economic Development*. Cambridge, MA: Harvard University Press.

Galbraith, J. (1973). *Economics and the Public Purpose*. Boston: Houghton Mifflin Company.

Galbraith, J. K. (1977). *The Age of Uncertainty: A History of Economic Ideas and their Consequences*. Boston and New York: Houghton Mifflin Company.

Galbraith, J. K. (1979). *The Nature of Mass Poverty*. Cambridge, MA, and London: Harvard University Press.

Galeano, L. A. (2012). "Paraguay and the expansion of Brazilian and Argentinian agribusiness frontiers." *Canadian Journal of Development Studies*, 33(4): 458–470.

Garland, E. (2008). "The elephant in the room: Confronting the colonial character of wildlife conservation in Africa. *African Studies Review*. 51(3): 51–74.

Gates, H. L. Jr. (2013). "The truth behind '40 Acres and a Mule'." *The African Americans*, www.pbs.org/wnet/african-americans-many-rivers-to-cross/history/the-truth-behind-40-acres-and-a-mule/ (accessed 28 June 2016).

Gauld, D. T., & Buchanan, J. B. (1959). "The principal features of the rock shore fauna in Ghana." *Oikos*, 10 (Fasc. 1): 121–132.

Geary, W. (1913). "Land tenure and legislation in British West Africa." *Journal of the African Society*, 12(47): 236–248.

General Secretariat of ECOWAS. (2014). "Update of the ECOWAS revised master plan for the generation and transmission of electrical energy: Final Report 1, Study Data." www.ecowapp.org/?page_id=136.

George, H. (1871). *Our Land and Land Policy*. Digitalized 2009 by Per Møller Andersen https://bibliotek1.dk/english/by-henry-george/our-land-and-our-land-policy (accessed 25 October, 2019)

George, H. ([1879] 2006). *Progress and Poverty*. New York: Robert Schalkenbach Foundation.

George, H. (1881). *The Land Question*. London: The New Age.

George, H. ([1883] 1981). *Social Problems*. New York: Robert Schalkenbach.

George H. (1885). "The crime of poverty." RSF, http://schalkenbach.org/library/henry-george/hg-speeches/the-crime-o f-po verty.html (accessed 15 January 2019).

George, H. ([1886] 1991). *Protection or Free Trade: An Examination of the Tariff 1979 Question, with Especial Regard to the Interests of Labor*. New York: Robert Schalkenbach Foundation. http://schalkenbach.org/library/henry-1981george/protection-or-free-trade/preface-index.html.

George, H. (1898). *The Science of Political Economy*. London: Kegan Paul, Trench, Trubner.

George, H. ([1892] 1981). *A Perplexed Philosopher*. New York: Robert Schalkenbach Foundation. www.schalkenbach.org/library/henry-george/.

George, S. (1996). "Review of *When Corporations Rule the World*." *Development in Practice*, 6(4): 371–375.

George, S. (2014). "The rise of illegitimate authority and the threat to democracy." *Journal of Australian Political Economy*, 72(Summer): 5–22.

Ghana News Agency. (2009a). "80% of lands without proper documentation." ghanaweb.com. www.ghanaweb.com/GhanaHomePage/NewsArchive/artikel.

Ghana News Agency. (2009b). "Cape coast: Lands commission registers 1285 lands in two years." ghanadistricts.com. http://capecoast.ghanadistricts.gov.gh/ (accessed 9 June 2010).

Ghana News Agency. (2010b). "Stool lands administrator urges journalists to specialize on land issues." *Ghana News Agency*, July 24.

Ghana Statistical Service (GSS). (2008). *Ghana Living Standards Survey: Report of the Fifth Round*. Accra: GSS.

Ghana Statistical Service. (2015). "Quarterly gross domestic product (QGDP): First quarter 2015." *GSS Newsletter*, June 17.

Gibbard, A. (1976). "Natural property rights." *Noûs*, 10(1): 77–86.

Gibson-Graham, J. K. (1996/2006). *The End of Capitalism (As We Knew It): A Feminist Critique of Political Economy*. Cambridge: Minnesota University Press.

Giddings, S. (2009). "The land market in Kampala, Uganda and its effect on settlement patterns." Report prepared (in January) for the International Housing Coalition, Washington, DC.

Gilbert, A. G. (2002). "On *The Mystery of Capital* and the myths of Hernando de Soto: What difference does legal title make?" *International Development Planning Review*, 24: 1–20.

Gilbert, A. G. (2012). "De Soto's *The Mystery of Capital*: Reflections on the book's public impact." *International Development Planning Review*, 34(3): v–xvii.

Gilberthorpe, E., & Rajak, D. (2017). "The anthropology of extraction: Critical perspectives on the resource curse." *Journal of Development Studies*, 53(2): 186–204.

Giles, C., & Pilling, D. (2018). "African nations slipping into new debt crisis." *Financial Times*, April 19. www.ft.com/content/baf01b06-4329-11e8-803a-295c97e6fd0b (accessed 11 August 2018).

Giles, R. (2016). *The Theory of Charges on Commonland*. Sydney: Association for Good Government.

Giles, R. (2017). *The Theory of Charges for Nature*. Sydney: Association for Good Government.

Gĩthĩnji, W. M. (2015). "Erasing class/(re)creating ethnicity: Jobs, politics, accumulation and identity in Kenya." *The Review of Black Political Economy*, 42(1): 87–110.

Gittings, R. (2010). *The Happy Economist: Happiness for the Hard Headed*. Sydney: Allen & Unwen.

Glaeser, E. L. (2011). *Triumph of the City*. London: Pan Books.

Glaeser, E. L., Ponzetto, G. A. M., & Tobio, K. (2014). "Cities, skills and regional change." *Regional Studies*, 48(1): 7–43.

Glassman, J. (2006). "Primitive accumulation, accumulation by dispossession, accumulation by 'extra-economic' means." *Progress in Human Geography*, 30(5): 608–625.

GLTN. (2011). GLTN Partners. www.gltn.net/en/suggest-link/gltn-partners-2. html (accessed 29 July 2011).

Goldstein, B. D., Osofsky, H. J., & Lichtveld, M.Y. (2011). The gulf oil spill. *The New England Journal of Medicine*, 364: 1334–1348

Good, K. (2008), *Diamonds, Dispossession and Democracy in Botswana*, James Currey, Suffolk.

Goodfellow, T. (2017). "Taxing property in a neo-developmental state: The Politics of urban land value capture in Rwanda and Ethiopia." *African Affairs*, 116(465): 549–572.

Gordon, R. J. (2013). "Not studying white, up or down, but around Southern Africa: A response to Francis Nyamnjoh." *Africa Spectrum*, 48(2): 117–121.

Gordon, R., Nell, M., & Bertoldi, A. (2007). "Overview of urban land as a commodity in South Africa: research findings and recommendations." Report submitted to Matthewed Nell and Associates (PTY) Ltd, June.

Gore, C. (1996). "Methodological nationalism and the misunderstanding of East Asian industrialization." *The European Journal of Development Research*, 8: 77–122.

Gore, C. (1997). "Irreducibly social goods and the informational basis of Amartya Sen's capability approach." *Journal of International Development*, 9: 232–250.

Gore, C. (2007). "Which growth theory is good for the poor?" *European Journal of Development Research*, 19(1): 30–48.

Gore, C. (2016). "The post-2015 moment: Towards sustainable development goals and a new global development paradigm." *Journal of International Development*, 27: 717–732.

Gore, C. (2017). "Late industrialisation, urbanisation and the middle-income trap: An analytical approach and the case of Vietnam." *Cambridge Journal of Regions, Economy and Society*, 10(1): 35–57.

Gould, J. (2006). "Strong bar, weak state? Lawyers, liberalism and state formation in Zambia." *Development and Change*, 37(4): 921–941.

Graham, E., & Ovadia, J. S. (2019). "Oil exploration and production in Sub-Saharan Africa, 1990-present: Trends and developments." *The Extractive Industries and Society*, 6(2): 593–609.

Grant, R., & Oteng-Ababio, M. (2012). "Mapping the invisible and real 'African' economy: Urban e-waste circuitry." *Urban Geography*, 33(1): 1–21.

Grant, R., Oteng-Ababio, M. & Sivilien, J. (2019). "Greater Accra's new urban extension at Ningo-Prampram: Urban promise or urban peril?" *International Planning Studies*, 24(3–4): 325–340.

Grant, Richard. (2009). *Globalizing City: The Urban and Economic Transformation of Accra, Ghana*. Syracuse, NY: Syracuse University Press.

Graphic Online. (2014). "Ghana, Cote d'Ivoire for Arbitration over Maritime Boundary." Graphic Online, September 24. http://graphic.com.gh/news/general-news/31108-ghana-cote-d-ivoirefor- arbitration-over-maritime-boundary.html.

Gray, L., & Kevane, M. (1999). "Diminished access, diverted exclusion: Women and land tenure in sub-Saharan." *African Studies Review*, 42(2): 15–39.

Green T. L. & Darity W. A., Jr., (2010). "Under the skin: Using theories from biology and the social sciences to explore the mechanisms behind the black–white health gap." *American Journal of Public Health*, 100(S1): S36–S40.

Green, Duncan. (2010). "Review of Paul Collier's *Plundered Planet: How to Reconcile Prosperity with Nature*." https://oxfamblogs.org/fp2p/the-plundered-planet-review-of-paul-colliers-new-book-and-impendingpersonal-crisis/.

Greenleaf Global. (2011). "Jatropha biofuel plantation update." *Greenleaf Newsletter*, November.

Gregory, R. G. (1976). "Some implications of the growth of the mineral sector." *The Australian Journal of Agricultural and Resource Economics*, 20(2): 71–91.

Grieves, V. (2008). "Aboriginal spirituality: A baseline for Indigenous knowledges development in Australia." *The Canadian Journal of Native Studies, XXVIII*, 2 (2008): 363–39

Grieves, V. (2009). "Aboriginal spirituality: Aboriginal philosophy; the basis of aboriginal social and emotional wellbeing." Cooperative Research Centre for Aboriginal Health Discussion Paper Series, No. 9.

Griffiths, A. (1983). "Legal duality: conflict or concord in Botswana?" *Journal of African Law*, 27(2): 150–161.

Griffiths, A. (1996). "Legal pluralism in Africa: The role of gender and women's access to law." *Political and Legal Anthropology Review*, 19(2, Anthropology Engaging Law (November 1996): 93–107.

Griffiths, A. (2000). "Gender, power, and difference: Reconfiguring law from Bakwena women's perspectives." *Political and Legal Anthropology*, 23(2): 89–106.

Grischow, J. (2008). "Rural 'community', chiefs and social capital: The case of Southern Ghana." *Journal of Agrarian Change*, 8(1): 64–93.

Groh, C., & Erickson, G. (2012). "The improbable but true story of how the Alaska Permanent Fund and the Alaska Permanent Fund Dividend came to be." In K. Widerquist & M. W. Howard, eds., *Alaska's Permanent Fund Dividend: Examining Its Suitability as a Model*. New York: Palgrave Macmillan, pp. 15–40.

Grossbard, S. (2010). "Independent individual decision-makers in household models and the new home economics." Discussion paper no. 5138, August.

*Guardian*. (2016). "Five West African countries ban 'dirty diesel' from Europe." December 10. www.theguardian.com/global-development/2016/dec/06/five-west-african-countries-ban-dirty-diesel-from-europe-nigeria-ghana.

Guillén, A. (2017). "Trump signs bill killing SEC rule on foreign payments." *Politico*, February 14. www.politico.com/story/2017/02/trump-sec-rule-foreign-governments -235013.

Gunn, C. (2011). "Workers' participation in management, workers' control of production: Worlds apart." *Review of Radical Political Economics*, 43: 317–327.

Gyampo, R. E. V. (2011). "Saving Ghana from its oil: A critical assessment of preparations so far made." *Africa Today*, 57(4): 49–69.

Gyampo, R. E. V. (2017). "Social media, traditional media and party politics in Ghana." *Africa Review*. DOI:10.1080/ 09744053.2017.1329806.

Gyimah-Boadi, E., & Prempeh, H. K. (2012). "Oil, politics, and Ghana's democracy," *Journal of Democracy*, 23(3): 94–108.

Gylfason, T. (2001). "Natural resources, education and economic development." *European Economic Review*, 45(4–6): 847–859.

Gylfason, T. (2011). "Natural resource endowment: A mixed blessing?" In R. Arezki, T. Gylfason, & A. Sy, eds., *Beyond the Curse: Policies to Harness the Power of Natural Resources*. Washington, DC: International Monetary Fund, pp. 7–34.

Gylfason, T. (2012). "Development and growth in resource-dependent countries: Why social policy matters." In K. Hujo, ed., *Mineral Rents and the Financing of Social Policy: Opportunities and Challenges*. Basingstoke: UNRISD/Palgrave, pp. 26–61.

Halevi, J., Harcourt, G. C., Kriesler, P., & Nevile, J. W. (2016). *Post-Keynesian Essays from Down Under, Volume 1: Essays on Keynes, Harrod and Kalecki – Theory and Policy in an Historical Context*. New York: Palgrave Macmillan.

Haila, A. (2016). *Singapore as a Property State*. Chichester: Wiley-Blackwell.

Hall, R. (2004). "A political economy of land reform in South Africa." *Review of African Political Economy*, 31(100): 213–227.

Hamilton, D., & Darity, W. Jr. (2010). "Can 'baby bonds' eliminate the racial wealth gap in putative post-racial America?." *Review of Black Political Economy*, 37(3,4): 207–216.

Hamilton, D., Darity, W. Jr., Price, A. E., Sridharan, V., & Tippett, R. (2015). *Umbrellas Don't Make It Rain: Why Studying and Working Hard Isn't Enough for Black Americans*. Oakland: Insight Center for Community Economic Development.

Hammond, F. (2008). "Marginal benefits of land policies in Ghana." *Journal of Property Research*, 25(4): 343–362.

Handelman, H. (2010). *The Challenge of Third World Development*. New York: Pearson Education.

Harcourt, G. C., & Kriesler, P. (2015). "Post-Keynesian theory and policy for modern capitalism." *Journal of Australian Political Economy*, 75(Winter): 26–41.

Hardin, G. (1968). "The tragedy of the commons." *Science* 162 (3859): 1243–1248.

Hardt, M., & Negri, A. (2000). *Empire*. Cambridge: Harvard University Press.

Hardt, M., & Negri, A. (2004). *Multitude: War and Democracy in the Age of Empire*. New York: Penguin.

Harris, N. (1987). *The End of the Third World: Newly Industrializing Countries and the Decline of an Ideology*. London: Penguin.

Harris, N. (1991). *City, Class, and Trade: Social and Economic Change in the Third World*. London and New York: I.B. Tauris.

Harrison, F. (2008). *The Silver Bullet*. London: The International Union for Land Value Taxation.

Harrison, G. (2011). "Poverty reduction and the chronically rich." *Review of African Political Economy*, 38(127): 1–6.

Harttgen, K., Klasen, S., & Vollmer, S. (2013). "An African growth miracle? Or: What do asset indices tell us about trends in economic performance?" *Review of Income and Wealth*, 59: S37–S61.

Hartwick, J. M. (1977). "Intergenerational equity and the investing of rents." *The American Economic Review*, 67(5): 972–974.

Harvey, D. (1973/2009). *Social Justice and the City*, revised edition. Athens and London: The University of Georgia Press.

Harvey, D. (1978). "The urban process under capitalism." *International Journal of Urban and Regional Research*, 2(1–4): 101–131.

Harvey, D, (2003). *The New Imperialism*. New York: Oxford University Press.

Hayek, F. A. (1945). *The Road to Serfdom*. London: The Institute of Economic Affairs.

Hays Recruiting Experts in Oil and Gas. (2012). *Oil and Gas Global Salary Guide*. Manchester, NH: Hays Plc.

Hays Recruiting Experts in Oil and Gas. (2013). *Oil and Gas Global Salary Guide*. Manchester, NH: Hays Plc.

Hays Recruiting Experts in Oil and Gas. (2015). *Oil and Gas Global Salary Guide.* Manchester, NH: Hays Plc.

Heilbrunn, J. R. (2014). *Oil, Democracy, and Development in Africa.* New York: Cambridge University Press.

Helliwell, J. F., Layard R, & Sachs, J. D. (2018). *World Happiness Report.* New York: The Earth Institute, Columbia University.

Hellum, A. (1998). Women's human rights and African customary laws: Between universalism and relativism-individualism and communitarianism. *The European Journal of Development Research,* 10(2): 88–104.

Henning, M. (2013). Africa and the middle class(es). *Africa Spectrum,* 48: 111–120.

Herbert-Cheshire, L., & Lawrence, G. (2002). Political economy and the challenge of governance. *Journal of Australian Political Economy,* 50: 137–145.

Highlife. (2014). *Highlife.* London: British Airways.

Hill, P. (1963). *The Migrant Cocoa-Farmers of Southern Ghana: A Study in Rural Capitalism.* New York: Cambridge University Press.

Hill, P. (1966). "A plea for Indigenous economics: The West African example." *Economic Development and Cultural Change,* 15(1): 10–20.

Hill, P. (1986). *Development Economics on Trial: The Anthropological Case for a Prosecution.* Cambridge: Cambridge University Press.

Hillbom, E., & Bolt, J. (2018) *Botswana: A Moder Economic History: An African Diamond in the Rough.* London: Palgrave.

Hilson, A. E. (2014). "Resource Enclavity and Corporate Social Responsibility in Sub-Saharan Africa: The Case of Oil Production in Ghana." PhD Diss., Aston University, UK.

Hilson, A., Hilson, G., & Dauda, S. (2019). "Corporate social responsibility at African mines: Linking the past to the present." *Journal of Environmental Management,* (241): 340–352.

Hirsch, M. (1966). *Democracy Versus Socialism.* New York: Robert Schalkenbach Foundation.

Hirschman, A. O. (1958). *The Strategy of Economic Development.* New Haven, CT, and London: Yale University Press.

Hirschman, A. O. (1984). "A dissenter's confession: 'The Strategy of Economic Development' revisited." In G.M. Meier & D. Seers, eds., *Pioneers in Development.* Oxford: Oxford University Press, pp. 87–111.

Hobson, J. M. (2004). *The Eastern Origins of Western Civilisation.* Cambridge: Cambridge University Press.

Hodgson, G. (2007). "Meanings of methodological individualism." *Journal of Economic Methodology,* 14(2): 211–226.

Hodgson, G. M. (2014). "What is capital? Economists and sociologists have changed its meaning: Should it be changed back?" *Cambridge Journal of Economics,* 38(5): 1063–1086.

Home, R., & Lim, H., eds. (2004). *Demystifying the Mystery of Capital: Land Tenure and Poverty in Africa and the Caribbean.* Sydney: Glass House Press.

Hooks, B. (1981). *Ain't I a Woman: Black Women and Feminism.* London: Pluto Press.

*Bibliography*

Hooper, M., & Ortolano, L. (2012). "Motivations for slum dweller social movement participation in urban Africa: A study of mobilization in Kurasini, Dar es Salaam, of mobilization in Kurasini, Dar es Salaam." *Environment and Urbanization*, 24: 99–114.

Hopkins A. G. (1973). *An Economic History of West Africa.* New York: Columbia University Press.

Hornby, D., Kingwill, R., Royston, L., & Cousins, B., eds. (2017) *Untitled: Securing Land Tenure in Urban and Rural South Africa.* Pietermarizburg: UKZN Press.

Hossein, C. S. (2016). "Money pools in the Americas: The African diaspora's legacy in the social economy." *The Forum for Social Economics*, XLV (4): 309–328.

Hossein, C. S. (2017). "Living Garveyism in the social economies of the African diaspora in the Canada and in the West Indies." *National Political Science Review*, 19(1): 169–186.

Howard, R. (1978). *Colonialism and Underdevelopment in Ghana.* London: Croom

Huber, M. T. (2013). *Lifeblood: Oil, Freedom, and the Forces of Capital.* London: University of Minnesota Press.

Hughes, T. (2003). "Managing group grievances and internal conflict: Ghana country." Working Paper Series of the Netherlands Institute of International Relations, 'Clingendael' Conflict Research Unit, Working Paper 11 June.

Hui, E. C., Yu, A., & Lam, R. (2010). "The impact of an announcement of land acquisition in auctions on real estate firms' stock return in Hong Kong." *Property Management*, 28(1): 18–32.

Hunt, D. (2004). "Unintended consequences of land rights reform: The case of the 1998 Uganda Land Act." *Development Policy Review*, 22(2): 173–191.

Hyötyläinen, M., & Haila, A. (2018). "Entrepreneurial public real estate policy: The case of Eiranranta, Helsinki." *Geoforum*, 89: 137–144.

Idrisu, M. (2014). "Ghana: skills shortages in the oil and gas industry: lessons from Ghana." *The Chronicle*, 11 February. www.reportingoilandgas.org/ghana-skills-shortages-in-the-oil-and-gas-industry-lessons-for-ghana/ (accessed 10 January 2015).

Ince, O. U. (2018). *Colonial Capitalism and the Dilemmas of Liberalism.* New York: Oxford University Press.

Insolvency Service. (2012). "International bio-diesel companies, Greenleaf Global, closed down following government investigation." Press release 12 April.

Institute of Statistical, Social and Economic Research (ISSER). (2012). *The State of the Ghanaian Economy in 2011.* Accra, Ghana: ISSER, University of Ghana.

International Finance Corporation (IFC). (2016). *IFC: The First Six Decades.* Washington, DC: IFC.

International Land Coalition. (2012). *Land Rights and the Rush for Land.* Rome: International Land Coalition.

International Monetary Fund (IMF). (2018a). *Fiscal Monitor 2018.* Washington, DC: IMF.

International Monetary Fund (IMF). (2018b). *World Economic Outlook 2018.* Washington, DC: IMF.

International Social Science Council. (2016). *World Social Science Report: Challenging Inequalities: Pathways to Just World.* Paris: UNESCO.

International Trade Union Confederation. (2010). "Annual survey of violations of trade union rights – Côte d'Ivoire." June 9. www.refworld.org/docid/4c4fec83c.html.

Issah, Z. (2013). "Stop foreigners from taking over our lands: Varsity registrar pleads with Supreme Court." *Daily Graphic*, 21 April.

ITLOS (International Tribunal for the Law of the Sea). (2015). "Press Release: Dispute concerning delimitation of the maritime boundary between Ghana and Côte d'Ivoire in the Atlantic Ocean (Ghana/Côte d'Ivoire). " April 25. www.itlos.org/fileadmin/itlos/documents/press_releases_english/PR_229_EN.pdf.

Jabbar, S. (2013). "How France loots its former colonies." *This Is Africa*, January 24. https://thisisafrica.me/france-loots-former-colonies/ (accessed 25 August 2018).

Jackson, C. (2003). "Gender analysis of land: Beyond land rights for women?" *Journal of Agrarian Change*, 3(4): 453–480.

Jacobs, S. (1998). "Past wrongs and gender rights: Issues and conflicts in South Africa's land reform." *The European Journal of Development Research*, 10(2): 70–87.

Jacoby, H. G., & Minten, B. (2007). "Is land titling in sub-Saharan Africa cost-effective?: Evidence from Madagascar." *World Bank Economic Review*, 21(3): 461–485.

Jamma, A. P., & Damji, B. H. (2012). "Dr. B.R. Ambedkar's thoughts on agriculture and its relevance to current agriculture in India." *Review of Research*, 1(vi): 1–4.

Jean-Yves, D., & Verdier-Chouchane, A. (2010). "Analyzing pro-poor growth in Southern Africa: Lessons from Mauritius and South Africa." (Working Papers Series No. 115). Tunisia: African Development Bank.

Jeffries, R. (1978). *Class, Power and Ideology in Ghana: The Railwaymen of Sekondi*. Cambridge: Cambridge University Press.

Jerven, M. (2013). *Poor Numbers: How We Are Misled by African Development Statistics and What to Do about It*. Ithaca, NY: Cornell University Press.

Jerven, M. (2014). *Economic Growth and Measurement Reconsidered in Botswana, Kenya, Tanzania, and Zambia, 1965–1995*. Oxford: Oxford University Press.

Jerven, M. (2015). *Africa: Why Economists Get It Wrong*. London; New York: Zed Books.

Jibao, S. S., & Prichard, W. (2015). "The political economy of property tax in Africa: Explaining reform outcomes in Sierra Leone." *African Affairs*, 114(456): 404–431.

Johnstone, N., & Wood, L. (1999). *Private Sector Participation in Water Supply and Sanitation: Realising Social and Environmental Objectives*. London: International Institute for Environment and Development.

Jones, E. (2010). "The Chicago school, Hayek and the Mont Pélerin Society." *Journal of Australian Political Economy*, 63(Winter): 139–155.

Joseph, R. A., & Johnston, R. (1985). "Market failure and government support for science and technology: Economic theory versus political practice." *Prometheus*, 3 (1): 138–155.

Judge, R. (2002). "Restoring the commons: Toward a new interpretation of Locke's theory of property." *Land Economics*, 78(3): 331–338.

Kalecki, M. (1945). "Full employment by stimulating private investment?" *Oxford Economic Papers*, 7: 83–92.

Kalecki, M. (1971). "Class struggle and the distribution of national income." *Kyklos*, 24: 1–9.

Kane, K., & Hipp, J. R. (2019). "Rising inequality and neighbourhood mixing in US metro areas." *Regional Studies*, 53(12): 1680–1695.

Kapp, K. W. (1950/1971). *The Social Costs of Private Enterprise*. New York: Shocken Books.

Kappel, R. (2014). "Neither hopeless nor rising." *GIGA Focus*, 1–8.

Karayalcin, C., & Yilmazkuday, H. (2014). "Trade and Cities." *The World Bank Economic Review*, 29(3): 523–549.

Karikari, I. (2006). "Ghana's Land Administration Project (LAP) and Land Information Systems (LIS) implementation: The issues," paper (Article of the Month) presented to the International Federation of Surveyors in February.

Karl, L. (1997). *The Paradox of Plenty*. Berkeley: University of California Press.

Kasanga, K. (2003). "Current land policy issues in Ghana." In P. Gropo, ed., *Land Reform: Land Settlement and Cooperatives*. Rome: FAO, pp. 141–154.

Kasanga, K., & Kotey, N. (2001). *Land Management in Ghana: Building on Tradition and Modernity*. Nottingham: IIED, Russell Press.

Katz, E. (2000). "Social capital and natural capital: A comparative analysis of land tenure and natural resource management in Guatemala." *Land Economics*, 76(1): 114–132.

Kea, P. J. (2010). *Land, Labour and Entrustment*. Leiden: Brill.

Keen, S. (2003). "Madness in their method." In F. Stilwell & G. Argyrous, eds., *Economics as a Social Science*. Melbourne: Pluto Press, pp. 140–145.

Kelly, L. D., Deaton, B. J., & Amegashie, J. A. (2019). "The nature of property rights in Haiti: Mode of land acquisition, gender, and investment." *Journal of Economic Issues*, LIII(3): 726–747.

Kemausuor, F., Obeng, G. Y., Brew-Hammond, A., & Duker, A. (2011). "A review of trends, policies and plans for increasing energy access in Ghana." *Renewable and Sustainable Energy Reviews*, 15: 5143–5154.

Kenji, T. V. (2018). "A manifesto for our time: Review of *The World We Wish to See* by Samir Amin (2008). " *Anti-Imperialism.Com*. https://countercurrents.org/2018/05/a-manifesto-for-our-time-review-of-the-world-we-wish-to-see-by-samir-amin-2008 (accessed 10 November 2019).

Kent, A., & Ikgopoleng, H. (2011). "City profile: Gaborone." *Cities*, 28: 478–494.

Kerekes, C., & Williamson, C. (2010). "Propertyless in Peru, even with a government land title." *American Journal of Economics and Sociology*, 69(3): 1011–1033.

Kettunen P. (2019). "The conceptual history of welfare state in Finland." In N. Edling, ed., *The Changing Meanings of the Welfare State: The History of Political Key Concept in the Nordic Countries*. New York: Berghahn Books.

Kevane, M., & Gray, C. (1999). "A woman's field is made at night: gendered land rights and norms in Burkina Faso." *Feminist Economics*, 5(3): 1–26.

Keynes, J. (1973). *The Collected Writings of John Maynard Keynes: The General Theory of Employment, Interest and Money* (II). London: Macmillan Cambridge University Press.

Klaeger, G. (2013a). "Dwelling on the road: Routines, rituals and road blocks in southern Ghana." *Africa*, 83(3): 446–469.

Kinyondoa, A., & Villanger, E. (2016). "Local content requirements in the petroleum sector in Tanzania: A thorny road from inception to implementation?" *The Extractive Industries and Society*, 4(2): 371–384.

Klaeger, G. (2013b). "Introduction: The perils and possibilities of African roads." *Africa*, 83(3): 359–366.

Klimina, A. (2018). "Rethinking the role of the state." In Joe, T-H., Chester, L., & D'lppoliti, C., eds., *The Routledge Handbook of Heterodox Economics: Theorizing, Analyzing and Transforming Capitalism*, London: Routledge, pp. 458–470.

Kludze, A. K. P. (1998). "Chieftaincy jurisdiction and the muddle of constitutional interpretation in Ghana." *Journal of African Law*, 42: 37–63.

Komenan, N. (2010). "Water and sanitation in Côte d'Ivoire: Before and after crisis." Working paper. October. Abidjan, Côte d'Ivoire: University of Cocody.

Konadu, K. (2009). "Euro-African commerce and social chaos: Akan societies in the nineteenth and twentieth centuries." *History in Africa*, 36: 265–292.

Konadu, K. (2015). *Transatlantic Africa, 1440–1888*. Oxford: Oxford University Press.

Koo, H. (2011). "Property rights, land prices, and investment: A study of the Taiwanese land registration system." *Journal of Institutional and Theoretical Economics*, 167(3): 515–535.

Korten, D. C. (1995). *When Corporations Rule the World*. Oakland, CA: Berrett-Koehler.

Korten, D. (1999). *Post Corporate World: Life After Capitalism*. West Hartford: Kumarian Press.

KOSMOS. (2010). "KOSMOS Energy reaches settlement agreement with Ghanaian government and Ghana National Petroleum Corporation." News Release, Accra, 20 December.

Kotey, N. (2004). *Ghana Land Administration Project Legislative and Judicial Review* (draft final report). Accra: Kotey and Associates.

Koulibaly, M. (2008). *Les Servitude du Pacte Colonial*. Abidjan: CEDA.

Koulibaly, M., Tete, R., & Taadhieu, S. (2011), "The servitude of the colonial pact: Interview with Professor Koulibaly." *The New African*, January 6, http://leo-kanisani.blogspot.com /2011/01/servitude-of-colonial-pact.html (accessed 25 August 2018).

Kranton, R. (2016). "Identity economics 2016: Where do social distinction and norms come from?." *American Economic Review: Papers and Proceedings*, 106(5): 405–409.

Krishna, A. (2008). *Poverty, Participation and Democracy: A Global Perspective*. New York and Cambridge: Cambridge University Press,.

Kudom-Agyemang, A. (2009). "LAP extended for two more years" in LAP, LAP news: A newsletter of the land administration project, Edn 2, 1, Ministry of Lands and Natural Resources, p. 8.

Kuecker, G. (2006). "Book review: *When Corporations Rule the World (second edition), The Post Corporate World: Life After Capitalism*." *Review of Radical Political Economics*, 38(3): 430–435.

Kwon, R. (2016). "Can we have our cake and eat it too? Liberalization, economic growth, and income inequality in advanced industrial societies." *Social Forces*, 95 (2): 469–502.

Klaeger, G. (2013a). "Dwelling on the road: Routines, rituals and road blocks in southern Ghana." *Africa*, 83(3): 446–469.

Lafargue, P. (1904). *The Right to be Lazy*. Ohio: Tere Haute Ind., Standard Publishing Co.

Lai, L. W.-C., & Chau, K. W. (2018). "A reinterpretation of Coase's Land Monopoly Model: Locational specificity and the betterment potential of land as de jure and de facto property." *Progress in Planning*, https://doi.org/10.1016/j.progress.2018.01.002

Lai, L. W.-C., & Chua, M. H. (2018). "Zoning and private property rights in land: Static and dynamic boundary delineation." *Habitat International*, 75, May: 105–113.

Lai, L. W.-C., & Lorne, F. (2006). "Planning by negotiation for sustainable development." *Economic Affairs*, 26(1): 54–58.

Laine, M. (2019). "Are the media biased? Evidence from France." *Journal of Economic Issues*, LIII(3): 774–798.

Lamont, M. (2013). "'The road to Sudan, a pipe dream?' Kenya's new infrastructural dispensation in a multipolar world." In U. Engel & M. J. Ramos, eds., *African Dynamics in a Multipolar World*. Leiden: Brill, pp. 154–174.

Land Administration Project (LAP). (2009). "LAP development objectives." About LAP, Official LAP website, www.ghanalap.gov.gh/index1.php?linkid=47&sublin kid=105 (accessed 23 December 2009).

Lange, S., & Kinyondo, A. (2016). "Resource nationalism and local content in Tanzania: Experiences from mining and consequence for the petroleum sector." *The Extractive Industries and Society*, 3: 1095–1104.

Lanjouw, J. O., & Levy, I. P. (2002). "Untitled: A study of formal and informal property rights in urban Ecuador." *The Economic Journal*, 112(482): 986–1019.

Larbi, W. O. (2011). "Ghana's land administration project: Accomplishments, impacts, and the way ahead." World Bank Conference on Land and Poverty Reduction, The World Bank, Washington, DC, 18–20 April.

Lawanson, T., & Oduwaye, L. (2014). "Socio-economic adaptation strategies of the urban poor in the Lagos metropolis, Nigeria." *African Review of Economics and Finance* 6(1): 139–160.

Lawrence, P. (2010). "Development by numbers." *New Left Review*, 62(March–April): 143–153.

Le Lannier, A., & Porcher, S., (2014). "Efficiency in the public and private French water utilities: Prospects for benchmarking." *Applied Economics*, 46(5): 556–572.

Lea, D. (2008). *Property Rights, Indigenous People and the Developing World: Issues from Aboriginal Entitlement to Intellectual Ownership Rights*. Leiden and Boston: Martinus Nijhoff Publishers.

Lehmann, C. (2012). "French Africa Policy Damages African and European Economies." *NSNBC*. https://nsnbc.wordpress.com/2012/10/12/french-africa-policy-damages-african-and-european-economies/ (accessed 25 August 2018).

Lentz, C. (2013). *Land, Mobility and Belonging in West Africa*. Bloomington: Indiana University Press.

Leonard, T. C. (2008). "Review of Richard H. Thaler, Cass R. Sunstein, Nudge: 'Improving decisions about health, wealth, and happiness'." *Constitutional Political Economy*, 19, 356–360.

Leonard, T. C., Goldfarb, R. S., & Suranovic, S. M. (2000). "New on paternalism and public policy." *Economics and Philosophy*, 16, 323–331.

Levitt, K. P. (2017). "Kari Polanyi Levitt on Karl Polanyi and the economy as a social construct." *Review of Social Economy*, LXXV(4): 389–399.

Lewis, W. A. (1965). *Politics in West Africa*. New York: Oxford University Press.

Lewis, W. A. (1985). *Racial Conflict and Economic Development*. Cambridge: Harvard University Press.

Lewonth, R., & Levins, R. (2007). *Biology under the Influence: Dialectical Essays on Ecology, Agriculture, and Health.* New York: Monthly Press.

Li, H., Lo, K., & Wang, M. (2015). "Economic transformation of mining cities in transition economies: Lessons from Daqing, Northeast China." *International Development Planning Review,* 37, 311–328.

Liberti, S. (2013). *Land Grabbing: Journeys in the New Colonialism.* London; New York. Verso.

Lines, K. & Makau, J. (2018). "Taking the long view: 20 years of Muungano wa Wanavijiji, the Kenyan federation of slum dwellers." *Environment & Urbanization.* DOI:10.1177/0956247818785327:1–18.

Lipton, J. E., & Barash, D. P. (2019). *Strength through Peace: How Demilitarization Led to Peace and Happiness in Costa Rica and What the Rest of the World Can Learn from a Tiny, Tropical Country.* New York: Oxford University Press.

Lipton, M. (2013). "Africa's national-accounts mess." *Journal of Development Studies,* 49 (12): 1765–1771.

López, A. J. (2007). "Introduction: The (Post)global South." *The Global South,* 1(1&2): 1–11.

Lucas, E. R. Jr. (1990). "Why doesn't capital flow from rich to poor countries?" *American Economic Review, Papers and Proceedings,* 80(2): 92–96.

Lummis, D. (1996). *Radical Democracy.* New York: Cornell University.

Lund, C. (2012). "Review of 'The Politics of Property Rights Institutions in Africa'." *Perspectives on Politics,* 10(2): 528–529.

Lynn, D. M. (2011). "The Dodd-Frank Act's specialized corporate disclosure: Using the securities laws to address public policy issues." *Journal of Business and Technology Law,* 6(2): 327–355.

Maathai, W. (2004). "Nobel Lecture." Nobelprize.org. www.nobelprize.org/nobel_prizes/peace/laureates/2004/maathai-lecture-text.html (accessed 10 December 2016).

Mabe, J. B., & Elias D. Kuusaana. (2016). "Property taxation and its revenue utilisation for urban infrastructure and services in Ghana." *Property Management* 34(4): 297–315.

Mabogunje, A. (1980). *The Development Process: A Spatial Perspective.* London: Routledge.

Maconachie, R. & Fortin, E. (2013). "'New agriculture' for sustainable development? Biofuels and agrarian change in postwar Sierra Leone." *The Journal of Modern African Studies,* 51: 249–277.

Mahali, A., Lynch, I., Tolla, T., Khumalo, S., & Naicker, S. (2018). "Networks of well-being in the Global South: A critical review of current scholarship." *Journal of Developing Societies,* 34(3): 1–28.

Makanga, D. (2009). "Rights-South Africa: Women want land to call their own." InterPress Service News. http://ipsnews.net/print.asp?idnews¼48015 (accessed 16 September 2010).

Mäki, U. (2018). "Rights and wrongs of economic modelling: Refining Rodrik." *Journal of Economic Methodology,* 25(3): 218–236.

Makki, F. (2012). "Power and property: Commercialization, enclosures, and the transformation of agrarian relations in Ethiopia." *The Journal of Peasant Studies,* 39(1): 81–104.

Mann, S., & Gairing, M. (2012). "Does libertarian paternalism reconcile merit goods theory with mainstream economics?" *Forum for Social Economics*, 41: 206–219.

Manirakiza, V. (2014). "Promoting inclusive approaches to address urbanisation challenges in Kigali." *African Review of Economics and Finance*, 6(1): 161–180.

Margold, S. (1957). "Agrarian land reform in Egypt." *American Journal of Economics*, Vol. 17, No. 1 , pp. 9–19.

Markey-Towler, B. (2019). "The new microeconomics: A psychological, institutional, and evolutionary paradigm with neoclassical economics as a special case." *American Journal of Economics and Sociology*, 78(1): 95–135.

Markusen, A. R. (1978). "Class, rent, and sectoral conflict: Uneven development in Western U.S. boomtowns." *Review of Radical Political Economics*, 10(3): 117–129.

Marmor, T. R. (1976). "Banfield's 'heresy." In H.H. Hochman, ed., *Problems of the Modern Economy: The Urban Economy*. New York: W.W. Norton and Company, pp. 278–282.

Marois, T. & Pradella, L. (2015). "Polarising development: Introducing alternatives to neoliberalism and the crisis." In L. Pradella & T. Marois, eds., *Polarizing Development: Alternatives to Neoliberalism and the Crisis*. London: Pluto Press, pp. 1–12.

Marshall, A. (1890). *Principles of Economics*, 8th edition. London: Macmillan and Co.

Martinussen, J. (1997). *Society, State and Market*. London: Zed Books.

Marx, K. (1852/1963). *The Eighteenth Brumaire of Louis Bonaparte*. New York: International Publishers.

Marx, K. (1867/1990). *Capital*, Vol. 1. London: Penguin Books.

Marx, K. (1894/1991). *Capital: A Critique of Political Economy*, Vol. 3. London: Penguin.

Marx, K. (1939/1993). *Grundrisse*. London: Penguin.

Marx, K. (1863/2000). *Theories of Surplus Value: Books I, II and III*. New York: Prometheus Books.

Marx, K. (1850/1969/2010) *The Class Struggles in France, 1848–1850, Selected Works*, Vol. 1. Moscow: Progress Publishers www.marxists.org/archive/marx/works/down load/pdf/Class_Struggles_in_France.pdf (accessed 9 November 2019).

Maseland, R. (2018). "Is colonialism history? The declining impact of colonial legacies on African institutional and economic development." *Journal of Institutional Economics*, 14(2): 259–287.

Matthewman, S. (2012). "Accidontology: Towards a sociology of accidents and disasters." *International and Multidisciplinary Journal of Social Sciences*, 1(2): 193–215.

Matthews, W. G. (2014). "Opportunities and challenges for petroleum and LPG markets in sub-Saharan Africa." *Energy Policy*, 64: 78–86.

Mattila-Wiro, P. (1999). "Economic theories of the household: A critical review." UNU WIDER Working Papers No. 159.

Mayer, A. (2016). *Naija Marxisms: Revolutionary Thought in Nigeria*. London: Pluto Press.

McFarlane, C. (2012). "The Entrepreneurial Slum: Civil Society, Mobility and the Co-production of Urban Development." *Urban Studies*, 49(13): 2795–2816.

Mckinsey Global Institute. (2010). *Lions on the Move: The Progress and Potentials of African Economies*. Washington, DC: Author.

McLennan, D. (2016). "The spatial patterning of exposure to inequality and its social consequences in South Africa: Work in progress." In *World Social Science Report, Challenging Inequalities: Pathways to Just World*. Paris: UNESCO, pp. 146–149.

Meadows, D. H., Meadows, D. L., Randers, J., & Bahrens, W. W. III. (1972). *Limits to Growth*. Washington, DC: Potomac Associates.

Measham, T. G., & Fleming, D. A. (2014). "Impacts of unconventional gas development on rural community decline." *Journal of Rural Studies*, 36: 376–385.

Medie, P. A., & Kang, A.J. (2018). "Power, knowledge and the politics of gender in the Global South." *European Journal of Politics and Gender*, 1(1–2): 37–54.

Mills, S., & Sweeney, B. (2013). "Employment relations in the neostaples resource economy: Impact benefit agreements and aboriginal governance in Canada's nickel mining industry." *Studies in Political Economy*, 91(Spring): 7–33.

Milonakis, D., & Meramveliotakis, G. (2013). "*Homo economicus* and the economics of property rights: History in reverse order." *Review of Radical Economics*, 45(1): 5–23.

Milonakis, D. (2012). "Introduction by the Guest Editor of the special issue." *Forum for Social Economics*, 41, 4–5.

Ministry of Education. (2010). *Education Strategic Plan 2010 to 2020: Volume 1, Policies, Strategies, Delivery, Finance*. Accra, Ghana: Ministry of Education, Government of Ghana.

Ministry of Energy. (2010). *Energy Sector Strategy and Development Plan*. Accra: Ministry of Energy, Government of Ghana.

Ministry of Finance and Economic Planning. (2012). *2013 Budget Statement*. Accra, Ghana: Ministry of Finance and Economic Planning, Government of Ghana.

Ministry of Finance and Economic Planning. (2013a). *2014 Budget Statement*. Accra, Ghana: Ministry of Finance and Economic Planning.

Ministry of Finance and Economic Planning. (2013b). *2014 Budget Statement: Appendix*. Accra, Ghana: Ministry of Finance and Economic Planning, Government of Ghana.

Ministry of Finance and Economic Planning. (2015). *The Budget Statement and Economic Policy of the Government of Ghana for the 2016 Financial Year*. Accra: MOFEP.

Ministry of Finance. (2018). *Budget of the Republic of Ghana*. Accra: Ministry of Finance.

Ministry of Lands and Forestry. (1999). *National Land Policy*. Accra: Ministry of Lands and Forestry.

Mireku. K.O., Kuusaana. E.D., & Kidido. J. K. (2016). "Legal implications of allocation papers in land transactions in Ghana: A case study of the Kumasi traditional area." *Land Use Policy*, 50: 148–155.

Mirowski. P. (1988a). *More Heat Than Light: Economics as Social Physics, Physics as Nature's Economics*. Cambridge: Cambridge University Press.

Mirowski. P. (1988b). "Energy and energetics in economic theory: A review essay." *Journal of Economic Issues*, xxii(3): 811–830.

Mishan, E. J. (1967). *The Costs of Economic Growth*. Middlesex: Penguin Books/Staples Press.

Mitchell-Walthour, G. (2018). *The Politics of Blackness: Racial Identity and Political Behavior in Contemporary Brazil*. Cambridge: Cambridge University Press.

Mkandawire, T. (2001). "Thinking about developmental states in Africa." *Cambridge Journal of Economics* 25(3): 289–314.

Mkandawire. T. (2015). "Neopatrimonialism and the political economy of economic performance in Africa: Critical Reflections." *World Politics*, 67(3): 563–612.

Mohan. J. (1966). "Varieties of African Socialism." *Socialist Register*: 220–266.

Molotch, H. (1970). "Oil in Santa Barbara and power in America." *Sociological Inquiry*, 40(1): 131–144.

Molotch, H. (1976). "The city as a growth machine." *American Journal of Sociology*, 82 (2): 309–332.

Molotch, H., & Lester, M. (1974). "News as purposive behaviour: On the strategic use of routine events, accidents, and scandals." *American Sociological Review*, 39(1): 101–112.

Moore, S. (1998). "Changing African land tenure: Reflections on the incapacities of the state." *The European Journal of Development Research*, 10(2): 33–49.

Motengwe, C. & Alagidede, P. (2017). "The nexus between coal consumption, $CO_2$ emissions and economic growth in South Africa." *Geography Research Forum*, 37 (December): 80–110.

Mouan. L. C. (2016). "Review of *the Petro-Developmental State in Africa: Making Oil Work in Angola, Nigeria and the Gulf of Guinea*." *The Extractive Industries and Society*, 3: 875–876.

Moyo, D. (2009). *Dead Aid: Why Aid Is Not Working and How There Is a Better Way for Africa*. New York: Farrar, Straus, and Giroux.

Moyo, S. (1998). "The Economic and Social Implications of Recent Land Designations." (Paper presented to the Friedich-Ebert-Stiftung (FES)/Zimbabwe Economics Society (ZES) seminar on "The Land Reform Challenge: An Economic and Social Perspective"), Harare, 27 February, 1998.

Moyo, S. (2011). "Land concentration and accumulation after redistributive reform in post-settler Zimbabwe." *Review of African Political Economy*, 38(128): 257–276.

Moyo, S. (2018). "Debating the African land question with Archie Mafeje." *Agrarian South: Journal of Political Economy*, 7(2): 211–233.

Moyo, S., Rutherford, B., & Amanor-Wilks, D. (2000). "Land reform and changing social relations for farm workers in Zimbabwe." *Review of African Political Economy*, 27(84): 181–202.

Moyo, S., & Yeros, P., eds. (2005). *Reclaiming the Land: The Resurgence of Rural Movements in Africa, Asia and Latin America*. London and Cape Town: Zed Books Ltd.

Mueller, D. C. (1976). "Public choice: A survey." *Journal of Economic Literature*, 14(2): 395–433.

Mugambwa, J. (2007). "A comparative analysis of land tenure law reform in Uganda and Papua New Guinea." *Journal of South Pacific Law*, 11(1): 39–55.

Muhammad, M., Mukhtar, M. I., & Lola, G. K. (2017). "The impact of Chinese textile imperialism on Nigeria's textile industry and trade: 1960-2015." *Review of African Political Economy*, 44(154): 673–682.

Muller, A., & Mbanga, E. (2012). "Participatory enumerations at the national level in Namibia: The Community Land Information Programme (CLIP). "*Environment and Urbanization*, 24: 66–75.

Munro, D. (2013). "Land and capital." *Journal of Australian Political Economy*, 70 (Summer): 214–232.

Murphy, G., & Siedschlag, I. (2013). "Human capital and growth of information and communication technology-intensive industries: Empirical evidence from open economies." *Regional Studies*, 47(9): 1403–1424.

Murphy, J. T., & Carmody, P. (2015). *Africa's Information Revolution: Technical Regimes and Production Networks in South Africa and Tanzania*. Oxford: Wiley Blackwell.

Murray, G. L. (1981). "The 'Gregory thesis': Where Does It Stand?" The University of Western Australia Discussion Paper 81.20, November. https://ecompapers .biz.uwa.edu.au/paper/PDF%20of%20Discussion%20Papers/1981/81–20.pdf (accessed 12 January 2015).

Murray, C. K. (2017). "Review of the Petroleum Resource Tax (PRRT). "Submission on behalf of Prosper Australia to the Australian Government Treasury on February 14. Melbourne: Prosper Australia.

Murrey, A., ed. (2018). *A Certain Amount of Madness: The Life, Politics and Legacies of Thomas Sankara*. London: Zed Books.

Mutambara, T. E. (2013). "Africa-Asia trade versus Africa's trade with the North: Trends and trajectories." *African Review of Economics and Finance*, 4(2): 273–299.

Mwakaje, A. G. (2012). "Can Tanzania realise rural development through biofuel plantations? Insights from the study in Rufiji District." *Energy for Sustainable Development*, 16(3): 320–327.

myjoyonline.com (2014). "Schlumberger local workers angry over huge expatriate salary disparities." *myjoyonline.com*, 8 March. www.myjoyonline.com/news/2014/ March-8th/slumberger-local-workers-angry-over-huge-salary-expatriate-dispari ties.php (accessed 25 May 2019).

Myrdal, G. (1944). *An American Dilemma: The Negro Problem and Modern Democracy*. New York: Harper and Brothers Publishers.

Ndikumana, L., & Boyce, J. K. (2011). *Africa's Odious Debts: How Foreign Loans and Capital Flight Bled the Continent*. London and New York: Zed Books.

Neary, P. J. (1982). "Real and monetary aspects of the 'Dutch Disease'." Working Paper No. 5. Dublin, Ireland: University College, Dublin Centre for Economic Research.

Nega, B., & Schneider, G. (2016). "Africa rising? Short-term growth vs. deep institutional concerns." *Forum for Social Economics*, 45(4): 283–308.

Nelson, C. (1968). "Changing roles of men and women: Illustrations from Egypt." *Anthropological Quarterly*, 41(2): 57–77.

Nembhard, J. G. (2014). *Collective Courage: A History of African American Cooperative Economic Thought and Practice*. State College: Pennsylvania State University Press, May.

Neubert, D. & Stoll, F. (2018). "The narrative of the 'African middle class' and its conceptual limitations." In Kroeker, L., O'Kane, D., & Scharrer, T., eds., *Middle Classes in Africa: Changing Lives and Conceptual Challenges*. Basingstoke and New York: Palgrave Macmillan, pp. 57–79.

New Economics Foundation. (2012). *The Happy Planet Index: 2012 Report*. London: Author. New York: Pluto Press.

New Economics Foundation, (2016). *The Happy Planet Index: 2016 Report*. London: Author. New York: Pluto Press.

Ngaruko, F. (2015). "Review of *Africa's Odious Debts: How Foreign Loans and Capital Flight Bled the Continent.*" *Journal of Economic and Social Thought*, 2(3): 226–223.

Ngoasong, M. Z. (2014). "How international oil and gas companies respond to local content policies in petroleum-producing developing countries: A narrative enquiry." *Energy Policy*, 73: 471–479.

Ngwane, T., Sinwell, L., & Ness, I., eds. (2017). *Urban Revolt: State Power and the Rise of People's Movements in the Global South*. Chicago: Haymarket Books.

Niehaus, I. (2013). "Anthropology and Whites in South Africa: Response to an unreasonable critique." *Africa Spectrum*, 48(1): 117–127.

Nik-Khah, E., & van Horn, R. V. (2018). "Planning the 'free' market: The genesis and rise of Chicago neoliberalism" (with Robert Van Horn). In D. Cahill, M. Cooper, M. Konings, & D. Primrose, eds., *The SAGE Handbook of Neoliberalism*, SAGE, pp. 98–112.

Njoh, A. (2007). *Planning Power: Town Planning and Social Control in British and French Colonial Africa*. London: University College London Press.

Njoh, A. J. (2003). "Urbanisation and development in sub-Saharan Africa." *Cities*, 20, 167–174.

Njoh, A. J. (2009a). "Ideology and public health elements of human settlement policies in sub-Saharan Africa." *Cities*, 26(1): 9–18.

Njoh, A. J. (2009b). "The development theory of transportation infrastructure examined in the context of Central and West Africa." *Review of Black Political Economy*, 36, 227–243.

Njoh, A. J. (2013). "Equity, fairness and justice implications of land tenure formalization in Cameroon." *International Journal of Urban and Regional Research*, 37(2): 750–768.

Nordic Council of Ministers. (2018). *Nordic Economic Review: Increasing Income Inequality in the Nordics*. Copenhagen: Nordic Council of Ministers.

Northrop, E. (2017). "A stable climate or economic growth?" *Review of Social Economy*, 75(4): 510–522.

Ntsebeza, L. (2005). *Democracy Compromised: Chiefs and the Politics of the Land in South Africa*. Boston: Brill Leiden.

Nwoke, C. N. (1984a). "The global struggle over surplus profit for mining: A critical extension of Marx's rent theory." Ph.D. Dissertation, Graduate School of International Studies, University of Denver, USA.

Nwoke, C. N. (1984b). "World mining rent: An extension of Marx's theories." *Review*, 8 (1): 29–89.

Nwoke, C. N. (1986). "Towards authentic economic nationalism in Nigeria." *Africa Today*, 33(4): 51–69.

Nwoke, C. N. (1990). "Oil power in international politics." *Nigerian Journal of International Affairs*, 16(1): 49–72.

Nwoke, C. N. (1991). "OPEC: A viable third world instrument of action in north-south dialogue." *Nigerian Forum*, 11(10, 11&12, October–December): 43–253.

Nwoke, C. N. (1995). "Foreign policies of developed countries towards Africa: Some conceptual issues." *Nigerian Forum*, 15(11&12, November–December): 1–18.

Nwoke, C. N. (2007). "The scramble for Africa: A strategic policy framework" *Nigerian Journal of International Affairs*, 33(2): 31–55.

Nwoke C.N. (2013a). "The illusion of a Euro-American partnership in development with Africa." *African Journal of International Affairs and Development*, 17(1&2): 68–94.

Nwoke, C. N. (2013b). *Rich Land; Poor People: The Political Economy of Mineral Rresource Endowments in a Peripheral Capitalist State*. Ibadan: College Press.

Nwoke, C. N. (2016). "Book review: *Oiling the urban economy: Land, labour, capital, and the state in Sekondi-Takoradi, Ghana*." *Review of Radical Political Economics*, 48 (4): 681–684.

Nyamnjoh, F. (2013). "From quibbles to substance: A response to responses." *Africa Spectrum*, 48(2): 127–139.

Nyamnjoh, F B. (2012a). "'Potted plants in greenhouses': A Critical Reflection on the Resilience of Colonial Education in Africa." *Journal of Asian and African Studies*, 47 (2): 129–154.

Nyamnjoh, F B. (2012b). "Blinded by sight: Divining the future of anthropology in Africa." *Africa Spectrum*, 47(2–3): 63–92.

Nygren, A., & Wayessa, G. (2018). "At the intersections of multiple marginalisations: Displacements and environmental justice in Mexico and Ethiopia." *Environmental Sociology*, 4(1): 148–161.

O'Connor, J. (1973). *The Fiscal Crises of the State*. New York: St. Martins Press.

O'Donnell, E. (2015). *Henry George and the Crisis of Inequality*. New York: Columbia University Press.

Obeng-Odoom, F. (2009). "Oil and urban development in Ghana." *African Review of Economics and Finance* 1(1): 18–39.

Obeng-Odoom, F. (2010). "Abnormal urbanisation in Africa: A dissenting view." *African Geographical Review*, 29(2): 13–40.

Obeng-Odoom, F. (2011). "The informal sector in Ghana under siege, *Journal of Developing Societies*, 2(3–4): 355–392.

Obeng-Odoom, F. (2012). "Beyond access to water." *Development in Practice*, 22(8): 1135–1146.

Obeng-Odoom, F. (2013a). "Africa's failed development trajectory: A critique." *African Review of Economics and Finance*, 4(2): 151–75.

Obeng-Odoom, F. (2013b). *Governance for Pro-Poor Urban Development: Lessons from Ghana*. London: Routledge.

Obeng-Odoom, F. (2013c). "Underwriting food security the urban way: Lessons from African countries." *Agroecology and Sustainable Food Systems*, 37(5): 614–628.

Obeng-Odoom, F. (2013d). "Do African cities create markets for plastics or plastics for markets?" *Review of African Political Economy*, 40(137): 466–474.

Obeng-Odoom, F. (2013e). "Resource curse or blessing in Africa's oil cities? Empirical evidence from Sekondi-Takoradi, West Africa." *City, Culture and Society*, 4(4): 229–240.

Obeng-Odoom, F. (2014a). *Oiling the urban economy: Land, labour, capital, and the state in Sekondi-Takoradi*. London: Routledge.

Obeng-Odoom, F. (2014b). "A new oil strategy for Africa." *Progress*, 1112: 9–12.

Obeng-Odoom, F. (2014c). "Review of ownership and control of oil." *The Extractive Industries and Society*, 1(2): 362–363.

Obeng-Odoom, F. (2014d). "Urban land policies in Ghana: A case of the emperor's new clothes?" *Rev Black Polit Econ*, 41(2): 119–43.

Obeng-Odoom, F. (2014e). "Green neoliberalism: Recycling and sustainable urban development in Sekondi-Takoradi." *Habitat International*, 41: 129–134.

Obeng-Odoom, F. (2014f). "Sex, oil, and temporary migration: The case of Vienna City, Sekondi-Takoradi, Ghana." *Extractive Industries and Society*, 1(1): 69–74.

Obeng-Odoom, F. (2015a). "Global political economy and frontier economies in Africa: Implications from the oil and gas industry in Ghana." *Energy Research and Social Science*, 10(Nov): 41–56.

Obeng-Odoom, F. (2015b). "The social, spatial, and economic roots of urban inequality in Africa: Contextualizing Jane Jacobs and Henry George." *The American Journal of Economics and Sociology*, 74(3): 550–86.

Obeng-Odoom, F. (2015c). "Sustainable urban development in Africa? The case of urban transport in Sekondi-Takoradi, Ghana." *American Behavioral Scientist*, 59(3): 424–437.

Obeng-Odoom, F. (2015d). "Oil rents, policy, and social development: Lessons from the Ghana controversy." United Nations Research Institute for Social Development (UNRISD) Research Paper, No. 2, May. Geneva: UNRISD.

Obeng-Odoom, F. (2016a). "Migration, African migrants, and the world: Towards a radical political economy." *African Identities*, 14(4): 1–13.

Obeng-Odoom, F. (2016b). "Understanding land reform in Ghana: A critical postcolonial institutional approach." *Review of Radical Political Economics*, 48(4): 661–680.

Obeng-Odoom, F. (2016c). "The meaning, prospects, and future of the commons: Revisiting the legacies of Elinor Ostrom and Henry George." *The American Journal of Economics and Sociology*, 75(2): 372–414.

Obeng-Odoom, F. (2016d). *Reconstructing Urban Economics: Towards a Political Economy of the Built Environment*. London: Zed.

Obeng-Odoom, F. (2016e). "Oil, construction, and economic development." In R. T. Abdulai, F. Obeng-Odoom, E. Ochieng, & V. Maliene, eds., *Real Estate, Construction and Economic Development in Emerging Market Economies*, Routledge, London, pp. 19–36.

Obeng-Odoom, F. (2016f). "Property in the commons: Origins and paradigms." *Review of Radical Political Economics*, 48(1): 9–19.

Obeng-Odoom, F. (2017a). "Unequal access to land and the current migration crisis." *Land Use Policy*, 62 (March): 159–171.

Obeng-Odoom, F. (2017b). "Urban governance in Africa today: Reframing, experiences, and lessons." *Growth and Change*, 48(1): 4–21.

Obeng-Odoom, F. (2018). "The contribution of J. R. Commons to migration analysis." *Evolutionary and Institutional Economics Review*, 15(1): 73–88.

Obeng-Odoom, F. (2019). "Economic cycles, economic crises, resource grabs, and expulsions." *International Critical Thought*, 9(1): 64–84.

Obeng-Odoom, F., & Gyampo, R. E. V. (2017). "Land grabbing, land rights, and the role of the courts." *Geography Research Forum*, 37 (December): 127–147.

Obeng-Odoom, F., & Marke, M. (2018). "The political economy of the Ebola virus disease." *Social Change*, 48(1): 18–35.

Obeng-Odoom, F., & McDermott, M. (2018). "Valuing unregistered land." Report for Royal Institution of Chartered Surveyors, London.

Obeng-Odoom, F., & Stilwell, F. (2013). "Security of tenure in international development discourse." *International Development Planning Review*, 35(4): 315–333.

Obi, C. (2009). "Nigeria's Niger delta: Understanding the complex drivers of violent oil-related conflict." *Africa Development*, XXXIV(2): 103–28.

Obrist, B., Cissé, G., Koné, B., Dongo, K., Granado, S., & Tanner, M. (2006). "Interconnected slums: Water, sanitation and health in Abidjan, Côte d'Ivoire." *The European Journal of Development Research*, 18(2): 319–336.

Odoom, I. (2015). "Dam in, cocoa out; pipes in, oil out: China's engagement in Ghana's energy sector." *Journal of Asian and African Affairs*, October: 1–25. DOI:10.1177/0021909615599419.

Ofori-Atta, K. (2019). "The Budget Speech of the Government of Ghana for the 2019 Financial Year Presented to Parliament on Thursday, 15th November 2018." Ministry of Finance, Accra.

Ojong, N. (2011). "Livelihood strategies in African cities: The case of residents in Bamenda, Cameroon." *African Review of Economics and Finance*, 3: 8–24.

Okechukwu, U., Ukiwo, U. O., & Ibaba, I. S., eds. (2012). *Natural Resources, Conflict, and Sustainable Development: Lessons from the Niger Delta.* London: Routledge.

Okoth- Ogendo, H.W.O. (2003). "The tragic African commons: A century of expropriation, suppression and subversion." *University of Nairobi Law Journal*, 1(1): 107–117.

Ollenu, N.A. (1962). *Principles of Customary Land Law in Ghana.* London: Sweet and Maxwell.

Onoma, A. K. (2009). *The Politics of Property Rights Institutions in Africa.* New York: Cambridge University Press.

Organisation of African Unity. (1993). "The Abuja Proclamation." Abuja, Nigeria, April 27–29.

Osei-Kojo, A., & Andrews, N. (2018). "A developmental paradox? The 'dark forces' against corporate social responsibility in Ghana's extractive." *Environment, Development and Sustainability*, industry https://doi.org/10.1007/s10668-018-0233-, pp. 1–21.

Ostrom, E. (1990). *Governing the Commons: The Evolution of Institutions for Collective Action.* New York: Cambridge University Press.

Oteng-Adjei, J. (2011). "Closing address by Hon. Dr. Joe Oteng-Adjei, Minister for Energy," on the occasion of the first Jubilee Oil Colloquium organised at KNUST (Kwame Nkrumah University of science and Technology), Kumasi, Ghana, 18 February.

Ovadia, J. S. (2012). "The dual nature of local content in Angola's oil and gas industry: Development vs. elite accumulation." *Journal of Contemporary African Studies*, 30 (3): 395–417.

Ovadia, J. S. (2013). "The making of oil-backed indigenous capitalism in Nigeria." *New Political Economy*, 18(2): 258–283.

Ovadia, J. S. (2014). "Local content and natural resource governance: The cases of Angola and Nigeria." *The Extractive Industries and Society*, 1(2): 137–146.

Ovadia, J. S. (2015). *"The role of local content Policies in natural-resource based development." Österreichische Entwicklungspolitik 2015. Rohstoffe und Entwicklung.* Wien: Österreichische Forschungsstiftung für Internationale Entwicklung (Austrian Development Policy, Annual Report 2015: Resources and Development. Vienna: Austrian Foundation for Development Research).

Ovadia, J. S. (2016a). *The Petro-Developmental State in Africa: Making Oil Work in Angola, Nigeria and the Gulf of Guinea.* London: C. Hurst & Co.

Ovadia, J. S. (2016b). "Local content policies and petro-development in sub-Saharan Africa: A comparative analysis." *Resources Policy*, 49: 20–30.

Ovadia, J. S. (2016c). "Local content policies, natural resource governance and development in the Global South" In H. Besada & K. J. Eyben, eds., *Governance of Natural Resources for Africa's Development*. London: Routledge, chapter 6.

Overå, R. (2017). "Local navigations in a global industry: The gendered nature of entrepreneurship in Ghana's oil and gas service sector." *The Journal of Development Studies*, 53(3): 361–374.

Owusu, G. A. (2008). "Gender, land tenure dynamics and livelihood: A comparison of the central and volta regions of Ghana using logistic regression analysis." *Studies in Gender and Development in Africa*, 1: 34–57, September.

Owusu, G. Y., with M. Rutledge McCall. (2017). *In Pursuit of Jubilee: A True Story of the First Major Oil Discovery in Ghana*. Houston: Avenue Lane Press.

Owusu, G., & Afutu-Kotey, R. (2010). "Poor urban communities and municipal interface in Ghana: A case study of Accra and Sekondi-Takoradi metropolis." *African Studies Quarterly*, 12(1): 1–16.

Owusu, George, Agyei-Mensah, Samuel, & Lund, Ragnhild (2008). "Slums of hope and slums of despair: Mobility and livelihoods in Nima, Accra." *Norsk Geografisk Tidsskrift – Norwegian Journal of Geography*, 62(3): 180–190.

Owusu-Ansah, A., Ohemeng-Mensah, D., Talinbe, R., & Obeng-Odoom, F. (2018). "Public choice theory and rental housing: An examination of rental housing contracts in Ghana." *Housing Studies*, 33(6): 938–959.

Owusuaa, D. (2012). "Gender and informality in the construction industry in Ghana's oil city Takoradi." Master's Thesis, Department of Geography, University of Bergen, Bergen.

Oya, C. (2007). "Agricultural maladjustment in Africa: What have we learned after two decades of liberalisation?" *Journal of Contemporary African Studies*, 25(2): 275–297.

Oya, C. (2011). "Agriculture in the World Bank: Blighted harvest persists." In K. Bayliss, B. Fine, & E. Van Waeyenberge, eds., *The Political Economy of Development. The World, Neoliberalism and Development Research*. London: Pluto Press, pp. 146–187.

Oya, C. (2012). "Contract farming in sub-Saharan Africa: A survey of approaches, debates and issues." *Journal of Agrarian Change*, 12(1): 1–33.

Oya, C. (2013). "Methodological reflections on 'land grab' databases and the 'land grab' literature 'rush.'" *The Journal of Peasant Studies*, 40(3); 503–520.

Ozkul, D., & Obeng-Odoom, F. (2013). "Temporary migration in Africa: Views from the Global South." *African Review of Economics and Finance*, 5(1): 1–6.

Padmore, G. (1956). *Pan-Africanism or Communism? The Coming Struggle for Africa*. London: Dobson.

Pádraig, C. (2016). *The New Scramble for Africa*, 2nd edition. Cambridge: Polity Press.

Paller, J. (2019). Democracy in *Ghana: Everyday Politics in Urban Africa*. Cambridge University Press.

Panda, P. & Agarwal, B. (2005). "Marital violence, human development and women's property status in India." *World Development*, 33(5): 823–850.

Panford, K. (2014). "An exploratory survey of petroleum skills and training in Ghana." *Africa Today*, 60(3): 56–80.

Panford, K. (2015). "The academy and the successful management of Ghana's petroleum resources." *Africa. Today*, 61(2): 78–107.

Panford, K. (2017). *Africa's Natural Resources and Underdevelopment: How Ghana's Petroleum Can Create Sustainable Economic Prosperity*. New York: Palgrave Macmillan.

Papyrakis, E. (2017). "The resource curse – What have we learned from two decades of intensive research: Introduction to the Special Issue." *Journal of Development Studies*, 53(2): 175–185.

Paton, J. (2010). "Labour as a (fictitious) commodity: Polanyi and the capitalist 'market economy.'" *The Economic and Labour Relations Review*, 21(1): 77–88.

Paul, M., Darity, W. Jr., & Hamilton, D. (2017). "Why we need a federal job guarantee." *Jacobin*, February, www.jacobinmag.com/2017/02/federal-job-guarantee-universal-basic-income-investment-jobs-unemployment/ (accessed 24 May 2019).

Paul, M., Darity, W. Jr., Hamilton, D., & Zaw, K. (2018). "Anti-poverty policy initiatives for the United States." *RSF: The Russell Sage Foundation Journal of the Social Sciences*, 4(3): 44–63.

Payne, G., Durand-Lasserve, A., & Rakodi, C. (2009). "The limits of land titling and home ownership." *Environment and Urbanization*, 21(2): 443–462.

Pearce, F. (2012). *The Land Grabbers: The New Fight over Who Owns the Earth*, Boston, MA: Beacon Press.

Peck, J. (2011). "Neoliberal suburbanism: Frontier space." *Urban Geography*, 32(6): 884–919.

Pedro, A. M. A. (2014). "Book review of *One Thing Leads to Another: Making the Most of the Commodities Boom in Sub-Saharan Africa*, by M. Morris, R. Kaplinsky & D. Kaplan." *The Journal of Development Studies*, 50(10): 1463–1464.

Pegram, J., Falcone, G., & Kolios, A. (2019). "Job role localisation in the oil and gas industry: A case study of Ghana." *The Extractive Industries and Society*, https://doi.org/10.1016/j.exis.2019.08.003

Peigo, N. D. F., & Ruas, J. A. G. (2015). "Rethinking 'energy nationalism': A study of the relationship between nation states and companies in the oil industry." *Brazilian Journal of Political Economy*, 35: 557–575.

Peil, M. (1972). *The Ghanaian Factory Worker: Industrial Man in Africa*. Cambridge: Cambridge University Press.

Peters, R. (2013). *Surabaya, 1945–2010: Neighborhood, State and Economy in Indonesia's City of Struggle*. Singapore: National University of Singapore Press.

Petrella, F. (1984). "Henry George's theory of state's agenda: The origins of his ideas on economic policy in Adam Smith's Moral Theory." *American Journal of Economics and Sociology*, 43(3): 269–286.

Phillips, J., Hailwood, E., & Brooks, A. (2016). "Sovereignty, the 'resource curse' and the limits of good governance: A political economy of oil in Ghana." *Review of African Political Economy*, 43(147): 26–42. DOI:10.1080/03056244.2015.1049520.

Pickvance, C. (1995). "Marxist theories of urban politics." In D. Judge, G. Stoker, & H. Wolman, eds., *Theories of Urban Politics*. London: Sage, pp. 253–275.

Pieterse, J. N. (1994). "Delinking or globalisation?" *Economic and Political Weekly*, 29 (5): 239–242.

Piketty, T. (2014). *Capital in the Twenty-First Century*. Cambridge, London: The Belknap Press of Harvard University Press.

Pinkovskiy, M., & Sala-i-Martin, X. (2014). "Africa is on time." *Journal of Economic Growth*, 19 (311–338).

Polanyi, K. ([1944] 2001). *The Great Transformation: The Political and Economic Origins of Our Time*. Massachusetts: Beacon Press.

Posel, D. & Rogan, M. (2018). "Inequality, social comparisons and income aspirations: Evidence from a highly unequal country." Paper presented at the 2018 AREF Conference on 22 August, University of Witwatersrand, Johannesburg, South Africa.

Poirine, B., & Dropsy, V. (2019). "Institutions, culture, and the tropical development gap: The agro-climatic origins of social norms about thrift and sharing." *Journal of Economic Issues*, LIII(3): 677–702.

Pressman, S. (2001). "State and government." In P. O'Hara, ed., *Encyclopedia of Political Economy*, Vol. 2. London: Routledge. pp. 1104–1107.

Price, G. (2018). "The emerging field of stratification economics: A unified social science theory of race and inequality?" In J. L. Conyers Jr., ed., Africana Social Stratification: *An Interdisciplinary Study of Economics, Policy and Labor*. London, New York, Lanham, Boulder: Lexington Books, pp. 13–19.

Pritchett, L. (2001). "Where has all the education gone?" *World Bank Economic Review*, 15(3): 367–391.

Public Eye. (2016). *Dirty Diesel: How Swiss Traders Flood Africa with Toxic Publication, Fuels*. Lausanne and Zurich: Public Eye.

Puka, L., & Szulecki, K. (2014). "The politics and economics of cross-border electricity infrastructure: A framework for analysis." *Energy Research & Social Science*, 4: 124–34.

Pullen, J. (2014). *Nature's Gifts: The Australian Lectures of Henry George and the Ownership of Land and Other Natural Resources*. Sydney: Desert Pea Press.

Rahnema, S. & Howlett, M. (2002). "Impediments to industrial policy: Overcoming path dependency in Canada's post staples transition." *Journal of Australian Political Economy*, 49(2 June): 114–135.

Ramaphosa, C. (2018). "This is no land grab." *Financial Times*, August 24.

Ramnarain, S. (2016). "Review of Economics, Culture and Development." *Review of Radical Political Economics*. DOI:10.1177/0486613416665831, 2016.

Rapley, J. (2004). "Development studies and the post-development critique." *Progress in Development Studies*, 4(4): 350–354.

Rapley, J.(1994). "New directions in the political economy of development." *Review of African Political Economy*, 21(62): 495–510.

Rasch, R. (2017). "Measuring the middle class in middle-income countries." *Forum for Social Economics*, 46(4): 321–336.

Reich, M. (1980). "Empirical and ideological elements in the decline of Ricardian economics." *Review of Radical Political Economics*, 12(1): 1–14.

Reifer, T. E. (2011). "Global inequalities, alternative regionalisms and the future of socialism." *Journal Fur Entwicklungspolitik*, XXVII(1): 72–94.

Reitz, C. (2016). "Accounting for inequality: Questioning Piketty on national income accounts and the capital-labor split." *Review of Radical Political Economics*, 48(2): 310–21.

Remoff, H. (2016). "Malthus, Darwin, and the descent of economics." Report. Working Paper Series. Netherlands Institute of International Relations 'Clingendael', Conflict Research Unit. Working paper 11.

Republic of Côte d'Ivoire. (2015). "Request for the Prescription of Provisional Measures Submitted by the Republic of Côte d'Ivoire under Article 290, Paragraph 1, of the

United Nations Convention on the Law of the Sea." www.itlos.org/en/cases/list-of-cases/case-no-23/.

Republic of Ghana. (2015). "Written Statement of Ghana in the Dispute concerning Delimitation of the Maritime Boundary between Ghana and Côte d'Ivoire in the Atlantic Ocean." www.itlos.org/en/cases/list-of-cases/case-no-23/.

Resnick, D. (2014a). "Urban governance and service delivery in African cities: The role of politics and policies." *Development Policy Review*, 32(S1): s3–ss17.

Resnick, D. (2014b). "Strategies of subversion in vertically-divided contexts: Decentralisation and urban service delivery in Senegal." *Development Policy Review* 32(S.1): s61–s80.

Reuters. (2017). "Shell battles Nigerian bommunities in high-stakes London lawsuit." Africa Independent. January 14. www.africanindy.com/ business/shell-battles-nigerian-communities-in-high-stakes-london-lawsuit-

Riddell, J. (2009). "World farmers' alliance challenges food profiteers." *Socialist Voice Pamphlet*, May: 3–11.

Rist, G. (2008). *The History of Development: From Western Origins to Global Faith*, 3rd edition. London: Zed Books.

Robinson, J. (1979/2009). *Aspects of Development and Underdevelopment*. Cambridge: Cambridge University Press.

Robinson, W. I. (2007). "Beyond the theory of imperialism: Global capitalism and the transnational state." *Societies without Borders*, 2: 5–26.

Robson, P. (1983). *Integration, Development and Equity: Economic Integration in West Africa*. London: Routledge.

Rodney, W. (1972/2011). *How Europe Underdeveloped Africa*. Baltimore, MD: Black Classic Press.

Rodrik, D. (2014). "An African growth miracle?" Richard H. Sabot Lecture, delivered at the Center for Global Development. Washington, DC, April 24.

Rostow, W.W. (1959). "The stages of economic growth." *The Economic History Review*, New Series, 12(1): 1–16.

Rousseau, J. J. (1776). *Discourse upon the Origin and Foundation on the Inequality Among Mankind*. London: R and J. Dodsley.

Rowlandson, J. (1996). *Landowners and Tenants in Roman Egypt: The Social Relations of Agriculture in the Oxyrbynchite Nome*. Oxford: Clarendon Press.

Rowthorn, R. (2014). "A note on Piketty's *Capital in the Twenty-First Century*." *Cambridge Journal of Economics*, 38: 1275–84.

Ruchira, T. (2017). "Hiding neoliberal coal behind the Indian poor." *Journal Australian Political Economy*, 78: 132–158.

Rutten, R. & Boekema, F. (2012). "From learning region to learning in a socio-spatial context." *Regional Studies*, 46(8): 981–992.

Sachs, J., & Warner, A. (1995). "Natural resource abundance and economic growth." NBER Working Paper Series no. 5398, December. Cambridge, MA: National Bureau of Economic Research.

Sahara Reporters. (2014). "Ghanaian oil workers strike; Claim expatriate workers are treated better." *Sahara Reporters*, October 29.

Said, E. W. (1978). *Orientalism*. New York: Vintage Books.

Sala-i-Martin, X., & Subramanian, A. (2012). "Addressing the natural resource curse: An illustration from Nigeria." *Journal of African Economies*, 22(4): 570–615.

Salih, M. A. M. (2001). "Natural Capital." In P. A. O'Hara, ed., *Encyclopedia of Political Economy*, Vol. 2. London: Routledge, pp. 779–780

Sam, K., Coulon, F., & Prpich, G. (2017). "Management of petroleum hydrocarbon contaminated sites in Nigeria: current challenges and future direction." *Land Use Policy*, 64(May): 133–144.

Samuelson, P. (1938). "A note on the pure theory of consumers behaviour." *Economica*, 5: 61–71.

Sandbrook, R., & Arn, J. (1977). *The Labouring Poor and Urban Class Formation: The Case of Greater Accra*. Montreal, QB: Centre for Developing-Area Studies, McGill.

Sarbu, B. (2014). *Ownership and Control of All*. London: Routledge.

Sarkodie, P. A., Agyapong, D., Larbi, G. O., & Owusu-Ansah, E. (2014). "A comparative study of the quality of wastewater from Tema Oil Refinery (TOR) against EPA standards and its effect on the environment." *Civil and Environmental Research*, 6(6): 85–91.

Sassen, S. (1991). *The Global City: New York, London, Tokyo*. Princeton: Princeton University Press.

Schafft, K. A., Glenna, L. L., & Green, B. (2014). "Local impacts of unconventional gas development within Pennsylvania's Marcellus shale region: Gauging boomtown development through the perspectives of educational administrators." *Society & Natural Resources*, 27(4): 389–404.

Schaps, K. & George, L. (2017). "Court rules Shell can't be sued in London for Nigeria oil spills." *Reuters*, January 26. www.reuters. com/article/us-shell-nigeria-court /court-rules-shell-cant-be-suedin-london-for-nigeria-oil-spills-idUSKBN15A1JV.

Scharrer, T., O'Kane, D., & Kroeker, L. (2018). "Introduction: Africa's Middle Classes in Critical Perspective." In T. Scharrer, D. O'Kane, & L. Kroeker, eds. *Middle Classes in Africa*. New York: Springer, pp. 1–31.

Schelling, T. C. (1971). "Dynamic models of segregation." *Journal of Mathematical Sociology*, 1: 143–186.

Schlatter, R. (1951). *Private Property: The History of an Idea*. New York: Russell and Russell.

Schmelzer, M. (2016). *The Hegemony of Growth: The OECD and the Making of the Economic Growth Paradigm*. New York: Cambridge University Press.

Schoneveld, G., German, L., & Nutakor, E. (2011). "Land-based investments for rural development? A grounded analysis of the local impacts of biofuel feedstock plantations in Ghana." *Ecology and Society*, 16(10), online. www.ecologyandsociety.org /vol16/iss4/art10/ (accessed 17 June 2015).

Schubert, C. (2012). "Pursuing happiness." *KYKLOS*, 65: 245–261.

Schultz, T. W. (1951). "A framework for land economics: The long view." *American Journal of Agricultural Economics*, 33(2): 204–215.

Schultz, T. W. (1961). "Investment in human capital." *The American Economic Review*, 51(1): 1–17.

Schumacher, E. F. (1973). *Small is Beautiful: Economics as If People Mattered*. London: Blond and Briggs.

Schumpeter, J. A. ([1912] 2003). "The theory of economic development." In J. Backhaus, ed., *Joseph Alois Schumpeter: Entrepreneurship, Style and Vision*, London: Kluwer Academic, pp. 61–116.

Schumpeter, J. A. (1928). "The instability of capitalism." *The Economic Journal*, 38 (151): 361–386.

Schumpeter, J. A. (1947). "The creative response in economic history." *The Journal of Economic History*, 7(2): 149–159.

Schumpeter, J. A. (1954). *Capitalism, Socialism, and Democracy*. London: George Allen & Unwin.

Scoones, I., Marongwe, N., Mavedzenge, B., Murimbarimba, F., Mahenehene, J., & Sukume, C. (2011). "Zimbabwe's land reform: Challenging the myths." *The Journal of Peasant Studies*, 38(5): 967–993.

Self, P. (1993). *Government by the Market?* London: Macmillan.

Selormey, E. E. (2013). "Citizen voice and bureaucratic responsiveness: FM radio phone-ins and the delivery of municipal and local government services in Accra Ghana." Ph.D. dissertation, Sussex University. Session2/Pages/Session2.aspx.

Sen, A. (1999). *Development as Freedom*. New York: Oxford University Press.

Shapiro, T. M. (2017) *Toxic Inequality: Toxic Inequality: How America's Wealth Gap Destroys Mobility, Deepens the Racial Divide, and Threatens Our Future*. New York: Basic Books.

Shawkat, Y. (2016). "Property market deregulation and informal tenure in Egypt: A diabolical threat to millions." *Architecture Media Politics Society*, 9(4): 1–17.

Shepphard, E. (2012). "Trade, globalization and uneven development: Entanglements of geographical political economy." *Progress in Human Geography*, 36(1): 44–71.

Shiozawa, Y. (2004). "Evolutionary economics in the 21st century: A manifesto." *Evolutionary and Institutional Economic Review*, 1(1):5–47.

Sihlongonyane, M. (2005). "Land occupations in South Africa." In S. Moyo, & P. Yeros, eds., *Reclaiming the Land: The Resurgence of Rural Movements in Africa, Asia and Latin America*. London and New York: Zed Books, pp. 142–164.

Sihlongonyane, M. F. (2012). "Review of *Africa's Odious Debts: How Foreign Loans and Capital Flight Bled the Continent*." *Development in Practice*, 22(8): 1147–1149.

Simatele, M.C.H., Schaling, E., & Alagidede, P. (2015). "Is Zambia ready for inflation targeting?." *African Review of Economics and Finance*, 7(2): 1–28.

Singh, R. J. & Huang, Y. (2011). "Financial Deepening, Property Rights and Poverty: Evidence from Sub-Saharan Africa." IMF Working Paper, WP/11/196.

Siu, R. C. S. (2019). "China's Belt and Road Initiative: Reducing or Increasing the World Uncertainties?" *Journal of Economic Issues*, LIII(2): 571–578.

Skillman, G. L. (2016). Special issue on "Inequality: Causes, Consequences, and Policy responses." *Metroeconomica*, 67(2): 204–209.

Smet, K. (2019). "The financialisation of primary sector MNES." *African Review of Economics and Finance*, 11(1): 199–219.

Smiley, S. L. (2017). "Defining and measuring water access: Lessons from Tanzania for moving forward in the post-Millennium Development Goal era." *African Geographical Review*, 36(2): 168–182.

Smith, J. (2016). *Imperialism in the Twenty-First Century : Globalization, Super-Exploitation, and Capitalism's Final Crisis*. New York: Monthly review Press.

Smith, L. T. (1999). *Decolonizing Methodologies Research and Indigenous Peoples*. London: Zed and Dunedin: University of Otago Press.

Sneyd, A. (2014). "Neopatrimonial African capitalism? Conceptual adventures via John Kenneth Galbraith. *ASPJ Africa & Francophonie*, (2nd Quarter): 21–27.

Songsore, J. (2011). *Regional Development in Ghana: The Theory and the Reality*. Accra: Woeli.

Soré, Z. (2018), 'Balai Citoyen: A New Praxis of Citizen Fight with Sankarist inspirations." In Murrey, A., ed., *A Certain Amount of Madness: The Life, Politics and Legacies of Thomas Sankara*, London: Zed Books, pp. 225–240.

Spiegler, P. M., & Milberg, W. (2013). "Methodenstreit 2013? Historical perspective on the contemporary debate over how to reform economics." *Forum for Social Economics*, 42: 311–345.

Stacey, P. (2019). *State of Slum: Precarity and Informal Governance at the Margins in Accra*, London: Zed Books.

Stadia Trustees. (2011). *"Trustees Diligence Visit Report: Greenleaf Global PLC, Republic of Togo."* London, Stadia Trustees.

Standing, G. (2009). *Work after Globalization: Building Occupational Citizenship.* Cheltenham, UK, & Northampton, USA: Edward Elgar.

Standford, J. (2008). *Economics for Everyone: A Short Guide to the Economics of Capitalism.* New York: Pluto Press.

Stein, H. (2011). "World Bank Agricultural policies, poverty and income inequality in sub-Saharan Africa." *Cambridge Journal of Regions, Economy and Society*, 4(1): 232–248.

Stevenson, M. (2014). "Public-private partnering in natural resource extraction." *Global Environmental Politics*, 14(3): 139–145.

Stewart, J. (2010). "Racial identity production dynamics and persisting wealth differentials: Integrating neo-institutionalist perspectives into stratification economics." *The Review of Black Political Economy*, 37: 217–222.

Stewart J.B. (2018). "Insights regarding black-white economic inequality from stratification economics." In Conyers J.L. Jr., ed., *Africana Social Stratification: An Interdisciplinary Study of Economics, Policy and Labor.* London, New York, Lanham, Boulder: Lexington Books, pp. 71–86.

Stilwell, F. (1993). *Economic Inequality: Who Gets What in Australia.* Sydney: Pluto Press.

Stilwell, F. (1995). *Understanding Cities and Regions.* Sydney: Pluto.

Stilwell, F. (2011). "The condition of labour, capital and land." Paper presented at the Conference of the Association for Good Government, Sydney; 2011.

Stilwell, F. (20120. *Political Economy: The Contest of Economic Ideas*, 3rd edition. Melbourne: Oxford University Press.

Stilwell, F. (2017). "Why emphasise economic inequality in development?" *Journal of Australian Political Economy*, 78: 24–47.

Stilwell, F. (2019). *The Political Economy of Inequality.* Cambridge: Polity Press.

Stilwell, F. & Jordan, K. (2004). "The political economy of land: Putting Henry George in his place." *Journal of Australian Political Economy*, 54: 119–134.

Stilwell, F. & Jordan, K. (2007). *Who Gets What? Analysing Economic Inequality in Australia.* Cambridge: Cambridge University Press.

Stoll, F. (2018). "The city and its ways of life: Local influences of middle-income millieus in Nairobi." In Ammann, C., & Förster, T., eds., *African Cities and the Development Conundrum*, Leiden and Boston: Brill, pp. 275–301.

Street, J. H. (1987). "The institutionalist theory of economic development." *The Journal of Economic Issues*, 21(4): 1861–1887.

Sunstein, C. R. (1986). "Legal interference with private preferences." *The University of Chicago Law Review*, 53: 1129–1174.

Sutton, I. (1984). "Law, chieftaincy and conflict in colonial Ghana: The Ada case." *African Affairs*, 83(330): 41–62.

Teppo, A. (2013). "Poor whites do matter." *Africa Spectrum*, 48(2): 123–126.

Tetteh, L. (2012). "Assessing safety culture: A special focus on the Ghana oil industry." Ph.D. Thesis submitted to University of Nottingham, UK.

Thaler, H. R. (2017). "From cashews to nudges: the evolution of behavioral economics," Nobel Prize Lecture, Stockholm, December 8. www.nobelprize.org/uploads/2018/ 06/thaler-lecture-slides.pdf (accessed 8 November 2019)

Thaler, H. R., & Sunstein, C. R. (2003). Libertarian paternalism. *American Economic Review*, 93: 175–179.

Thaler, H. R., Sunstein, C. R., & Balz, J. P. (2012). Choice architecture. In E. Shafir. ed., *The Behavioral Foundations of Public Policy*. Princeton, NJ: Princeton University Press, pp. 428–439.

*The Economist* (1977). The Dutch disease. *The Economist*, 26 November: 82–83.

*The Economist* (2014). Is college worth it? *The Economist*, 5–11 April: 27–28.

*The Economist* (2019). "Inequality illusions." *The Economist*, 30 November–6 December: 11–12.

The Editors (2012). "The agrarian question: Past, present and future." *Agrarian South*, 1(1): 1–10.

Thornycroft, P. (2012). "Zimbabwean killed in Ghana land dispute." *Pretoria News*, 19 April. www.iol.co.za/pretoria-news/zimbabwean-killed-in-ghana-land-dispute -1279566 (accessed 10 November 2019).

Tiba, S. (2019). "Modeling the nexus between resources abundance and economic growth: An overview from the PSTR model." Resources Policy, 64(December): https://doi.org/10.1016/j.resourpol.2019.101503

Tieleman, J., & Uitermark, J. (2019). "Chiefs in the city: Traditional authority in the modern state." *Sociology*, 53(4): 707–723.

Todaro, M., & Smith, S. (2006). *Economic Development*. London: Pearson Addison-Wesley.

Tomer, J. (2001). "Social and organizational capital." In P. O'Hara, ed., *Encyclopedia of Political Economy*, Vol. 2. London and New York: Routledge, pp. 1049–1051.

Tordo, S., Warner, M., Manzano, Osmel, & Anouti, Y. (2013). *Local Content Policies in the Oil and Gas Sector*. New York: World Bank.

Toulmin, C. (2008). "Securing land and property rights in sub-Saharan Africa: The role of local institutions." *Land Use Policy*, 26: 10–19.

Traore, N. (2000). "Financing the urban poor: SODECI's experience in Cote d'Ivoire." Presentation in Nairobi, June 19–22.

Tullow Oil PLC. (2010). *Corporate Social Responsibility Report*. London: Tullow Oil PLC.

Tullow Oil PLC. (2012). *Corporate Social Responsibility Report*. London: Tullow.

Tullow Oil PLC. (2015). *Corporate Social Responsibility Report*. London: Tullow.

Turner, L. (2010). "Toward a black radical critique of political economy." *The Black Scholar*, 40(1): 7–19.

Turok, I., & McGranahan, G. (2013). "Urbanization and economic growth: The arguments and evidence for Africa and Asia." *Environment and Urbanization*, 25: 465–482.

Twineyo-Kamugisha, E. (2012). *Why Africa Fails: The Case for Growth before Democracy*. Cape Town: Tafelberg.

Ubink, J. (2002). "Courts and peri-urban practice: Customary land law in Ghana." *University of Ghana Law Journal*, 22: 25–77.

Ubink, J. (2007). "Traditional authority revisited: popular perceptions of chiefs and chieftaincy in peri-urban Kumasi, Ghana." *Journal of Legal Pluralism*, 55, 123–161.

Ubink, J. (2008). *Traditional Authorities in Africa: Resurgence in an Era of Democratisation*. Leiden: Leiden University Press.

Ubink, J., & Quan, J. (2008). "How to combine tradition and modernity? Regulating customary land management in Ghana." *Land Use Policy*, 25(2): 198–213.

Uemura, T. (2007). "Exploring potential of global tax as a cutting edge-measure for democratizing global governance." *International Journal of Public Affairs*, 3: 112–129.

Uemura, T. (2012). "From Tobin to a global solidarity levy: Potentials and challenges for taxing financial transations towards an improved global governance." *Économique Áppliquee*, LXV(3): 59–94.

Uetela, P, & Obeng-Odoom, F. (2015). "Gas and socio-economic transformation in Mozambique: Some preliminary evidence." *Journal of Energy and Development*, 41 (1&2): 47–66.

Ulriksen, M. S. (2011). "Social policy development and global financial crisis in the open economies of Botswana and Mauritius." *Global Social Policy*, 11(2–3): 194–213.

UN ECA (United Nations Economic Commission of Africa). (2011). "Minerals and Africa'sDevelopment: The International Study Group Report on Africa's Mineral Regimes." Addis Ababa, Ethiopia.

UN ECA (United Nations Economic Commission of Africa). (2013). "Harmonizing Policies to Transform the Trading Environment: Assessing Regional Integration in Africa VI." Addis Ababa, Ethiopia. www.uneca.org/sites/default/files/PublicationFiles/aria_vi_english_full.

UN-HABITAT (2003). *The Challenge of Slums*. London and Sterling, VA: Earthscan Publications Ltd.

UN-HABITAT (2008a). *The State of African Cities 2008: A Framework for Addressing Urban Challenges in Africa*. Nairobi, Kenya: UN-HABITAT.

UN-HABITAT (2008b). *State of the World's Cities 2008/2009*. London: Earthscan.

UN-HABITAT (2009). *Ghana: Accra Urban Profile*. Nairobi: UN-HABITAT.

UN-HABITAT (2011). *Housing Profile in Ghana*. Nairobi, Kenya: UN-HABITAT.

UN-HABITAT. (2010). *The State of African Cities: Governance, Inequality and Urban Land Markets*. Nairobi: UN-HABITAT.

UN-HABITAT. (2013). *Unleashing the Economic Potential of Agglomeration in African Cities*. Nairobi: UN-HABITAT.

UN-HABITAT. (2014). *State of African Cities: Re-imagining Sustainable Urban Transitions*. Nairobi: UN-HABITAT.

UN. (2015). *MDGs Report 2015*, New York: UN.

UNDP. (1990). *Human Development Report*. New York: Oxford University Press.

UNDP. (2010). *Human Development Report 2010*. New York: Palgrave Macmillan.

UNDP. (2011). *Human Development Report 2011*. New York: Palgrave Macmillan.

UNDP. (2016). *Human Development Report 2016*. New York: UNDP.

United Nations Conference on Trade and Development (UNCTAD). (2016). *African Continental Free Trade Area: Advancing Pan-African Integration: Some Considerations* Geneva: UNCTAD.

United Nations Conference on Trade and Development (UNCTAD). (2018). "The African Continental Free Trade Area: The Day after the Kigali Summit." UNCTAD, No. 67, May.

United Nations Conference on Trade and Development (UNCTAD). (2007). World Investment Report: Transnational Corporations, Extractive Industries, and Development. Geneva: UNCTAD. http://unctad.org/en/pages/PublicationArchive .aspx?publicationid5724.

United Nations Office of the High Commissioner on Human Rights (UNOHCHR). (2016). Draft Report on the Second Session of the Open-Ended Intergovernmental Working Group on Transnational Corporations and Other Business Enterprises with Respect to Human Rights. Geneva: OHCHR. www.ohchr.org/EN/HRBodies/ HRC/WGTransCorp/Session2/Pages/Session2.aspx.

United Nations Office of the Special Advisor on Africa (OSAA) and the NEPAD-OECD Africa Investment Initiative. (2016). "Gross domestic product Africa fact sheet." www.oecd.org/investment/investmentfordevelopment/47452483.pdf (accessed 9 August 2016).

Ura, K., Alkire, S., Zangmo, T., & Wangdi, K. (2012). *An Extensive Analysis of GNH Index*. Bhutan: The Centre for Bhutan Studies.

Valdovinos, J. (2015). "Transnational Corporations in Water Governance. Veolia and Suez in Mexico and the United States (1993–2014)." Geography. Universite de la Sorbonne nouvelle - Paris III, 2015. https://tel.archives-ouvertes.fr/tel-01222539/ document.

Valentine, T. R. (1993). "Mineral-led economic growth, drought relief, and incomes policy income distribution in Botswana Reconsidered." *American Journal of Economics and Sociology*, 52(1): 31–49.

Valiente-Riedl, E. (2016). "To be free and fair? Debating fair trade's shifting response to global inequality." *Journal of Australian Political Economy*, 78: 159–185.

Van Alstine, J., Manyindo, J., Smith, L., Dixon, J., & Ruhanga, I. A. (2014). "Resource Governance Dynamics: The Challenge of 'New Oil' in Uganda." *Resources Policy*, 40: 48–58.

van Noorloos, F. (2014). "Transnational land investment in Costa Rica: Tracing residential tourism and its implications for development." In M. Kaag & A. Zoomers, eds., *The Global Land Grab: Beyond the Hype*. London: Zed Books, pp. 86–99.

Veblen, T. ([1923]/2009). *Absentee Ownership: Business Enterprise in Recent Times: The Case of America*. New Brunswick and London: Transactions Publishers.

Verma, R. (2013). "The Tiger and the Dragon: A neoclassical realist perspective of India and China in the oil industry in West Africa." Ph.D. Thesis, Department of International Relations, LSE, London.

Vinciguerra, V. (2013). "How the Daewoo attempted land acquisition contributed to Madagascar's political crisis in 2009." In S. J. T. M., Evers, G. Campbell, & M. Lambek, eds., *Contest for Land in Madagascar: Environment, Ancestors and Development*. Leiden: Brill, pp. 221–246.

Wadho, W. A. (2014). "Education, rent seeking and the curse of natural resources." *Economics & Politics*, 26(1): 128–156.

Walker, C. (1998). "Land reform and gender in post-apartheid South Africa." United Nations Research Institute for Social Development (UNRISD).

Walker, M. (2015). "Advancing student well-being and agency: The outline of a 'capabilities friendly' approach." *South African Journal of Higher Education*, 29 (5): 279–296.

Walker, M. (2016). "Context, complexity and change: Education as a conversionfactor for non-racist capabilities in a South African University." *Race, Ethnicity and Education*. http://dx.doi.org/10.1080/13613324.2015.1095176.

Wallerstein, I. (1961). *Africa: The Politics of Independence and Unity*. Lincoln and London; University of Nebraska Press.

Ward, K. (2010). "Towards a relational comparative approach to the study of cities." *Progress in Human Geography*, 34(4): 471–487.

Waring, M. (1988). *Counting for Nothing: What Men Value and What Women are Worth*. Wellington: Allen & Unwin/Port Nicholson Press.

Warren, R. (2017). *The Debate on Postcolonial Theory and the Specter of Capital*. London: Verso.

Watkins, M. H. (1963). "A staple theory of economic growth." *The Canadian Journal of Economics and Political Science/Revue canadienned'Economique et de Science politique*, 29(2): 141–158.

Watson, V. (2013). "African urban fantasies: Dreams or nightmares?" *Environment and Urbanization*, 26(1): 1–17

Wayessa, G .O. (2018). "'The master plan is a mater killer': Addis Ababa master plan and popular resistance in Oromia, Ethiopia." Unpublished manuscript, University of Helsinki.

Wayessa, G. O. & Nygren A. (2016). "Whose decisions, whose livelihoods? Resettlement and environmental justice in Ethiopia." *Society and Natural Resources*, 29(4): 387–402.

Weber, M. ([1930]/2001). *The Protestant Ethic and the Spirit of Capitalism*. London: Routledge.

Weber, M. (1920/2019). *Economy and Society* (newly edited by Tribe K). Cambridge, MA: Harvard University Press.

Weeks, J. (2011). "Review of *Africa's Odious Debts: How Foreign Loans and Capital Flight Bled the Continent.*" *African Arguments' Insiders' Newsletter*, October 5. http:// africanarguments.org/2011/10/05/review-africas-odious-debts-african-arguments-by-leonce-ndikumana-and-james-k-boyce/ (accessed 12 August 2018).

Weeks, J. (2014). *Economics of the 1%: How Mainstream Economics Serves the Rich, Obscures Reality and Distorts Policy*. London and New York: Anthem Press.

Wenar, L. (2008). "Property rights and the resource curse." *Philosophy and Public Affairs*, 36(1): 1–32.

Wengraf, L. (2018). *Extracting Profit: Imperialism, Neoliberalism and the New Scramble for Africa* Chicago: Haymarket Books.

Westbrook, D. A. (2004). *City of Gold: An Apology for Global Capitalism in a Time of Discontent*. London: Routledge.

Westbrook, D. A. (2017). "Prolegomenon to a defense of the city of gold." *Real-World Economics Review*, 78: 141–147.

Weszkalnys, G. (2008). "Hope and oil: expectations in São Tomé e Príncipe." *Review of African Political Economy*, 35(3): 473–482.

Weszkalnys, G. (2009). "The curse of oil in the Gulf of Guinea: A view from São Tomé and Príncipe." *African Affairs*, 108(433): 679–689.

Whitehead, A., & Tsikata, D. (2003). "Policy discourses on women's land rights in sub-Saharan Africa: The implications of the re-turn to the customary." *Journal of Agrarian Change*, 3(1&2): 67–112.

Wiegratz, J. (2016), *Neoliberal Moral Economy: Capitalism, Socio-Cultural Change and Fraud in Uganda*. New York and London: Rowman and Littlefield International.

Wiener, J. B. (2011). "What begat property?" *History of Political Economy*, 43(2): 353–360.

Wilde, A., Adams, I., & English, B. (2013). *Fueling the Future of an Oil City: A Tale of Sekondi-Takoradi in Ghana*. Silver Spring, MD: Global Communities. www.global communities.org/publications/2013-ghana-fueling-the-future-of-an-oil-city.pdf (accessed 23 May 2019).

Wilkinson, R., & Pickett, K. (2010). *The Spirit Level: Why Greater Equality Makes Societies Stronger*. New York: Bloomsbury Press.

Wilkinson, R., & Pickett, K. (2018). *The Inner Level: How More Equal Societies Reduce Stress, Restore Sanity and Improve Everyone's Well-Being*. New York: Penguin Press.

Williams, R. B. (2017). "Wealth privilege and the racial wealth gap: A case study in economic stratification." *Review of Black Political Economy*, 44: 303–325.

Williamson, O. E. (1981). "The modern corporation: origins, evolution, attributes." *Journal of Economic Literature*, 19(4): 1537–1568.

Williamson, O. E. (2002). "The theory of the firm as governance structure: From choice to contract." *Journal of Economic Perspectives*, 16(3): 171–195.

Williamson, O. E. (2009). "Transaction cost economics: The natural progression." Nobel Prize Lecture December 8, Stockholm.

Wilson, W. J. (1987). *The Truly Disadvantaged: The Inner City, the Underclass, and Public Policy*, Chicago: University of Chicago Press.

Wilson, W. J. (1992). "Another look at the truly disadvantaged." *Political Science Quarterly*, 106(4): 639–656.

Wilson, W. J. (2009). *More than Just Race: Being Black and Poor in the Inner City*. New York: W.W.Norton.

Wiredu, B. (2007). *2007 Budget Statement of Ghana*. Accra, Ghana: MOFEP.

Wisborg, P. (2012). "Justice and sustainability: Resistance and innovation in a transnational land deal in Ghana." paper prepared for presentation at the Annual World Bank conference on land and poverty, Washington, DC, 23–26 April.

Women in Law and Development in Africa (WiLDAF). (2006). *Shadow report to Ghana's third, fourth and fifth reports on the implementation of the CEDAW in Ghana*. Accra: WiLDAF.

Women in Law and Development in Africa (WiLDAF). (2011). *The WiLDAF Voice*, October. Accra: WiLDAF.

Woodman, G. (1996). *Customary Land Law in the Ghanaian Courts*. Accra: Ghana Universities Press.

Woodson, C. G. (1990/1933). *The Mis-Education of the Negro*. Trenton, NJ: Africa World Press, Inc.

Woodson, T. S. (2016). "Review: *Why Economists Get It Wrong*." *Science and Public Policy*, 43(4): 578–579.

World Bank. (1975). "Land reform," Sector Policy Paper, Pub 440, May, The World Bank, Washington, DC.

World Bank. (1988). *Oil Windfalls: Blessing or Curse?* Oxford: Oxford University Press.

World Bank. (1993). *The East Asian Miracle: Economic Growth and Public Policy.* New York: Oxford University Press.

World Bank. (2003a). "Land policies for growth and poverty reduction," World Bank, Washington, DC.

World Bank. (2003b). "Project appraisal document on a proposed credit in the amount of SDR 15.1 million (US$20.5 million equivalent) to the Republic of Ghana for a Land Administration Project," The World Bank. Report no.25913.

World Bank. (2009). *World Development Report 2009: Reshaping Economic Geography.* Washington, DC: World Bank.

World Bank. (2010). *Rising Global Interest in Farmland: Can It Yield Sustainable and Equitable Benefits?* Washington, DC: World Bank.

World Bank. (2015). "Republic of Cote d'Ivoire Urbanization Review," Report No: AUS10013 Washington, DC: World Bank.

World Bank. (2017). "World Bank Development Indicators (for Ghana)." http://data .worldbank.org/country/ghana.

World Health Organization. (2013). *Global Status Report on Road Safety.* Geneva: World Health Organization.

Writers for the 99%. (2012). *Occupying Wall Street: The inside story of an action that changed America.* Melbourne: Scribe Publications.

Wunder, T. A. (2019). "Fighting childhood poverty: How a universal child allowance would impact the U.S. population." *Journal of Economic Issues*, LIII(2): 537–544.

Wynne, A., & Olamosu, A. (2015). "Review: *Africa: Why Economists Get It wrong.*" ROAPE.net. http://roape.net/2015/12/01/africa-why-economists-get-itwrong/ (accessed 13 October 2016).

Yaro, J. A., & Tsikata, D. (2013). "Savannah fires and local resistance to transnational land deals: The case of Dipale in Northern Ghana." *African Geographical Review*, 32 (1): 72–87.

Yates, D. A. (2014). "Port-Gentil: From forestry capital to energy capital." In J. A. Pratt, M. V. Melosi, & K. A. Brosnan, eds., *Energy Capitals: Local Impact, Global Influence.* Pittsburgh: University of Pittsburgh Press, pp. 159–180.

Yergin, D. (2009). *The Prize: The Epic Quest for Oil, Money and Power.* New York: Free Press.

Yimovie, S-C. (2018). "Re-reading Sankara's philosophy for a praxeology of debt in contemporary times." In Murrey, A., ed., *A Certain Amount of Madness: The Life, Politics and Legacies of Thomas Sankara.* London: Zed Books, pp. 180–193.

Yngstrom, I. (2002). "Women, wives and land rights in Africa: Situating gender beyond the household in the debate over land policy and changing tenure systems." *Oxford Development Studies*, 30(1): 21–40.

Yokying, P., & Lambrecht, I. (2019). "Landownership and the gender gap in agriculture: Disappointing insights from Northern Ghana." International Food Policy Research Institute (IFPRI) Discussion Paper, 01847.

Yoo, D., & Harris, E. (2016). "Conditions of successful land reform: A study of Micronesia." *Australian Economic History Review*, 56(3): 292–316.

Yoo, D., & Steckel, R. (2016). "Property rights and economic development: The legacy of Japanese colonial institutions." *Journal of Institutional Economics*, 12(3): 623–650.

Young, A. (2012). "The African growth miracle." *Journal of Political Economy*, 120: 696–739.

Zack-Williams, A. (2016). "Book review: *Africa: Why Economists Get It Wrong.*" *Review of African Political Economy.* doi:10.1080/03056244.2016.1249705.

Zack-Williams, A. (2013). "Neo-imperialism and African development." *Review of African Political Economy*, 40(136): 179–184.

Zeilig, L. (2017). "Burkina Faso: from Thomas Sankara to popular resistance." *Review of African Political Economy*, 44(151): 155–164

Zein-Elabdin, E .O. (2016). *Economics, Culture and Development.* New York: Routledge

Zhang, Y.-H. (2013). "On Samir Amin's strategy of 'delinking' and 'socialist transition.'" *International Journal of Business and Social Research*, 3(11): 101–107.

Ziai, A. (2015). "Post-development: Premature burials and haunting ghosts." *Development and Change*, 46(4): 833–54.

Zouache, A. (2017). "Race, competition, and institutional change in J. R. Commons." *The European Journal of the History of Economic Thought*, 24(2): 341–368.

Zouache, A. (2018). "Institutions and the colonisation of Africa: Some lessons from French colonial economics." *Journal of Institutional Economics*, 14(2): 373–391.

# Index

community land rights, 86–87, 90–92, 115
  individualist perspective on, 85–86
  land tenure and, 90–92
  social capital and, 90–91
Community Organization Resource Centre,
    South Africa, 208
comparative advantage, 288–289
compartmentalization, 3–5, 36–37, 51
constitutional political economy, 263
context, stratification economics and, 40
contracts, TNCs and, 231–232
Cooper, Frederick, 22, 269
Corden, Max, 12, 127
corporate social responsibility (CSR), 146, 160,
    181–182, 184–185
corruption, 153–154, 250–251
Costa Rica, 245–246
Cote d'Ivoire, 259, 260–261, 263, 269
  Abidjan in, 176–177, 179–180, 190
  CIAPOL in, 270
  energy access and, 274
  environmental pollution in, 209, 270
  Ghana dispute with, 266–267
  oil industry in, 209, 260–261, 266–267, 272
  refining capacity and, 272
  SODECI in, 177–180, 191–192
  TNCs in, 176–181, 232
  water in, 176–180
Cousins, Ben, 99, 102
credit, 115
  formalization and, 116
  microfinance and, 67
  Schumpeter on, 69
  Uganda and, 105, 106
Crenshaw, Kimberlé, 46
CSR. *See* corporate social responsibility
cultural difference, Global South and, 4
cultural dominance, neoclassical economics
    on, 48–49
culture, ix–x, 14
  anthropology of Africa and, 17–18
  historical approaches to, 22
  institutional economics and, 39
  neoclassical economics and, 38–39
  neopatrimonialism and, 16–17
  of poverty, 10–11
  property economics and, 65
  stratification economics and, 40
cumulative causation, of inequality, 166,
    185–186, 235, 236, 283
currency, 287. *See also* exchange rates

debt of Africa and, 165–166, 167, 169–170
  French, 165–166
  reparations and, 240–241
current expropriations, managing, 242–255
  Africa-wide commons and, 246–248
  beyond growth and, 243–244
  happiness and, 244–246
  state restructuring and, 248–252
  taxes and, 242
  work, restructuring, and, 252–255
customary land, 116–117
  land reform and, 14, 15
  social capital approach to, 116
  South Africa and, 99, 101, 114
  World Bank on, 87
customary land law, 93, 95–98, 104–106, 112,
    114

Dakar Appeal, 263
Daly, Herman, 243, 265
de Beauvoir, Simone, 9
de La Grandville, O., 201
dead capital, 59, 67, 69
Debreu, Gerard, 201
debt
  development economics and, 24
  HIPC initiatives and, 161
debt, of Africa, 161–170, 198–199
  aid and, 169–170
  capital flight and, 168, 169–170
  colonialism and, 163–167, 198
  currency and, 165–166,
    167, 169–170
  floating interest rates and, 167
  Ghana and, 169
  international financial system and, 163–164,
    167–169, 198–199
  protectionism and, 161, 198
  slavery and, 163–164, 198
  standard explanation of, 161–163
  weapons sales and, 168, 169
debt forgiveness, 161
DED framework, 175–176
deforestation, 271–272
Deininger, Klaus, 13–14, 87
de-linking, 220–221, 233–234
democratization, of work, 252–255
Demsetz, Harold, 31, 86
dependency theory, 8, 233
Devarajan, S., 204
development, political economy of, 7–10